Globalization and the National Security State

NORRIN M.
RIPSMAN
and
T. V. PAUL

GLOBALIZATION AND THE NATIONAL SECURITY STATE

OXFORD
UNIVERSITY PRESS
2010

Oxford University Press, Inc., publishes works that further
Oxford University's objective of excellence
in research, scholarship, and education.

Oxford   New York
Auckland   Cape Town   Dar es Salaam   Hong Kong   Karachi
Kuala Lumpur   Madrid   Melbourne   Mexico City   Nairobi
New Delhi   Shanghai   Taipei   Toronto

With offices in
Argentina   Austria   Brazil   Chile   Czech Republic   France   Greece
Guatemala   Hungary   Italy   Japan   Poland   Portugal   Singapore
South Korea   Switzerland   Thailand   Turkey   Ukraine   Vietnam

Published by Oxford University Press, Inc.
198 Madison Avenue, New York, New York 10016

www.oup.com

Oxford is a registered trademark of Oxford University Press.

Cataloging information for this title is available from the Library of Congress.

ISBN: 978-0-19-539390-3; 978-0-19-539391-0 (pbk.)

9 8 7 6 5 4 3 2 1

Printed in the United States of America
on acid-free paper

PREFACE

THE ONSET OF INTENSIFIED GLOBALIZATION since the 1990s has affected every aspect of state functions, including national security. However, the extent of this impact is yet to be fully assessed. Many existing works make sweeping generalizations regarding the relationship between globalization and security, often without offering sufficient empirical evidence. Our work was motivated by the need for such an empirical analysis in light of national and international experience during the past two decades of accelerated globalization. This book evaluates the impact of globalization in its different manifestations on the national security state at both the macro and micro levels during 1991–2007. We do this by first assessing several propositions relating to the relative absence of war, patterns in arms spending and troop levels, the role of private and nongovernmental organizations in the conduct of national defense, and the significance that countries assign to nontraditional security threats. We then examine the national security policies of different categories of states—great powers, states in cooperative zones, states in enduring rivalry zones, and weak nations—to assess if and how they have responded to the myriad of challenges presented by globalization.

The genesis of this book was from a joint paper we presented at the International Studies Association world conference in Budapest in June 2003. Subsequently, we published two co-authored articles in the journals *International Studies Review* (7, no. 2 [June 2005]: 199–227) and *Millennium* (33, no. 2 [December 2004]: 355–380). In the introduction and chapters 1 and 2, we draw upon sections of these articles. Our work has greatly benefited from presentations at a number of institutions worldwide. During the past five years, we conducted interviews and workshops in several countries, including Australia, Chile, Columbia, Ethiopia, India, Peru, Singapore, South Africa, Taiwan, Tanzania, Uganda, United Arab Emirates, United States, Vietnam, and Zambia. The institutions include Academic Staff College, Trivandrum; Addis Ababa University, Ethiopia; African Centre for the Constructive Resolution of Disputes (ACCORD), Durban, South Africa; Bangalore University; Calicut University; Center for Human Rights, Bhubaneswar; Center for Security Analysis, Chennai; Chilean Diplomatic Academy, Santiago; Chilean War College, Santiago; Cochin University, Kochi; Finnish Institute of International Affairs, Helsinki; Goa University; Gulf Research Center, Dubai; the Hebrew University of Jerusalem; Ho Chi Minh City University, Vietnam; Indian Institute of Management, Ahmadabad; Jaipur University; Kannur University; Kerala International Center, Trivandrum; Kerala University, Trivandrum; Loyola College, Chennai; Madurai Kamaraj University; Maharajas College, Ernakulum; Mahatma Gandhi University, Kottayam; Mangalore University; National Chengchi University, Taipei; National Defense College of the Philippines, Manila; S. Rajaretnam School of International Studies, Singapore; Stella Mary's College, Chennai; Taiwan Foundation for Democracy, Taipei; Thevara S. H. College, Kochi; Udaipur University; University of Dar Es Salaam; University of Peace, San Jose, Costa Rica; and Utkal University, Bhubaneswar.

Many individuals in the countries just mentioned helped us in organizing our visits and conducting our research. We are particularly grateful to Jean-Marc F. Blanchard, Chris Demchak, Patrick James, Steven Lobell, Derek McDougall, Baldev Raj Nayar, and Pradeep Taneja for comments on portions of this manuscript. Able research assistance was offered by Bahar Akman, Heloise Blondy, Margaret Foster, Nadine Hajjar, Sandra Helayel, William Hogg, Liz Kawasaki-Smith, Sebastien Mainville, Imad Mansour, Theodore McLauchlin, Mahesh Shankar, Jessica Trisko, and Stéfanie von Hlatky. Much of the financial assistance for this project came from Fonds de recherche sur la société et la culture (FQRSC), Quebec, through a team grant for the Globalization and the National Security State project (with Michel Fortmann and John Hall as comembers with us). Additional funding was obtained through the McGill University—University of Montreal Research Group in International Security through a grant from the Security and Defense Forum, Ottawa, James McGill Chair, and the Social Sciences and Humanities Research Council of Canada. We thank David McBride, editor of Oxford University Press, for his enthusiasm for the book. We greatly appreciate the constant support of our families throughout this endeavor.

CONTENTS

Globalization and the National Security State

Introduction: National Security State
in the Era of Globalization

S INCE ITS INCEPTION AS A SOCIAL INSTITUTION, the primary purpose of
the nation-state has been to provide security within a geographically
defined territory against both external and internal threats. Throughout
many political, economic, and social changes, ranging from the emergence of
nationalism, the industrial revolution, two world wars, and the development
of nuclear weapons, the state has remained at the forefront of organized protection, and the protection of national security has been its hallmark.
However, during the contemporary era, when economic, political, and social
interaction expanded beyond national boundaries to reach a global scale,
many believe that the state is losing its relevance not only as a welfare provider, but also as a guarantor of security. Consequently, many theorists assert
that globalization has begun to dismantle the national security state.

To substantiate their arguments, these scholars cite a number of recent
trends, including the relative absence of major interstate wars, the avoidance
of intense balance-of-power politics, declining military expenditures, and the
increase of transnational actors in the security arena. Moreover, they point to
the proliferation of nontraditional security challenges, particularly in the
areas of transnational terrorism, the environment, and drug trafficking, sup-
planting traditional military security concerns. Globalization theorists argue
that because these new challenges are transnational in nature, they have
affected all states and they require collective action, because the traditional
state-centered approaches to security planning are not suited to deal with
them effectively. In general, they contend that most states have responded to

the new threats by altering the architecture of their national security establishments and by pursuing cooperative security, both nationally and internationally. Those states that have failed to adjust their pursuit of national security accordingly have suffered as a consequence and will face disruptions in the future that will undermine their competitiveness both economically and in the security arena.[1]

These globalization theses, however, remain in the realm of conjecture, because no systematic testing of their predictions for the national security state has been undertaken. The purpose of this book, therefore, is to test the main elements of the globalization and security paradigm against the behavior of the world's national security apparatuses from the end of the Cold War through 2008. Although eighteen years is a short period to assess large historical processes and changes, in our view, the empirical data are sufficient for a reasonable preliminary assessment of the globalization–security relationship.[2] We do so in two stages. First, we explore whether there has been a shift in the way security is being pursued at the global level. We investigate whether there has been a significant reduction in global military expenditures or military manpower during this period of globalization's rapid spread, whether there has been a reduction in the number of interstate wars, whether the global security agenda has turned its attention to confronting new nontraditional security challenges, and whether nonstate actors, such as nongovernmental organizations (NGOs) and intergovernmental organizations, have begun to play a greater role in security affairs.

Second, we consider—on a selected country-by-country and region-by-region basis—whether and to what extent globalization has affected the national security state during this period. This allows us to consider whether the effects of globalization, if they manifest themselves in the national security realm at all, do so evenly or unevenly across states and regions. Most globalization arguments are presented as if transnational political and economic forces are transforming national security states uniformly throughout the world. In contrast, we consider whether the relative power and position of a state in the international system determine the degree to which these changes affect it. This makes intuitive sense, because realist writings on security emphasize that the great powers shape global forces more than global forces shape them. Thus, we examine the security practices and defense doctrines of contemporary states to determine whether different categories of states (i.e., major powers, middle powers, and weak states) are being affected differentially by these changes. In addition, we check for regional variations, because it is reasonable to expect that states in less conflict-prone regions (e.g., western Europe, Southeast Asia, and Latin America) might be more subject to the effects of globalization than those in regions plagued by enduring interstate rivalries (e.g., the Middle East and South Asia).

Our findings are threefold. First, global trends are not fully consistent with the globalization school's predictions. Although worldwide military spending dropped initially during the early 1990s, it climbed back up again at the end of the 1990s and the beginning of the twenty-first century. In fact, it seems the national wealth bolstered by economic globalization has encouraged many states to increase military expenditures and to modernize their armed forces. Furthermore, global and regional security institutions have not stepped up to supplant the primacy of the state in the provision of security. And, although there has been a measurable decline in the incidence of interstate war during the period under investigation, it is by no means clear that this can be attributed exclusively or even primarily to globalization, rather than the more compelling alternative explanations of the end of the Cold War and the consequent rise of American hegemony, or the spread of technology that promotes defense/deterrence dominance. Second, the globalization school's claims about national security policy are overstated, because states of all types pursue more traditional security policies than globalization theorists would expect. In addition, in many instances when national security states have conformed to the school's expectations, strategic circumstances—rather than globalization—appear to be the cause. Third, to the extent that globalization has affected the pursuit of national security, it has done so unevenly. States in stable regions have transformed their national security establishments the most to meet the challenges of globalization, whereas those in conflict-ridden regions have done so the least, although the latter are tremendously affected by many negative forces associated with globalization. The great powers have adapted to globalization only when it was consistent with their own strategic imperatives. Finally, the very weak or failed states of sub-Saharan Africa have had their fragile national security establishments buffeted by the pressures of globalization, which have added further impetus to state collapse.

The remainder of this introduction will proceed with our definition of the terms *globalization* and *national security state*, a discussion of our fourfold framework for distinguishing the responses to globalization of four different categories of states, a note on our methodology, and a brief overview of the book.

What Is Globalization?

Globalization is a frequently used buzzword in contemporary political discourse, but it is rarely used with precision and appears to mean different things to different people. Indeed, the political science literature is replete with economic, political, social, and cultural definitions of globalization that focus on very different, although related, phenomena.[3] Economic definitions of *globalization* denote an expansion of the scale of economic activity beyond the nation-state, manifested in "the expansion of market relations, ubiquitous commodification and the communications revolution that mediated them."[4] To Jagdish Bhagwati, for example, economic globalization "constitutes integration of national economies into the international economy through trade, direct foreign investment (by corporations and multinationals), short-term capital flows, international flows of workers and humanity in general, and flows of technology."[5] As a result, in a globalized world, economic management, decision making, production, distribution, and marketing are organized on a global scale, which limits the nation-state's ability to regulate its own economic interests, and makes national welfare heavily dependent on the international market.[6] In effect, economic globalization essentially comprises the two parallel phenomena of heightened economic interdependence and transnationalism.[7]

Economic interdependence refers to the interconnectedness of the world economy, such that a change in the economic conditions of one country would bring about changes in the economy of others; moreover, a disruption of normal economic relations would impose costs upon multiple states.[8] States need not be symmetrically dependent on international exchange; it is enough that they all would incur at least some costs if economic patterns were to alter. Some theorists, such as Gerald Schneider, Katherine Barbieri, and Nils Petter Gleditsch, equate economic interdependence and globalization, defining globalization merely as "the contemporary surge in economic interdependence."[9] We reject this as unsatisfying in that it fails to capture the transnational nature of decision making, production, distribution, and communication that are essential features of globalization. Indeed, economic interdependence is merely the product of a large volume of interstate transactions; globalization begins with a high volume of cross-border transactions, but also implies an increase in the scale of transactions beyond the level of the nation-state (i.e., transnationalism). For example, Hans-Henrik Holm and Georg Sørensen comment:

> Whereas intensified economic interdependence involves more of the same in the sense that economic intercourse between national economies increases, true economic globalization invokes a qualitative shift toward a global economic system that is no longer based on autonomous national economies, but on a consolidated global marketplace for production, distribution, and consumption.[10]

Thus, the second component of globalization is transnationalism, or the increased ease with which goods, services, and business entities can cross national boundaries as a result of revolutionary advances in communication and transportation technologies.[11] Transnationalism thus gives greater impetus to nonstate actors, such as private corporations, to set the international economic agenda and circumvent the state. Although mere economic interdependence may be the conscious result of state strategies, globalization is now driven less by states than by nonstate actors.

This economic dimension, or economic engine, is the most crucial aspect of globalization. There is disagreement on the precise starting point of economic globalization. Some scholars believe that there was more economic globalization during the pre-World War I period in terms of higher flows of merchandise, capital, and labor.[12] To others, globalization dates back to the sixteenth century when European states began to expand to different regions of the world as colonial rulers. Still others, however, believe that the contemporary phase of globalization is more intensive and qualitatively different as a result of the crossing of several thresholds in the global economy: the ratio of global production has increased vis-à-vis national production, global trade assumed more than a quarter of world economic output, economic production is increasingly organized on a global basis largely by multinational corporations (MNCs) that are not bound by geographical or territorial constraints, direct foreign investment has increased by an order of magnitude, money markets have rapidly been internationalized with advanced information technology and global capital markets functioning 'round the clock, and a world consumer culture has been created with individual consumers becoming more global in their consumption patterns and orientations.[13]

What is clear, however, is that the world economy has become truly global during the past fifteen years. Although total world exports in 1990 totaled just under $4.6 trillion, that figure more than doubled to just under $11 trillion by 2004.[14] The composition of trade also shifted further away from primary commodities to manufactured goods. Thus, although in 1980, 54.2% of world exports consisted of manufactured goods, and in 1990 that figure increased to 70.5%, by 1999, 76.5% of world exports were manufactured products.[15] This means that states are not only using the global market to purchase resources that they might not possess in sufficient quantity domestically, but they are buying goods that they produce domestically from the international market to take advantage of lower prices and greater efficiency abroad. Global foreign direct investment (inward stock) has also ballooned from just more than $2 trillion to more than $9.5 trillion from 1992 to 2004.[16] In addition, the number of transnational corporations operating worldwide increased from about 35,000 parent companies with about 150,000 foreign affiliates in 1990 to about 78,411 parent companies in 2007 with more than 777,000 foreign affiliates.[17] In 1990, these foreign affiliates generated about $1.5 trillion, or less than 7% of the gross world product. By 2006, they generated more than $4.7 trillion, or more than 10% of the gross world product, indicating the growing transnationalization of the world economy.[18] Thus, in economic terms, globalization has transformed the world economy.

Political definitions of globalization emphasize the actions states have taken to adapt to the new global economic environment and, in particular, the decline of the welfare provision and income redistribution components of the state.[19] It also refers to the spread of the liberal democratic system (along with free markets) throughout much of the globe as the most acceptable form of political governance.[20] *Social* definitions of globalization take two forms. Some see globalization as the expansion of social relations on a global scale as a result of economic and technological changes. Shaw, for example, views it as "the quality involved in the worldwide stretching of social relations."[21] Others, more concerned with social conflict, focus on the social impact, at both the local and global levels, of the distribution of gains and losses that economic globalization entails.[22] Indeed, globalization has had the profound effect of widening income disparities and exacerbating the North–South divide.

Cultural definitions of globalization focus on the degree to which cultural identities increase in scale, as people shift their allegiance from national or subnational units to supranational ones.[23] This occurs, in James H. Mittelman's estimation, as social relations between peoples increase worldwide, with events happening at different locations around the globe affecting all the world's peoples and shaping their identities. Thus, as the "locus of power gradually shifts in varying proportions above and below the territorial state," cultural identities will follow suit.[24] In Alex Inkeles's view, globalization implies cultural convergence, which "involves the movement of national populations away from diverse indigenous cultural patterns towards the adoption of attitudes, values and modes of daily behavior that constitute the elements of a more or less common world culture."[25]

Finally, some argue that globalization is a multifaceted phenomenon, proceeding in parallel along multiple dimensions. Holm and Sørensen, for example, define it as "the intensification of economic, political, social, and cultural relations across borders."[26]

We argue that, if we are to use the term *globalization* meaningfully as a causal variable, we must conceptually distinguish it from its effects. Therefore, it is not useful to conflate the phenomenon of globalization with the reactions of states or nonstate actors to it, as some theorists do. *In our view, all these images of globalization share a concern with the expansion of socioeconomic and sociopolitical activities beyond the state on an international and transnational scale.*[27] Thus, for us, globalization entails the widespread operation of businesses on a global, rather than a national, level; the ease with which individuals and groups can communicate and organize across national frontiers; the global transmission of ideas, norms, and values that might erode national cultures in favor of a broader global culture; the increasing participation of states in international political, economic, and military organizations; the spread of particular forms of political institutions, such as representative democracy, to vast areas of the globe; and the increasing participation of individuals from multiple countries in international NGOs.[28] Globalization, therefore, is a vast, multifaceted enterprise that proceeds both outside the state and within it, spurred on by businesses, consumers, social groups, states, and international institutions as they organize the economic, political, and cultural spheres beyond the nation-state.[29]

The sources of the intense phase of globalization are a matter of debate among analysts. To more geopolitical and critical theorists, the main source of contemporary globalization was the hegemonic power of the United States, along with powerful MNCs, both American and international, and Washington's institutional allies, the World Bank and the International Monetary Fund (IMF).[30] This does not mean that globalization is continually shaped or controlled by the hegemonic power consciously, as the diffusion of wealth to other states would mean the relative weakening of the hegemonic power itself. Some of the leading players in international mergers and acquisitions, in fact, are from developing economies, such as China, India, and Brazil. However, geopolitical and critical scholars, such as Helleiner, view globalization as a political project of the United States, and, as such, as driven by political determinants, not technological or economic determinants. Others contend that economic efficiency concerns and technological changes have been the main driving force of globalization. They argue that technological innovations have lowered the costs of moving goods and providing services, that the potential efficiencies from international integration have increased dramatically, and that governments that fail to take advantage of these trends face increasing opportunity costs.[31] A country's acceptance of globalization, however, may be determined by a number of internal factors, which include the attitudes of national leadership, their willingness to emulate other states, regime type, the size of the state, the arrival of liberalizing coalitions to power, and favorable social and political conditions, such as economic development and literacy.[32] As Jeffry Frieden contends:

> Globalization is still a choice, not a fact. It is a choice made by governments that consciously decide to reduce barriers to trade and investment, adopt new policies toward international money and finance, and chart fresh economic courses. Decisions made by each government are interconnected; international finance, international trade, and international monetary relations depend on the joint actions of national governments around the world. National policies and relations among national governments are the sources of globalization and determine its staying power...Globalization needs supportive governments and supportive governments need domestic political support.[33]

What Is the National Security State?

There are three related meanings of the *national security state*,[34] with slightly nuanced implications for the object of our study. We address each of these meanings, which broaden the range of effects that we look for when exploring the effect of globalization in the national security arena.

The first definition of the national security state is the real-state associated with realism: a state that accords primacy to the protection of national borders, physical assets, and core values largely through military means.[35] As a result of the anarchical nature of the international system, states must provide for their own security, because they cannot turn to a higher authority to protect them, nor can they rely on the guarantees or good behavior of other states.[36] Self-help and relative gains concerns are the norm, and security can only be achieved through the acquisition and maintenance of a robust military capability. Consequently, although states have other purposes, such as providing domestic order and welfare, national security takes priority over all others in the hierarchy of state interests, because without territorial security, all national values would suffer.[37] According to this view, then, all states are—first and foremost—national security states.

This realist position accords well with the view of some historical sociologists who contend national security was the central reason for the rise and preeminence of the nation-state above all other social institutions in the modern age. The state, according to them, arose in Europe in modern times as a result of its war-making function and has since been accorded primacy because of the persistence and centrality of that role.[38] States thus remain the "principal referent objects of security because they are both the framework of order and the highest source of governing authority."[39] During the postwar years, although the welfare state has encroached upon the national security role of the state, the state has survived as the preeminent national security organ. In this realist image, then, the national security state is a constant entity, at least as long as the international system remains anarchic.

Two other uses of the term *national security state* are also relevant. Daniel Yergin and others refer to states that have institutionalized the provision of security and prioritized it over all other functions of state as national security states. Yergin refers to the enactment of the National Security Act in the United States in 1947 and its construction of institutions, such as the National Security Council and the Central Intelligence Agency, to oversee and conduct the pursuit of national security, as the foundation of the national security state.[40] In this image, not all states are national security states, or "garrison states."[41] National security states would engage in activities related to trade and economic welfare, but would not grant them the same priority as military security, and would be willing to subvert economic advantages, civil liberties, and virtually all other values to the provision of security.[42] In contrast, other states—such as Richard Rosecrance's trading states—are more likely to pursue economic goals while reducing their focus on military-related behavior. Thus, unlike the realist image, the national security state is not a constant; the degree to which states prioritize national security and engage in military balancing depends on a variety of factors, including the international environment and domestic political factors.

A final, institutional, understanding of the national security state is that, in any state, the political institutions responsible for the conduct of foreign security policy collectively constitute the national security state.[43] These institutions and the strategies they pursue may vary considerably both across states and within the same state over time. Some national security states are more autonomous of key societal interest groups, legislatures, and the public at large; others are constrained. Some are well funded; others possess limited means. Some rely heavily on armaments and internal balancing; others favor alliances and cooperative security. Thus, it makes sense to refer to particular national security states, rather than "the national security state" as a category.

When we use the term *national security state* in this book, we refer, to some extent, to all these meanings. We are clearly interested in the extent to which globalization has affected both the centrality of the pursuit of national security to the state's mission and the centrality of the state to the national and international pursuit of security. In other words, we wish to explore whether globalization, by rendering the state incapable of securing its population, has finally killed the realist image of the national security state, or whether the real-state has merely adapted to changing conditions. But we are also interested in whether the constraints and opportunities of a globalized world have shifted states away from the security practices described by the second definition of the national security state, and toward the provision of wealth or welfare that characterizes the trading state. Finally, we wish to examine the degree to which globalization has altered the nature of the security institutions of the state referred to by the third definition, both globally and within specific states, and the means through which these institutions pursue security.

Power, Position, and Globalization: A Systemic Framework for Assessing the Impact of Globalization

As we shall see in chapter 1, because globalization is posited to be a global phenomenon, affecting all countries and regions of the world, the globalization school's approach to international security predicts changes at the global level without much variation across states and regions. For this reason, we begin our analysis of the contemporary pursuit of security with an exploration of global trends. Nonetheless, there are compelling reasons to supplement the global picture with a more targeted investigation of different types of states and different regions. To begin with, not all states have globalized their economies to the same degree. Thus, like Christopher Coker, we might expect the security effects of globalization on states in the western, capitalist, developed world to be different from its effects on the developing world.[44]

There are also theoretical reasons to test for differential effects of globalization. Realists contend that international phenomena affect states differently, depending on their relative power and position within the international system.[45] Typically, major powers, by virtue of their superior power resources—which help them both to maintain their independence vis-à-vis international pressures and to shape them—are least affected by international political, economic, and military changes. Yet, they simultaneously are best able to take advantage of changes in economic organization and military technologies to enhance their power. Thus, realists might expect the major powers to be in command of globalization—making concessions to it only when it increases their power advantage over others—rather than at its mercy. In addition, a state's geostrategic position in the international system also affects its foreign and defense policy responses to systemic pressures. It is possible, therefore, that responses to globalization may also vary depending on a state's international position. All things being equal, we might expect that regional powers located in stable regions would be the most affected by the pressures of globalization, because their incentives to resist global pressures are likely to be low, absent a powerful existential threat. States engaged in enduring rivalries (in regions of conflict) might be more resistant to its pressures because they are most eager to preserve their autonomy to defend their national and regional interests. Finally, very weak or failed states might be completely unable to buffer themselves from the pressures of globalization and, therefore, might be utterly at their mercy.

After we investigate whether there are system-level indicators that globalization has changed the pursuit of security during the contemporary era, the balance of this book will investigate whether globalization has indeed affected the pursuit of national security by examining the experiences of these four groups of states, which we will define more concretely before proceeding.

MAJOR POWERS AND GLOBAL SOCIAL FORCES

Major powers are the most powerful states in the international system and are, therefore, its key military security actors. They maintain global power projection capabilities, which allow them to claim international leadership positions. These states acquire military capabilities not simply to defend their homelands, but also to maintain coercive power over secondary states and balance against rival states and potential rivals. They are also distinguished by their global interests and how they are perceived by other states.[46] In recent years, major power status has been broadened to include *structural power*, which denotes the superior capacity of a state in terms of threatening, defending, and denying the security of other states from violence; controlling the system of goods and services; determining the structure of finance; and exerting the highest influence over the acquisition and dissemination of knowledge.[47]

Among the major powers, security behavior varies depending on whether they are hegemonic, status quo, declining, or rising powers.[48] In the post-Cold War system, in terms of their overall power attributes and dispositions, the United States has emerged as the status quo hegemonic power and China has become the rising challenger. For the bulk of the globalization era, Russia was the declining/greatly weakened great power, with a decline that was very palpable across many dimensions of national power, particularly military (conventional), economic, and demographic.[49] During the past couple of years, however, Russian oil wealth has led to a resurgence of Russian power and a desire to recapture its great power influence. These different structural situations should affect their approaches toward security and military power. Thus, we consider how globalization has affected the national security establishments of each of these three major powers. We do not consider Great Britain and France as major powers, and include them in the next category, both because their major power attributes have declined considerably over the years and because they have been active members of the European Union (EU), which makes them less great powers in their own right than participants in an aspiring great power bloc. Although India has several parameters of a rising power, we also do not include it in the chapter on the great powers, given that we address it more comprehensively in the chapter on enduring rivals.

STATES IN COOPERATIVE REGIONAL SUBSYSTEMS

Among the next level of powers, some find themselves in regional subsystems with relatively stable security environments. Two types of stable subsystems are possible. In the first, regional cooperation is highly developed and institutionalized. Members of the EU, who have already established a pluralistic security community, are the best example of this category of states.[50] The second is a subsystem in which states have achieved some cooperative institutional arrangements and lack protracted militarized rivalries, but have not yet formed a true security community. These include Southeast Asia and the southern cone of Latin America, where states are in the process of building security communities around the Association of Southeast Asian States (ASEAN) and El Mercado Común del Cono Sur (Mercosur), respectively. Because the states in these regions do not face powerful existential challenges and have less of a need than the major powers to project power beyond their region, we might expect them to have responded most positively to the pressures of globalization. After all, they have the fewest incentives to bear the burden of resisting global pressures to retain national control of their national security establishments. To test the globalization propositions on this category of state, we shall examine three regions—highly stable western Europe, moderately stable Southeast Asia, and relatively stable Latin America—by considering both how the region as a whole has responded to contemporary changes, as well as how leading states in these regions have responded.

STATES IN COMPETITIVE REGIONAL SUBSYSTEMS

Other regional powers inhabit competitive regional subsystems characterized by protracted conflicts and enduring militarized rivalries. These conflicts are driven by intractable issues such as territory, ideology, or identity, and the conflict relationships among states in these regions spill into most spheres of their interstate interactions.[51] These states enjoy no credible security protection from outside and are frequently targets of economic and military sanctions by the major powers, which are often heavily involved in regional affairs. Some of the larger states in these regions seek regional hegemony, whereas some face major power intervention in their internal affairs. Moreover, because of the chaotic security environments these states face, their military planning and preparations are typically based on worst-case assumptions.

Two regions rife with such rivalries are South Asia and the Middle East. In the former, regional security is dominated by the territorial conflict between nuclear rivals India and Pakistan. In the latter, regional dynamics are conditioned by the Arab–Israeli conflict, inter-Arab competition for leadership of the Arab world, and American clashes with the Gulf states (particularly Iran and Iraq) as the United States attempts to secure its oil interests in the region. We can assume that if any states should want to resist the forces of globalization and retain national control of their military apparatuses as sovereignty protecting instruments, it should be these, because the cost of relinquishing national control could be the highest. To assess how globalization has affected this category of state, we shall consider how South Asia and the Middle East are adjusting to contemporary changes as regions, as well as how leading regional actors are responding.

WEAK STATES

The final category of states we consider are weak states. A weak state has three major characteristics: (1) *security deficiency* (the state is often unable to provide basic security to its citizens, because military and police forces tend to be weak), (2) *participation deficiency* (civil society tends to be absent or dysfunctional; free, open political participation is deficient or extremely limited; and political power tends to lie in the hands of a small oligarchical elite); and (3) *infrastructure deficiency* (the physical infrastructure of the state is poorly maintained because resources are improperly extracted and taxes are not collected regularly or sufficiently [The state could be heavily indebted to external donors and the government has great difficulty meeting its daily financial needs.]).[52] Many are beset with problems of internal conflict driven by ethnic rivalries and political and economic inefficiencies. Their state institutions often lack legitimacy, and state laws receive little compliance from citizens.[53] The capacity of these states to protect citizens from predators is also minimal. Weak states lack both what Michael Mann calls "despotic power" (the power of the state elite over civil society) and "infrastructural power" (the institutional capacity of the state to penetrate the territory and implement decisions effectively).[54] They are also the most affected by external shocks, the impact of which they often cannot cushion or control.

The African continent offers the best examples of weak and failing states, although some exist in the Middle East, Central Asia, South Asia, and Latin America as well. There are, however, variations within this category. Several states, including Somalia, Nigeria, Sudan, Sierra Leone, Liberia, and Angola, have a "volatile mix of armed conflict, unstable political institutions, limited resources and inevitably, a 'bad neighborhood' of similar crisis ridden states." Others, such as Senegal, Mali, Ghana, and Benin, however, have been able to avoid violent conflicts and are "negotiating risky transitions toward democracy."[55]

This suggests that not all weak states are failed or failing states. Although a weak state shows a mixed record in terms of the three characteristics mentioned earlier, a *failing* state approaches the failed category unless remedial measures are taken to stem the tide of decline and disintegration. A *failed state* exhibits an extreme level of state weakness; the societies of these states "are tense, deeply conflicted, dangerous, and contested bitterly by warring factions. In most failed states, government troops battle armed revolts led by one or more rivals."[56] Thus a failed state has little capacity to intervene and end its internal conflicts. A state may remain weak and stagnate or it may move up and down in the weak, failing, or failed category.

We would expect that globalization would have the most destabilizing effect on these weak states, which already are losing their grip on national sovereignty and defense. To test the globalization propositions on this group, we will assess sub-Saharan Africa as a whole, rather than focus on individual states, because their very weakness makes it difficult to get reliable data on them.

Study Design

To determine whether globalization has affected contemporary international security, we conduct a number of case studies to assess whether there is congruence between the globalization school's predictions and the contemporary pursuit of security in different states, regions, and settings.[57] Our approach to this analysis is as follows. We begin by identifying specific propositions from the globalization literature pertaining to globalization's likely effect on different aspects of the pursuit of national security. In particular, we address two types of propositions. First we explore three core propositions about the way the pursuit of security should change at the global level if globalization theorists are correct, including the frequency of interstate wars, the level of global manpower and military spending, the degree to which terrorism has transformed the global security agenda, and the prominence of multilateral security-providing institutions. To these, we add ten propositions about the way in which national security apparatuses should have changed under the influence of globalization. These propositions are clustered into three groups: three pertaining to the security environment that states face, five relating to the strategies that states use to secure themselves, and two concerning the reliance of states on nontraditional actors to achieve security.

We then test the four global-level propositions against the global record of the years between the end of the Cold War and 2008—the era of globalization's entrenchment. For this, we rely primarily on data sources such as the International Institute for Strategic Studies (IISS) or the Stockholm International Peace Research Institute (SIPRI), which publish global conflict, military spending, and manpower data annually, as well as United Nations (UN) statistics on multilateral interventions and peacekeeping and peace-building operations. Then we investigate the state-based propositions with two types of data from the same time period. For propositions such as those relating to manpower and defense expenditures, which can easily be tested through reliable independent data sources, we rely on both national and regional data provided by the IISS or SIPRI. For propositions that are more difficult to assess directly with quantitative data, such as the degree to which national security establishments have shifted their emphasis to new security threats, we examine the national security doctrines and/or policy statements of each state, together with its recent behavior, to determine whether each reflects such "globalized" concerns. Although official doctrines and policy statements may, at times, merely reflect declaratory policy, rather than actual policy, they do represent a good first cut at the logic that animates the state's national security strategy, the threats that matter most to its security establishment, and the degree to which it has evolved to meet the demands of a globalized world. Moreover, these documents can often be revealing not only by their statements, but also by their omissions. Thus, as we shall see, the omission of any serious reference to the importance of multilateral regional security organizations in Russian, South Asian, and Middle Eastern doctrines—despite the obvious rhetorical imperative of paying lip service to them—casts significant doubt on the centrality of such institutions in the contemporary era, at least for these states. Nonetheless, we explore military doctrines critically and, when possible, seek external data and secondary source analyses to corroborate our conclusions.

Overview of the Book

We explore the globalization school's predictions for the pursuit of security in chapter 1. First we examine the various strands of the demise of the state argument, including those of hard globalization proponents, soft globalization proponents, and commercial liberals, as well as two other groups with claims that are compatible with our definition of globalization, democratic peace theory, and constructivist arguments about the spread of globalized political norms. We then cull out of these positions a set of common propositions about the effect globalization is likely to have on the way states pursue security. We identify macro-level propositions about the level of interstate war, aggregate defense spending, the prominence of transnational terrorism, and the role of multilateral institutions at the international system level. Then we identify state- and region-specific propositions about the national security strategies and architectures of individual states.

In chapter 2 we investigate global trends from 1991 to 2008. In particular, we inquire whether the macro-level propositions identified in chapter 1 have been borne out. Therefore, we consider whether the level of interstate conflict has declined, whether global defense spending has decreased, whether the threat of global terrorism has begun to supplant interstate warfare on the global security agenda, and whether regional and global multilateral security institutions have begun to supplant states as the primary security providers, as many globalization scholars have predicted. Our conclusion is that global trends are not very consistent with the globalization-kills-the-national-security-state hypothesis. Moreover, to the extent that certain features of the contemporary international system (such as the general reduction in interstate wars) are consistent with the globalization school's predictions, it remains unclear whether globalization is the sole cause (or even the primary cause) or whether something potentially less enduring—such as American hegemony, the defense/deterrence dominance of contemporary military technology, or a lull after the all-encompassing global clash that was the Cold War—may have been more instrumental.

Chapters 3 through 6 present our examination of the differential impact of globalization across regions and types of states during the same time period. Each chapter investigates the degree to which the ten specific propositions of the state-in-demise approach correspond with the contemporary security apparatuses and practices of different categories of states. Chapter 3 looks at the major powers: the United States, China, and Russia. Chapter 4 focuses on regional powers in two types of stable regions, with an examination of states in western Europe (a mature security community) and Southeast Asia and Latin America (stable regions that have not yet become pluralistic security communities). In chapter 5, we concentrate on regional powers in areas characterized by enduring rivalries, with a focus on the Middle East and South Asia. Chapter 6 examines the lot of the very weak and failed states of sub-Saharan Africa. We conclude that states of all four types continue to pursue far more traditional security policies than globalization theorists predict. To the extent that globalization does matter, though, its impact on security policies appears to vary across states and regions. States in stable regions have had their security policies affected by globalization the most, whereas those in regions of enduring conflict have been affected the least. The great powers have adapted to global economic trends when it served to maximize their power advantage over others, but resisted them when they sought to undermine national autonomy over national security policy. Finally, globalization has helped accelerate the dependence of weak states on the international security market, but it is not the primary cause of their inability to pursue traditional national security policies.

The final chapter summarizes the conclusions reached in this study and considers why many of the globalization school's predictions have fallen far from the mark. In this regard, we compare the globalization and security approach with past state-in-demise arguments linked to other social, economic, or technological changes, such as the rise of the trading state, the invention of dynamite, and the development of thermonuclear weapons. We contend that the state as a security-providing institution was not swept away by these changes, principally because, as complex adaptative systems, states both adapted to and controlled these changes. Similarly, we argue that, at least in the security realm, states have to this point been able to adapt to the pressures of globalization, and the great powers—particularly the United States—have been able to exert some control over it. Thus, although not completely absent, globalization's effect on the security practices of states has been muted, particularly among great powers and those states that face considerable regional security dilemmas.

CHAPTER 1 | Globalization and National Security:
Key Propositions

A S WE INDICATED IN THE INTRODUCTORY CHAPTER, our conception of
globalization is a broad one that centers on the expansion of a multiplic-
ity of socioeconomic and sociopolitical activities on a transnational scale. As
a result, there are a wide variety of theoretical arguments about the changing
nature of national and international security that we classify as globalization
hypotheses, because they identify the engine of change as a particular transnational economic, political, or social process. In this chapter we detail
numerous strands of the globalization-alters/kills-the-national-security-state
argument and draw out common hypotheses from these disparate arguments
about the way global processes should affect the pursuit of security.

Varieties of the Globalization Thesis

Several types of globalization and security approaches exist in the literature,
differentiated by the nature of the global processes that supposedly drive
national changes and the depth of change they envision. In this section we
identify seven types of arguments. Hard economic globalization theorists
assume that the increasing scale of the global economy has already made the
state obsolete, both as a means of managing and regulating the economy and
as a provider of national security. In contrast, soft economic globalization
approaches contend that the growth of a truly global economy has meaningfully affected the state's functions, but only in an incremental manner, with

radical change a possibility over the longer term. These are the prototypical globalization school arguments, but we identify five more approaches as globalization-type approaches, because they also posit changes in state behavior caused by global political and economic processes.

Commercial liberals argue that the growth of global trade and investment has had a more punctuated effect, making states less likely to use force against economic partners. *Democratic peace theorists* contend that the global spread of democratic political norms and institutions reduces the willingness of democracies to use force to resolve disputes with others who share their norms and institutions. The *global norms approach* assumes that the spread of political norms—particularly those respecting human rights—across national boundaries has restricted the state's ability to pursue certain proscribed types of national security policies. The *global culture approach* maintains that the displacement of national identities and cultures by global referents has led to a cultural convergence that stabilizes international relations. Last, *postmodern warfare theorists* argue that the ease with which people can move, organize, and communicate across national boundaries in a globalized era has not only changed the nature of warfare, but has paralyzed the ability of even powerful states to provide effectively for their security. We shall consider each of these approaches in turn and subsequently derive testable hypotheses from the composite "globalization school."

Although we use the shorthand *the globalization school* or *globalization theorists* for the group of arguments we are testing, it is important to note that these terms represent a composite of a variety of different and often-competing arguments that are related only in that they explore the effects of the phenomenon of globalization on the pursuit of national security. We believe it is useful to cull and investigate a set of core propositions flowing from this school in much the same way that international relations scholars have done with disparate realist arguments (united by their emphasis on the impact of international anarchy on international politics) and liberal arguments (united by their emphasis on the impact of individuals and institutions on international politics).[1] However, we acknowledge the diversity of the literature in this area and the contending views it has generated among enthusiasts and opponents.

To some "hard" globalists, globalization has already ushered in drastic changes to every aspect of the state's functions, and affects all aspects of national and international economic, political, social, and cultural relations. Martin Shaw summarizes their arguments:

> For globalization theorists, contemporary change often has the relentless aspect of a single process—or a closely related set of processes—through

which the market system colonizes new social space. Globalization ren-
ders territorial boundaries irrelevant—or in the more cautious versions
which have become increasingly prominent, less significant. It also nul-
lifies the cultural, political and technical boundaries that defined distinct worlds, isolated some social relations from world markets, and
inhibited communications.[2]

Ardent proponents, such as Kenichi Ohmae, contend that, under the irre-
versible influence of modern information technology, genuine borderless
economies are emerging. The resulting new incentives, opportunities, and
constraints have affected business behavior and the values, judgments, and
preferences of citizens all over the world.[3] Under these circumstances, the
state is an obsolescent institution, ill equipped to control its economic destiny, provide for the welfare of its citizens, or ensure its own security. The
supreme mobility of capital and labor make it easy for businesses to escape
national regulations and shop around for the most hospitable environment
within which to operate. The state is, therefore, severely limited in the
restrictions it can place on business activities. Nor, as more and more production and distribution take place beyond national boundaries, can the state
shield its citizens from economic shocks (such as refinery fires, strikes, inclem-
ent weather, or natural disasters) that take place halfway around the world. In
Susan Strange's formulation, "[w]here states were once the masters of markets, now it is the markets which, on many crucial issues, are the masters over
the governments of states."[4] And, because globalization implies deterritorial-
ization or "the end of geography," the core basis of state power has eroded.[5]
Thus, to the extent possible, states have already realized their futility and
have scrambled to join both regional and global institutions in an attempt to
find more appropriate ways of regulating their economies. After all, if the
problems are transnational in nature, the solution must be, as well.[6]

Gilpin summarizes the case of hard-core globalization enthusiasts in more
measured terms:

A quantum change in human affairs has taken place as the flow of large
quantities of trade, investment, and technologies across national borders has expanded from a trickle to a flood. Political, economic, and
social activities are becoming worldwide in scope, and interactions
among states and societies on many fronts have increased. As integra-
tive processes widen and deepen globally, some believe that markets
have become, or are becoming, the most important mechanism determining both domestic and international affairs. In a highly integrated

global economy, the nation-state, according to some, has become anachronistic and is in retreat.[7]

Thus, the changes are not merely economic. Other hard globalization theorists have argued that the cohesiveness of the state as a social institution has eroded. Throughout its existence, the state provided both internal and external security and economic productivity, in large part because it was able to command the loyalty of its citizens and harness it toward national goals. Some argue, however, that under the weight of global social forces, the individual citizen's loyalty to the state has declined and will decline further in the future. Without war as a mechanism to foster national loyalty and patriotism (as we shall see later, globalization scholars presume that interstate war is declining), there is nothing equivalent in sight to generate the "glue" that this social institution provided nation-states for centuries.[8]

In the security theater, too, hard globalization theorists assume that the state has outlived its utility. As modern technology has made national borders porous, the state cannot effectively prevent hostile groups from entering national territory and harming its citizens. Indeed, as terrorist attacks in the United States, Spain, Israel, India, and elsewhere during the past few years indicate, not even states with modern capitalist economies or powerful military establishments can secure their populations reliably. Furthermore, globalization has brought with it a whole range of problems, such as pandemic diseases and transnational organized crime, which affect states far more than traditional international military threats do. Therefore the national security state has been overtaken by these contemporary challenges, for which it is ill equipped to respond, at the same time as the primary purpose of the national security establishment—interstate warfare—is declining in frequency.

Moreover, the argument goes, as states become more enmeshed into the global economy, they are compelled to pay more attention to wealth-making as opposed to war-making activities. There is also an inherent assumption (similar to many writings on economic interdependence) that when states seek more wealth through increased economic interactions, overseas trade, foreign direct investment (FDI), and capital markets, they have to appear less threatening to others and, consequently, modify their traditional security policies. The economic conditions, often set by leading lender institutions such as the World Bank and the IMF, require states to reduce their focus on military spending while encouraging liberalization of their economies, because the opportunity costs involved in war making are expected to be higher than the economic benefits that accrue from conflict.[9] Economic liberalization also would encourage domestic actors and coalitions that favor wealth over societal actors who pursue military might and war making. As a result, the state's focus on security has diminished, and the type of threats that proliferate in a globalized world are those that states are ill equipped to counter.

"Soft" globalization theorists agree that a profound revolution in human affairs is underway, but they contend that changes have been taking place incrementally and that it will take time until they are fully manifest. Therefore, rather than seeing the state as outmoded in the contemporary international environment, they view it as facing increasingly difficult economic, political, and security-related challenges with which its existing standard operating procedures are unable to cope. As Jonathan Kirshner writes: "The intensification of economic exchange, the information revolution, and pressures for marketization are changing (though not always diminishing) the nature of state power and state capacity, affecting the balance of power between states, and creating new sources of and axes of conflict between them."[10] As a result, the state has already been forced to adapt to new circumstances, to embrace nonstate actors as well as regional and global international institutions that can assist it in meeting the challenges of a globalized world, and, on occasion, it has been unable to provide its signature economic and security goods to its citizens.[11] Indeed, in the economic realm, the ability of states to protect their citizens from the global market has greatly diminished, because globalization has already stripped the state of much of its autonomy and the state must avoid actions that sap its competitiveness in the international marketplace.[12] Eventually, the cumulative weight of these global changes will force the state to give way to sociopolitical institutions that are more appropriate for a globalized world.

In the security theater, according to soft globalization arguments, states are increasingly reluctant to use heavily military-oriented approaches to resolve interstate problems, for many of the same reasons suggested by hard globalization theorists.[13] Although they do not believe that globalization has yet knocked the state off its national security perch, soft globalization theorists believe that the porousness of national borders, the global nature of contemporary threats to international security, and the economic disincentives for using force are combining to make states increasingly willing to seek partners beyond the state to assist in the provision of security. Moreover, because of the growing desire for wealth acquisition through economic liberalization and trade, states are starting to focus less on conquest and matters of national security than in the past.[14] Although in the past, great powers engaged in warfare for the control of land and resources to maintain their power and prosperity, conquest and occupation of land has now become difficult. Indeed, during the contemporary era, many argue that controlling land physically is no longer that vital for prosperity, because trade, commerce, and specialization in knowledge-intensive industries can make a nation prosperous, and the factors of production now include information and new technology.[15] Aversion to conquest is bolstered by the intense nationalism that is prevalent in almost all parts of the world, which has combined with asymmetric strategies that occupied peoples can use to make occupation costly.[16] Therefore, soft globalization scholars would expect states to have less intense traditional security dilemmas and be less eager to capture the territory of others.

As a result, according to soft globalization accounts, activities surrounding war making are no longer the primary focus of states, the proof of which lays in the dramatic decline of interstate wars since the end of the Cold War in 1991. Even major powers (barring the United States, perhaps) are conducting their limited competition through "soft geopolitics," with less emphasis on open arms races, crises, and war.[17] In their view, major security threats are no longer heavily military oriented, but consist of terrorism, drug trafficking, disease, ecological disasters, mass migration, and widespread poverty.[18] Notions of "human security" as opposed to military security increasingly affect the preferences of policy makers in many countries.[19] With the decline of geopolitical conflicts, it is argued that the military in most advanced states has become more focused on internal and international crime fighting or policing as opposed to waging interstate wars.[20] The pursuit of internal security issues has decreased the importance of the state as the national security provider, as protection from external threats has traditionally been the core function of the nation-state and the key source of its legitimacy and power over society.[21] And, to deal with external threats to security from transnational sources, states have been increasingly relying on private security providers, NGOs, and international institutions, which are better suited to combat these new threats.[22] Thus, soft globalization scholars argue, the state's role in the security theater is gradually changing and eroding under the pressures of economic globalization.

A precursor to the economic globalization position that still remains as a distinct and more limited argument is commercial liberalism. Commercial liberals maintain that as trade and investment flow freely across national boundaries, states grow increasingly interdependent. As a result, they become reluctant to use force against trading partners, both because of the opportunity costs of force in terms of lost trade and investment, and because trade is more efficient than force as a means of securing a state's basic needs.[23]

In a globalized world, the implications of commercial liberalism are more profound as economic interdependence becomes more widespread. Furthermore, as transnational actors, such as MNCs, take more control over the trading agenda under globalization, they undermine national efforts to protect defense and security-related industries, as well as supplies of strategic goods.[24] And as multinationals become more transnational, producing different components of their products in different countries and assembling at plants across the globe, the states that host them are generally careful not to undertake military ventures across borders, because they would suffer heavily in economic terms if war breaks out.[25] Stephen Brooks argues that the globalization of world production has made it even more economically unprofitable to conquer territory, especially because states can use MNCs as a means of extracting materials, wealth, and goods from foreign territories.[26] Therefore, globalization scholars in the commercial liberal tradition would expect that, more than ever, states should be both unwilling and unable to fight large-scale wars to resolve disputes among themselves, even if they involve territorial issues.

More sophisticated versions of commercial liberalism contend that not only will states respond to economic disincentives to use force, they will also organize themselves differently to perpetuate the gains of an interdependent world. Richard Rosecrance, for example, believes that unprecedented levels of global economic interdependence have ushered in a qualitative alternative to the national security state: the trading state. Recognizing that wealth and power no longer derive from military might, trading states embrace economic interdependence and shun the economic nationalist's concern for autarky. Therefore, unlike their military–political counterparts, they specialize in particular industrial activities in which they enjoy a comparative advantage to derive the maximal benefit from the international economy.[27] Under these favorable economic circumstances, military competition becomes not only unnecessary, as wealth becomes divorced from the physical control of territory, but also counterproductive, because it would disrupt the basis of economic prosperity.[28] Moreover, as the global business environment depends on mobile information technology, relying on workers, capital, and information that cross national boundaries with unprecedented ease, the trading state becomes a "virtual state" that has no interest in territorial security or conquest.[29]

Meanwhile, Etel Solingen argues that the economic liberalization that has been taking place globally since the early 1990s led economically and politically liberalizing elites to undermine the power of their militaries deliberately, to attract foreign capital, investment, and market access.[30] In other words, economic interdependence leads states not only to eschew the use of force now by affecting national security decision making, it also causes them to alter the architecture of the state to make the future use of force less likely.

In our view of globalization, we can also identify democratic peace arguments as another form of globalization theory, concerned as they are with the spread of common democratic norms and institutions worldwide. To democratic globalization theorists, the widespread democratization of countries in most regions of the world has diminished the likelihood of war.[31] They argue that democracies rarely fight each other; these states deliberately find nonviolent means to resolve conflict among themselves for both institutional and normative reasons. Democratic domestic political institutions requiring governments to mobilize the public and the legislature in support of war slow down the resort to force, create time to resolve crises and conflicts with other democracies without violence, and require the government to furnish legitimate reasons for using force.[32] Furthermore, their domestic political norms of tolerance, compromise, and the rejection of coercion as a legitimate means of securing consent are externalized to their foreign relations with similar political systems.[33] Thus, according to the theory, the globalization of democracy should lead to greater military restraint and reluctance to use military force.[34]

A fifth set of globalization-related arguments is put forward by normative schools, which believe that several global norms have emerged in recent decades that have conditioned state behavior in the security arena. These norms affect issues of considerable importance, such as state sovereignty and territorial integrity, humanitarian intervention, and the acquisition and use of certain weapons, such as land mines. Of greatest significance, Mark Zacher claims that a norm of territorial integrity has become embedded, making it virtually impossible for states to alter borders by force and receive international recognition.[35]

International human rights norms have also been cited as affecting the behavior of states vis-à-vis their citizens.[36] Norms against war crimes and genocide, although broken in Rwanda and Yugoslavia, have become focal points in an emerging normative international framework with the arrest and prosecution of some leaders who perpetrated such crimes. The newly constituted International Criminal Court further augmented this position. Furthermore, norms regarding the production, sale, use, and deployment of weapons that cause undue harm to civilian populations have also led some states to alter their security behavior. In this regard, norms against the use of nuclear weapons, the nuclear nonproliferation regime, and the treaty to ban antipersonnel land mines may all represent a growing trend to curtail the national security behavior of states.[37] The increasing presence of norms in the security arena suggests, therefore, that a nascent global normative order may have emerged that challenges the traditional state-centric military security approach of states.[38]

A sixth line of argument posits that the emergence of a putative global culture will foster a more peaceful world, because a global civil society is emerging that is founded on democratic regimes and civil societies based on a consensus on civic virtues.[39] As different groups—especially humanitarian NGOs, human rights advocates, and transnational terrorist organizations— are able to use new technologies such as the Internet and satellite television to communicate across national boundaries, they are able to fight for common causes and thereby undermine traditional boundaries set by states, classes, or communities.[40] Thus, national identities are weakening while transnational associations are strengthening. Moreover, over time, the exposure of all the world's population to the same media, music, movies, books, and so forth, is creating a world culture that unites, rather than divides, the world's population.[41] Thus, the globalization of culture, it is argued, should reduce international conflict.

In the aftermath of the September 11 terrorist strike on the United States, a seventh line of globalization arguments has come to the fore. Accordingly, the attacks on the United States show that even the most sophisticated military power in the world could not prevent a major assault on its financial and military nerve centers by a deeply committed and highly organized group of individuals of various nationalities using civilian aircraft as a weapon. Furthermore, it has proved very difficult to combat the scourge of terrorism. The conventional attacks on states, such as Afghanistan, that harbor and sponsor terrorism have achieved only limited success, because terrorists can flee to other locales and countries. The irony of transnational terrorism, therefore, is that it uses some of the key instruments of globalization—transportation and communication networks—although terrorists seem to be fighting the spread of the western cultural ethos that promotes global values, which they believe are threatening "local religions and cultures."[42]

These competing images of globalization vary in both the intensity of the change, as well as the intervening variables (be they political norms, economic incentives, or political institutions) through which global changes affect the pursuit of national security. They all agree, however, that the phenomenon of globalization has profound implications for the national security state, which is increasingly ill-equipped to confront the challenges of the modern world. In the next section, we cull a representative set of propositions about the pursuit of national security that are consistent with all or most of these approaches.

Key Propositions

GLOBAL-LEVEL PROPOSITIONS (PG)

As the preceding discussion shows, the arguments that globalization theorists make regarding the pursuit of security are broad and sweeping, and they come from different directions. Although there is no single integrated theory of globalization and the state, nearly all versions of it focus on the weakening of the nation-state as the primary unit of international politics, and the decreasing importance of military security in the behavior and national policies of states. However, if the core arguments on the state's security function that are present in most globalization theses are valid, then changes should be visible in the following areas on a global scale.[43]

PG1: Interstate Conflict Should Decline

First, if the theses are correct, there would be a major decline in interstate armed conflicts worldwide, as states increasingly seek the economic gains of globalization, a constructive global culture emerges, and democratic norms and institutions spread. In other words, both the need for and the utility of interstate conflict should have subsided with the economic and social changes that have occurred. As Zaki Laidi suggests, "there would seem to be a close relationship between the relative decline of interstate violence and the weakening role of states in the global process."[44] This trend should be reinforced by the unprecedented level of destruction made possible by modern weapons technology, available on the global arms markets, which should increase the physical and economic costs of warfare.[45] Consequently, although the weakening of the state may lead to more frequent challenges from within—in other words, intrastate conflicts—states in a globalized world should be less willing to use force beyond their borders.

PG2: Worldwide Defense Spending and Military Manpower Should Be Declining

As interstate war becomes less common, the *raison d'être* of armed forces would be undercut. For, although military apparatuses would still be of some utility in fighting low-intensity conflicts (LICs), they would no longer need to be as large as they were when the primary threat was full-scale warfare among rival states. As a result, maintaining traditional armies would be unnecessarily costly and, therefore, economically irrational. Consequently, as more states adapt to the new globalized environment, they would drastically reduce their military forces and substantially cut military expenditures. The result would be a global reduction in money spent on military security and fewer soldiers in traditional armies.

PG3: Multilateral Regional and Global Institutions Should Be Increasingly Important in the Provision of Security

A third global change is what David Held and Anthony McGrew call "the internationalization of security," or the growing importance of multilateral regional and global institutions as central actors in the security theater.[46] In their view, changes in the nature of global security challenges require a response above the level of the nation-state. Because security threats are increasingly coming from nonstate actors (such as insurgents and terrorists who organize and operate across state borders), global health pandemics (such as AIDS, SARS, and H1N1), and ecological and environmental threats, the need for a response coordinated above the level of the nation-state is self-evident, according to globalization theorists, because the state is geographically limited. With broader geographical reach and greater aggregate resources, regional and global institutions should be more effective in responding to the new international security agenda. For this reason, globalization theorists would expect the increasing involvement of international institutions in the provision of security.

PG4: The Incidence of Global Terrorism Should Have Increased Dramatically

As communications technology allows people and groups to organize on a global scale, and porous borders allow them to infiltrate countries and move weapons and materiel across national borders, terrorism should emerge as a truly global challenge. In other words, although terrorism has been a problem for particular states and regions in the past, it was not a problem that affected all states. In a globalized world, however, transnational terrorist groups have global reach and can carry out operations against multiple targets across the world with relative ease and, therefore, require a global effort to combat.[47] Moreover, as goods move more easily across national boundaries, transnational terrorist organizations may be able to access the international black market for fissile materials (perhaps from a cash-starved Russia or ideologically motivated actors in Pakistan) and threaten devastating nuclear attacks.[48] Given these enormous stakes, therefore, counterterrorism efforts should be occurring on a transnational basis, too, to meet the threat effectively.

By examining these four key areas, we will assess the extent to which changes have taken place on a global scale, whether these changes are caused by globalization, and whether they are sustainable. To assess whether changes have occurred within states and across regions, the next section culls specific state-level propositions from the globalization literature about the effect of globalization on the state's pursuit of security.

STATE-LEVEL PROPOSITIONS (PS)

The emerging globalization literature assumes that several features of the contemporary international system—principally, the nature of technology, the interdependence of national economies, and the ease with which people, goods, services, and ideas cross national borders—have transformed the way in which states pursue national security. We identify three categories of changes that should be evident at the national level if the literature is correct: (1) changes in the challenges states face, (2) changes in the national security strategies states use to secure themselves, and (3) a challenge to the exclusivity of the state as a provider of national security. We discuss each of these issues in turn.

With regard to *the challenges states face*, according to the globalization literature, the nature of threats to national security has changed during the contemporary era. States traditionally organized to defend themselves against rival states, which were the only actors that could amass sufficient capabilities to threaten their interests. Two processes have altered this dynamic. First, the overwhelming destructive capability of modern military technology decreases the likelihood of traditional interstate wars, because even the winner of a modern war between states with roughly equal capability would suffer extensively.[49] Thus, wars tend not to be all-encompassing "Clausewitzian interstate wars," but rather LICs, involving smaller states with lower levels of technology, and frequently are civil or ethnic wars, insurgencies, or counter-insurgencies.[50] Our first state-level proposition, therefore, is that:

> *PS1: A shift in the nature of wars from Clausewitzian interstate wars to "wars of a third kind"—civil ethnic wars and wars between small states— has taken place*

Second, in a globalized and wired world, states cannot easily prevent hostile groups from recruiting and organizing across the globe, hacking computers and interfering with global commerce, or transporting hazardous materials, money, or weapons across national borders.[51] As a result, smaller, substate actors have the ability to challenge nation-states by disrupting their economies, spreading disease, or engaging in terrorist activities.[52] This amounts to a shift from ordinary interstate warfare as the primary purpose of states to an increasing emphasis on what Michael Klare calls the new challenge of "postindustrial warfare," or a global assault by unprofessional, ideological combatants, operating in deprived areas, targeting civilians and businesses.[53] Thus, an increasing focus of national security agendas should be countering terrorism. Our second proposition, therefore, is:

PS2: States have increasingly shifted their national security establishments to counter the challenge of postindustrial warfare and, in particular, terrorism

As borders become porous and global transactions increase, the safety and security of populations will be threatened by a host of nontraditional threats, including the spread of disease and environmental degradation. Furthermore, mass migrations of disaffected populations, as a result of ecological change or economic dislocations, could hasten the spread of these ills.[54] As a result, these nontraditional areas have become "securitized" and should be increasingly targeted by national security establishments.[55] In a globalized world, therefore, national security policy should have well-developed economic, environmental, and human health dimensions. Our final challenge-related proposition, then, is:

PS3: National security increasingly includes nondefense areas of trade, ecology, migration, and health, because threats are increasingly economic, environmental, and disease related

With regard to the *strategies states pursue,* in large part because of the redefinition of national security threats, the globalization thesis asserts that states are changing the way they organize their national security apparatuses and the types of security strategies they use. To begin with, the need for offensive military doctrines that predicate national defense on the ability to seize military objectives on enemy territory has declined during the contemporary era. Because traditional interstate wars are declining in frequency, the utility of offensive doctrines is extremely limited. Furthermore, because the conquest of territory no longer yields extractable gains in a globalized world, and because trade and investment are more efficient than conquest, there is no practical incentive for offense. Perhaps most significant, with the spread of nuclear weapons to more countries, the deterrent power of these weapons means that great powers can achieve their basic security objectives more efficiently through nuclear deterrence. Therefore, states no longer need offensive strategic doctrines and are increasingly relying upon more economical and efficient defense and/or deterrence.[56] Our fourth proposition, therefore, is:

PS4: National military doctrines are abandoning offense in favor of defense/ deterrence

In addition to switching military doctrines, some claim that, in response to economic globalization, countries have forgone traditional balance-of-power politics (or "hard balancing") altogether, and no longer base their national security strategies on alliances and military buildups at the global and regional levels. Instead they have adopted noncoercive strategies, such as "soft balancing" (using diplomatic and institutional means), "bandwagoning," buck passing, and free riding, or transcending balance-of-power politics altogether.[57] Soft balancing, especially, has become attractive to second-tier major powers such as Russia, China, and France because (1) they no longer fear losing their existential security from the hegemonic power and (2) the United States is a much more "constrained power" than previous dominant states were.[58] These strategies, they argue, are more appropriate in an era in which the use of force is economically counterproductive and military technology makes offense ineffective. Our fifth proposition, therefore, is:

PS5: States increasingly prefer to counter powerful rivals with soft balancing and other less competitive strategies, rather than traditional hard balancing

The shift away from offense and hard balancing has further implications for the size and shape of national armed forces. Without an emphasis on occupying and controlling territory, large, expensive, standing armies should no longer be the staple of the national security state. This logic is reinforced by technological advances in warfare that encourage states to rely on more efficient high-tech weaponry, instead of traditional, manpower-based military apparatuses.[59] As a result, globalization theorists expect a decline in national conscription and overall defense spending, because paying, mobilizing, and supporting service people is the most cost-intensive component of the defense budget. Military establishments are, therefore, supposed to be becoming smaller, more mobile, and more potent.[60] Our sixth and seventh propositions are:

PS6: National conscription and the size of the military apparatus should decline

and

PS7: Defense spending should decline as traditional military apparatuses become of less utility

Finally, as it increasingly faces lower intensity challenges and threats by individuals and groups, rather than traditional interstate battles, the national security state is shifting from a war-fighting apparatus to a crime-fighting and policing apparatus, not only externally, but internally as well.[61] As a result, traditional armies, navies, and air forces—which are appropriate for interstate battles, but not geared to maintaining domestic order—should find their position within national security establishments eroding. Meanwhile, intelligence agencies, border and coast guards, police, and special operations forces should increasingly become the face of the national security state. Our final strategy-related hypothesis, therefore, is:

PS8: Military establishments are shifting from war fighters to police forces

With regard to *the monopoly of the state as security provider*, globalization theorists conclude that the emergence of new threats and the contraction of national military apparatuses have not only changed the national security strategies states pursue, but they have also eroded the exclusivity of the state as a provider of national security, because the state is incapable of meeting its security needs on its own.[62] Instead, national security establishments are increasingly compelled to look both inside and outside the state to form partnerships that can provide security more economically and more effectively.[63] Inside the state, national armed forces are enlisting the services of private companies that can assist them in data gathering, data processing, monitoring, guarding prisoners and installations, and training personnel.[64] In some areas of the world, most notably Africa, states are even using private militias supplied by international security companies to perform some of the traditional functions of national armies, such as securing government buildings and suppressing rebellions.[65] Thus, the "marketization" of security "should redistribute power over the control of force" and hence the "oft-assumed collective monopoly of states over violence should suffer a blow."[66]

In addition, because counterterrorism and counterinsurgency operations depend on winning the hearts and minds of the local population, states are relying on the friendlier faces of NGOs—which often have greater expertise and experience than states in humanitarian areas, and are driven not by parochial national interests, but by broader humanitarian principles—as a means of delivering humanitarian aid and thereby fostering stability.[67] These organizations can also help alleviate the dire poverty and disease that can contribute to mass migration and the spread of economic dislocations and disease, which globalization scholars assume comprise a core component of the contemporary security agenda. Our ninth proposition, therefore, is:

PS9: States are privatizing security by including nonstate actors in defense activities

According to the globalization literature, states are also looking for assistance outside the state, as they realize they are no longer the appropriate institution to provide security when the threats transcend the scale of the nation-state. Therefore, globalization theorists expect states pursue security increasingly within the context of multilateral frameworks, particularly regional security organizations, such as the North American Treaty Organization (NATO), ASEAN, the African Union (AU), and the Organization of American States (OAS).[68] Security in a globalized world, therefore, should be increasingly regionalized.[69] Our final state-level proposition, then, is:

PS10: States increasingly pursue security through regional institutions

The balance of this book investigates the validity of these propositions to determine whether and to what degree globalization has affected the pursuit of security to this point. In the next chapter, we examine the global picture to assess whether the macro-level changes represented by propositions PG1 through PG4 accurately reflect the contemporary international security environment. Subsequent chapters will test the state-level hypotheses across regions and categories of states.

CHAPTER 2

The Global Security Environment

Has globalization brought about meaningful changes in the global security environment? Has it produced macro-level changes in the nature of threats, actors, and security behavior in the international system? In this chapter, we test the macro-level propositions (PG1–PG4) that we developed in chapter 1 to assess the changes that may have occurred at the global level as a result of globalization during the period we investigate (1991–2008). This chapter also offers a first cut at broader issues relating to globalization and its impact on the security behavior of states in an aggregate sense, before we delve into its effects on specific categories of states and regions.

Interstate and Intrastate Wars

A key measurable argument of the globalization thesis pertains to the amount of interstate wars in the international system.[1] According to PG1, interstate wars should have decreased in number and frequency as globalization advanced, as a result of the economic disincentives to waging war, the spread of democratic governance, and global normative, cultural, and technological constraints on the use of force. As a corollary, we should expect that the percentage (if not the number) of global conflicts that are intrastate conflicts should have increased, as interstate warfare declines.

On this measure, there is strong supporting evidence; there has been a considerable decrease in the number of interstate wars since the end of the Cold War. Even intrastate wars, after peaking in 1991, declined substantially by 1999. In 1991, fifty-one states, representing 33% of all independent countries, were engaged in some form of serious conflict, many of which were interstate wars. By 1999, this total had declined by half, both in the number of cases and the percentage of involved states, indicating a preponderance of intrastate wars.[2] Indeed, only two of the twenty-five conflicts (involving twenty-three countries) with a thousand or more battlefield deaths in 2000 were interstate conflicts.[3] This decline continued from 2001, when twenty-four armed conflicts occurred in twenty-two locations, to 2006, when all seventeen major armed conflicts were intrastate.[4] The vast majority of the post-Cold War conflicts consist of civil wars, terrorism, or political violence—in other words, intrastate conflicts—even when more than one state is involved.[5] Indeed, prior to the 2003 war against Iraq, Ted Robert Gurr and Monty Marshall observed that "[t]he Iraqi invasion of Kuwait and the subsequent 1991 US-led Gulf War to expel the invaders is the only unambiguous interstate war during the post-Cold War era."[6] Thus, states seem to be less willing than in the past to resort to military force in the face of conflict situations, especially with their neighbors.

It is difficult, however, to assess the exact cause of the decline in interstate warfare, which may be overdetermined. Economic globalization could be one of the significant factors, but it is by no means clear whether it is the key explanatory variable. Other factors that might be responsible for the reduction of traditional warfare include the end of the Cold War, the preponderance of American power and the consequent transformation of the international system to near unipolarity in military terms, and, above all, the technological changes that obstruct offense and support defense and/or deterrence. We shall briefly consider these alternative explanations.

The Cold War was the defining feature of the post-World War II world, with the globe divided into two competing camps led by nuclear-armed superpowers, and a third, much weaker, nonaligned block of nations. This division contained war between the superpowers largely through mutual deterrence. It also spurred and exacerbated conflicts on the periphery of the two competing blocs and in the Third World, as the United States and the Soviet Union engaged in proxy wars for control of, or influence over, Korea, Vietnam, Afghanistan, the Middle East, and many African and Latin American nations.[7] The collapse of the Soviet Union, followed by improved economic and political relations between the West and the former communist states of central and eastern Europe (including Russia), has eliminated both a key source of interstate conflict as well as superpower support for warring states in the less developed world.[8] Indeed, the end of conflicts in southern Africa, Cambodia, and Afghanistan during the early 1990s can, in large measure, be attributed to the ending of the Cold War.

Furthermore, the collapse of the Soviet Union has left the world with only one superpower with political, economic, and military resources that far exceed its leading competitors. According to hegemonic stability theorists, this condition of unipolarity, or hegemony, is conducive to peace and stability, because the hegemonic leader can use its power resources to foster cooperation. Specifically, the hegemonic leader regulates the international system by setting the rules of the global economy and geopolitical competition. It secures compliance with its rules by providing selective incentives to those who comply and by coercing those who do not.[9] Using this logic, William Wohlforth expects that American hegemony should provide unprecedented stability to the international system.[10]

Finally, technological changes that have altered the offense–defense balance may also have dampened the frequency of interstate warfare. Offense–defense theorists contend that when technology favors the offense, the security dilemma between states is intensified because the costs of failing to respond to a threat are likely to be high. As a result, states have an incentive to preempt rivals when in doubt, and conflict becomes more likely. Furthermore, when it is difficult to distinguish between offensive and defensive weapons, the security dilemma is similarly intensified, because states can have little confidence in their estimates of adversary intentions and must, consequently, always assume the worst. In contrast, when technology favors defense, and when it is easy to distinguish between offensive and defensive weapons, the security dilemma is greatly reduced, because states can have confidence in their assessment of adversary intentions, and the costs of error are low.[11] As Robert Jervis explains, the advent of nuclear weapons creates a defense- (or deterrent-) dominant world. These weapons, after all, are not useful for conquering territory and extracting resources. Instead, they are used to deter an adversary's attack on the holder's territory, a fundamentally defensive purpose. Moreover, in a nuclear world, it is easy to distinguish an adversary with a defensive/deterrent posture from one with an offensive posture (the latter will be investing disproportionately in conventional military capability). Therefore, in his view, nuclear weapons have made interstate conflict between states that possess them far less likely.[12]

These are compelling explanations of the decline in interstate war during the past fifteen years. This is not to say that economic globalization and its explosive expansion of the global economy did not play a role. Furthermore, observers have also linked reduced warfare to globalization-related explanatory variables, such as changes in values, ideas, and norms (e.g., the anti-imperial norm), the spread of democracy, and the mitigating role of international institutions, giving some credibility to the globalization thesis.[13] Clearly the decline of interstate warfare is overdetermined and cannot confidently be attributed to the advent of globalization. Nor is there credible evidence that globalization was either a necessary or sufficient condition for this decrease. We cannot, though, conclusively reject globalization as a contributing factor to the decreasing frequency of interstate wars.

A related question that needs to be answered is the following: If states and other international actors are not fighting wars to settle disputes, to what alternative strategies are they resorting? According to the globalization thesis, in an economically interdependent world, states and international institutions should increasingly rely on economic statecraft and other soft power approaches to security, as opposed to military instruments. Nonviolent policy instruments would also face fewer obstacles in terms of global political norms. Therefore, the degree to which states use economic statecraft instead of military force to achieve national security objectives may be a related indicator of the affect of globalization on the pursuit of security.

During the past fifteen years, economic statecraft has indeed played a more prominent role on the international stage. There are two principal strategies of economic statecraft—economic sanctions and economic incentives, which seek to influence a target state by manipulating the market either to impose economic costs on states that fail to comply with one's wishes (sanctions) or convey economic benefits to those that do comply (incentives).[14] The latter strategy, economic incentives, has gained prominence on the international stage since 1990. Although they have historically been both underused and understudied, during the post-Cold War era, economic incentives have been used by states and international institutions to an unprecedented extent.[15] Several high-profile examples include American, Japanese, and Korean incentives to North Korea in their attempt to terminate the latter's nuclear weapons program; American and Russian economic incentives to induce the Ukraine to give up its Soviet-era nuclear weapons; EU incentives to eastern European states in an effort to stabilize the treatment of minorities; and western incentives to the Palestinian Authority to persuade it to clamp down on terrorism.

The global use of economic sanctions as a policy alternative may also have increased in the globalization era. Kimberly Ann Elliott and Barbara L. Oegg, for example, document fifty-one applications of economic sanctions from 1990 to 1999, a 50% increase from the thirty-four episodes of the 1980s. Multilateral UN sanctions have also increased during this time period, with eleven documented cases in the 1990s, compared with only two from 1970 to 1989.[16] Indeed, sanctions have become one of the preferred instruments, particularly of the United States and American-led international institutions, to ensure compliance with international law, the protection of human rights, and a host of other multilateral objectives.[17]

It is not clear, however, whether economic sanctions have replaced the use of force, because some of these sanctions were imposed either just before or after intense military campaigns. In 1990, for example, the UN imposed economic sanctions against Iraq to induce Saddam Hussein to withdraw his troops from Kuwait. Yet, in January 1991, before sanctions were given time to work, the UN commenced a U.S.-led military campaign to force Iraq to withdraw. The postwar UN sanctions against Iraq also failed to prevent a subsequent U.S.-led military coalition against Iraq in 2003. Moreover, rather than relying on economic statecraft, the United States and its allies used force against Serbia in 1999 in response to its ethnic cleansing of Kosovar Albanians, and against Afghanistan in 2001 because of its hospitality to Osama bin Laden and his terrorist network. Thus, economic sanctions have been companions of, or precursors to, the use of force, rather than its replacement.[18]

Finally, although sanctions were used with greater frequency during the 1990s, between 2000 and 2006, economic sanctions were employed only sixteen times (even less frequently than during the 1980s).[19] So the 1990s may have been an aberration, rather than a new trend in favor of economic instruments of statecraft, rather than military ones.

The reluctance of states to advance their aims solely through economic statecraft may reflect a strong current of theoretical skepticism toward economic instruments. Robert Pape, for example, argues that economic sanctions have rarely been effective—except in restricted situations when the target is a very weak, dependent, or vulnerable state, or when the demands made by the "sanctioner" are minimal—in forcing changes to the foreign or security policies of states. He concludes, therefore, that they are not a reliable alternative to the use of military force.[20] Others agree that sanctions often fail because they inspire a rally-around-the-flag effect that strengthens the target state's government, because they encourage the target state to adapt through substitution, conservation, securing access to other suppliers of embargoed goods, or redirecting the costs of sanctions from domestic supporters of the regime to opposition groups, and because they are difficult to maintain over long periods of time.[21] Even proponents of economic sanctions acknowledge that they only work a small percentage of the time,[22] and that their main contribution is frequently third-party signaling, rather than compelling a change in target-state policy.[23]

Nor is there strong evidence that nonstate market pressures can compel states to change their security policies. Thus, although Stephen Brooks argues that the fear of losing FDI has a powerful effect on state security calculations, more recent evidence suggests that FDI flows into a state do not necessarily decrease as the state becomes embroiled in international conflicts.[24] Thus, states need not fear the indirect sanction of the market.

There is some anecdotal evidence that economic calculations may sometimes help alter state security policies. For example, *New York Times* columnist Thomas Friedman has argued that during the summer of 2002, India chose not to attack Pakistani camps training militants to launch incursions into Indian Kashmir in part because of the pressures exerted by the computer software industry—a major source of India's economic growth—fearing that the economy would suffer incalculable harm if a war were to break out in the region.[25] Even in this case, however, the Indian escalation options were limited by Pakistan's possession of nuclear weapons and U.S. diplomatic and military involvement in the region. Therefore, economic calculations might not have been the main driving force behind the Indian decision.

To sum up, then, the decline in the frequency of interstate wars is a major development in world politics. Although this finding is consistent with the globalization school's expectations, it remains unclear whether this is part of a broader trend, and whether it is caused principally by globalization. There are too many compelling alternative explanations to attribute the reduction in interstate warfare to the effects of globalization. Furthermore, although economic statecraft is on the rise, on balance states are not overwhelmingly replacing the use of force with economic instruments, as globalization theorists would expect. Therefore, although PG1 is confirmed by our analysis, we cannot be confident that the causal relationships it posits fully hold. We do not, however, discount that economic globalization may be a factor among the several variables causing this outcome.

Military Spending and Size of Armed Forces

Another core proposition (PG2) of the globalization and security paradigm is that global military spending should decline considerably under the pressures of economic globalization and economic liberalization.[26] After all, if interstate conflict is declining, states no longer need costly, labor-intensive manpower-based armies. Instead, they can pare down their armed forces and concentrate on cheaper defensive and deterrent technology to provide for their drastically reduced security needs. Although we investigate this on a state-by-state and region-by-region basis in the next chapters, in this chapter we examine how global spending has fared during the period under investigation.

There was, indeed, a major decline in global military spending beginning in the late 1980s, when world military expenditures fell by more than 30% from almost $1.2 trillion in 1988 to $834 billion in 1999 (in 2005 constant U.S. dollars and exchange rates), before increasing slowly thereafter to $892 billion in 2001. After the terrorist attacks against the United States in 2001 transformed the international security environment, world military spending increased by a further 6.2% in real terms in 2002 to $948 billion, and then jumped consistently each year, reaching a total of almost $1.15 trillion in 2006 (in 2005 constant U.S. dollars and exchange rates).[27]

It would stretch credulity to claim that the earlier short-term decline was brought about by globalization. In fact, the end of the Cold War, which is akin to the end of a major war, was the immediate cause of this change.[28] After this all-encompassing global conflict was resolved, most states no longer needed to compete at the intense Cold War level and, therefore, could contemplate a peace dividend. Furthermore, the collapse of the Soviet Union and the Warsaw Pact, and the subsequent economic decline of Russia reduced a substantial portion of total global spending on armed forces. The number of proxy wars supported by the superpowers also declined, resulting in fewer weapons transfers to competing groups.

Moreover, if globalization is the key factor inhibiting arms spending, what explains the increase in military spending since 1999, even before the 2001 terrorist attacks? The increase in defense spending by western states is particularly problematic for the globalization-kills-the-national-security-state school, because it is precisely these trading states that should focus on trade, interdependence, and multilateral security arrangements as the sources of security, rather than military spending. Yet the twenty-five biggest spenders on defense include several trading states, including many western liberal states. At the top of the list is the United States, which has increased its defense budget considerably, especially since the 2001 terrorist attacks. Under the Future Year Defense Plan for fiscal years (FYs) 2007 to 2011, the United States will spend about $2.4 trillion with budget authority for national defense projected to increase in real terms from $463 billion in FY 2007 to $482 billion in FY 2009 and then decrease to $477.2 billion in FY 2011 (all at constant FY 2007 prices).[29] This figure does not include estimated future spending for wars and cost overruns. Thus, it is estimated that actual U.S. spending for 2008, for example, would, in reality, be approximately $690 billion when additional outlays for Iraq and Afghanistan are taken into account.[30] At these levels, the United States is spending almost as much on defense as the rest of the world combined.

However, the United States is not the only trading state to spend heavily on defense. Japan, a key trading state, accounted for 45% of East Asia's military expenditures in 1999, whereas China, a growing trading state, has been increasing its average annual budget by 10% in real terms since 1995. Similarly, in 1999, Malaysia—another trading state—increased its defense budget by 39% in real terms.[31] In 2000, South Korea increased its defense budget by 2.8%. In Southeast Asia, Thailand has been pursuing a major boom in military spending: 20% in 1999 and 7% in 2000.[32] Likewise, Singapore, a small trading state, is in the forefront of acquisition of the latest military gadgetry. What we can see in some of these instances is that the trading state and the traditional territorially oriented national security state can go hand-in-hand, as they did in the past.[33] Thus, the economic gains of globalization do not appear to be restraining the willingness of states to spend on defense.

Global arms sales data provide another useful resource in assessing the impact of global forces on the state's security function. According to the Congressional Research Service (CRS), the global arms market (measured in terms of arms transfer agreements, rather than actual annual sales) has not contracted dramatically in recent years, but it has not grown considerably either. Indeed, international arms sales grew by 5% from $43.4 billion in 1999 to $45.6 billion in 2000, before dropping 30% during the next three years to $31.7 billion (all figures in 2006 constant U.S. dollars). The following year (2004), they shot right back up again to $41.7 billion, before climbing to $46.3 billion—an increase of more 46% over two years. Yet, by 2006, global arms sales had settled back again to $40.3 billion.[34, 35] Yet, SIPRI reports that, since 2002, actual global arms imports have increased steadily and consistently from $16.8 billion to $26.8 billion in 2006 (both figures in 1990 constant U.S. dollars), or by almost 60% in four years.[36] It is not clear, therefore, whether states are increasingly relying on the global market to access military goods. If the SIPRI report is correct, it might mean that globalization has spelled the end of autarky as a means of pursuing security, rather than the end of traditional national security establishments themselves. This would be a significant globalization-induced trend. Although, in the past, states preferred to protect their national defense industries to ensure adequate supplies in the event of a wartime embargo, states today may eschew autarky to procure the best equipment available most economically on the international market.[37] Conversely, if the picture painted by the CRS is correct, reliance on the global arms market may not be increasing significantly during the contemporary era.

A related indicator of the impact of globalization on the national security state is the number of people actively serving in armed forces worldwide. After all, if globalization makes traditional national security operations obsolescent, then we should see a marked drop in the size of military apparatuses. Although we consider this proposition on a national and regional basis in subsequent chapters, we briefly consider the global picture here. There does, indeed, seem to have been a reduction in the size of global military manpower—from just less than 28 million in 1985 to less than 23 million in 1994, less than 22 million in 1999, 20.5 million in 2002, and 19.8 million in 2006.[38] Once again, however, it is not clear whether we can fairly attribute this reduction to globalization. Where the size of armed forces has been reduced, it has been, in many cases, the result of technological innovations.[39] Large land armies are unlikely to remain high on national agendas, because modern weaponry can achieve many tasks assigned previously to military personnel. Furthermore, as with the initial reduction in defense spending, the reduction in global manpower is also consistent with the peace dividend sought by most countries at the end of the Cold War.

There would appear, therefore, to be no significant and consistent trend to lower national military spending, despite the pressures of globalization. Furthermore, although there is evidence of a consistent reduction in global manpower, it may be an artifact of other influences—namely, technological sophistication and the end of the Cold War. A possible change that we might be able to trace to globalization and its creation of a truly global arms market is that states may be increasingly supplying their defense establishments through the international market, thereby abandoning efforts at national autarky in the areas of weapons development and procurement. To this point, however, the data on arms transfers—perhaps because many are unreported black market transactions—are not clear enough to support such a conclusion. As we shall see in chapters 3 and 5, there also appears to be a close relationship between the increasing military spending of countries such as China and India, which have been steadily globalizing their economies and reaping benefits by way of increased foreign currency reserves and gross domestic product (GDP) growth rates. These states, awash with cash, are now in the forefront of new weapons purchases. For instance, India is planning to buy 126 modern aircraft to replace its aging fleet. Similarly, China has ratcheted up its military spending on new equipment and modernization during the globalization era.[40] In this regard, globalization is having exactly the opposite effect from that expected by most globalization theorists, as increased globalization leads to increased military spending and arms competition.

International Institutions and Transnational Actors

According to globalization theorists, in a globalized world, international institutions and transnational actors should play an increasing role as security providers. Intergovernmental organizations (IGOs) should complement state security strategies by coordinating policy in a multilateral framework to combat threats that reach beyond state borders. In addition, transnational NGOs should play a leading role in constraining conflict behavior among states by monitoring and generating international norms of conduct. These norms may be codified in rules adopted by IGOs, which should further constrain state behavior. Thus, in principle, states should be reluctant to resort to force in abrogation of UN Security Council resolutions, or to violate guidelines issued by authoritative regional organizations that are heavily involved in their particular jurisdictions.[41] Moreover, these organizations, organized as they are on a larger scale, should be better equipped to respond to the problems of a globalized world than the nation-state. Thus, whether it is to combat terrorism, stop the spread of infectious diseases, or contain ethnic conflicts that threaten to spill over borders—all elements of the new security agenda that globalization theorists describe—we should expect to see increased IGO and NGO involvement.[42]

Different varieties of institutions and transnational actors are relevant here. International IGOs seem to have gained prominence during the immediate aftermath of the Cold War, as there has been a mushrooming of institutions at both the regional and global levels. There was much talk, led by U.S. President George H. W. Bush, of a new world order based on these institutions.[43] These institutions, especially the UN—when the five permanent members of the UN Security Council were in agreement—have played a pivotal role in peacekeeping and peace-building operations. Indeed, from 1996 to 2002, international organizations organized an average of more than fifty peacekeeping and peace-building missions per year, with the UN directly responsible for almost half of them.[44] This represents a substantial increase in UN peacekeeping operations. Indeed, the 1940s and '50s each witnessed only two such operations, and although no decade from the 1960s to the 1980s experienced more than six, during the 1990s there were an unprecedented thirty-six UN peacekeeping operations. By May 2008, the UN had initiated eight peacekeeping operations in the new millennium. Thus, in the eighteen years since 1990, the UN fielded more than twice as many peacekeeping operations as it did in its first forty-two years.[45] This represents a substantial increase in involvement by the UN in regional conflict theaters since the end of the Cold War. This upsurge in UN peacekeeping activities may be explained by globalization, but it may also be caused by the end of the Cold War conflict between the great powers of the UN Security Council.

Despite this apparent surge in IGO activities, however, the power of the United States was necessary for international institutions to intervene in conflict theaters like the Persian Gulf, Cambodia, Yugoslavia, Ethiopia, Eritrea, and East Timor, and even in humanitarian interventions in places like Somalia and Haiti.[46] At the same time, many of the UN-led operations have been insufficient to handle the tasks, have not been fully funded, or, worst of all, have been selective. In almost all the interventions by the UN, power politics and security considerations of the permanent five (P-5) members of the UN Security Council were crucial. Indeed, the United States engineered interventions by the UN in Iraq in 1991 and by NATO in Yugoslavia to advance its own foreign policy agenda, and has tended to ignore these institutions when their policies diverge.[47] Although the United States has warmed up to the UN in the aftermath of the terrorist attacks of September 11, the UN is not a key player in the war against terrorism Washington has initiated. In 2003, the United States, after failing to gain support from the UN Security Council for its military operations against Iraq, simply ignored the council. At the beginning of the twenty-first century, the expectation of some globalization theorists that international institutions could supplant national security establishments remains unfulfilled. As U.S. power and interests diverge more rapidly from other states, including allies, the UN Security Council is likely to be marginalized in the future despite—or, perhaps, because of—efforts by countries such as France, Russia, and China to constrain U.S. unilateralism through their veto power.

Regional security organizations, such as NATO, the OAS, ASEAN, and the AU, also seek to provide security to members within a multilateral framework. Regional organizations can provide a forum for dispute resolution, can initiate concerted efforts to ameliorate conditions that inspire conflict, or can engage in peacemaking or peacekeeping operations, often with greater legitimacy than outsiders to the region. Since 1997, regional organizations have participated in peacekeeping operations even more frequently than the UN. In 1997, the UN coordinated twenty-five missions compared with twenty-nine missions organized by regional security organizations. The difference was most striking in 2001, when regional security organizations coordinated thirty-two operations to the UN's nineteen—almost 70% more.[48] In addition, the 1999 intervention in Kosovo was conducted under NATO auspices, as was the 2001 war against Afghanistan.

Africa, in particular, has been a region of increasing interventions by regional institutions as peacekeepers and peacemakers. The AU organized an intervention in Burundi in 2003, and peacekeeping activities in the Darfur region of Sudan since 2003. The Economic Community of West African States (ECOWAS) has set up an armed monitoring group (the ECOMOG), which intervened in Liberia and Sierra Leone in 1997.[49] The Southern African Development Community (SADC) has also attempted to promote regional stability and security, by intervening in Congo and Lesotho.[50]

ASEAN has maintained a relatively low-key approach toward security issues, because of its principles of nonintervention in each others' internal affairs, but it has, in recent years, increased coordination in the issue areas of terrorism, piracy, and drug trafficking. The ASEAN Regional Forum (ARF) has been active in building confidence among member states and regionally involved states, especially the major powers. The Shanghai Cooperation Organization (SCO) is another effort by China, Russia, and central Asian states to deal with regional security issues through institutional means.

Nonetheless, there is reason to doubt the degree to which states rely on these institutions. After all, although the United States used NATO as a multilateral fig leaf for its operations against Serbia and Afghanistan, it did not hesitate to embark on the 2003 campaign against Iraq when it determined that NATO (and the UN) was not inclined to act in accordance with perceived American national interests. In addition, African regional efforts remain partial and often meet with only limited success as a result of weak state capacities and divergent policy preferences. Thus, it is by no means clear that states have decided to pursue security within multilateral institutions, rather than through state-centered means.

If the globalization thesis is correct, transnational actors, including global financial institutions, MNCs, and NGOs should also play important international security roles. In fact, in key areas in which they specialize, they should compete with states on an almost equal footing. According to global norms theorists, nonstate actors can help to shape the international security environment in different ways. First, they can work to change the policies of particular states by providing national governments with important policy-relevant information, by stimulating domestic political pressure on the government, and by supporting parties and candidates that support their political positions. Second, they can seek to change the global environment within which security is pursued by generating and promoting global norms, setting the agendas of global discourse and the agendas of international institutions, and by helping to draft international treaties and international laws to govern the conduct of states and other international actors. Last, they can enhance security "in the field" by providing humanitarian assistance to at-risk groups and by generating global popular boycotts against regimes and actors that threaten people and states.[51]

The empirical record, though, seems mixed. Some NGOs do play a key role in today's international arena, but only in selected areas. There has been a significant increase in transnational advocacy networks in issue areas ranging from human rights, world order, women's rights, development, and peace. Indeed, in the 1950s, there were fewer than a hundred such groups active at the international level. By 2003, that number ballooned to approximately 1,011.[52] This is a remarkable increase, but it does not mean that these groups have dramatically altered the nature of international politics.

Some of these nonstate actors have been successful in transcending state objections and in helping to get security treaties concluded, albeit on a limited scale. An important example has been the Global Land Mines Treaty, largely the result of efforts by the International Campaign to Ban Landmines, which united more than one thousand NGOs in fifty-five countries.[53] This effort, however, failed to get the United States or other key producers of the weapons—such as Russia, China, and India—on board. NGOs have also been active at global conferences, both as critics and as sources of information and mobilization of international coalitions. Some NGOs have been key players in helping to provide humanitarian aid in war-torn areas, often in association with UN agencies.

Despite the increased activities and presence of NGOs, their influence has been confined to a few specific security issues and, therefore, has been—at best—episodic. On core issues involving the major powers—nuclear arms control (barring the conferences that led to the Nuclear Non-Proliferation Treaty (NPT) extension, Comprehensive Test Ban Treaty [CTBT], and the Chemical Weapons Convention), NATO's eastward expansion, national and theater missile defense, and the increasing militarization of space—there has been very little NGO interest or participation. In fact, in the arms control and disarmament area, NGOs, especially peace movements, were perhaps more effective during the peak of the Cold War (i.e., during the Reagan and Gorbachev years). During the conferences that led to the NPT extension and the conclusion of the CTBT, NGOs were present merely as observers or as helpers to national delegations. Without the active interest and the prodding of the key negotiating states, these treaties would not have been concluded.[54] No NGO group has ever come close to offering the comprehensive security package that nation-states offer, both internally and externally. Having a say in a specific security issue is not the same as challenging the state in a whole host of security issues in which the state and the state alone has the upper hand. As Hoffmann contends, international civil society remains "embryonic"; it represents a small segment of mostly advanced states, and often possesses only limited independence from governments.[55]

A final potential institutional means of providing security in a globalized world centers on international financial institutions (IFIs), such as the World Bank, the IMF, and the regional development banks. These institutions have, at times, attempted to use economic aid as a tool for changing national security policies. In particular, many of these institutions have been increasingly using criteria such as the military expenditures of the recipients and imposing conditions that include reductions in defense spending. In some cases, they have even imposed sanctions and forced recipients to reduce military spending (e.g., Pakistan after its nuclear tests in 1998).[56] In other instances, the IFIs have used their financial power to force recipients to follow policies consistent with international humanitarian law and UN Security Council resolutions. For instance, donor pressure was very much instrumental in the extradition of former Yugoslavian President Slobodan Milosevic to the International Criminal Tribunal in the Hague.[57] The important question, however, is how independent these actors are, because in most cases the sanctions were the result of specific policy preferences of the western countries that hold significant voting rights in these institutions.[58] Moreover, the target states have been generally weak or vulnerable developing states and are, therefore, "sovereign" in only a limited sense. Thus, although IFIs may be able to compel a comparatively weak state, like Pakistan, to alter its security policies marginally, it is by no means clear that it would be able to have as much impact on a more institutionalized state with a more stable economy. The number and function of IFIs and other transnational actors may be increasing, but they are not yet equal or superior to states, except for very weak actors in the international system. As these institutions increasingly focus on the reconstruction and development of war-torn societies, and as they place more emphasis on effective governance and fiscal management by states, it is possible that they may increase their influence in the security policies of states. However, what these institutions seek is not the displacement of the state, but its reform and effectiveness.

It would be difficult, therefore, to conclude that multilateral security-providing institutions and international non-governmental organizations (INGOs) have supplanted—or even greatly diminished—the role of the state in the security area. Instead, although these organizations increasingly attempt to intervene in the provision of security, they are too heavily dependent on the powerful state actors to have any real independent impact.

Transnational Terrorism as a Global Security Challenge

One type of transnational organization deserves special consideration for its impact on the global security environment. According to some globalization theorists, *transnational terrorist organizations*—groups that operate across national boundaries and use violence against civilian targets to inspire widespread societal terror as a means of securing political objectives—are especially adept at exploiting globalization's assault on national borders to challenge nation-states. In the process, they are said to transform the meaning of security, the threats that states and other international actors seek to counter, and the tools these actors use to achieve security. Specifically, according to globalization theorists, the fact that terrorists are organized transnationally and that they use modern communication systems makes it difficult for the nation-state to provide security in the modern world, and international organizations have not yet adapted to their challenge either.[59] Moreover, small terrorist groups are able to amass immense destructive power that was formerly the "monopoly of states," thus undercutting the primacy of states in the security area and requiring security coordination at the global level.[60] Furthermore, as well-organized groups, such as al Qaeda, attack targets across the globe with increasing frequency, they should replace the scourge of interstate war as the leading threat to global security in the modern world.[61] Although we investigate the degree to which individual states have adapted to terrorism in the following chapters, in this section we consider whether it has had an impact at the system level.

The empirical record on this point, at least during the twenty-first century, is favorable to the globalization thesis. Although states in the twentieth century faced rather localized terrorist threats—such as Palestine Liberation Organization (PLO) and Hamas attacks against Israel, Irish Republican Army (IRA) attacks against Great Britain, and Basque separatist attacks against Spain—since September 11, 2001, the most salient feature of international politics has been the global war against terrorism. Most significant, a single transnational network, al Qaeda, has conducted large-scale bombing operations against civilians in as diverse a group of states as the United States, Spain, Great Britain, Indonesia, Kenya, Egypt, Saudi Arabia, Afghanistan, and Iraq. Worldwide, in 2007, there were more than 14,000 terrorist incidents, resulting in more than 22,000 deaths—an astounding total, indicating the magnitude of the terrorist challenge.[62] The responses to terrorism have also, in large part, transcended the nation-state, with broad antiterrorism coalitions; efforts, however weak, to define and combat terrorism in the

UN and other international institutions; and multilateral efforts to share intelligence and deport those suspected of participating in terrorist attacks abroad.

The impact of global terrorism, however, has been even more profound than these indicators would suggest, even if some would question the magnitude of the threat.[63] The September 11 terrorist attacks in the United States suddenly highlighted a fundamental challenge to the state-centric security paradigm throughout the world. Traditional notions about war between territorially defined political entities have been bloodied by the arrival of transnational terrorism. Nor can states, themselves, hope to stop transnational terrorists without reestablishing the tight border controls that are inimical to economic productivity in a globalized world. This problem is compounded by the spread of democracy throughout much of the globe. As more and more regimes accept the package of personal rights (including the freedom of movement and freedom from unwarranted search and seizure) that is a necessary prerequisite of democracy, it becomes harder for states to monitor and halt terrorist activity.

To the extent that states have enacted intrusive measures to combat terrorist attacks, transnational terrorism has had another ironic consequence. Although globalization is allowing the spread of transnational terrorism, the war against terrorism may be adversely affecting several dimensions of globalization, especially the free flow of skilled labor and capital, and the spread of democratic regimes. Some measures states have taken to combat terrorism have strengthened the illiberal states that are supposedly helping to fight terrorism. Thus, for example, the Pervez Musharraf regime in Pakistan, founded as it was on a military coup against a democratically elected government, was strengthened for a period by American aid and support as an ally in the war against terrorism. And even liberal states, such as the United States and Great Britain, have enacted legislation—such as the Patriot Act in the United States—that increases the scope of the state and reinforces sovereignty. Some EU states, such as France and Holland, have also strengthened the state with tougher immigration regulations to clamp down on immigrant communities that do not share the dominant values of their culture.[64]

Although the increase in transnational terrorism has affected the state as a security actor in multiple ways, it does not mean that the nation-state will simply collapse in the face of the terrorist menace.[65] States are slowly adapting to this menace, as evident in U.S. policies. Washington's homeland security programs have shown that the state could come up with new solutions to the problem, although foolproof security against terrorism may remain a false hope. Moreover, the challenge posed by international terrorism may not be all that unique, as in other historical eras states also confronted important challenges by other nonstate actors. Piracy, in particular, was a challenge to both great power navies and commerce for hundreds of years, and it is still occurring in pockets of the world. Even at its peak, the struggle against piracy did not replace traditional great power security competition, even in the naval realm, or undermine the primacy of the state.[66] And, as Hedley Bull contends, in eighteenth- and nineteenth-century Europe, states coexisted and shared the stage with chartered companies, revolutionary and counterrevolutionary political parties, and national liberation movements.[67] Moreover, even prior to the al Qaeda threat, terrorism had been a perennial problem for states such as Russia, Great Britain, India, and many Middle Eastern states, especially Israel. Thus, the presence of powerful nonstate actors is not a new phenomenon in world politics.

To the extent that global terrorism does reflect a qualitative change from these previous nonstate actor challenges to the primacy of the nation-state, it does so because of the growing transnational reach of terrorists and their increasing ability to inflict damage and panic on the United States, the global hegemon. Indeed, the terrorists were able to reach the United States heartland and attack the very citadels of American power—the Pentagon and the World Trade Center. Nonetheless, the war against terrorism has paradoxically strengthened the American state both internally and internationally. Internally, the state has consolidated its policing, border surveillance, and intelligence-gathering capabilities in the Department of Homeland Security, and has increased its powers of surveillance within the Patriot Act. Internationally, the Bush administration's response to September 11 has been heavily military oriented, with wars and policing actions in Afghanistan and Iraq, based on the administration's doctrine of "preemption" and "prevention."[68] In this regard, the American state is stronger and more central to the provision of national security after the September 11 attacks than ever before. Other states, both in the West and elsewhere, have responded to the threat of global terrorism in similar manners, by ratcheting up the national security state, rather than replacing it. Indeed, Vladimir Putin has responded to the terrorist threat of Chechen separatists by bolstering state authority and the national security state at the expense of civil liberties.[69] Other states, such as Great Britain, Argentina, Brazil, Canada, and Australia, have also enacted tougher new counterterrorism laws since September 11 that increase state monitoring of citizens and business transactions.[70] Although, as Philip Cerny suggests, this attempt at reasserting state control may engender backlashes, it has not, as yet, undermined state primacy in the provision of security, at least not on a global scale.[71]

Conclusion: Limited Changes at the Global Level

Our examination of global-level propositions reveals limited support for the argument that globalization has dramatically altered the pursuit of security. The most powerful evidence for a transformation in international security is the decline of interstate warfare and the global response to transnational terrorism. In addition, states may increasingly be relying on the international arms market, rather than pursuing autarky, to supply their national security apparatuses. The decline in traditional warfare, however, cannot solely and clearly be attributed to globalization. Other explanations based on the increase of unipolarity and the end of the Cold War need to be taken into account. Furthermore, we have found no evidence that globalization has led to lower levels of military spending and, although international institutions and international NGOs have increasingly involved themselves in international security operations (particularly UN peacekeeping operations, which have become more frequent), they have not done so on the scale that globalization scholars would have expected, and their impact on global security remains limited. Thus, the only compelling evidence of a major transformation of global security is the worldwide explosion of terrorist activity and the concerted global effort to combat this new public enemy. Although important, this is hardly evidence of a sea change in the international pursuit of security.

Furthermore, when we consider only the global picture, we find little evidence that globalization has fundamentally eroded the state's central role in international security. Indeed, the evidence in support of this globalization claim is weak. States continue to arm, military spending has been on the rise during the period we assessed, multilateral security organizations and international NGOs still wield significantly less influence in the security theater than the nation-state, and the challenge of global terrorism—although it has altered the missions of national security establishments—may only have reinforced the role of the state in the security realm. And, although the number of international peacekeeping operations by international organizations has increased, these operations have depended upon great power participation, particularly that of the United States, to be successful. Thus, at the global level, the case for the kind of global transformation described by globalization theorists appears to be either overstated or premature.

In the next four chapters we investigate our state-level propositions on a state-by-state and regional basis to explore whether national security establishments have responded to globalization as the state-in-demise school predicts, and whether globalization has affected all states equally.

CHAPTER 3 | The Major Powers

IF GLOBALIZATION HAS TRULY REVOLUTIONIZED THE WAY STATES PURSUE SECURITY, then we should expect to see dramatic changes in the security policies of the states that have traditionally been the most important security actors: the major powers. If the national security establishments of these states have been largely immune to the influence of global economic and social forces, then we should question the extent of the "global transformations." Conversely, if the major powers, which have typically had the most independence internationally and have essentially ruled the security environment, are now powerfully constrained by globalization, then we should have strong evidence in support of the state-in-demise hypothesis. In this chapter we test the state-level propositions developed in chapter 1 against the national security doctrines and practices between 1991–2008 of the three most powerful states in the contemporary international system: the United States, Russia, and China.

Each of these major powers occupies a different position in the international system in the period we are investigating. The United States is the world's hegemon, with global interests and responsibilities. China is the rising challenger without commitments on the same scale or breadth as the United States, but with growing geopolitical and economic interests in Asia, Africa, and Latin America. Because these types of states have traditionally been the world's dominant security actors, we would consider major alterations in the way that they pursue security to be powerful support for the globalization school. Alternatively, because Russia began the past fifteen years as the weakened major power, with diminished economic and political resources to conduct itself in the geopolitical arena, we should expect it to operate with a rather scaled-back national security state. Therefore, we would consider the pursuit of traditionally oriented security policies by the Russian national security establishment to constitute an important challenge to the globalization hypotheses. In addition, we will look for trends regarding each of the globalization hypotheses in the national security behavior of all three major powers.

The United States

More so than any other international actor, the United States is the most important litmus test of the impact of globalization on the pursuit of national security. If the world's greatest power, possessing the world's largest economy and by far its most powerful military apparatus, has had its national security establishment transformed by globalization, its behavior would necessarily create a powerful global ripple effect, dominating the international system as it does. In contrast, if the international trendsetter continues to prepare for and wage interstate wars, and spend on traditional military goods, other states would be compelled to do the same. We therefore pay particular attention to the American national security state.

THE NATURE OF THREATS

The United States offers inconsistent support for proposition PS1 (*changing nature of wars*). During the period under investigation, the United States has been embroiled in several wars of various kinds. On the one hand, it has participated in LICs, such as the civil war in Somalia, and has fought in limited-scale operations in support of substate actors, such as the NATO bombing campaign against Serbia in 1999 to protect the Albanians of Kosovo province. These nontraditional engagements are consistent with the transformations that globalization theorists predict. Furthermore, the U.S. Department of Defense (DoD), in its assessment of contemporary security challenges to the United States, observes that "[i]n the post-September 11 world, irregular warfare has emerged as the dominant form of warfare confronting the United States, its allies and its partners."[1] Nonetheless, it has also fought in more traditional—if atypical—interstate wars. In particular, it played the primary role in two wars against Iraq (1990–1991 and 2003) and the 2001 war against Afghanistan. These wars, which pitted American and coalition forces against the national armed forces of the opposing state, cannot properly be called LICs or "wars of a third kind." Thus, there is no evidence that the United States has abandoned traditional warfare in favor of LICs.

There is more support, however, for PS2 (*postindustrial warfare*). Indeed, the United States has been targeted by the al Qaeda terrorist network both at home and abroad (in Saudi Arabia, Yemen, Kenya, and elsewhere). The notorious attack on the World Trade Center in 2001, in particular, highlighted its vulnerability to terrorism on its own shores at the very heart of its economic power base. As a result, the United States has become embroiled not only in outright wars, but also in classic postindustrial warfare campaigns, including limited strikes at terrorist targets, intelligence gathering and monitoring, attempts to disrupt the financing of terrorism, and efforts to provide economic and political assistance to states in which the terrorists might make inroads. It is significant, in this respect, that the primary thrust of the George W. Bush administration's first national security doctrine, published in 2002, was combating terrorism and states that support terrorism worldwide.[2] The 2006 doctrine, published four years after the September 11 attacks, still includes as its second mission, "[to] [s]trengthen alliances to defeat global terrorism and work to prevent attacks against us and our friends," although a careful read of that document reveals that combating terrorism is actually its central focus.[3] Furthermore, the U.S. State Department's 2006 "Trends in Terrorism" states that although al Qaeda operations have been disrupted, the Jihadist threat is "increasing in both number and geographic dispersion" and that "if this trend continues, threats to U.S. interests at home and abroad will become more diverse, leading to increasing attacks worldwide."[4] In July 2007, the National Intelligence Estimate by the National Intelligence Council assessed that although the worldwide antiterrorism campaign has "constrained" the ability of al Qaeda to attack the American homeland, the United States will face "a persistent and evolving terrorist threat," at least for the next three years as terrorists adapt and improve their capabilities.[5] Clearly, the United States devotes a considerable amount of its attention to postindustrial warfare.

Nonetheless, with regard to proposition PS3 (*changing threats*), there is only limited evidence that the United States has recast its national security policies radically to address the new economic, ecological, and public health threats that globalization theorists believe constitute a significant component of the "new security agenda." To be sure, U.S. policy statements do devote some attention to these new concerns. The 2002 U.S. National Security Strategy, for example, identifies a variety of goals and threats, in addition to traditional military security. It assumes that "[a] strong world economy enhances our national security by advancing prosperity and freedom in the rest of the world." Therefore, the promotion of economic development and free trade is a component of U.S. strategic doctrine.[6] This priority is reiterated in the 2006 revision, more than a fifth of which is devoted to economic development, creating an open world economy, and enhancing energy security.[7]

Furthermore, the 2006 document contains a section that outlines the challenges of national security in an era of globalization, including "public health challenges like pandemics (HIV/AIDS, avian influenza) that recognize no borders"; "[i]llicit trade, whether in drugs, human beings, or sex, that exploits the modern era's greater ease of transport and exchange"; and "[e]nvironmental destruction, whether caused by human behavior or cataclysmic megadisasters such as floods, hurricanes, earthquakes, or tsunamis." Most significant, it contends that "[p]reparing for and managing these challenges requires the full exercise of national power, up to and including traditional security instruments."[8] Thus, U.S. strategic planning addresses a wide variety of "new" security threats, as globalization theorists would expect.

Nonetheless, from the structure of the document it is clear that these threats take a back seat both to traditional security threats and to the new overriding priority of combating terrorism as well. Indeed, the globalization section is relegated to the last two pages of the document, almost as an afterthought. Moreover, as DoD planning indicates, the spending priorities of the national security establishment still overwhelmingly favor traditional defense-related procurement at the expense of the new security issues, excluding combating terrorism. Thus, the *Quadrennial Defense Review* describes an expensive reorientation of U.S. forces to meet the lower level state and substate challenges the United States is likely to face in the future that is rather military in nature, rather than economic, medical, environmental, or other.[9] This could reflect the institutional lag time that is necessary for a large and complex governmental apparatus, encompassing a vast array of actors with entrenched interests, to adapt to changed circumstances. Indeed, interviews we conducted with both U.S. State Department and Pentagon officials suggest that the decision-making elite in both departments have embraced the new security priorities, but that they expect that it will take time to overcome the vested interests arrayed against a corresponding reallocation of the national security budget.[10]

At best, then, there is only mixed evidence that the U.S. national security establishment has been compelled by the new globalized security environment to retool itself to meet the nontraditional threats identified by the globalization and security paradigm. Although it does occasionally fight LICs, the United States still wages traditional interstate warfare. And, although it pays increasing lip service to "new security" threats, such as poverty alleviation and the spread of pandemics, it continues to prioritize traditional threats and a conventional military posture. The only, not insignificant, change in

U.S. strategy that suggests a globalization of its agenda is the increasing emphasis on fighting global terrorism after the September 11 attacks.

THE STRATEGIES STATES PURSUE

In terms of the strategies that the United States is using to meet its security objectives, there is little to suggest that globalization has radically altered the American approach to national security. Regarding proposition PS4 (*defensive and deterrent doctrines*), for example, during the early post-Cold War era, because the United States faced no credible challengers, Washington's military doctrine was largely defensive and deterrent—targeting potential long-range challengers and instability in critical regions, such the Middle East and the Persian Gulf— although the political component of American grand strategy sought to expand the American sphere of influence by spreading democracy and market economies.[11] In light of the September 11 terrorist attacks, however, the U.S. strategic doctrine has regained an offensive posture. Most striking, the grand strategy of "preemption" that President Bush unveiled in September 2002 emphasizes "destroying the threat before it reaches our borders" and "convincing or compelling states to accept their sovereign responsibilities." It boldly claims that "the best defense is a good offense"; thus, the United States can no longer rely on a reactive posture to weapons of mass destruction (WMD).[12] Bush's 2006 national security doctrine, with its opening statement, "It is the policy of the United States to seek and support democratic movements and institutions in every nation and culture, with the ultimate goal of ending tyranny in our world," indicates the continuation of the proactive military posture that led to wars of regime change in Afghanistan and Iraq.[13] To be sure, the new security blueprint avoids any mention of utilizing military means to promote democracy and states that "freedom cannot be imposed; it must be chosen."[14] Nonetheless, it promises ominously to "employ the full array of political, economic, diplomatic, and other tools at our disposal," evoking echoes of Iraq and Afghanistan.[15]

Moreover, when addressing the threat of WMD proliferation in the 2006 document, the administration reaffirmed its policy of military "preemption," stating the following:

> Our strong preference and common practice is to address proliferation concerns through international diplomacy, in concert with key allies and regional partners. If necessary, however, under longstanding principles of self-defense, we do not rule out the use of force before attacks occur, even if uncertainty remains as to the time and place of the enemy's attack. When the consequences of an attack are potentially so devastating,

we cannot afford to stand idly by as grave dangers materialize. This is the principle and logic of preemption.[16]

Clearly, the United States is no longer merely counting on its overwhelming military and technological superiority to dissuade adversaries from attacking it. Instead, Washington aims to use its military power, when deemed necessary, to remold the world to enhance its security.

With no viable contenders in sight, the United States has not needed to engage in traditional hard balancing behavior since the end of the Cold War. Nonetheless, although it increasingly relies on soft balancing strategies, it still uses hard balancing, as well, which calls proposition PS5 (*soft balancing*) into question. After the collapse of the Soviet Union, the only potential challenger on the horizon appears to be China, with its large population, its rapidly growing economy, its nuclear arsenal, and its conventional force modernization program. To counter the Chinese threat, much of U.S. grand strategy focuses on soft balancing, by spreading American cultural influence and maintaining international political institutions—such as NATO—that reinforce American primacy. In Asia, America has been engaging in a more direct balancing strategy vis-à-vis China that crosses the line into hard balancing territory. U.S. efforts to increase its alignment with Japan and build up a relationship with India need to be seen in this context. The United States–India nuclear accord, which the U.S. Congress approved in December 2006, is meant to improve strategic and economic relations between the world's two largest democracies, but it also has a soft balancing and prebalancing strategy dimension to the extent that both parties view it as a way to contain China, a rising power. Especially interesting is the avowed willingness of the United States to help India obtain great power status as a means of containing China. Furthermore, as we shall see, Congress and the Pentagon continue to spend heavily on defense, which they justify largely in terms of the potential Chinese threat.[17]

In the regional contexts also, the United States uses both hard balancing and soft balancing, using military and economic carrots and sticks to contain the ambitions of states such as Iran and North Korea. The UN has been a central instrument for both efforts, although diplomacy with regional powers in the form of six-party talks has been Washington's preferred route to deal with the North Korean nuclear problem. Therefore, in multiple theaters, American strategy continues to use traditional hard balancing together with softer policy instruments.

There is considerable support for the globalization school when it comes to proposition PS6 (*manpower*). During the past two decades, the size of the American armed forces declined sharply. In 1985–1986, before the Cold War ended, the United States had more than 2.1 million people in active service. That figure dropped steadily throughout the 1990s to a low of less than 1.4 million in 2000–2001. Even after the September 11 terrorist attacks, active U.S. manpower rose only marginally in 2002–2003 to more than 1.4 million, and it has increased only somewhat since then to just more than 1.5 million in 2007.[18] It remains to be seen whether the protracted conflict in Iraq will lead to an elevation of troop levels in the future. For the time being, however, U.S. military manpower trends are consistent with globalization school expectations.

At least on the surface, American defense spending figures during the 1990s fit the globalization thesis expectations (proposition PS7), although figures from the new millennium are hard to reconcile with that trend. The U.S. defense budget decreased considerably during the first decade after the Cold War. It decreased steadily from more than $424 billion in 1992 to less than $329 billion in 1998 (all figures in 2005 constant U.S. dollars), where it remained, with only small increases, until 2002, when it jumped back to more than $387 billion (representing a one-year increase of more than 12%).[19] It increased again in subsequent years to almost $529 billion in 2006, which, in real terms, was considerably more than the United States was spending during the last years of the Cold War. Moreover, that figure is likely to continue to increase as the DoD increases the size of its special forces by one third, while maintaining conventional force strength and purchasing more flexible weapons and information technology systems.[20] The rapid recovery of the U.S. defense budget early during the twenty-first century makes it difficult to attribute the initial decrease in American defense spending to the pressures of globalization, rather than to the relatively stable world of unipolarity after the Soviet Union's defeat.[21] Indeed, the substantial increase in U.S. defense allocations after the September 11 attacks suggests that the changing threat environment, rather than international economic forces, shapes American defense spending.

Of course, the 2006 *Quadrennial Defense Review* suggests another possibility. That document, which breaks down the DoD's massive spending priorities, indicates that the many new and variegated challenges that the United States faces in the new millennium, including lower level asymmetric challenges from terrorists and other nonstate actors, policing operations, and interdictions (of WMD components and other controlled materials), together with the complexity of information-based warfare in the age of globalization, require both more sophisticated and more expensive equipment.[22] To this extent, it may indicate that globalization is affecting defense spending (at least by the greatest world power), but that it is having the reverse effect of that expected by most of the globalization school. Rather than reducing defense spending, the overwhelming new challenges caused by globalization require a significant increase in spending on high-tech defense goods that are more appropriate than traditional arsenals, as Anthony Giddens suggests.[23]

U.S. security behavior during the past fifteen years also provides some support for proposition PS8 (*shift from war fighting to policing*). Although it has retained its focus on war fighting, the American national security establishment has simultaneously added a policing dimension to its military missions to fight terrorism, to interdict drug smugglers and organized crime, and to provide domestic order. Most significant, in its war against terrorism, the Bush administration has constructed a new security institution, the Department of Homeland Security, to prevent future attacks on U.S. soil. This department, which controls border crossings, intelligence gathering and analysis, and other policing and monitoring apparatuses, is a centerpiece of President Bush's post-September 11 national security approach.[24] But even before 2001, the United States was using its military apparatus to combat narcotics trafficking and to assist Latin American states in their efforts to defeat drug cartels and smugglers. This counternarcotics mission remains a part of U.S. national security doctrine.[25]

The American strategic repertoire, therefore, represents a mix of the traditional and the new. Clearly, American manpower has declined, and the military apparatus is increasingly performing policing-type operations to meet contemporary threats. In addition, it is modernizing its armed forces to combat the asymmetric, often substate, challenges it is increasingly facing. But Washington continues to use traditional hard balancing strategies and, since September 11, the United States has ramped up its defense spending and has developed a broad-reaching offensive doctrine, which represents a large measure of continuity with the national security state of old, rather than a radical departure from it. This could mean that the United States is at the cusp of a transition of its security strategies and that domestic interest group squabbles are responsible for Washington's slow pace of adaptation to new environmental conditions. Alternatively, it could mean that the stable environment that prevailed during the early post-Cold War era led to a different national security repertoire, but that the recent challenges to American security interests have prompted a return to more traditional security behavior.

THE MONOPOLY OF THE STATE AS A SECURITY PROVIDER

The United States does not appear to have ceded its role as the world's leading security actor in any meaningful way either to substate actors or to international institutions. In particular, there is little evidence in support of proposition PS9 (*nonstate actors*). It is striking, for example, that the Bush administration's most recent national security blueprint makes no mention of cooperation with private institutions or NGOs in their official doctrines as a means of achieving national security objectives, even those promoting international development or alleviating poverty.[26]

It is true that after September 11, Washington has begun to encourage private–public partnerships to facilitate homeland defense against terrorist attacks.[27] Furthermore, the Pentagon does rely on outsourcing to supply and service much of its equipment.[28] In its reorganization, the DoD also views contractors as one of the four "elements of the Total Force," although it is not clear whether these contractors are private security companies, or merely participants in the department's supply chain.[29] Of greatest interest, the United States has begun to contract private security companies in support of some of its overseas activities.[30] Thus, such companies have played a limited role in the war against the Taliban in Afghanistan and Saddam Hussein's forces in Iraq, and a more important role in the fight against drug cartels in South America (e.g., the $2 billion Andean Regional Initiative).

The use of private firms in support of operations in post-Saddam Iraq is instructive. Private firms have been engaged to train U.S. troops and to provide security for U.S. personnel and installations in postwar Iraq.[31] Moreover, estimates released in December 2006 counted nearly 100,000 government contractors operating in Iraq and several thousand subcontractors—a figure ten times larger than the number the United States had deployed during the first Gulf War. The tasks assigned to them include "providing security, interrogating prisoners, cooking meals, fixing equipment, and constructing bases that were once reserved for soldiers." The main private companies involved are Dyncorp International, Blackwater USA, Kellogg, Brown and Root, and MPRI, a unit of L-3 Communications. Labor Department statistics show that 650 contractors have died in Iraq since 2003.[32]

It is also estimated that under the George W. Bush administration, the expenses on private contractors soared from $207 billion in 2000 to $400 billion in 2006, because they were also used for domestic security and rehabilitation work after hurricane Katrina.[33] Despite this, it would appear that, although it is increasingly using private security providers in a supporting role, Washington is reluctant to cut costs by delegating critical national security tasks to private organizations.

Similarly, American strategy does not rely on regional institutions (proposition PS10) to any great degree. To be sure, it cooperates with them on specific, lower level security activities, such as countering the smuggling of WMD materials and stabilizing regional hotspots, such as the Balkans or Afghanistan.[34] Moreover, it looks to regional institutions as a means of advancing region-specific goals of American foreign policy. Thus, the Bush administration's 2006 national security doctrine mentions NATO, the Organization of American States, the African Union, ASEAN, and the Asia–Pacific Economic Cooperation (APEC) as organizations that can advance their region-specific objectives.[35]

In practice, though, successive U.S. administrations have utilized international institutions when these institutions were prepared to support American policy unconditionally, but have pursued other options when these institutions sought to block American goals. Thus, although George H. W. Bush forged the 1991 Gulf War coalition under the UN, the Clinton administration, meeting opposition from Russia and China within the UN Security Council, conducted the 1999 bombing campaign against Serbia under NATO auspices. And, in 2003, facing widespread opposition within the UN Security Council and French, German, and Belgian opposition within NATO, George W. Bush elected to work with an ad hoc "coalition of the willing" to prosecute the second Gulf War, even at the risk of interallied relations. This fair-weather reliance on multilateral institutions is, in fact, codified in American doctrine. In principle, the Bush administration states that "[o]ur priority is pursuing American interests within cooperative relationships."[36] When push comes to shove, however, it states that "we must be prepared to act alone if necessary, while recognizing that there is little of lasting significance that we can accomplish in the world without the sustained cooperation of our allies and partners."[37] It would appear, therefore, that the American reliance on multilateral security frameworks is episodic and instrumental, as American interests take primacy for American policy makers.

From the evidence presented here, we must conclude that the argument that globalization has transformed American national security policy is overstated. From 1991 to 2008 Washington continued to focus on traditional military security threats, responds to them with a rather traditional mix of policy instruments, and keeps itself—rather than nonstate actors and international institutions—as the principal security actor. Nonetheless, some important changes are evident, especially in the increasing American attention to the threat of transnational terrorism and the dramatic increase of policing-type operations as a key component of its security strategy.

China

China presents us with another critical test of the globalization arguments. With the demise of the Soviet Union and China's rapid economic expansion, China has become the leading potential challenger to American primacy in the international system. In the past, rising challengers launched considerable campaigns of military spending and political challenges that frequently led to arms races, intensive great power security competition, and war.[38] If globalization has meaningfully altered the face of security in the contemporary era, we should see China pursuing rather different strategies as it rises in power.

THE NATURE OF THREATS

In practice, Chinese behavior during the period under investigation provides some support for proposition PS1 (*changing nature of wars*). Since the end of the Cold War, China has not participated in any interstate wars. The Chinese were not active participants in the 1991 Gulf War or the American-led war against Afghanistan in 2001, and they expressed strong opposition to both the bombing of Serbia in 1999 and the 2003 Gulf War.

It is clear from Chinese military doctrine, though, that their military planners, too, still contemplate national defense primarily in terms of traditional interstate warfare. The principal defense policy objective articulated by the 2006 Chinese white paper on defense was "to basically reach the strategic goal of building informationized armed forces and being capable of winning informationized wars by the mid-21st century." This clearly is cast in terms of traditional interstate warfare, even if the weapons are more advanced. Furthermore, the first of five central objectives of the People's Liberation Army (PLA) was "[u]pholding national security and unity," which included "guarding against and resisting aggression, defending against violation of China's territorial sea and air space, and borders; opposing and containing the separatist forces for 'Taiwan independence' and their activities," as well as to contain terrorism.[39] To achieve these traditional goals, China is modernizing its strategic forces to facilitate "the defense of Chinese sovereignty and national territory against threats or attacks from all manner of opponents."[40]

Moreover, it may use traditional military means, if necessary, to "uphold national unity," which could potentially mean a war to regain Taiwan or prevent it from declaring its independence from China. As the white paper states: "By pursuing a radical policy for 'Taiwan independence,' the Taiwan authorities aim at creating 'de jure Taiwan independence' through 'constitutional reform,' thus still posing a grave threat to China's sovereignty and territorial integrity, as well as to peace and stability across the Taiwan Straits and in the Asia–Pacific region as a whole," which is complicated by American support for the regime in Taipei.[41]

This thinly veiled threat suggests that it is by no means clear that China will avoid interstate wars in the future.

China has also had to confront secessionists and substate actors using terrorist tactics, in line with proposition PS2 (*postindustrial warfare*). In particular, in the Xinjiang province, Beijing has been challenged by ethnic Uyghur secessionists, whom China characterizes as affiliated with an East Turkestan terrorist network. The 9-million-strong Uyghurs aspire to autonomy, and elements within them have engaged in sporadic terrorist activities. China has responded fiercely, suppressing their movement for the large part. Notable incidents include an armed uprising in April 1990, bombing episodes in 1992–1993, the arrest of suspected terrorists during 1996–1997, the Guhulja incident in February 1997 when large-scale protest demonstrations took place, attacks, and assassinations of Chinese businessmen and officials in 2000 and 2002. Between 1998 and 2001, three leaders from the movement were killed. However, a study of the Xinjiang problem that discusses these incidents suggests that the threat of Uyghur separatism is exaggerated by Chinese officials and media, and the outside world has little information other than what the Chinese supply. In the post-September 11 world, China and some of its central Asian neighbors have made every effort to link Uyghur separatists with al Qaeda.[42]

Similarly, China has used the American-led war on terrorism to ratchet up its suppression of Falun Gong, a religious movement with tens of millions of followers. Alarmed at the group's ability both to penetrate Chinese society and to mobilize protests, such as a 10,000 strong silent protest outside the communist leadership headquarters in 1999, the government of Jiang Zemin banned the movement, and the Chinese state has treated it as a terrorist organization.[43] In addition, China has portrayed the independence movement in Tibet as a terrorist threat, and has used military means to suppress it, most prominently in the buildup to the Beijing Olympics.[44] The targets of Chinese national security policy are, therefore, broadening to include some of the substate and transnational actors that globalization theorists identify, which the Chinese state is forced to combat in nontraditional ways. In this regard, combating terrorism is a very prominent mission identified by the 2006 Chinese defense white paper.[45]

In contrast, the Chinese national security establishment provides only limited support for proposition PS3 (*changing threats*), as official Chinese doctrine makes rhetorical references to nontraditional security threats, but casts its security policy primarily in terms of more traditional threats (and, of course, fighting terrorism). Although, previously, Chinese defense policy statements made no reference to the new security agenda,[46] the 2006 document asserts: "Security issues related to energy, resources, finance, information and international shipping routes are mounting. International terrorist forces remain active; shocking terrorist acts keep occurring. Natural disasters, serious communicable diseases, environmental degradation, international crime and other transnational problems are becoming more damaging in nature."[47] Furthermore, it explicitly links defense policy with the goal of economic prosperity.[48]

Nonetheless, when it comes to articulating the essence of Chinese national security policy, the document identifies as the primary purpose to entail "[u]pholding national security and unity, and ensure the interests of national development. This includes guarding against and resisting aggression; defending against violation of China's territorial sea and air space, and borders; opposing and containing the separatist forces for 'Taiwan independence' and their activities; taking precautions against and cracking down on terrorism, separatism and extremism in all forms." The remaining priorities refer to the technological and diplomatic means through which these traditional security objectives are to be met, with no mention of nontraditional concerns, aside from terrorism.[49] Nor has Chinese security behavior, focused as it is on Taiwan and an armed forces modernization program, given us reason to conclude that China's national security establishment has switched its focus to nontraditional threats. And anecdotal evidence of Beijing's lackluster response to a potential SARS pandemic in 2003 suggests that the Chinese government does not take new threats as seriously as they might.[50]

Therefore, the Chinese national security establishment remains focused on traditional security threats, even as they currently participate in fewer interstate wars and have changed their declaratory language to identify a broader range of nontraditional security concerns. The only shift in focus of the Chinese security state is the increasing attention it pays to subnational threats from terrorists and secessionist movements. This, though, does not constitute strong evidence for the globalization school's hypotheses.

THE STRATEGIES STATES PURSUE

The strategies and instruments China has used to meet its contemporary security needs also appear relatively traditional, with certain exceptions. Regarding proposition PS4 (*defensive and deterrent doctrines*), for example, there would appear to be some ambiguity. The official Chinese military doctrine is decidedly defensive in orientation, although it is difficult to reconcile certain Chinese foreign policy goals with a defensive doctrine. The preamble to the 2006 defense statement asserts: "The Chinese government . . . pursues a defense policy which is purely defensive in nature."[51] China's declaratory foreign security policy, moreover, is based on the principles of peaceful coexistence, mutual respect for sovereignty and territorial integrity, noninterference in other states' internal affairs, mutual nonaggression, and the resolution of all international issues by peaceful means.[52] Most significant, the principle of no first use of Chinese nuclear weapons reinforces this defensive/deterrent posture.[53]

Nonetheless, some of China's stated foreign security policy goals are more outward looking and potentially offensive. In particular, because the Chinese government would view a movement toward Taiwanese independence as a serious threat to Chinese sovereignty and unity, Chinese military doctrine clearly leaves open the possibility of offensive operations against Taiwan. Moreover, as a military confrontation with Taiwan may embroil China in a war with Taiwan's erstwhile protector, the United States—whom the 2006 white paper acknowledges is being unhelpful by supplying Taiwan with arms, despite being officially committed to a "One China" policy—it would appear that Chinese strategists may actually be contemplating the initiation of a great power war to achieve their political aims.[54] Other issues, such as separatism, border disputes with India, and close relations with North Korea and Pakistan, raise additional questions about the "defensive" nature of the Chinese doctrine. Furthermore, Beijing has recently expanded its naval presence into the Indian Ocean and the Pacific by setting up facilities in Myanmar, and constructing ports and other facilities that have dual use in countries like Pakistan. We can best represent Chinese military doctrine, therefore, as somewhat of a hybrid or "calculative" approach consistent with its "peaceful rise approach."[55]

Moreover, to the extent that China is currently eschewing offense in the international system, it may have less to do with globalization than relative Chinese weakness compared with the global hegemon, the United States. A central principle of Chinese national security strategy is Deng Xiaoping's injunction that the Chinese must "bide our time and build up our capabilities" until they can act decisively on the international stage.[56] Therefore, China may simply be avoiding offense in the short term.

China has been actively pursuing soft balancing (proposition PS5) since the 1990s, using largely institutional mechanisms. In fact, China sees hard balancing vis-à-vis the United States as both unachievable and undesirable in the short run. The reasons are twofold. To begin with, Chinese leaders fear being denied access to the American market, which it views as essential to achieve its economic goals, because active military competition with the United States could result in Washington taking measures to impose an economic embargo on its rival. Perhaps of even greater significance, China has found allies wanting in the pursuit of a hard balancing coalition. China and Russia have made occasional efforts at building such an alliance, but both balked at anything other than a limited entente.[57] China has, however, used its UN Security Council veto power as a tool to contain American unilateralism. During the Kosovo crisis, China made consistent efforts along with Russia to prevent U.S.-led intervention and also to deny UN approval for the action. During the events leading to the Iraq invasion, China—along with Russia and France—made efforts at the UN to prevent the invasion and, since 2003, opposed the war, blocking UN approval.[58] China has also been expanding to regions such as Africa and Latin America, developing regional economic alliances intended to balance U.S. and western influence in these regions, especially in the competition for oil. In addition, China has been actively participating in regional institutions in the Asia–Pacific, especially APEC and the Shanghai Cooperation Council, which it has helped to create. These institutions, although focused considerably on trade and other economic issues, also offer China a platform from which to engage and constrain the influence of other great powers, particularly the United States, in the region.[59]

As predicted by proposition PS6 (*manpower*), Chinese military manpower has steadily declined from 3.9 million in 1985–1986 to less than 2.3 million in 2007, as part of a coordinated governmental plan to reduce manpower and make the military more efficient through the acquisition of weapon systems that capitalize on the revolution in military affairs and the "informationalization" of warfare, a major preoccupation of the 2006 defense white paper.[60] This dramatic reduction in great power military manpower is clearly consistent with the globalization school's predictions.

Chinese defense spending during the eighteen years of our study does not conform to the globalization school's proposition PS7 (*defense spending*), because, after an early post-Cold War dip, it has risen considerably in recent years. In 1992, China spent an estimated $16.5 billion on defense. After declining to an estimated $14.6 billion in 1994, it has surged every year since then to an estimated $49.5 billion in 2006.[61] This represents more than a tripling of Chinese defense spending during the past twelve years! And, indeed, by the Chinese government's own estimates, Chinese defense spending has risen by an average of 15.36% annually between 1990 and 2005 (9.64% when adjusted for inflation).[62] These recent increases no doubt reflect both the rapid advance of the Chinese economy and its desire to modernize its South Sea fleet.[63] During the past fifteen years, China's economy grew by a staggering 580%, generating more aggregate wealth that can be devoted to national security goals.[64] As a result of this new wealth, and to protect it, the

Chinese government has sought to revamp its South Sea fleet in an effort to improve its power projection capabilities in the Straits of Malacca, through which 80% of Chinese imports pass. This modernization program has brought the fleet both new submarines and surface ships, including the LUDAI class destroyer with enhanced air defense systems. Nonetheless, spending on the theater will likely continue until China solves the "Malacca Dilemma," or the insufficient operational range of the PLA Air Force and PLA Navy Air Force in the Straits.[65]

The Chinese experience, then, is inconsistent with predictions of lower defense spending in the age of globalization. Its preoccupation with Taiwan and the South China Sea fleet suggests that its spending decisions continue to be dictated by rather traditional calculations of national interest. Indeed, recent Chinese behavior suggests that if globalization is likely to affect national investments in procurement at all, it is likely to have the opposite impact. For, like China, as other less-developed states reap the economic gains that the global market makes possible, they, too, might have more resources to invest in national defense.

Despite its rather traditional primary mission, the Chinese military offers some support for proposition PS8 (*shift from war fighting to policing*). After all, China also charges its national security apparatus with "taking precautions against and cracking down on terrorism, separatism and extremism in all forms."[66] The principal organization charged with domestic public order is the People's Armed Police Force (PAPF), which is a branch of the national security establishment, charged by the defense white paper "to perform guard duties, handle emergencies, combat terrorism, and participate in and support national economic development."[67] In practice, however, policing tasks are not limited to the PAPF, because the PLA also contributes to counterterrorist and public order operations. One need only consider the military's response to the 1989 Tiananmen Square protests, its crackdown on the Falun Gong, or its recent suppression of unrest in Tibet to see that internal policing is part of its bailiwick.

The Chinese military thus remains at the heart of Chinese national security strategy and continues to envisage the use of force on an interstate basis to achieve its security objectives. Its doctrine is potentially offensive—even though its declaratory policy is defensive and deterrent only—and it continues to spend heavily on military goods in an effort to modernize its capability to fight an interstate war, potentially over Taiwan or, perhaps, its border with India. Some innovation is apparent, however, as the military reduces its manpower (relying more on higher technology weapons) and increasingly engages in policing-type activities. Similarly, although it continues to balance against the United States in traditional terms, such as increasing defense spending and modernizing its armed forces, it avails itself primarily of soft-balancing diplomatic techniques vis-à-vis the United States, rather than forming military alliances or coalitions against the hegemon.

THE MONOPOLY OF THE STATE AS A SECURITY PROVIDER

The Chinese defense policy statement continues to view the business of national security as a state-centric endeavor. Consequently, it does not identify any role for nonstate actors, such as private companies or NGOs. Indeed, because the state plays a central role in the Chinese economy, there are no truly private companies in China that are completely independent of Beijing.[68] In addition, we have found no evidence of widespread use of nonstate actors to advance Chinese security goals. We conclude, therefore, that China offers no support for proposition PS9 (*nonstate actors*).

With regard to proposition PS10 (*regional institutions*), however, the Chinese national defense policy does identify a role for international security cooperation and regional institutions, stating: "China pursues a new security concept featuring mutual trust, mutual benefit, equality and coordination, and adheres to the Five Principles of Peaceful Coexistence. It works to promote good-neighborliness, mutual benefit and win–win, and endeavors to advance international security cooperation and strengthen military relations with other countries." In particular, it credits ASEAN, the grouping of ASEAN plus China, Japan, and the Republic of Korea, the SCO, and the ASEAN Regional Forum with playing "a major role in promoting peace, stability and prosperity in the Asia–Pacific region" and helping to combat nontraditional security challenges, such as terrorism, the drug trade, proliferation issues, and disaster relief.[69] The bulk of the document, though, lays out a rather independent defense policy, which suggests that the Chinese state remains at the forefront of the pursuit of Chinese security, relying on regional institutions to help cope with challenges that do not directly affect what the government views as the core interests of Chinese sovereignty and security.

Our analysis of Chinese national security strategy from 1991 to 2008 indicates that the international system's rising contender is conducting its challenge using a mix of both traditional and nontraditional means. Nonetheless, many of the changes that are consistent with the globalization hypotheses—such as the shift to a defensive or deterrent doctrine, the inclusion of a host of nontraditional threats in the preamble to the national security blueprint, or the reliance on multilateral institutions to achieve key security objectives—appear to be declaratory only and are not reflected in actual behavior. Indeed, China is using the proceeds of its economic boom to spend heavily on national defense, continues to contemplate offensive operations and a potential interstate war in an effort to reunite Taiwan with the mainland, and still views the national security state as the principal security actor. Consequently, although some of the changes in the Chinese national security apparatus—in particular, its treatment of terrorism as an important security threat, its reduced manpower, and the growing importance of policing-type missions—are hardly inconsequential, they do not yet constitute the transformation in the pursuit of security to which globalization theorists have pointed.

Russia

Of the three major powers, Russia has been the most constrained in security behavior during the period we assess, because of the political and economic decline of its predecessor the Soviet Union. As a result, it has been more inward looking for most of the past two decades, as it tried to consolidate its hold on breakaway republics and restore its shattered economy. This may be only a temporary situation, and there is evidence to suggest that newfound Russian oil wealth and the high commodity prices that prevailed until autumn 2008 began to lead former president and current Prime Minister Vladimir Putin to act more boldly on the international stage, particularly within what Russia views as its "Near Abroad."[70] Constraints on Russian power during the early post–Cold War era, however, mean that Russian security policies are not as good indicators of the effect of globalization as China's or the United States', because it has been overdetermined that Russia should spend less on defense, reduce its involvement in interstate wars, and rely on other actors to achieve its security objectives. Nonetheless, if we find that even a constrained great power like Russia during the early period continued to pursue traditional security policies or that Russia's recent economic resurgence has led to greater interstate competition, that would constitute important evidence against the globalization school.

THE NATURE OF THREATS

Initially, Russian behavior as an independent state was consistent with proposition PS1 (*changing nature of wars*), although Russian military doctrine is not. Since the collapse of the Soviet Union, for example, although Russia has fought a protracted counterinsurgency campaign against well-organized bands of rebels in Chechnya, has intervened in Tajikistan's civil war, and has supported the secessionist movements in the Georgian's regions of Abkhazia and South Ossetia, it had largely avoided active participation in interstate conflicts.[71] Nonetheless, the most recent Russian national security doctrine remains focused on traditional interstate warfare as the primary mission of the armed forces. Although it acknowledges that the risk of an attack on Russia has declined, it still relies on both conventional and nuclear weapons "to deter (prevent) aggression against it and (or) its allies."[72] Coupled with Russia's battered economy and domestic difficulties, which may explain its recent reluctance to fight interstate wars as a temporary expedient in function of its current priorities, there would appear to be no basis for assuming that Russia has stopped preparing for interstate wars in the new era. Indeed, the Russian conflict with Georgia in summer 2008, Moscow's increasingly belligerent stand toward the Ukraine, and its warnings that if NATO were to proceed with the installation of a missile shield in Poland, that could lead to war all suggest that with increasing oil wealth, Russia has become more assertive and more likely to contemplate interstate warfare as a means of achieving its great power ambitions.[73]

Russia's interminable war with Chechen separatists provides considerable support for proposition PS2 (*postindustrial warfare*). During the bloody counterterrorism campaign resulting from the first Chechen war (1994–1996), Chechen rebels have targeted not only the Russian military, but also civilian interests. And, although the Russian army had initially recaptured all the breakaway republic's urban areas after their December 1994 offensive, it was unable—for more than a decade—to defeat the guerrilla forces, which took refuge in the forbidding mountain terrain and struck unconventionally in Chechnya, in Moscow, and elsewhere in Russia, targeting not only military personnel, but also apartment buildings, entertainment complexes, and even an elementary school.[74] Clearly, the Chechen campaigns represent a nontraditional, non-Clausewitzian form of warfare, where victory does not depend upon massing firepower against a clearly defined enemy on the battlefield.

Regarding proposition PS3 (*changing threats*), Russian military doctrine does identify some new security threats in the contemporary security environment. Specifically, it lists "prevention of ecological and other emergencies and elimination of their consequences" as one of the Russian Federation Armed Forces missions.[75] Nonetheless, in the key sections outlining the main external and internal threats Russia faces, only traditional military, sovereignty protection, and counterterrorist concerns are enumerated.[76] Thus, nonmilitary security remains a low priority for Russia.

On the whole, then, Russian national security policy since the cold war does not match the globalization school's prediction about threats and orientation. True, it did not wage interstate wars for the first fifteen years after it emerged from the Soviet Union, it has increasingly confronted the challenge of postindustrial warfare in the form of secessionists and terrorists, and it acknowledges—at least in principle—that environmental issues have some role in national security discussions. Nonetheless, in light of its increasing assertiveness, its saber rattling in Georgia, the Ukraine, and Poland, and the fact that Russian doctrine and planning continue to privilege traditional security threats, it can hardly be asserted that the Russian national security establishment has been moderated by globalization.

THE STRATEGIES STATES PURSUE

In terms of the means Russia uses to meet its security threats, official Russian doctrine does suggest a new approach to security, although its recent behavior remains much more traditional in scope. Of the three major powers, for example, Russia's national security doctrine offers the most support for proposition PS4 (*defensive and deterrent doctrines*). The most recently articulated Russian military doctrine, for example, begins by stating: "[T]he Military Doctrine is defensive in nature . . . with a firm resolve to defend national interests and guarantee the military security of the Russian Federation and its allies." The priority given to defense is conditioned by the strategic environment, which is characterized by "a decline in the threat of the unleashing of a large-scale war, including a nuclear war." In this more stable environment, Russia maintains its nuclear forces solely as a means of deterring both nuclear and conventional attacks on Russia and its allies from nuclear-armed states.[77] Thus, offense gets almost no play within Russian military doctrine.

This doctrine, however, is at odds with recent Russian behavior. Russia's initiation of offensive operations against Georgia in August 2008 in response to Georgia's attack against the separatist South Ossetian region suggests a somewhat resurgent Russia that is not unwilling to use offensive operations to expand its influence in its Near Abroad. In fact, Russian troops occupied several Georgian cities and relinquished them only after intense mediation by French President Nicolas Sarkozy on behalf of the European Union.[78] Furthermore, Russia's interference in Ukrainian domestic politics and its steadfast refusal to allow the Ukraine and Georgia to join NATO or Poland to deploy missile defenses also suggest the prospect for offensive Russian military operations in the future. Indeed, in June 2007, the Kremlin threatened to deploy nuclear missiles targeting western missile defense emplacements in eastern Europe. And in August 2008, a high-ranking Russian general threatened war with Poland if it deployed missile defenses.[79] It would appear, therefore, that Russia's late-Cold War decline and internal political and economic strains simply made it unfeasible for Russia to pursue offensive goals outside its core territory during the initial post-Cold War era, but Russian economic resurgence resulting from its oil wealth has led to a more assertive and potentially offensive Russian great power.

Russia had also initially switched from hard balancing to soft balancing (proposition PS5) during the early post-Cold War era, but it has begun to resort to harder balancing options, including military threats, of late. With its collapse as a superpower and the disintegration of the Warsaw Pact, Russia lost its chief balancing instruments vis-à-vis the West. Although nuclear weapons offer a certain amount of capacity to balance the United States, this asset has been less than useful in the era of globalization. Furthermore, to Russia's chagrin, NATO has been steadily expanding to former members of the Warsaw Pact, as well as constituent states of the USSR, including the Baltic states, which reduces its power to balance. Thus, Russia initially attempted to balance against the United States and the West only very minimally. Although it made occasional overtures to China and India to form limited coalitions, both have refrained from joining such an option for fear of losing their economic links with the United States. Russia, therefore, adopted a mixture of "bandwagoning" and soft balancing policies to face the power of the United States. The soft balancing efforts were most prominent in Russia's participation in UN Security Council deliberations and its threatened veto along with other like-minded major powers. In this manner, it played a leading role in blocking UN approval for the Kosovo and Iraq interventions. It also formed tacit coalitions and ententes with China in the first instance, and France and Germany in the second, to raise substantial costs for the United States in terms of diplomatic support and global approval for its military intervention.[80] Its escalation of threats against NATO expansion into the Ukraine and Georgia in 2008, and its deployment of missile defenses in eastern Europe, however, suggest the beginnings of a return to a hard balancing strategy.

In terms of manpower (proposition PS6), Russian behavior has been remarkably consistent with the globalization school's expectations. During the past twenty years, Russian manpower dropped dramatically from 5.3 million in active service in 1985–1986 to just less than 4 million in 1990–1991 and less than 1 million in 2002–2003, before increasing marginally to just more than 1 million in 2007. Of course, the pre-1992 IISS figures include all of the Soviet Union, which makes meaningful comparison difficult. When we consider, though, that the Russian republic encompassed more than half of the USSR's population, this decline of more than 80% is considerable.[81] There would appear to be little reason to attribute this primarily to the effects of globalization, rather than a Russian retreat inward after the collapse of its eastern European empire.

Russian military expenditures follow the same pattern as their American counterparts and, therefore, do not confirm proposition PS7 (*defense spending*). Although Russian defense spending declined sharply from an estimated $42.5 billion in 1992 to a low of approximately $13.6 billion in 1998, it almost tripled again to $34.7 billion between 1998 and 2006. It would, of course, be a heroic assumption to attribute the initial collapse in the Russian military budget to the pressures of globalization, rather than to the dire economic circumstances that Russia faced after the Cold War. Indeed, the sharp climb upward during the past decade reflects a rapid increase in state revenue resulting from the increase in the price of oil and the renationalization of petroleum companies as well as the reactivation of conflict in the Caucasus. It is entirely possible, therefore, that the more assertive Russian security behavior witnessed in 2007 and 2008 will lead to a significant increase in Russian defense spending in the coming years, unless the recent sharp decline in oil prices are to persist and sap Russia's ability to spend on defense.

Russian security policy also provides evidence in support of proposition PS8 (*shift from war fighting to policing*). Most significant, the Russian military doctrine lists among its national security goals combating "organized crime, terrorism, smuggling and other illegal activities on a scale threatening to the Russian Federation's military security." In addition, it targets "illegal activities by extremist nationalist, religious, separatist, and terrorist movements, organizations, and structures aimed at violating the unity and territorial integrity of the Russian Federation and destabilizing the domestic political situation in the country."[82] No doubt this focus is a direct response to the terrorist campaign waged by Chechen separatists, who have created threats to public order not simply in Chechnya, but in the capital and other cities, as well. As a result, part of the mission of the Russian national security establishment is crime fighting and maintaining domestic order.

Russian national security strategies thus conform only partially to the globalization school's expectations. Since the end of the Cold War, Russia has cut military manpower drastically, and has utilized its security apparatus to conduct counterterrorism and policing operations. Of late, though, Russia has begun to engage in hard balancing in the form of military threats against NATO and its eastern European allies, and it has conducted offensive operations against Georgia. Thus, there is reason to believe that Russian leaders have begun to return to more traditional security policies emblematic of great power competition.

THE MONOPOLY OF THE STATE AS A SECURITY PROVIDER

Moscow has also been reluctant to devolve national responsibility for security to actors either above or below the state. Russia is, however, prepared to make use of nonstate actors (proposition PS9) to assist in the provision of security under the direction and control of its national security establishment. Thus, although the official Russian national security doctrine makes no mention of either private security companies or NGOs, Moscow has been employing private security contractors in a far more active military role than the United States. Indeed, not only has Russia used private contractors to defend strategic facilities in Azerbaijan, Armenia, and Kazakhstan, but about 40% of the Russian fighting force in Chechnya was comprised of privately contracted soldiers fighting alongside the regular Russian army.[83] We have found no evidence of Russia delegating important security-related tasks to NGOs, though, most probably because the independent organizations are less likely to operate under Moscow's direct control.

Of the three major powers, Russian military doctrine devotes the least attention to regional security frameworks (proposition PS10). As one of the last elements of the policy, it states: "The Russian Federation attaches priority importance to the development of military (military–political) and military–technical cooperation with CIS [Commonwealth of Independent States] Collective Security Treaty states on the basis of the need to consolidate the efforts to create a single defense area and safeguard collective military security."[84] Nonetheless, it prefaces this by emphasizing that military cooperation is a "state's prerogative" that it exercises "on the basis of its own national interests."[85] This is hardly a strong endorsement of regional institutions. Nor is Russia a member of the leading European security institutions. Most significant, it remains outside NATO and the EU, although it consults with them.[86] Clearly, then, Moscow continues to view the Russian state as the sole relevant actor in the provision of Russian security.

As we would expect of a weakened power, Russian national security strategy during the period of our study fits the globalization school's expectations far better than the other two major powers. In particular, Russia has oriented its scaled-back national security establishment to address new threats—primarily those posed by subnational secessionists and terrorist movements—and uses nontraditional strategies and instruments for national security. Surprisingly, the only area in which Russia has retained a more traditional focus is in its rejection of NGOs and international actors as partners in the provision of national security, although it does make extensive use of private military companies. The Russian experience, then, clearly does not provide us with evidence against the globalization hypotheses. Nonetheless, as Russian decline has made many of the changes it has made to its national security policy largely overdetermined, it provides only limited support for the globalization school. Its behavior must, therefore, be interpreted in light of the behavior of the other great powers.

Conclusions

As might be expected based on their relative positions in the international system, the three major powers are pursuing different approaches to security during the contemporary era. While Russia, the weakened power, was retrenching and rebuilding, thus producing policies that (until recently) were largely consistent with the globalization hypotheses, the United States and China—the dominant power and the rising challenger, respectively—have continued to pursue security in more traditional interstate terms, even as they adapt to new circumstances, such as the challenge of global terrorism. As Russian oil wealth facilitates the country's economic and strategic recovery, we are seeing increasing evidence that Russia, too, intends to pursue a more traditional security policy focused on interstate challenges and great power competition.

Table 3.1 summarizes the results of our analysis of major power security doctrine and practice of the post-Cold War era. Each proposition for which we have found strong support appears shaded; we have partially shaded cells for propositions for which we have found limited support; and, we have left unsupported propositions unshaded. A quick glance at the table and its vast white areas indicates that, as a category, the great powers provide only limited support for the globalization hypotheses. Indeed, the security behavior and doctrines of the great powers as a group are inconsistent with six of the ten state-based propositions. Only with regard to propositions PS2 (*postindustrial warfare*), PS6 (*manpower*), and PS8 (*policing*) is there strong confirming evidence of the globalization claims. These are important changes, which indicate, in particular, a recognition of and reaction to the growing threat from transnational terrorists, but on balance, the major powers continue to pursue security in a fairly traditional manner.

It is particularly significant that the United States and China continue to spend heavily on traditional military defense goods during the twenty-first

TABLE 3.1 The Major Powers and Propositions Regarding Globalization

Propositions	United States	China	Russia	Overall
PS1: shift to low-intensity conflicts	Inconsistent with proposition	Consistent practice, inconsistent doctrine	Largely inconsistent with proposition	No trend
PS2: shift to postindustrial warfare	Consistent with proposition	Consistent with proposition	Consistent with proposition	Consistent with proposition
P3: face new threats	Somewhat consistent	Largely inconsistent with proposition	Somewhat consistent	Somewhat consistent with proposition
P4: defensive doctrines	Inconsistent	Largely inconsistent	Consistent doctrine; inconsistent behavior	Largely inconsistent with proposition
P5: soft balancing	Inconsistent	Largely consistent	Somewhat consistent with proposition	Partially consistent with proposition
P6: less manpower	Consistent with proposition	Consistent with proposition	Consistent with proposition	Consistent with proposition
P7: lower defense budgets	Inconsistent with proposition	Inconsistent with proposition	Consistent with proposition	Largely inconsistent with proposition
P8: shift to policing actions	Somewhat consistent with proposition	Somewhat consistent with proposition	Consistent with proposition	Consistent with proposition
P9: privatize to nonstate actors	Largely inconsistent	Inconsistent	Somewhat consistent	Largely inconsistent with proposition
P10: pursue security through regional institutions	Largely inconsistent	Somewhat consistent	Inconsistent	Inconsistent with proposition

Dark shading indicates propositions that are largely consistent with evidence. Light shading indicates propositions that are somewhat consistent with century and continue to plan for interstate warfare in which they take the initiative. It would seem, therefore, that major power military spending and planning since the end of the Cold War has continued to reflect relative power and interests, rather than the pressures of globalization, although it remains possible that globalization itself may actually be responsible for the increased spending, as states seek high-tech solutions for the new security challenges they face. Furthermore, the fact that all three great powers view the state as the key security actor and the cornerstone of national security policy, to the exclusion of meaningful participation from nonstate actors and international institutions, leads us to doubt the extent to which globalization has washed away the state-centric security paradigm.

These findings raise important questions. To begin with, to what extent is the experience of these eighteen years representative of the globalization era? More specifically, to what extent are our findings merely an artifact of other important causal events in the international system, without which the security policies of the great powers would have conformed to the globalization school's expectations? To be sure, their security behavior might have looked considerably different had the September 11 terrorist attacks against the United States not occurred. During the early post-Cold War era, it appeared that the military doctrines of all three major powers were indeed becoming defensive and deterrent in nature, and their defense spending had declined sharply. Perhaps the response to the September 11 terrorist attacks makes it appear that national security is proceeding as usual, masking great changes that globalization has wrought.

Our inclination is that this is not the case. After all, after the early post-Cold War peace dividend, both American and Chinese defense spending began to climb again in the late 1990s, a few years before September 11. Furthermore, the initial post-Cold War situation created an atypical situation of stability that could not endure indefinitely. The early 1990s found the former Soviet Union without the means to carry out an offensive strategy, and the United States without a significant challenger. It is easy for us to understand the temporary retrenchment of the national security state in this period as a product of the resulting stability, rather than as a reaction to emerging globalization. Finally, because transnational terrorism is one of the quintessential challenges of the globalization era—that the globalization literature, indeed, focuses on it as a fundamental change—it would be a gross error brimming with irony to presume that a large-scale transnational terrorist attack halted progress toward more globalized security establishments and temporarily caused a return to "business as usual" in the security theater. For if the most striking manifestation of globalization causes states to revert to traditional modes of national security, then surely any changes manifest in the early part of the era were not profound and may have been induced by other causes.

Moreover, the Russian experience leads us to believe that it was the initial period of retrenchment, rather than the more recent competition, that represents the aberration. The retreat of the Russian security state after 1990 seems to have been the result of the economic constraints imposed by the Soviet Union's economic collapse, rather than by globalization. As oil revenues climbed during the past few years, Russia has reverted to a much more assertive and competitive approach to national security.[87]

Another issue is whether it is early enough for us to judge whether and how globalization has altered the pursuit of security. Perhaps it will take time for states to adapt to the monumental changes brought about by globalization. Adaptation may be especially complicated by resistance from key vested interests with heavy stakes in the business of national security. These could include elements of the military, corporations that supply defense-related goods, governmental institutions, and other participants of the so-called military–industrial complex who have gained power and wealth as pillars of the national security state, and who stand to lose a great deal if threats and spending priorities were to change.[88] Indeed, many of the U.S. State Department and Pentagon officials we interviewed acknowledged that the American understanding of national security in the new era had changed, but that practice had not yet caught up because of the influence of hawks in the Pentagon and their allies in Congress, who resisted changes to spending priorities because of the threat from China. Thus, although American decision makers have begun to view poverty among the global have-nots as the leading cause of global insecurity and the primary emerging threat to American interests, they spend little on poverty reduction, while they continue to spend heavily on big-ticket defense items that are most useful for interstate warfare.[89] Moreover, we can see from the evolution of both Chinese and American national security doctrines in the last half of this decade that more attention is paid to the "new security agenda" in the more recent documents, even if they still play second fiddle to more traditional concerns. Thus, it is possible that, over time, national security planning will evolve to reflect the globalization school's expectations.

In our view, this is a serious objection that we cannot easily dismiss. It is entirely possible that, within the next few decades, after states overcome the opposition of vested interests, globalization will have caused a profound metamorphosis in the way states pursue security. Studying major power security policies and behavior of the first eighteen years of the rise of globalization, however, we have no basis for reaching such a conclusion. Instead, we have observed some important, but limited, changes (mostly regarding the adaptations states have made to the terrorist threat), whereas the bulk of national security activity goes on largely as it has.

On the whole, then, the major powers do not provide strong evidence for the globalization propositions. Most of the propositions find little support in American and Chinese national security doctrines. These states continue to prepare for traditional interstate wars, spend on defense when their interests demand it, and eschew meaningful participation in national defense by regional and private actors. Only in the areas of manpower and the inclusion of postindustrial warfare and policing operations do they behave as globalization theorists would expect them to. Russian security policy and behavior was initially more consistent with the globalization hypotheses, but it, too, has diverged from a globalized security agenda in recent years. Because all three major powers have deviated from the globalization school's expectations, the weight of the evidence suggests that globalization has not yet transformed the way the major powers pursue security. We now turn our attention to a second category of states—leading states in stable regions—to see how they have been affected by globalization.

CHAPTER 4 | States in Stable Regions

A SIDE FROM THE MAJOR POWERS, there are other important security
actors whose power, interests, and influence are more limited, but still
are key players in the affairs of their own region and who also participate, to
some degree, on the world stage. We divide these second-rank powers
into two groups. This chapter focuses on second-tier powers that inhabit
relatively stable regions, leaving those that are in regions of enduring rivalry
for chapter 5.

The very stability of their regions should mean that these states face fewer
security threats and, consequently, a reduced security dilemma. As a result,
we should expect less resistance to the pressures of globalization from these
states, because the costs of devolving state control over national security will
be low, as will the need to prepare for interstate warfare. These states, then,
should be less inclined to spend on traditional defense goods, more apt to
refocus their national security establishments to meet the new threats that
are brought by globalization, and more willing to share responsibility for
meeting these threats with nongovernmental actors and international institutions. Our purpose in this chapter is to investigate whether that, indeed,
has been the case. We will explore the experiences of second-rank powers in
two types of stable regions. First we will investigate the pursuit of security in
western Europe, which has made the transition from a region of war and
instability to a stable region of democratic states, constituting a pluralistic
security community.[1] Then we will shift our attention to South America and
Southeast Asia, regions without enduring rivalries that are enjoying protracted stability, but that contain some nondemocratic states and have not
yet achieved the status of pluralistic security communities.

Because the very stability of these states and their low security dilemmas make them the most likely cases for the globalization hypotheses, it would not constitute strong support for the globalization school if we find significant changes in the way they pursue security during the period under analysis (1991–2008). After all, these states have very weak incentives to resist the economic and political logic of globalization by retaining strong national control over the pursuit of security. Conversely, if even these rather secure states continue to follow traditional security practices, this would constitute powerful evidence against the national-security-state-in-demise propositions.

Western Europe

During the Cold War, the states of western Europe were on the frontline of the geopolitical divide. Prior to that, they were embroiled in centuries of internecine war and conflict. Yet, the end of the Cold War found this previously troubled region ensconced in unprecedented peace, stability, and security. All the states in the region are liberal democratic and participate together in cooperative political, economic, and military· organizations, principally the European Union and NATO. Consequently, they have committed to resolving their conflicts with each other peacefully and do not pose military threats to one another. Indeed, they represent, in Waever's estimation, the quintessential pluralistic security community.[2] Nor, after the collapse of the Soviet Union, do they face any serious threats from states outside the region.

Facing this unprecedented period of interstate security, no states should be as willing as these to depart from traditional security practices and doctrine, because the costs of relinquishing tight state control and scaling back preparation for interstate warfare are likely to be low. In this chapter we investigate the security policies of the two leading national security states in the region: Britain and France. We restrict our focus to these two states because they are the only states in the region that possess nuclear weapons and are western Europe's two veto-holding permanent members of the UN Security Council. The only other leading power in the region, Germany, has a constitutionally truncated national security apparatus as a result of conditions imposed upon it after World War II and, therefore, is not representative of second-tier powers. For propositions PS6 and PS7 (*manpower* and *defense spending*), we will also consider the experiences of the region as a whole. If even the secure states of western Europe continue to pursue traditional national security strategies and persist in retaining state primacy in the security arena, this would cast doubt on the globalization hypotheses.

THE NATURE OF THREATS

The two key states of western Europe provide little support for proposition PS1 (*changing nature of wars*). To be sure, they have not fought a traditional interstate war on their own soil since World War II came to an end. Nonetheless, they participated in both the international coalition against Iraq in the 1991 Gulf War and the NATO-led operations against Yugoslavia in 1999. The United Kingdom also played a significant role in the 2001 war against Afghanistan and the 2003 war against Iraq. Thus, in practice, they have continued to wage interstate warfare in extraregional territories in the era of globalization.

On a doctrinal level, the British have begun to move away from interstate warfare as the primary motivating threat, but clearly have not abandoned it as a major mission of the armed forces. Thus, the 2003 British defense white paper acknowledges that "[t]here are currently no major conventional military threats to the UK or NATO," and that "[t]he largest operation envisaged was a regional conflict." Nevertheless, it concluded that Great Britain retained "[t]he need for modern and effective armed forces equipped and supported for rapid and sustainable deployment on expeditionary operations, usually as part of a coalition." Moreover, it presumed that "a requirement to retain the basis on which to reconstitute larger capabilities in the event of a re-emerged strategic threat to NATO remained."[3]

French strategic planning is even more traditional in focus, cast largely in terms of poles of power. Indeed, in a policy speech to the French military establishment, former President Jacques Chirac cautioned against treating international terrorism as the sole or even the primary threat that France faces. "One should not," he declared, "yield to the temptation of restricting all defense and security-related considerations to this necessary fight against terrorism. The fact that a new threat appears does not remove all others." Instead, he warned:

> Our world is constantly changing and searching for new political, economic, demographic and military equilibria. It is characterized by the swift emergence of new poles of power. It is confronted with the appearance of new sources of imbalance, in particular the sharing of raw materials, the distribution of natural resources, and changing demographic equilibria. These changes could result in instability, especially if concurrent with the rise of nationalisms.

Furthermore, he noted, "one should not ignore the persistence of more traditional risks of regional instability. There are risks of this kind everywhere in the world, unfortunately."[4] There is every reason to believe that new President Nicolas Sarkozy views the world in similar terms, even if his foreign policy alignments have departed significantly from Chirac's.[5] Thus, although the Europeans have also participated in numerous lower level conflicts—such as the bombing campaign against Serbia—and peacekeeping operations, there is no basis for concluding that they have fundamentally or irrevocably shifted their focus away from traditional-style military engagements.

They have, however, begun to devote considerable attention to battling terrorism and the challenge of postindustrial warfare (proposition PS2). Both Great Britain and France have had extensive experience with terrorism. For decades, the British were targeted by IRA terrorism, whereas the French were periodically attacked in the 1980s and '90s by Algerian terrorist groups and Corsican separatists in what David C. Rapoport calls the second and third waves of terrorism.[6] It required the advent of global terrorism on a massive scale, however, for counterterrorism to reshape their national security concept. French defense planners, for example, now acknowledge that global terrorism threatens western Europe almost as much as it does the United States.[7] Thus, they are beefing up their special forces to fight terrorism and the spread of weapons of mass destruction.[8]

Since September 11, 2001, the British government has made combating global terrorism the number one priority of its national security establishment. As the 2003 British defense white paper asserts: "International terrorism and the proliferation of WMD represent the most direct threats to our peace and security." To this end, the main security mission of British forces is "[t]o deliver security for the people of the United Kingdom and the Overseas Territories by defending them, including against terrorism." Therefore, "[a]s well as confronting the threat directly, we are working with our partners to tackle the conditions that promote terrorism and provide ready recruits and to deny terrorists funding and freedom of movement."[9] This white paper, however, was written before the July 7, 2005, terrorist attacks by al Qaeda operatives against the British underground and bus network. These devastating attacks have highlighted the importance of fighting terrorism and have thus solidified it as the number one concern of the British military establishment.[10] Subsequent arrests, such as the sweeping August 2006 operation against terrorists who aimed to bomb transatlantic flights departing from England, indicate the magnitude of national security resources the British have devoted to this endeavor. Thus, postindustrial warfare has, indeed, begun to dominate western Europe's security agenda.

Furthermore, in western Europe, now that Cold War threats have disappeared, most defense establishments have turned their attention to a host of new security threats, as expected by globalization scholars (proposition PS3). The United Kingdom, for example, acknowledges that "[t]here are currently no major conventional military threats to the UK or NATO," and thus devotes sections of its defense blueprint not only to the threats of global terrorism and the proliferation of WMD, but also the economic and environmental dimensions of national security.[11] Thus, for example, the 2003 defense white paper cautions that

> [a]s the world's population continues to grow (particularly in North Africa, the Middle East, Latin America and much of Asia), demographic pressures will have more of an impact on international security. Religious and ethnic tensions, environmental pressures and increased competition for limited natural resources may cause tensions and conflict—both within and between states. The UK may not remain immune from such developments; regional disputes can swiftly become internationalised, and may have a major impact on the global economy, energy security, and our allies and partners.[12]

Moreover, failing states on the fringes of Europe and their attendant ills, "[i]nternal conflict, poverty, human rights abuse and famine can all create the conditions for mass population movements, adding to pressures on neighbouring countries or emerging as a surge in migration to Europe," which can threaten British interests.[13] Similarly, *Strategic Trends 2007–2036*, published by the U.K. Ministry of Defense in May 2007, identified a number of security fault lines emerging during the next two decades, as global prosperity increases and integration into the global economy proceeds. Notably, the document forecasts tremendous global climate changes, considerable relative deprivation, income inequalities, and scarcity of resources, such as water and energy, which may inspire the use of force to secure these resources.[14] Thus, the United Kingdom is attempting to grapple with globalization and its impact on security in a multidimensional fashion. French policy, while more traditional in focus, still includes organized crime and trafficking in arms and drugs as potential security threats.[15]

On the whole, western Europe provides more support for the globalization hypotheses on threat definition than the major powers. In particular, in addition to their growing emphasis on counterterrorism and postindustrial warfare, these states are also increasingly defining their security objectives in terms of nontraditional threats and the new security agenda. Nonetheless, they still continue to fight and prepare for traditional interstate wars.

THE STRATEGIES STATES PURSUE

The means that western European states use to secure themselves in the new era also appear to have changed somewhat. For example, their military doctrines all reflect the relatively stable strategic context of the post-Cold War era and, hence, are largely defensive and deterrent in orientation (proposition PS4), although the threat of global terrorism may be in the process of introducing more interventionist and proactive elements to this doctrine. The 2001 British defense white paper predicated its security strategy on maintaining the NATO alliance as a deterrent to larger challengers, remaining engaged in likely trouble spots, such as the Balkans, stabilizing potential flash points, and combating transnational crime, terrorism, and political extremism through careful intelligence, monitoring, and, if necessary, military means.[16] Clearly, this orientation emphasizes caution and the promise of retaliation, rather than offense. The emphasis of the 2003 defense white paper retains this largely defensive and deterrent approach. Nonetheless, its approach to international terrorist threats is somewhat less reactive. Although the British have not yet adopted a more offensive "preemption" policy, like the United States, they do note the requirement for "rapidly deployable forces able to respond quickly to intelligence and achieve precise effects in a range of environments across the world."[17] Thus, toward nonstate threats, the British defense posture may not merely be defensive and deterrent.

French military doctrine also remains largely defensive and deterrent in orientation, although its goals have shifted. The French nuclear arsenal remains the bedrock of French national security planning. "For in the face of the concerns of the present and the uncertainties of the future," Chirac argued, "nuclear deterrence remains the fundamental guarantee of our security. Wherever the pressure comes from, it also gives us the ability to keep our freedom to act, to control our policies, to ensure the durability of our democratic values."[18] In addition to nuclear deterrence, however, under Chirac, the emphasis of the French conventional defense strategy became to project power in tandem with France's European allies to prevent conflicts abroad and to intervene in ongoing armed conflicts.[19] Although these are somewhat outward-looking goals, with the aim of expanding French influence worldwide, they do not appear to be offensive in nature.

The states of western Europe also appear to have abandoned hard balancing (proposition PS5) against the leading power, the United States, in recent years. Great Britain, for one, has tended "to bandwagon" with the United States, participating with Washington in each of the American-led military operations since the end of the Cold War, and has endorsed the broad outlines of American foreign policy in the Middle East, toward Iran, Afghanistan, and its war on terrorism.[20] Although the French leadership has been less comfortable with American leadership and more publicly critical of it, the French, too, have avoided traditional hard balancing behavior. Thus, rather than forging anti-American alliances or challenging the United States militarily, France has organized political opposition to Washington's leadership both within the UN Security Council and NATO, as it did over American efforts to build international support in 2002 for a strike against Iraq. And, under Chirac in crisis situations resulting from the 2006 Israeli–Hezbollah war and the Iranian pursuit of nuclear weapons, France has acted more like a veto-playing partner of the United States, bargaining with it and constraining its policy, rather than balancing against it. President Sarkozy has even reduced French soft balancing against the United States, and has emerged as Washington's leading supporter on matters such as Iranian nuclear weapons.[21]

Within the region more broadly, Germany and Belgium joined France in actively opposing the U.S.-led war on Iraq in 2002 and 2003, whereas a few states such as Spain and Italy, and new NATO members, such as Poland, supported Washington. Thus, European states that disagreed with Washington engaged in soft balancing by opposing U.S. policy in NATO, the EU, and, most prominently, in the UN Security Council. In the latter forum, they joined hands with other leading opponents of the war: Russia and China.[22]

During the past two decades, the total military manpower of NATO Europe dropped to just more than 2.2 million in 2007 from almost 3.3 million in 1986 (despite the inclusion of new eastern European NATO members since the late 1990s), providing considerable support for proposition PS6 (*manpower*).[23] This decrease, moreover, was consistent throughout region, because every country in western Europe reduced its military manpower.

During the same period, however, the states of western Europe behaved only somewhat consistently with proposition PS7 (*defense spending*). In the wake of the Soviet threat, defense spending for all of western Europe clearly declined—from less than $282 billion in 1990 to $243 billion (in 2005 constant U.S. dollars) in 1996.[24] The regional total increased thereafter, climbing to almost $262 billion in 2004 before settling back to $255 billion in 2005. This figure is clearly lower than the immediate post-Cold War highs, but the recent increase suggests that the end of the Cold War may have had more to do with the initial decrease than globalization. Both the British and

French experiences appear to fit the regional pattern well. Although British defense spending dropped from $62.3 billion in 1991 to less than $47.5 billion in 1999, this reduction was almost completely reversed by 2004, when spending jumped to almost $60.2 billion (all figures in 2005 constant U.S. dollars), before dropping slightly to $59.2 billion by 2006. French spending declined from a post-Cold War high of almost $57.9 billion in 1991 to less than $50.2 billion in 2001, before increasing less dramatically to almost $54 billion in 2004, and settling back to $53.1 billion in 2006. Thus, defense spending for the region and its leading security actors reflects an initial decrease, followed by a steady increase into the new millennium.[25]

There is also clear evidence that western Europeans have altered their national security apparatuses to allow them to engage in the policing-type operations that are necessary components of counterterrorism and counternarcotics campaigns (proposition PS8). The 2003 British defense white paper comments that "[w]hile centred on the need to confront international terrorism abroad rather than waiting for attacks within the UK, the New Chapter also recognized the valuable contribution Defence could make to home defence and security in support of the Home Office and civil authorities."[26] In particular, it identifies a role for the armed forces in civil air defense, the control of shipping, counterterrorist operations and hostage release, and support for the activities of the police services of northern Ireland.[27]

French doctrine also recognizes that "the abolition of distances, the downgrading of borders and the development of terrorism as a type of war contributes to a partial erasure of the boundaries between internal and external security," making internal policing a key component of national security policy.[28] French plans to upgrade forces for international peacekeeping and peace-building operations further highlights the importance of policing operations to French security planning.[29]

In most of these aspects, then, the western European states have changed the national means they use to pursue security, reducing their armed forces, eschewing offense and hard balancing, and embracing nontraditional policing missions.

THE MONOPOLY OF THE STATE AS A SECURITY PROVIDER

Given the changed threat environment in western Europe and the altered means that leading states in the region are using to address these challenges, we would expect that the globalization school's predictions about the reduced primacy of the state in defense planning would also be supported in the region. To a limited extent, this appears to be the case with respect to the role of private actors in the pursuit of defense-related goods, although the national security state does not appear to be outsourcing the bulk of its defense activities or relying on NGOs to any large degree (proposition PS9). Although the 2001 British defense white paper makes no reference to coordinating defense activities with private actors, the 2005 defense acquisition blueprint has clearly moved in that direction. For example, the new document asserts the following:

> [T]he nature of acquisition is evolving and we face an increasingly demanding and complex environment. Closer collaborative engagement between us and our industrial suppliers will be vital if we are to continue to deliver the improvements that the Armed Forces and UK taxpayers demand. The increasing pace of technological change, linked to a demand for delivery of projects that combine new equipment with other elements such as through-life support and training as an integrated capability present challenges that both the Department and industry must face together.[30]

Therefore, the Ministry of Defense is required to coordinate closely with industry and to rely on a series of public–private partnerships to meet defense needs.[31]

For economic reasons, the French defense procurement strategy also relies on public–private partnerships to

> achieve tighter control of the overall life cycle cost of equipment through closer involvement of companies in every stage of the equipment's life; reduce costs by making available to third parties any potential capacity not used by the armed forces; share expenses over a period consistent with equipment lifetime, allowing equipment to be handed over and, in some cases, reducing the unit price. In addition to their economic and financial impact, these new procurement methods have implications (varying according to the operation) for a number of issues—organization, state ownership, social aspects—as well as contractual or tax consequences.[32]

Neither country, though, appears to have embraced outsourcing of national security tasks to private companies. Furthermore, aside from a brief mention of coordination with NGOs in the 2001 British defense white paper, concluding that "[j]oint (and coalition) thinking must be the foundation of doctrine, with a shift in emphasis over the period from joint to fully integrated, interagency operations, involving OGDs (other government departments) and NGOs,"[33] neither the British nor the French security strategies seem to rely on these organizations to any significant degree in their planning. Thus, although both countries are clearly increasing their emphasis on private–public partnerships, we do not see evidence yet of a radical devolution of national security to nonstate actors.

To a far greater degree, British and French defense doctrines emphasize cooperation with regional security institutions as central to the pursuit of security (proposition PS10). They disagree, though, on which regional security institutions are most relevant. France gives strategic priority to the EU as a security institution, which it views as "the basis of collective defense in Europe."[34] In contrast, British doctrine "recognises the preeminence of NATO as the alliance upon which Europe and North America depends for collective defence and global crisis management."[35] It also commits itself to strengthening the EU's Common Foreign and Security Policy (CFSP), but views it as complementary to NATO, which is the primary security institution, rather than a competing framework.[36] This disparity may result from the fact that France has not been a member of NATO's integrated force structure since 1966. If so, then French policy may become more NATO oriented if President Sarkozy makes good on his pledge to return France to NATO.[37] Interestingly, although the 2001 white paper made mention of the World Trade Organization, the G7 and G8, the Organization for Economic Cooperation and Development (OECD), and the Organization for Security and Cooperation in Europe (OSCE) as other important institutions that foster stability,[38] the 2003 document makes no mention of them. Moreover, although the British view cooperation with the UN and NATO as important for achieving national security goals, they are prepared to act independently of these institutions when disagreements exist:

> The UK's national security and economic interests are best protected through working closely with other members of the international community. While Iraq exposed differing views within the UN Security Council, NATO and the EU over the handling of that crisis, it does not undermine our continued commitment to the development of these organisations. But we also need the flexibility to build coalitions of the willing to deal with specific threats when necessary.[39]

The French similarly emphasize that they must retain their freedom to decide whether to participate in allied operations or to act independently.[40] The split within Europe over participation in the 2003 coalition against Iraq—in which Great Britain, Italy, and Spain supported the United States, but France, Germany, and Belgium, among others, did not—highlights the degree to which states are still willing to put national considerations ahead of a collective, multilateral approach to security. Thus, although both leading western European powers clearly count on multilateral security institutions of one sort or another to maintain their security, they both continue to place state and national interests above collective ones.

Overall, the policies pursued by the second-rank powers of western Europe have been remarkably consistent with the globalization propositions. With the exception of their continued involvement in, and planning for, interstate warfare, their limited use of private companies and NGOs as security agents, and their recent increases in defense spending, their doctrines conform to the bulk of the globalization school's expectations. This would be very strong evidence for the globalization-transforms-the-national-security-state argument, if these states were not most likely candidates for the globalization hypotheses given the unprecedented security they enjoy in the contemporary era. In addition, we must examine the security policies of noteworthy states in other stable regions before we reach any conclusions about their security behavior. The next section, therefore, considers the security policies of leading states in a second stable region: South America.

South America

The states of South America constitute another region of protracted stability, although not of the same depth or quality as western Europe. Although some regional rivalries remain, such as that between Argentina and Brazil for regional supremacy, the major players in the region have not waged war with each other for decades.[41] Participation in Mercosur, the regional economic organization, moreover, has sought to create a wider range of common interests among the South American states. Nonetheless, to date, the region lacks institutions of regional political integration akin to those in Europe, and not all states in South America have made the successful transition to stable democracy. Perpetual political instability and insurgency in Colombia, the volatility of the Chavez regime in Venezuela, and the region's frequent economic crises further distinguish South America from the steadier ship of western Europe. Therefore, the region does not currently constitute a pluralistic security community.[42]

It is important for us to evaluate the degree to which the South American experience conforms to the globalization school's propositions. To this end, we examine the security behavior and doctrines of two of the region's leading powers, Argentina and Brazil, and the defense spending and manpower of the region as a whole. These actors are appropriate because they are the leading economic and military powers of the region, and both countries have, at times, flirted with the option of pursuing nuclear weapons.[43] If we find correspondence between recent European security practices and those in South America, it would bolster the conclusion that the national security states in stable regions have embraced the logic of globalization. Conversely, if South American states continue to pursue traditional security policies, it could imply that the changed security behavior in western Europe may be attributable to the peculiar stability of a pluralistic security community, rather than to the advance of globalization.

THE NATURE OF THREATS

The leading powers of South America provide only partial support for proposition PS1 (*changing nature of wars*). The region, as a whole, has largely avoided interstate wars since the end of the Cold War, with few notable exceptions, such as the border conflict between Peru and Ecuador. This does not mean that the region has been exactly "peaceful." David R. Mares argues that there has been a sort of "violent" peace in the region characterized by several militarized disputes, although they rarely reach the level of interstate war.[44] In this relatively stable climate, the national security doctrines of the leading states lack a clearly defined purpose. Nonetheless, the Brazilian military establishment intends to retain the capability to wage traditional wars. For, after observing how the current international environment has stabilized, the 2002 Brazilian White Paper on defense argues: "But the country has not been entirely free of risks. Despite its status as a peaceful member of the international community, Brazil could be forced into externally generated conflicts which might threaten its patrimony and its vital interests."[45] And the 2005 White Paper asserts that "the concept of security has been enlarged to include the fields of politics, military, economics, social, environmental and others. However, external defense remains the primary role of the armed forces in its interstate context."[46] Thus, the White Papers offer rather traditionally oriented strategy guidelines to the Brazilian armed forces.[47]

In Argentina, the only South American country to participate in the 1991 Gulf War coalition, the 2001 revision of the January 2000 White Book on defense remains cast in traditional interstate terms, although the primary threats it identifies are farther afield, particularly in Asia and the Middle East.[48] It does, however, acknowledge that

[t]oday, internal tensions constitute the most important source of international conflicts.... An objective observation of the international scene allows one to note that the greatest threats to peace in the post-Cold War era are unstable states rendered aggressive, regional wars, ethnic and religious conflicts, interstate conflicts or, more frequently, intrastate ones.[49]

In practical terms, Argentine doctrine has shifted away from fighting traditional interstate wars toward interoperability with alliance partners for peacekeeping and other purposes. Thus, its 2000 defense White Paper vaguely states: "The main goal of our policy regarding the military is the modernization and reorganization of the Armed Forces, adapting them to the new world requirements, including the redefinition of military missions and the promotion of jointness."[50] It would be hard to classify this as a shift from interstate wars to low-intensity conflicts (LICs), though.

Further afield from the American war on terrorism, South American defense policies vary in their emphasis on counterterrorism and postindustrial warfare (proposition PS2). The 2005 Brazilian defense White Paper makes only a brief mention of terrorism, asserting that "[t]ransnational criminal activities of various nature and international terrorism are threats to peace, security, and the democratic order."[51] Overall, though, the document appears to be far more concerned with transnational organized crime and the drug trade than with counterterrorism.[52] In contrast, Argentina—which has a history of high-profile terrorist attacks, particularly against its Jewish community—identifies international terrorism and extremism as a key challenge for the armed forces.[53] Both countries, however, having been identified by the United States as part of the high-risk "triborder region" with Paraguay (where Hamas and Hezbollah have fund-raising operations), and have signed the Inter-American Agreement on Terrorism under the auspices of the OAS to facilitate cooperation against terrorism throughout the Americas, although this does not mean they have internalized combating terrorism as a primary national security mission.[54] At best, then, we can conclude that there is only partial support for proposition PS2.

In contrast, there is very strong support in the region for proposition PS3 (*changing threats*). Indeed, given the remoteness of credible international threats to regional participants, their definition of national security has been broadened to address a wide range of nontraditional threats. Argentina's 2000 White Paper on national defense, for example, includes among its "main defense interests," "[e]conomic and social growth, [s]cientific and technological development, [p]rotection of the Nation from the drug trafficking [*sic*] and international terrorism, [r]enewable and non renewable [*sic*] resources, [and] [e]nvironmental protection."[55] Thus, a key mission of the Argentine military instrument is to assist "national and international efforts towards a better standard of living" and efforts at environmental protection.[56] Its 2001 revision of this document states even more clearly that "[t]he strategic environment is also characterized by new threats to peace: drug traffic, illegal and massive migrations, and environment degradation."[57]

Among the greatest security threats identified by the Brazilian government is the vastness and small population of the Amazon region, which make it susceptible to drug traffickers, transnational criminal organizations, terrorists, and incursions by the Revolutionary Armed Forces of Colombia (FARC) and other subnational rebel groups.[58] Brazil's 2002 defense White Paper charged the military with the task of interdicting the drug trade and operations in the Amazon to promote economic development and environmental protection.[59] In addition, the 2005 document asserts both that "[t]he question of the environment remains one of the greatest concerns for humanity," and that "[t]he increasing exclusion of significant portions of the world's population from the processes of production and consumption and from the access to information constitutes a potential source of conflict."[60] Clearly, South American states have begun to "securitize" a host of nontraditional issue areas, in line with the globalization school's hypotheses.

On the whole, then, the leading states of South America show some evidence of a shift in the nature of threats they prioritize in the new security environment, but they appear to be somewhat more reluctant than western Europeans to refocus their national security apparatuses exclusively to meet these new challenges.

THE STRATEGIES STATES PURSUE

The strategies used by the leading South American powers have also altered somewhat, but not nearly to the degree that Great Britain and France have changed their security architecture.

Without credible national security threats, the major states in South America have even less need for offensive doctrines in the contemporary era. Thus, in accordance with proposition PS4 (*defensive and deterrent doctrines*), Argentina's primary defense goals are the preservation of the "[s]overeignty and independence of the Argentine Nation; [i]ts territorial integrity; [i]ts right to self-determination; [t]he protection of the life and freedom of its people."[61] Because these vital interests are currently not in jeopardy, Argentina's international security policy largely consists of cooperation with allies and the international community, prevention of WMD proliferation, and the pursuit of arms control.[62]

Because Brazil similarly faces no serious challenges to its traditional security interests, Brazilian military doctrines summarize its defensive and deterrent nature as follows:

> The preventive source of our National Defense resides in the valuation of diplomacy as the first instrument to solve conflicts and in a strategic position based on the existence of credible military capabilities apt to generate a deterrent effect. Furthermore, Brazil rejects wars of conquest.[63]

Indeed, the chief mission of the Brazilian armed forces is to "react to aggression," rather than to achieve proactive security objectives.[64] South American doctrines, at least the larger states in the region, then, have abandoned offense, as globalization scholars would predict. Nonetheless, the more restrained national security doctrines of states in this region may also be merely an artifact of frequent military *coups d'etat*, which may have encouraged civilian governments to restrain the military and curtail the possibility of the armed forces reasserting themselves domestically.[65]

South America offers limited evidence in support of proposition PS5 (*soft balancing*). During the 1990s, most South American states adopted liberal economic ideas (following the Washington consensus), democratic modes of governance, and somewhat pro-U.S. foreign policies. However, this began to change during the early twenty-first century as economic globalization and liberalization failed to bring the resources or policy frameworks to address the growing inequalities and absence of progress for the poorer sections of these countries. The Bush administration's unilateralist policies increasingly began to face considerable opposition in many Latin American countries. Several of them, including Venezuela, Ecuador, Bolivia, Brazil, and Peru, elected left-leaning and populist political leaders who mounted strong opposition to U.S. economic and security policies in the region and beyond. Although much weaker than great power soft balancing efforts, these left-leaning states have engaged in soft balancing toward the United States by forming coalitions with Cuba and engaging China as a lead investor in the region. Venezuela's Hugo Chavez, especially, has taken several steps akin to soft balancing, particularly by forming anti-U.S. ententes with other Latin American states and offering counterpositions at the UN and other regional gatherings and institutions.[66] However, they have avoided the major arms buildups and formal alliances characteristic of hard balancing.

The armed services in the Caribbean and Central and Latin America have maintained rather steady numbers during the past two decades, after increasing briefly during the late 1980s and early 1990s. In 1988, there were more than 1.3 million active servicepeople in the region. After rising to a high of more than 1.5 million the following year, this figure has settled back down to more than 1.3 million again in 2007.[67] This provides little support for proposition PS6 (*manpower*).

Furthermore, the South American experience departs from that of western Europe (and the globalization school's expectations) in its defense spending (proposition PS7). Because its security climate was largely unaffected by the collapse of the Soviet Union, it did not pare its defense expenditures in the 1990s. Instead, South America experienced a sizable increase in regional defense spending during the past fifteen years. In 1991, the region spent less than $14.7 billion on defense; by 2002, that figure rose to almost $27.4 billion, an increase of more than 86% in real terms, climbing a little further by 2006 to $29.1 billion (all figures in 2005 constant U.S. dollars). This represents a drastic increase, rather than the sharp downward trend predicted by globalization scholars or that initially exhibited by the western Europeans, who reduced spending by 9% in real terms during the same period. Moreover, during this period, some leading regional players (including Brazil, Chile, and Colombia) increased their investment in defense substantially. Most striking, the Brazilian defense budget ballooned from less than $5.9 billion in 1991 to just less than $15.4 billion in 2002—an increase of 161%—before settling back to $13.4 billion in 2006.[68]

Conversely, in accordance with proposition PS8, the leading states of the region have shifted a good portion of their national security apparatus to policing roles, as opposed to traditional war fighting. Indeed, Brazil's new security dilemma—trying to justify the military establishment's existence in a stable region—has led the military to redefine itself as a police apparatus. Thus, according to the 2002 defense white paper, Brazil uses its military forces primarily to combat drug trafficking, to participate in international peacekeeping forces, and to provide public security to its larger cities, particularly Rio de Janeiro.[69] Interestingly, the 2005 document recognizes the role of the armed forces "as guarantor of law and order," but declines to specify exactly how it is to perform this role, because that "is regulated by separate legislation."[70] It highlights the centrality of this role, however, in sparsely populated areas—especially in the Amazon region, where narcotics trafficking, transnational crime, and other activities detrimental to the state thrive. Thus, "[t]he presence of the state, and primarily of the armed forces, along our borders, is a necessary condition for the achievement of our stabilization and development objectives in the Amazon."[71]

Although the Argentine military doctrine prioritizes traditional defense, it acknowledges that "[t]he armed forces of the Republic of Argentina, like others in the world, play an important role in supporting other state agencies in charge of the operational aspect of the fight against illegal activities."[72] Specifically, the armed forces are tasked with participation in three kinds of policing missions: "[o]perations in support of the Security and Police Forces in interior security operations,...[o]perations destined to preserve units or infrastructures of the armed forces and to re-establish order,...[o]perations destined to re-establish interior security when facing extreme situations in which the Security Forces are insufficient to restore the State of Law."[73] Clearly, policing-type activities are making up an increasing proportion of their national security missions.

The strategies South American states are pursuing in the contemporary era, therefore, provide some support for the globalization school, but equally offer some challenges. Although these states have abandoned offensive doctrines and have embraced policing missions as part of their security agenda, they have simultaneously doubled regional defense spending and have not reduced military manpower.

THE MONOPOLY OF THE STATE AS A SECURITY PROVIDER

Nor does the region show clear evidence of shifting the locus of security outside the state. Indeed, the leading regional powers in South America provide only weak support for PS9 (*nonstate actors*). Neither Argentina nor Brazil made any reference to outsourcing or relying on private security organizations in their military doctrines.[74] Nonetheless, some states in the region, including Brazil, participate in the American-led Andean Regional Initiative, which relies on private security companies together with U.S. troops to provide security and stop the drug trade.[75] NGOs have also garnered little attention within South American defense planning. The Brazilian White Paper, for example, makes no mention of NGOs. The January 2000 Argentine White Paper discusses cooperation between the armed forces and environmental NGOs, but does not foresee a role for humanitarian and other NGOs as providers of national security.[76] It would appear, therefore, that nonstate actors have not yet become meaningful partners in the provision of security.

Leading South American states have, though, embraced the emerging regional security institutions (proposition PS10) as a means of stabilizing their security environments. According to its January 2000 defense White

Paper, Argentina's defense establishment regards several regional initiatives and institutions as critical for maintaining regional stability.[77] The first is the OAS, "the region's premier forum for multilateral dialogue and concerted action," whose mission is "to promote good governance, strengthen human rights, foster peace and security, expand trade, and address the complex problems caused by poverty, drugs and corruption."[78] Two other initiatives—the Contadora Process for Central American security and the larger Rio Group that grew out of it to resolve Latin American crises more broadly—with their dispute resolution and peacekeeping mechanisms were also deemed important security-providing mechanisms. In addition, the 2000 Argentine White Paper views the enlargement of the Mercosur as "an element of stability" and "an important tool to face the new global challenges."[79] The 2001 White Paper update directly credits these organizations with stabilizing South American security and emphasizes their centrality to the Argentine national security strategy.[80]

Brazil similarly views the region's nascent institutions as useful developments for Brazilian national security. The 2005 defense White Paper notes with satisfaction:

> Among the processes that help reduce the possibility of conflicts in our strategic environment, there are some that stand out: the integration process through Mercosur, the Andean Community of Nations, and the South American Community of Nations; the close relationship between the Amazonian countries through the Amazon Cooperation Treaty Organization; the intensification of our cooperation and commerce with African countries, facilitated by ethnic and cultural bonds; and the consolidation of the Zone of Peace and Cooperation of the South Atlantic.[81]

Therefore, the document continues, "As a consequence of its geopolitical position, it is important for Brazil that it deepens the regional integration process of South America, which should be extended, of course, to the area of regional defense and security."[82]

Another relevant regional security-related institution not mentioned in the defense white papers, but of critical importance for managing regional competition is the Argentine–Brazilian Agency for Accounting and Control of Nuclear Materials (ABACC), which monitors their civilian nuclear activities. ABACC was the institutional means by which the two states abandoned their nuclear pursuits in the 1990s.[83] Thus, although the region's institutions are not as well developed or entrenched as those in Europe, the major actors in the region are increasingly looking to multilateral mechanisms as a means of providing greater security in the future.

Overall, then, South America does provide support for the globalization hypotheses, but to a much more limited degree than western Europe. Certainly, South American states have reorganized the national security apparatus to respond to new threats, have adopted primarily defensive doctrines, are increasingly conducting policing-type operations with their armed forces, and have embraced multilateral security-providing institutions as partners in the pursuit of security. Yet, their doctrines have not fully moved from interstate war fighting to LICs, and not all key regional players have embraced postindustrial warfare or nonstate actors as key components of their national security strategies. Moreover, the region has actually increased both its defense spending and its military manpower during the past decade, which flies in the face of the globalization hypotheses. In the next section, we will consider one final region of broad-based stability, Southeast Asia, to determine whether there are any generalizable patterns across the stable regions.

Southeast Asia

The relatively stable region of Southeast Asia offers another good testing ground for the globalization school's propositions on national security. The states in the region have, in general, embraced economic globalization and an institutional mode of cooperation, although many of them remain nondemocratic or quasi-democratic polities. If globalization has any major effect on national security policies, this is perhaps one of the most likely regions where such an impact could be manifested. Southeast Asia contains ten states, with varying degrees of economic and political development. The region took the institutional path in 1967 with the founding of the Association of South-East Asian Nations (ASEAN), which included six initial members: Brunei, Indonesia, Malaysia, the Philippines, Singapore, and Thailand. By 1999, it was expanded to include all states in the region, with the addition of Cambodia, Laos, Myanmar, and Vietnam.

Because Southeast Asia does not yet constitute a pluralistic security community and, with its mix of dictatorships and quasi democracies, is unlikely to do so for the foreseeable future, it is, perhaps, the least stable of the three stable regions explored in this chapter. Therefore, it will allow us to determine whether the convergence of western Europe with the globalization propositions is merely an artifact of the nature of political community in the region, or whether the greater divergence of Latin American experiences from the propositions is merely an aberration.

THE NATURE OF THREATS

Regarding proposition PS1 (*changing nature of wars*), Southeast Asian states have not engaged in interstate wars since the more than a decade-long Vietnamese intervention in Cambodia ended in 1991. What is remarkable about this absence of wars is that Southeast Asia had been the theater of one of the major conflicts during the post–World War II era: the Vietnam War. Later on, it witnessed a war between China and Vietnam (1979) and a military intervention by Vietnam in its neighboring country, Cambodia (1978–1991). Moreover, the region had witnessed periodic crises over the Philippine claims to Malaysia's Sabah region, the confrontation between Indonesia and Malaysia in the 1960s, and the occasional discord between Malaysia and Singapore.[84] Since the founding of ASEAN in 1967, however, there have been no major interstate wars or military crises among the organization's original founding members. New members—Vietnam, Cambodia, Laos, and Myanmar—have also not waged any interstate wars after they joined ASEAN in 1989, although in 2001–2002, Thailand and Myanmar engaged in limited military clashes over the control of border posts.[85]

Southeast Asian nations have attempted to solve their remaining territorial disputes through diplomacy. For instance, they have resorted to multilateral dialogue mechanisms to resolve their disputes over islands in the South China Sea, especially over the Spratly Islands with China.[86] Vietnam and China have improved their relations after settling the border dispute and have made limited progress on joint exploration of oil and natural gas in the Gulf of Tonkin.[87] However, the region is likely to be affected by the possible competition arising from the rise of China and India as well as the maritime policies of regional states and great powers that seem increasingly focused on balance-of-power politics, an uninterrupted oil supply, and challenges such as piracy. ASEAN states may also increase their maritime buildup as a result of the great power naval competition in the region.[88]

Although ASEAN nations have avoided interstate military conflict during the past fifteen years, and (as we shall see later) some face separatist insurgencies, it is not clear that they have shifted their strategic attention solely to LICs. Nonetheless, the complete absence of interstate warfare in the region during the globalization era and the adoption of defensive doctrines by them (a theme we discuss later) lead us to conclude that proposition PS1 is consistent with events in Southeast Asia.

Proposition PS2 (*postindustrial warfare*) does bear considerable evidence in Southeast Asia. States in the region have been confronting wars fought by ethnic separatists groups (e.g., Aceh separatists in Indonesia, Mindanao rebels in the Philippines, Muslim rebels in Southern Thailand, and the Karin resistance group in Myanmar, among several others) who are dissatisfied with their lack of political autonomy and economic opportunities.[89] The insurgency by the minority Muslim community in southern Thailand has been especially bloody, notably since 2004. Nearly 1,900 people have died in the clashes with insurgents in three southern Thai provinces, and the struggle shows no signs of abating in 2007.[90]

The region has also seen a proliferation of transnational terrorist networks that have been particularly active in Muslim-majority states, such as Indonesia and Malaysia, and Muslim-minority states, including Thailand and the Philippines. In Indonesia, these threats have manifested in several high-profile suicide bombings of foreign tourist centers and hotels such as the 2002 bombings in Bali and Jakarta. al Qaeda has established training facilities in the region and has been actively recruiting locally for its global war.[91] It has also found receptive audiences in many of the internal insurgent groups. The groups that al Qaeda has supported include the Moro Islamic Liberation Front and the Abu Sayyaf Group in the Philippines, the Lashkar Jundullah in Indonesia, the Kumpulan militants in Malaysia, Jemmah Salafiyah in Thailand, the Arakan Rohingya National Organization and the Rohingya Solidarity Organization in Myanmar, and, most prominent, the Jemaah Islamiah, which wants to establish an Islamist state in Indonesia.[92]

Regional states have responded both individually and collectively to these new security threats. However, their individual responses to the terrorist challenge have been uneven, varying according to state capacity. Singapore and Malaysia, states with high capacity, have taken decisive independent steps. Notably, Singapore has increased its security standards in the areas of maritime, land, and air transport; improved its border control and infrastructure protection; established new agencies, such as the Home Front Security Office and the Joint Counter-Terrorism Center to combat terrorism; and reinvigorated its National Security Secretariat.[93] Lower down the state capacity ladder, the Philippines and Thailand have made some efforts, but have not addressed the threat in a systematic manner. They have, though, stepped up their cooperation with the United States in the antiterrorism campaign, and Manila allowed the stationing of U.S. troops on its soil for counterterrorism operations and training.[94] Finally, the Indonesian state has been unable to forge an effective counterterrorism strategy, largely because it lacks sufficient resources to face the large problem it encounters.[95] Nonetheless, Jakarta, too, cooperates with the U.S. war on terrorism and, despite constraints, by mid 2007, it seemed to have made some major strides against terrorism, especially by arresting leaders of the Jemaah Islamiah, although smaller splinter groups have taken their place.[96] It is clear, however, that the challenge of postindustrial warfare has become a central problem for many of the states in the region.

National security threats indeed seem to be changing, in line with proposition PS3 (*changing threats*). In this region, new and old threats have become somewhat enmeshed, whereas the former have assumed more prominence during the era of globalization that we address. These threats include high levels of economic disparities (despite impressive annual growth rates), ecological disasters, demographic challenges (especially posed by refugees and internally displaced persons), ethnic and religious conflicts, trading in illegal drugs, trafficking in human beings (especially women and children), communicable diseases such as HIV/AIDS, pandemic diseases such as SARS and avian flu, energy security, piracy on Southeast Asian waters (especially the Straits of Malacca), and cyber crime (such as financial fraud and cyber terrorism).[97] We will consider each of these challenges briefly, before turning to national doctrines to demonstrate that these problems are viewed as security threats by states in the region.

Environmental problems generated by fast economic changes and the depletion of natural resources, especially forests, water, and fisheries stocks, have been quite salient in the region. The forest fires in Indonesia's Sumatra islands in 1997, in particular, plunged the whole region in a smoke-induced haze, making breathing difficult for millions of people for weeks. Similar problems have recurred in subsequent years as a result of Indonesian farmers clearing their lands annually for agriculture, a practice that Jakarta has not been able to stop.[98]

Refugees, both economic and victims of ethnic violence, have been a recurring problem for the region. These migrations occur as a result of the uneven development of states in the region as well as internal violence caused by ethnic conflicts and state policies. Indonesian and Philippine workers and refugees in Malaysia, and Cambodian and Myanmar refugees in Thailand have often generated tensions within and among states.[99]

The Asian financial crisis in 1997–1998 showed how intensely the region is interdependent as plummeting currency values in one country began to spread to others rapidly. The decline has since reversed, but the region's susceptibility to global economic forces was revealed during this crisis.[100]

The rapid economic growth of China and the increasing maritime trade via the Straits of Malacca have led to piracy, which many ASEAN states now view as a threat to national security. Singapore has taken the lead in combating the menace of piracy with the help of other regional states as well as Japan, the United States, and India.[101]

That the states of the region are increasingly treating these challenges as security matters is evident in concerted efforts to address these issues within ASEAN, as evidenced by the ASEAN Vision 2020 statement and the Hanoi Action Plan.[102] However, ASEAN states are far from undertaking the concerted collective efforts needed to face these challenges, which are increasingly manifold as a result of globalization and the uneven economic development of member states.

Individual states now emphasize internal and nontraditional security threats in their threat assessments. Although Indonesia emphasized "the primacy of domestic security by solving internal sources of security threats such as Communist insurgency, ethnic tensions, economic malaise, and social divisions within its far-flung archipelago," the "Malaysian concept of comprehensive security emphasized non-military sources of security threats," which are seen as "inseparable from political stability, economic success and social harmony."[103] Indonesia's first defense white paper, issued in 1997, talked about globalization, which it suggests has made "domestic and external affairs almost inseparable." The military, however, considers internal security threats, including extremists from the Communists and Islamic fundamentalists, as paramount and it fears that globalization might foster individualism and unglue national unity.[104] The 2003 Indonesian defense white paper, however, after acknowledging several nontraditional security threats, still lists the main role of the Indonesian armed forces as national defense, maintenance of sovereignty and unity of regions, carrying out military operations other than war, and participation in regional and international peacekeeping.[105] It does, though, identify nontraditional security challenges relevant to Southeast Asia, including terrorism, human and weapons smuggling, drug trafficking, money laundering, illegal immigration, environmental destruction, deforestation, and water security.[106] Its national security policy gives considerable importance to these issues, but full success is not expected any time soon.[107]

Cambodia's 2000 defense white paper listed several nontraditional challenges to the country, including economic threats, demographic threats (including HIV/AIDS), geographical threats (such as maritime border protection), and environmental threats.[108] Thailand's military doctrine assumes that "potential conflicts or threats seem to be more internal, non-military threats that stem from economic, social or environmental problems. There are no major threats from our immediate external environment."[109] Therefore,

Thailand bases its national defense on a "Total Defense Concept," with two components: "national development, which aims at strengthening internal security and focuses on the development of border areas and the well-being of citizens," together with broader involvement in national defense "among regular forces, local forces and citizen soldiers."[110] Furthermore, in May 2001, the Thai government declared that drugs pose a "threat to national security" and it engaged in military operations for the eradication of the drug trade, which led to border clashes with Myanmar forces.[111] Finally, in its foreign policy statement of October 2004, Vietnam described its efforts with other countries and international institutions "to address common challenges such as epidemics, poverty, transnational crimes, environmental pollution, and drug trafficking."[112] Clearly, the states of the region have begun to pay more attention to nontraditional security concerns.

Thus, the nature of threats addressed by Southeast Asian nations bears testimony to the globalization hypotheses presented in chapter 1. Although they increasingly talk about it, we cannot be certain, however, to what extent states in the region have made these nontraditional threats priorities for their national security establishments. Despite statements in policy blueprints about Southeast Asian security in terms of its wider dimensions, including human security, it would be difficult to endorse William Tow's assertion that ASEAN states have "embraced socially constructed concepts that reflect greater orientation towards the welfare of the individual."[113] Nonetheless, it is fair to conclude that the security agenda has broadened considerably in the region.

THE STRATEGIES STATES PURSUE

With regard to the strategies states in the region are pursuing to counter these threats, the record is mixed. Certainly, there is evidence that almost all Southeast Asian states have abandoned offensive doctrines and are increasingly pursuing defensive and deterrent doctrines in accordance with PS4 (*defensive and deterrent doctrines*). The most comprehensive approach to defense has been by Singapore. The concept of "Total Defense," which it adopted in 1984, has been upgraded to include a number of traditional and nontraditional threats and the strategies to confront them. The doctrine asserts that "warfare has changed" in the new century as "wars are no longer limited to the battlefield. Instead potential aggressors can strike in less obvious, non-military ways.... Total Defense is divided into five aspects— Military Defense, Civil Defense, Economic Defense, Social Defense, and Psychological Defense."[114] Thailand also relies on a Total Defense concept and calls its strategy, "defensive," as does Cambodia.[115] Indonesia maintains "a doctrine of national defense called Total People's Defense, based on experiences during the struggle for independence." According to this doctrine, Indonesian forces would wage territorial guerilla warfare with the support of the population to repel an enemy state attack.[116] It is definitely a defensive and internally focused doctrine. Malaysia relies on a "defensive defense posture," while emphasizing "deterrence" and "total defence."[117] Vietnamese officials stated that during the 1990s, Vietnam eschewed offense, pinning its national security goals on developing "as many friends as possible, as close relations as possible with outside world [sic], and more international relations and international trade," similar to China's approach.[118] Thus, regional states appear to be casting their national security policies in terms of defense and deterrence, as globalization theorists would expect.

Regarding proposition PS5 (*soft balancing*), the evidence is mixed. Southeast Asian states use a combination of institutional balancing, "bandwagoning," and alliances to achieve security goals. In particular, they have increasingly used institutional mechanisms for binding great powers that can potentially upset the regional security architecture, especially China. Although the ASEAN states do not see any near-term Chinese threat of direct attack, they have expressed concern over future conflict and the need to balance against China using soft approaches such as institutional binding. Allan Whiting, who held interviews in six ASEAN countries— Indonesia, Singapore, Malaysia, Thailand, the Philippines, and Vietnam— contends that all these states view ASEAN as a source of soft balancing of Beijing in the near term.[119] They also view the United States, which remains the most powerful actor in the region, as the potential "balancer" of China, although they have used the ASEAN Regional Forum (ARF) dialogue to prevent great power rivalry and intense balance-of-power politics in the region.

The Southeast Asian states also have used ASEAN and other institutional forums such as APEC to reduce the threat of great power military involvement. Moreover, they have manipulated the rivalries of one regional power against the other (e.g., China and India) to prevent a future hegemony by either of the two rising powers of Asia. Some states in the region, such as Singapore, Thailand, and the Philippines, have also been actively aligning with the United States, especially in counterterrorism operations since the September 11 attacks, as a form of hard balancing in an effort to keep regional challengers in check.[120] Overall, however, we cannot conclusively say that states in the region pursue one single approach—hard balancing, soft balancing, or institutional balancing—to secure themselves. It seems they have adopted a combination of strategies, going from one end of the spectrum to the other, but not actively embracing a single approach.[121]

Furthermore, the region has reduced its military manpower during the past two decades, in accordance with proposition PS6. In 1990, the region fielded more than 2.3 million people in active service. This figure rose somewhat in 1991, before dropping to less than 1.8 million in 1994. This figure rose again to more than 2 million in 2003, but it has since settled back at around 1.9 million, where it was in 2007. Different regional players, however, have been following divergent trends. Indonesia, for example, has steadily grown its armed forces from 283,000 in 1990 to 302,000 in 2007. Thailand followed a similar pattern, whereas Vietnam cut its standing army considerably from more than 1 million in 1990 to 455,000 in 2007. On the whole, though, there is evidence that military manpower is decreasing in the region.

The region offers no support, though, for proposition PS7 (*defense spending*). Defense spending by ASEAN member states has almost doubled in real terms (adjusted for inflation) from an estimated $8.6 billion in 1988 to more than $15.8 billion in 2006 (all figures in 2005 constant U.S. dollars).[122] Most of the leading states in the region followed this pattern. Notably, Singapore more than tripled its defense budget during this period from less than $1.9 billion in 1988 to more than $5.8 billion in 2006, Indonesia increased from less than $1.9 billion to almost $3.7 billion, and Malaysia had a threefold increase from less than $1 billion to almost $3 billion. Thailand was the only real outlier, increasing from more than $2.1 billion in 1988 to a high of more than $3.2 billion in 1996, before dropping again to less than $2 billion in 2000, a figure it has hovered around ever since.

The increase in defense spending was not prompted by fears of interstate war, but was in part the result of modernizing outdated weapon systems, and the regional states' participation in the U.S.-led war on terrorism after September 11, 2001. The strategic rationale, such as maritime defense, conflict over the Spratly Islands, and internal political dynamics involving the armed forces also seem to be affecting defense spending.[123] It is clear, though, that globalization has not caused states to scale back their militaries.

Proposition PS8 (*shift from war fighting to policing*) does seem to be applicable to the region. Most of the militaries in the region prepare for waging internal battles as opposed to external wars. When confronting insurgent groups, their behavior is akin to strong-armed police forces, although they may not be the best prepared for such roles. The Philippine army and the Thai army, in particular, have been very active in suppressing rebel groups fighting for autonomy. Indeed, Singapore's army may be the only one in the region actively preparing primarily for interstate war, rather than domestic insurgency.

On balance, then, Southeast Asian states pursue a mix of security strategies in the contemporary era, some corresponding to the globalization school's expectations and others not. They have clearly rejected offensive doctrines, cut back on manpower-based militaries, and have reduced their emphasis on military-based strategies. Nonetheless, their military spending has ballooned, and they use both traditional hard balancing and soft balancing approaches to the regional great power.

THE MONOPOLY OF THE STATE AS A SECURITY PROVIDER

Despite the presence of institutional mechanisms for regional order and stability, states remain the chief security providers in the region. Indeed, the role of nonstate actors as security managers (PS9) seems rather limited in Southeast Asia. The states in the region, like other developing states, are still very sensitive about issues relating to sovereignty and defense policy. Indeed, the power of the Westphalian sovereignty norm was strongly evident in the fact that even ASEAN meetings, which as we shall see were quite important to regional actors, for a long time refused to discuss security issues in deference to the institution's norm of noninterference in each others' internal affairs. This may well be a result of the fact that the states in the region are fairly new and are concerned about losing their autonomy, similar to other developing countries. For this reason, not surprisingly, NGOs are typically not utilized in the provision of security within the region. According to Dent, security policy in most of these states "is still a highly secretive matter in which non-governmental actors—or even civilian politicians in some cases—are allowed no significant role."[124]

However, NGOs in general are credited with advancing nontraditional security issues in different countries, especially Indonesia, Malaysia, the Philippines, and Thailand.[125] Some NGO groups such as the ASEAN People's Assembly, the ASEAN Institute of Strategic and International Studies, and the Council for Security Cooperation in the Asia–Pacific (CSCAP) have engaged in Track-2 (nonofficial-level) diplomacy and have made partial inroads in broadening the security discourse to include nontraditional items, especially human security issues.[126] A network known as Peace, Disarmament, and Symbiosis in the Asia Pacific has organized conferences on human security issues, and the People's Forum held parallel conferences with the APEC summits. The ASEAN People's Assembly is yet another group campaigning for a more human-centered regional security agenda.[127] It is difficult to say how much influence these groups have on state policies. Moreover, as Brian Job states, "security issues considered in Track-2 forums continue to be defined largely by states. The various elements of comprehensive security beyond traditional military threats have gained a place on the agenda, but internal security matters have been kept off the table."[128] Thus, NGOs are attempting to influence the ideas underlying security dialogue in the region, but they have not been treated as partners in the performance of security tasks.

Private security providers have not been that active in individual countries of the region. However, one area where they have become prominent players for more than a decade is the fight against piracy in Southeast Asian waters, especially in the Malacca and Singapore straits. They have been performing services such as risk assessment and consulting, training of crews and military personnel, supply of armed guards for ships and ports, crisis response, investigation and recovery of hijacked vessels, rescue of crew members, and protection of fishermen against attacks by pirates.[129] Other than in the area of antipiracy operations, security remains a very state-centric issue, and the roles of private security organizations and nongovernmental agencies are marginal or nonexistent.

There is evidence that Southeast Asian states are increasingly utilizing regional security institutions to provide for their security (proposition PS10). The security institutions of Southeast Asia are manifold and well institutionalized. ASEAN has been the main institutional forum for the region for more than three decades. Initially ASEAN shied away from security issues, leaving them to bilateral frameworks. However, during the 1990s, ASEAN began to consider security issues in a limited fashion. It was not until May 2006, though, that ASEAN defense ministers met for the first time in a formal setting and launched an annual meeting with the intent of creating conditions for an ASEAN Security Community.[130]

This security community idea emerged in December 1997, when ASEAN leaders adopted ASEAN Vision 2020. Its avowed purpose is to create a "concert of Southeast Asian nations, outward looking, living in peace, stability and prosperity, bonded together in partnership in dynamic development and in a community of caring societies."[131] The concert includes, among other things, Southeast Asia as a Zone of Peace, Freedom and Neutrality; territorial disputes resolved by peaceful means; a region free from nuclear weapons where all nuclear states adhere to the protocols of the Southeast Asia Nuclear Weapon Free-Zone; and the ARF as an established means of confidence building.[132] At their Bali Summit in October 2003, ASEAN leaders signed the ASEAN Concord II, with the explicit aim of building an

ASEAN Security Community.[133] This initiative however, remains a long-term project.

ASEAN states formed the ARF in 1994, with a membership of all ASEAN member states, Australia, Canada, China, the EU, India, Japan, the Democratic Republic of Korea, the Republic of Korea, Mongolia, New Zealand, Pakistan, Papua New Guinea, the Russian Federation, and the United States. The ARF has emerged as a major venue to discuss regional security issues such as the relationship among the major powers, nonproliferation, counterterrorism, transnational crime, and conflict in the South China Sea and the Korean Peninsula. The ARF annual meetings have offered an important venue for the states to engage their neighbors and major power actors diplomatically, especially the rising China. As an institution, it has been reasonably successful in the areas of confidence building and the exchange of information on military doctrines, arms acquisitions, and military exercises. In recent years, it has especially focused on the prevention of terrorism and intelligence sharing among member states.[134] However, "progress towards preventive diplomacy and the development of mechanisms for conflict resolution have so far been hampered by fears that they would open the floodgates for intervention into members' internal affairs."[135]

ASEAN responses to security challenges have been mostly in organizing meetings at the ministerial and official levels to exchange views and coordinate policy responses. The institution's approach to infectious diseases has been to promote openness and transparency, whereas, for terrorism, it has promoted the "sharing of intelligence." ASEAN has also promoted maritime security initiatives like joint patrols and contingency planning. "All these efforts are in an early and tentative stage with concrete results as yet uncertain."[136]

Regional states accord high value to their ASEAN participation. For instance, Malaysia's foreign policy overview states: "Malaysia believes that the existence of ASEAN has encouraged patterns of behavior that reduce risks to security by enhancing bilateral relations as well as fostering habits of open dialogue on political and security matters including establishing confidence building measures," and that "a strong and successful ASEAN is not only an economic necessity but also a strategic imperative."[137] The Philippines has placed among its national foreign and security goals the "enhancement of national security through bilateral, regional and multilateral institutions"; and the "[u]tilization of development diplomacy to attain economic security." It further asserted that "[t]he Asia–Pacific region faces challenges that may only be surmounted through collective efforts. The security of the region can thus be effectively addressed through cohesive, dynamic and viable cooperation by the member countries in major regional and international groupings such as ASEAN, ARF, APEC and ASEM [Asia-Europe Meeting]."[138] Similarly, Laos has pledged to

> expand its relations and cooperation with the international community as well as contribute actively to the regional integration, particularly the integration of ASEAN member countries with the aim of enhancing the role of the Lao PDR [People's Democratic Republic's] as an efficient partner of the countries in Southeast Asia and other regions in the world.[139]

In contrast, though, the Malaysian security doctrine provides only limited scope for regional security institutions, stating "[e]ven though it recognizes the importance of regional cooperation and external assistance, Malaysia believes that self-reliance should continue to be the cornerstone of its defence."[140]

Some argue that Southeast Asia is starting to emerge as a limited or second-tier security community with interstate war becoming unthinkable among states in the region.[141] They argue that the "ASEAN way" of cooperation, based on limited institutional engagement, has helped change state behavior through "socialization inside international institutions," and "persuasion" as well as by providing "modes of behavior," through "habits of cooperation."[142] However, as newly emerging states in the region have been extremely sensitive to the norms of sovereignty and nonintervention in each other's internal affairs, they are reluctant to allow ASEAN too much authority over regional security.[143] Instead, the "ASEAN way" comprises less of a proactive regional security provider than a sociocultural norm complex of sovereignty, the nonuse of force, and the peaceful settlement of disputes founded on "informality," "consultations," and "consensus," rather than a supranational security architecture.[144] These nonintervention principles include refraining from criticizing the actions of governments toward their own people, and denying recognition and sanctuary to groups that seek to overthrow a neighboring state's government. However, ASEAN governments are encouraged to support member state policies against subversive groups.[145] This nonintervention principle may be one of the reasons why the Southeast Asian states (unlike in South Asia or the Middle East) have avoided interstate violence, but continued with high levels of internal violence. The absence of institutionalized restraints on internal repression based on regionwide democratic norms is also the reason why ASEAN has yet to form a proper pluralistic security community similar to the EU.

To sum up, then, although ASEAN and its associated institutions is viewed by most regional actors as a central component of regional security, member states fiercely resist its encroachment into areas of sovereign state authority in the security area.

The Southeast Asian region provides reasonable evidence in support of many of the propositions advanced in chapter 1. In particular, it has developed strong, but limited, multilateral regional institutions to achieve national security goals and has changed its security focus to address a host of nontraditional security challenges. However, it also exhibits some of the traditional security characteristics, in terms of deep concerns for state sovereignty and the nonintervention principle, and increased levels of military spending. In addition, regional institutions have been built with the intention of not replacing traditional instruments such as the balance of power or American preponderance, but as supplements to these frameworks. Two scholars of the region thus contend that, in Southeast Asia, both "balancing mechanics and regional community dynamics will coexist (as is already happening), at times comfortably and other times, not."[146]

Conclusion

As we would have expected, the experience of the leading powers in stable regions since 1990 has been more consistent with many of the globalization school's hypotheses on security than that of the major powers. In particular, as Table 4.1 indicates, our analysis has confirmed a greater integration of regional security institutions into national security plans, greater priority given to nontraditional threats, and the complete abandonment of offensive doctrines. These states also share the major powers' newfound focus on combating terrorism and developing an internal policing dimension to their national security establishments.

Nonetheless, even among these stable regions, a number of the globalization propositions are flatly contradicted. Of note, although the western European states initially reduced both defense spending and military manpower, that trend has been largely reversed in recent years, whereas South America and Southeast Asia have actually increased regional expenditures during the period under investigation. In addition, we have found no evidence that the leading states in these regions have begun to offload important national security tasks to NGOs or private security corporations. Finally, despite the development of important multilateral security institutions in these regions, it is clear that states in these regions still value sovereignty and

TABLE 4.1 Stable Regions and Propositions Regarding Globalization

Propositions	Western Europe	South America	Southeast Asia	Overall
PS1: shift to low-intensity conflicts	Inconsistent with proposition	Inconsistent with proposition	Consistent with proposition	No trend
PS2: shift to postindustrial warfare	Consistent with proposition	Partially consistent with proposition	Consistent with proposition	Largely consistent with proposition
P3: face new threats	Consistent with proposition	Consistent with proposition	Consistent with proposition	Consistent with proposition
P4: defensive doctrines	Consistent with proposition	Consistent with proposition	Consistent with proposition	Consistent with proposition
P5: soft balancing	Partially consistent with proposition	Partially consistent with proposition	Partially consistent with proposition	Partially consistent with proposition
P6: less manpower	Consistent with proposition	Consistent with proposition	Inconsistent with proposition	Partially consistent with proposition
P7: lower defense budgets	Partially consistent with proposition	Inconsistent with proposition	Inconsistent with proposition	Inconsistent with proposition
P8: shift to policing actions	Consistent with proposition	Consistent with proposition	Partially consistent with proposition	Largely consistent with proposition
P9: privatize to nonstate actors	Inconsistent with proposition	Inconsistent with proposition	Inconsistent with proposition	Inconsistent with proposition
P10: pursue security through regional institutions	Partially consistent with proposition	Partially consistent with proposition	Partially consistent with proposition	Partially consistent with proposition

Dark shading indicates propositions that are largely consistent with evidence. Light shading indicates propositions that are somewhat consistent with evidence. Propositions that are largely inconsistent with evidence are unshaded.

independence of action, and are prepared to depart from institutional policies when it suits them. Thus, these states continue to pursue rather traditional security strategies and retain strong national roles in the pursuit of security, despite shifting their focus to new types of threats that have been "securitized."

Overall, then, the experience of the stable regions provides less support for the globalization and security argument than we would have expected. The role of the state as a security provider in these regions may recede further in the future, as regional security institutions entrench themselves and continue to reduce traditional security concerns. To this point, however, if even these states, which face the least intense security dilemmas, have not altered their national security apparatuses drastically in response to the challenge of globalization, we must conclude that a state-centric, interstate war-oriented security architecture remains strong. In the next chapter we shift our focus to security behavior in regions of enduring rivalry, where we would expect to find even less evidence of a transformation in the way states pursue security.

| States in Regions of Enduring Rivalry

I N CHAPTER 4, we considered the security behavior of second-tier powers in regions characterized by broad-based stability. Other second-rank powers, however, inhabit regions mired in perpetual conflict or are themselves embroiled in enduring rivalries. Such rivalries typically involve entrenched territorial conflicts that take new significance because of religious, ideological, or nationalistic differences, which create perpetual "militarized competition" between the rivals.[1] Of all the states of the international system, these states face the most acute security dilemmas, because war is always possible for them. Consequently, we should expect that these states would be the most reluctant to abandon traditional, state-centric approaches to national security, because the costs of relinquishing national control over security and neglecting to prepare for interstate war could include defeat in war. If even these states have adapted their national security strategies in accordance with the globalization school's propositions, that would constitute powerful evidence that globalization has fundamentally altered the national security state. Alternatively, if these states continue to privilege traditional forms of defense and security, this may indicate that changes we have witnessed in more stable regions may be epiphenomenal of the stability of those regions in the post-Cold War era, rather than the impact of globalization.

In this chapter we examine two regions of enduring rivalry: the Middle East and South Asia. The Middle East, which has experienced numerous interstate wars since World War II and is constantly in a state of at least low-level tensions on account of the enduring rivalry between the State of Israel and its Arab neighbors, is the prototypical unstable region in which persistent crises may ignite to war at any time. South Asian regional tensions revolve around the Indo-Pakistani enduring rivalry, which has also erupted in war four times since 1947. We will evaluate the security policies of leading second-rank states in these two troubled regions, as well as the defense postures of these broader regions, to determine what effect globalization has had on their national security states.

The Middle East

Long the forum for great power competition during the colonial era, the Middle East did not find stability as a by-product of decolonization. Central to this instability is the 1947 UN decision to partition the former British mandate of Palestine into two states: one Jewish and one Arab. Arab states rejected the UN partition plan, declaring war on the new State of Israel immediately to eliminate it from what they viewed as Arab land. Failing to resolve the issue in the 1948–1949 war, the Arab states maintained a war of attrition against Israel, punctuated by two wars: the 1956 Sinai War, in which Israel attempted to capitalize on British and French anger over Nasser's nationalization of the Suez Canal to weaken its primary adversary with a preventive war, and the 1967 war, in which multiple Arab states again prepared a concerted effort to eliminate the Jewish state, but were preempted by a successful Israeli attack.[2] After Israel captured territory from Syria, Jordan, and Egypt in the 1967 war, the Arab goal changed from eliminating the Jewish state to recapturing these territories. The conflict remained no less intense, however, with a war in 1973 in an attempt by Egypt and Syria to regain the territories, and an Israeli invasion of Lebanon in 1982 in an attempt to silence PLO artillery attacks. Although Israel has signed peace treaties with Egypt (1979) and Jordan (1994), and has begun a peace process with the PLO under the framework of the Oslo Agreement (1993), the conflict has remained intractable, because it involves not only a territorial dispute, but a clash over core territory (Jerusalem and the Temple Mount) that is significant on both religious and national grounds.[3]

Not all Middle Eastern wars, however, have been Arab–Israeli contests. A variety of internecine wars and lower level conflicts in the Arab/Islamic world have taken place throughout the years between Iran and Iraq, Egypt and Libya, and Syria and Lebanon.[4] In 1991, both Arab states and external powers participated in the Gulf War coalition against Iraq. In addition, not only is the Middle East the primary exporter of terrorism worldwide, it is daily the scene of low-level violence, such as rocket firings, suicide bombings, and air strikes, which all have the potential to escalate to interstate wars.[5]

To evaluate the impact of globalization on security in the Middle East, we will examine the national security doctrines and defense behavior from 1991–2008 of two leading states in the region who have been key players in the enduring rivalry—Israel and Egypt—as well as one key state on the fringes of the region, which nonetheless plays an important, often indirect, role in regional dynamics: Iran. In addition to comparing the experiences of these states with the globalization school's propositions, we also consider data on defense expenditures and military manpower for the entire region.

THE NATURE OF THREATS

In the Middle East, there is only limited evidence of states spurning traditional security threats in favor of a new security agenda. To begin with, proposition PS1 (*changing nature of wars*) is overstated for the region. Although low-intensity conflicts (LICs) abound in the region, most Middle Eastern states have attempted to retain the capacity to wage both traditional interstate wars and also smaller scale wars and counterinsurgencies. Israel, faced with two major Palestinian *intifadas* (uprisings) in the West Bank and Gaza since the mid-1980s, must not only prepare its armed forces for a major interstate war (potentially against Syria or Iran), but also for a day-to-day counterinsurgency.[6] Despite signing the Camp David Accords and formally ending its enduring rivalry with Israel, Egypt, too, has structured its defense forces to wage interstate wars. As Hillel Frisch observes: "Almost all of Egypt's capabilities, equipment, and deployment of forces are concentrated on one front, to engage one opponent only: the Israel Defense Force. The Egyptians have made this explicit since the Badr-96 exercises in 1996, in which they specifically named Israel as the training target."[7] As a moderate Arab regime, however, it must also be wary of a potential Islamist uprising, which has always seethed just below the surface in Egypt.[8]

Even Iran, whose defense minister makes no mention of counterinsurgencies or LICs in his comments on Iranian military doctrine,[9] focuses considerable attention on the destructive potential of LICs in its very unstable neighborhood. Iraq, Turkey, Tajikistan, Afghanistan, and Pakistan are all facing insurgencies of different degrees that could destabilize Iran. If the Kurds, in particular, were to achieve their independence from Iraq and Turkey, that would place considerable pressure and territorial demands on Teheran.[10] Thus, Iran has much to fear from insurgent groups in its region. Yet Iran's focus on erasing the State of Israel from the map indicates that it still contemplates interstate warfare as an important goal of its armed forces.[11] Moreover, now that the United States has dispensed with Teheran's traditional enemy, Iraq, the bulk of their strategic planning is preoccupied with the possibility of a conventional war with the United States.[12] Thus, the leading states in the region continue to prepare for interstate warfare, even though lower intensity challenges occupy a good deal of their attention.

All states in the region have had to adapt to postindustrial warfare (proposition PS2) because of the ubiquity of terrorist groups. No state has suffered more from terrorism than Israel. Since the mid 1960s, groups such as the PLO, Hamas, and Islamic Jihad have conducted frequent bombing campaigns against Israeli civilians both in territories across the Green Line and within the pre-1967 borders. Since September 2000 alone, according to Magen David Adom, the Israeli equivalent of the Red Cross, more than 1,100 people in Israel were killed by terrorism and Palestinian violence.[13] In addition, Iranian-supported Hezbollah forces in southern Lebanon have maintained guerrilla operations against Israeli soldiers and civilians in neighboring Israeli villages, which in fact sparked an interstate war in 2006.[14] Egypt, too, has had to deal with its share of domestic terrorism, much of which has targeted foreign tourists in Cairo and in resort towns on the Red Sea.[15] In fact, of all the regimes in the region that we investigated, Iran is the only one not to suffer from terrorism to any significant degree, nor to prepare to combat it, despite the defense minister's claim that Iran is preparing its forces to combat "state terrorism."[16] Instead, Iran appears to use postindustrial warfare as an integral component of its regional strategy, by promoting and supporting groups such as Hezbollah and Hamas.

There is very little evidence, however, of leading Middle Eastern states adopting the new security agenda and its changing threats (proposition PS3). Israeli military doctrine, for example, identifies the following missions: "To defend the existence, territorial integrity and sovereignty of the state of Israel; [t]o protect the inhabitants of Israel and to combat all forms of terrorism which threaten the daily life."[17] It makes no reference to organized crime, threats from diseases, drug trafficking, or economic threats, except insofar as it acknowledges that mobilization should be conducted in a manner that does not overtax the fragile Israeli economy.[18] Of course, the Israeli government is concerned about two demographic trends that could have profound security implications. First, the declining rate of Jewish immigration to Israel could hamper the state's long-term ability to secure itself in a hostile region.[19] Second, economic, social, demographic, and religious changes in the Arab Middle East also could exacerbate the Israeli security situation by radicalizing moderate neighbors.[20] These newer threats, though, concern the Israeli security establishment precisely because they could affect the likelihood and severity of interstate wars in the region. We, therefore, treat them as rather traditional concerns.

Egyptian security policy is similarly cast in terms of preventing war, protecting sovereignty, and defending against aggression, without mention of new threats.[21] The only real concession the Egyptian military establishment has made to the new security agenda is its treatment of economic prosperity as an important component of national security.[22] In contrast, according to the Iranian defense minister, Iran addresses "a broad spectrum of threats," including "foreign aggression, war, border incidents, espionage, sabotage, regional crises derived from the proliferation of weapons of mass destruction, organized crime, and state terrorism." In essence, however, only organized crime fits in the category of "new security" threats, and the defense capabilities that Iran is pursuing (especially the potential for nuclear weapons) are geared primarily toward military-style, interstate threats.[23] As Iran gears for a possible confrontation with the United States, Israel, and, potentially, the international community, over its nuclear enrichment program, it is clear that traditional threats continue to dominate its security agenda.

Thus, Middle Eastern states remain preoccupied with traditional security threats and the potential for interstate warfare, as one would expect from a region that has witnessed many recent wars. At the same time, the key players in the region have increasingly had to deal with lower intensity conflicts and postindustrial warfare, particularly the challenge of transnational terrorism. Nonetheless, because both terrorism and LICs have been indigenous to the region for decades, it would be difficult to attribute them to the advent of globalization, which manifested itself only during the 1990s.

THE STRATEGIES STATES PURSUE

If national security threats in the Middle East have not changed much in the era of globalization, the strategies that that states pursue show even less evidence of being "globalized." Regarding proposition PS4 (*defensive and deterrent doctrines*), therefore, although the declaratory doctrine of some key regional powers is purely defensive and/or deterrent in nature, their behavior and planning indicate that potential for offense, preemption, or prevention clearly exists. The Israeli government, for example, states that its military doctrine is "defensive on the strategic level" with "no territorial ambitions," resting on the conventional superiority of the Israeli defense forces and whatever unconventional weapons it may possess.[24] Nonetheless, because the first principle of Israeli security policy is that it cannot afford to lose a war, it is possible that regional changes could lead to preventive strikes, such as the

1981 bombing of Iraq's nuclear reactor, the bombing of a suspected nuclear site in Syria in 2007, or limited strikes on state sponsors of terrorism, such as its strike against Syria in 2003. Indeed, the protracted crisis over the Iranian nuclear program has raised speculation that Jerusalem might be compelled to launch a limited attack on Iranian facilities.[25] In addition, the government of Ariel Sharon was willing to reoccupy areas under Palestinian Authority control temporarily in response to terrorist attacks and his successor, Ehud Olmert, was willing to wage war against Lebanon and Gaza to stop Hezbollah and Hamas incursions and rocket attacks. One would expect that current Israeli Prime Minister Binyamin Netanyahu, a sharp critic of his predecessors' dovishness, would also be willing to consider such offensive policy instruments if Hamas and Hezbollah rocket attacks were to escalate.

Other leading Middle Eastern states also report defensive postures. Most credible, Egypt—which is attempting to solidify its relationship with Washington and rebuild its economy—lists as its strategic priorities to "[p]revent war and contribute to the stability and peaceful development in the region; [p]rotect the sovereignty of all territories and territorial boundaries within its international borders; [m]aintain the integrity, security, and stability of the country; and [d]efend itself against any act of aggression."[26] However, it has also beefed up its offensive capabilities during the past two decades. According to Frisch, "much as [the statements of the Egyptian military elite] stress deterrence, they equally emphasize that this can only be achieved through efforts to enhance offensive capabilities, commensurate with the potential foe's strength. Nor can war with Israel be entirely ruled out."[27] Thus, Egypt is either pursuing defensive capabilities to enhance deterrence, or its doctrine may gradually be shifting to a more offensive one. For its part, Iran also claims to pursue a policy of "strategic deterrent defense" against unspecified threats.[28] By threatening to absorb a first strike and then retaliate with all means available, its goal is to discourage adversaries who favor preemption (i.e., the United States) by making such a move too costly.[29] Its open support of Hezbollah strikes against Israel from Lebanon, President Ahmedinejad's threats to wipe Israel off the map, and its growing military arsenal, including submarines, warships, Shihab ballistic missiles, and, potentially, nuclear capabilities, suggest an offensive dimension to Iranian policy.[30] Thus, all three of these key regional players appear to include offensive forces and options in their game plan, even if they stress defense and deterrence in their official statements.

The Middle East does not appear to be a region of soft balancing against American hegemonic power in contradiction to proposition PS5. Certainly, Israel—a state that is considerably dependent on its American ally for military hardware and critical diplomatic support—has had no interest in balancing American power.[31] Egypt, too, which has benefited from American economic and military aid since the 1980s and has profited from Washington's view of it as a moderate Arab regime, does not want to be seen as a participant in balancing coalitions against the United States.[32] Thus, Cairo has attempted to cast itself as a moderate on the Israeli–Palestinian conflict and participated in the 1991 American-led Gulf War coalition alongside other Arab states. Nonetheless, President Hosni Mubarak's opposition to the 2003 Gulf War, which was quite vocal and sought to restrain the United States together with other dissenters, does constitute a degree of soft balancing.

It is Iran, however, that has embraced hard balancing and asymmetric balancing against the global hegemon. Iran has opposed the entire thrust of American foreign policy in the Middle East and Persian Gulf. Not only has its rhetoric been consistently anti-American, it has also defied Washington by assisting Shi'ite insurgents in Iraq, fostering instability in Lebanon through its Hezbollah proxies, and supporting terrorist organizations such as Hamas and Hezbollah.[33] Most significant, the Iranian nuclear program, which Teheran is unwilling to open up for international inspectors, suggests a willingness to balance against U.S. hegemony in the region by developing the means to deter American actions against Iranian interests and, at a minimum, an American preventive attack against Iran.[34] By provoking and escalating a crisis over its nuclear program, the Iranian government is clearly engaged in traditional hard balancing *par excellence*, relying on national military capabilities and the potential for nuclear deterrence.[35]

Military manpower in the region increased somewhat and then reached a plateau during the past two decades, providing little support for proposition PS6 (*reduced manpower*). In 1985, the total number of active military personnel in the region was more than 2.5 million.[36] That number rose rapidly during the late 1980s to almost 3.5 million by 1990, before stabilizing at around 2.9 million people in active service between 1992 and 2003. By 2007, the total declined to slightly less than 2.8 million, but it is too early to conclude that this represents a trend in accordance with the globalization school's propositions. The three regional states on which we are focusing reflect the region's divergence from the globalization hypothesis. During the past two decades, Israel increased its active service complement from 141,000 in 1990 to around 175,000 during the 1990s, before reducing that figure slightly to around 168,000 in 2003—a figure it has held constant since. Iran increased its armed forces from just more than 500,000 in 1989 to 545,000 in 2007. Egypt remained rather steady with 450,000 active forces in 1989 and 1990, and a similar number from 1997 through 2003, with small dips in between. After increasing its armed forces by almost 10% to 486,500 in 2004, by 2007 Egypt pared some of that increase to settle at 469,000. Thus, neither the region as a whole nor its key players provide clear evidence of a reduction in military manpower in response to globalization.

During the early 1990s, it looked like the Middle East was achieving the expectations of proposition PS7 (*reduced defense spending*), as regional spending plummeted from $50.7 billion in 1991 to $40.7 billion in 1996 (all figures in 2005 constant U.S. dollars).[37] This decrease, however, may have been merely epiphenomenal of the end of the Cold War, which eliminated the Soviet Union as a weapons supplier to Arab states, such as Syria and Iraq, as well as the stability and goodwill created by the initial Gulf War coalition. By mid-decade, however, regional defense spending began to climb again, ballooning to more than $57.1 billion in 2001. Moreover, between 2003 and 2005, regional defense spending jumped a full 24% to $70.5 billion, before settling back to $69.1 billion in 2006. Leading regional antagonists, such as Israel ($8 billion in 1992 to $12.5 billion in 2005), Egypt ($2.2 billion in 1992 to $2.8 billion in 2003), and, most notably, Iran (an almost fivefold increase from less than $1.9 billion in 1992 to more than $9.8 billion in 2006) increased their defense budgets considerably during the decade. Thus, regional practice is at odds with the globalization school's expectations.

The Middle East provides ample evidence in support of PS8 (*shift from war fighting to policing*). Faced with successive Palestinian *intifadas*, the Israeli national security establishment has devoted considerable resources during the past two decades to policing activities in the Gaza Strip and the West Bank. In addition, a good deal of its mission is to interdict terrorist infiltration from the Palestinian Authority to conduct attacks within Israel. Therefore, policing has become a central feature of its national security activities.[38]

The Egyptian government, which is under steady pressure from Islamist forces in the country, also relies heavily on its armed forces to act as police-type forces domestically. Although the mainstream Islamist opposition from the Muslim Brotherhood is primarily a populist electoral challenge that the ruling party deals with mainly by resisting electoral reforms that would allow multiparty elections, more radical Islamist groups, such as the Jamaa'at al-Jihad and the Jama'a al-Islamiyya, have used terrorist tactics aimed both at the regime and at foreigners. During the 1990s, in particular, their low-level insurgency claimed more than 1,300 lives. This challenge has forced Mubarak's national security establishment to pay more attention to policing and interdiction operations.[39] And, since 1994, the cleric-dominated Iranian government, challenged at various times by more progressive opposition forces, has had to use its *Basij* paramilitary force to help quell domestic protests, such as the widespread student protests of 2003.[40] Consequently, although Middle Eastern states do not dwell upon policing missions in their official statements on defense policy, there is every reason to believe that they are part of the military establishment's purpose. This pattern, though, existed well before the onset of globalization.

On balance, then, Middle Eastern states continue to pursue very traditional security strategies in the contemporary era. They continue to spend heavily on national defense, maintain military manpower, and retain the capacity for offensive military operations. Moreover, this region provides one of the few contemporary instances of a state (Iran) that is attempting hard balancing against American power. Thus, despite the increasing use of policing-type operations by the leading states in the region, we must conclude that the strategies they are pursuing are at odds with the globalization school's propositions.

THE MONOPOLY OF THE STATE AS A SECURITY PROVIDER

Nor is there strong evidence that Middle Eastern states are relinquishing their central roles as security providers. Regarding proposition PS9 (*nonstate actors*) we found no evidence, either in doctrine or actual behavior, that Israel or Egypt have started to outsource their security policies or rely significantly on NGOs. In contrast, Iran has, for years, attempted to advance its security agenda by training and funding terrorist organizations, such as Hezbollah and Hamas, to wreak havoc on regional rivals.[41] Nonetheless, the core Iranian security functions are performed by the Iranian national security state.

The states of the region have also not utilized multilateral regional institutions as a means of providing security (proposition PS10). Indeed, the Middle East has no overarching security institutions. Because few Arab states recognize Israel's existence, it is excluded from those institutions that do exist. Therefore, Israel relies on itself and extraregional allies—notably the United States—to secure itself in a hostile environment. The main Arab security institution is the Arab League, an organization designed to foster cooperation among Arab states, defend their sovereignty, and advance common Arab goals.[42] This institution has largely been stymied by geopolitical competition between its members and, therefore, has been largely ineffective as a regional security organization.[43] Instead, the Arab states largely rely on themselves and on ad hoc coalitions to pursue their security interests.

The pursuit of security in the contemporary Middle East remains remarkably traditional despite the pressures identified by the globalization school. Except for the increasing sensitivity of these states to terrorism and their consequent resort to policing-type national security actions to counter the terrorist threat, none of the globalization propositions finds much support in this region. Most notable, leading Middle Eastern states still spend heavily on defense, continue to contemplate offensive military operations, and, above all, jealously guard the central role of the state in both directing and administering their national security policies. In the next section we will examine a second region of perpetual rivalry, South Asia, to consider whether the Middle Eastern resistance to security globalization is a unique phenomenon or is more broadly generalizable across unstable regions.

South Asia

South Asia offers another fertile theater for exploring the globalization–security nexus in a region of perpetual discord. The defining feature of politics in this region of eight states (India, Pakistan, Bangladesh, Nepal, Bhutan, Maldives, Sri Lanka, and Afghanistan) has been the enduring rivalry between India, which occupies more than 70% of the region's geographical area and population, and its smaller neighbor, Pakistan. The core area of dispute remains Kashmir, which Pakistan claims on the grounds of the religious nature of the 1947 partition plan. Since 1947, India and Pakistan have fought three major wars (1947–1948, 1965, 1971) and one minor war (1999), three of which were over Kashmir.[44] The introduction of nuclear weapons to the arsenals of both antagonists has since increased the stakes, and potential costs, of conflict. The China–India dyad constitutes another critical nuclear rivalry in the region. This antipathy began as a territorial rivalry during the early 1960s, although it has now emerged as a rivalry for power and status. In recent years, both pairs of rivals have engaged in peace talks aimed at settling their border disputes, with economic calculation being one of the motivations for finding a solution to their decade-long conflicts.[45]

To evaluate whether globalization has affected the security postures of states in South Asia, we will examine the security policies and practices of the two leading states in the region, India and Pakistan, as well as broader regional defense spending and military manpower patterns.

THE NATURE OF THREATS

With respect to proposition PS1 (*changing nature of wars*), the two leading South Asian states have waged both traditional interstate wars and LICs since they emerged as independent states in 1947. They fought three major interstate wars—in 1947–1948, 1965 and 1971—and engaged in several crises during the Cold War era. During the post-Cold War era (more relevant to the advent of intensified globalization), there has been one interstate confrontation, the Kargil war of 1999, which meets the 1,000 battle deaths threshold that entitles it to the designation "war."[46] At the same time, the globalization era has coincided with an increase in limited and asymmetric wars in Kashmir and various parts of Pakistan. Pakistan had already been facing violence between its disparate ethnic and religious groups—for example, Sunni versus Shia—as well as rebellion from extremist groups sympathetic to the Taliban and Wahhabi forms of Islam. These conflicts are especially prevalent in the Northwest Frontier Province, along its border with Afghanistan, especially in Pashtun-dominated areas of Baluchistan and Waziristan.

Much of this, however, was not caused by globalization, per se, but resulted from an alliance of convenience between Islamic fundamentalist groups and the Pakistani Army and intelligence services in the wake of the Afghan war and its aftermath under the leadership of General Zia ul-Haq.[47] The availability of Mujahedin fighters after the Soviet withdrawal from Afghanistan in 1989, which had nothing to do with globalization, allowed Pakistan to wage its asymmetric war in Kashmir.[48] In addition, Pakistan increased its support for insurgency in Kashmir as it acquired nuclear weapons capability during the late 1980s. Thus, the link between globalization and increased insurgency in Pakistan is only tenuous. Globalization may have assisted the spread of rebellion and facilitated the communication between rebel groups, but the source of the substate challenges lay elsewhere.

It seemed possible for a period, however, that major interstate wars in the region might decline in the future, as a result of Indo-Pakistani peace talks since 2004, which resulted in a reduction in tensions between the two rivals. These talks led to the implementation of several confidence-building measures and have partially opened up the borders in Kashmir. It was not clear to what extent these peace talks are attributable to globalization. Certainly, as we discuss later, economic globalization and the desire to spread economic prosperity to the region were secondary considerations for the peace process. Strategic concerns, however, were the driving factors. Pressure from Washington has contributed to the dynamism of this process.[49] Furthermore, sections of the Pakistani elite also consider the necessity for "peace now," when Pakistan has some leverage, rather than allowing India's high economic growth rate to widen the power disparity between the two states.[50] The fragility of such peace processes between these adversaries, which always find ways of unraveling during an enduring rivalry, have come to the fore with the November 2008 terrorist attacks on Mumbai carried out by individuals apparently trained and equipped by rogue state security elements in Pakistan.

As far as military doctrines are concerned, the two leading states of South Asia, ever on the verge of interstate war, have primarily geared their military strategies to wage traditional-style interstate wars with both conventional and nuclear arsenals. Nonetheless, there is some variation in the degree to which their military apparatuses have engaged in preparation for LICs. The Pakistani military policy focuses almost exclusively on waging a war against India, on the premise that "if we lower our defences below a certain threshold we could be facing the spectre of extinction."[51]

Indian policy is more complex, because it is complicated by a less intense rivalry with China and the fear of insurgency in Kashmir fueled by outside powers. Therefore, it supplements its focus on interstate wars with an emphasis on containing local insurgencies and small-scale border wars.[52] In December 2006, for example, the Indian army for the first time produced a "Doctrine for Subconventional Warfare" in which it recognized that "total war" was becoming less relevant and the prospects for interstate conventional wars were receding. This has resulted in an impetus for subconventional warfare and internal challenges such as "militancy, insurgency, proxy war and terrorism." It advocated the use of overwhelming force against external aggression; but, toward internal groups, a chance to shun violence, and surrender and join the national mainstream by focusing on a strategy of "winning the hearts and minds" of the insurgents' support base.[53] This doctrine suggests some level of adaptation by the Indian army to the new security environment. Nonetheless, the Indian army doctrine concludes that asymmetric wars could become "adjunct of and influence conventional wars themselves," but are unlikely to "replace conventional war."[54] The national security objectives contained in the Indian Defense Ministry web page focus largely on threats from Pakistan and nonstate actors supported by the neighboring country.[55] Although there has been an upsurge in LICs in South Asia in recent years, neither recent experience nor doctrine provides strong evidence of a shift away from interstate warfare.

These two conflict-ridden states also face the threat of terrorism and extremism, and therefore must combat postindustrial warfare (proposition PS2). Traditionally, India has encountered Kashmiri separatists who use terrorist tactics both within Kashmir and elsewhere in India. During the post-September 11 era, India has faced heightened terrorist challenges, including the December 2001 attack on the Indian parliament and the coordinated attacks in different parts of the country, especially in Mumbai in July 2006 and November 2008. Terrorism thus receives the highest level of attention in India, although it is largely the purview of the Home Ministry, which has created internal security mechanisms to face the challenge.[56]

What is interesting is that, in the wake of the September 11 attacks against the United States, Pakistani participation in the U.S.-led war against terrorism has led it, too, to fear a backlash by Muslim extremists and to battle terrorism domestically, although terrorism still remains an active part of Pakistan's strategy in its conflict with India in Kashmir. Since 2002, many Muslim fundamentalist groups turned against President Pervez Musharraf, who turned extended support to the U.S.-led war on terrorism in neighboring Afghanistan. His banning of militant groups such as Laskar-e-Taiba and Jaish-e-Mohammed alienated them, although these groups shortly afterward reappeared in different manifestations. Groups such as Harkat ul-Mujahideen and Harkat al-Jihad-al-Islami have had strong links with the Taliban and turned against Musharraf as a result of these actions. The Pakistani leader himself became the target of several failed assassination attempts, and his peace overtures to India further alienated many of the radical groups. The violent activities in the Red Mosque in Islamabad and the bloody ouster of the ultraradicals by the Pakistani military in July 2007 were further evidence of a rift between the government and terrorist groups.[57] Thus, although the patronage of Jihadist organizations by the Pakistani state, especially elements of the army and intelligence services, seems to continue, Pakistan has begun to make combating terrorism part of its security mission.[58]

Certainly, on a regional level, South Asian states are confronting a plethora of new challenges that are often securitized by states (proposition PS3). The subcontinent contains one of the largest numbers of HIV/AIDS cases and other communicable diseases such as malaria and tuberculosis. India alone is reported to contain between 3 and 5 million HIV/AIDS cases.[59] The region is also plagued by environmental challenges, as well as the scourge of organized crime and drug trafficking.[60] Furthermore, economic considerations appeared to have been facilitating recently stalled peace talks between India and Pakistan. India wanted to solve its border disputes to focus on economic growth and attract foreign investment, whereas Pakistani military leaders seemed to have come to the realization that they cannot win a war outright with India and that they will lag behind economically if some form of settlement is not achieved with India.[61]

The two regional antagonists have taken somewhat different approaches to the emerging threats of the new security agenda. Pakistani security goals remain focused on military threats from India and threats to domestic order by Islamic extremist groups. Little attention in official policy pronouncements is devoted to "new security" threats.[62] To the extent that the Pakistani government does address "new" security threats, it is with other state institutions, rather than with the national security establishment. Thus, for example, it treats contagious diseases, such as AIDS, as under the jurisdiction of the health ministry and not as part of the defense jurisdiction.[63] Consequently, there is little evidence that Pakistan has drastically restructured its national security establishment to focus on new threats.

In contrast, Indian policy pronouncements are increasingly paying attention to nontraditional threats. The 2004 defense doctrine, for example, observes that "this region is witnessing an unprecedented proliferation in small arms and narcotics trafficking which, in turn, threaten the stability of states and societies. Trans-border migration on economic grounds also raises serious security concerns."[64] The defense ministry's official website also mentions, in its enumeration of the threats that India faces, that "India is also affected by the trafficking in drugs and proliferation of small arms."[65]

Nonetheless, although India clearly faces a variety of nontraditional threats (environmental security, food security, organized crime, attacks by ultraradical groups or Naxalites, and drug trade), Indian security officials have continued to focus primarily on the traditional military challenges to the state. Indeed, according to a former foreign secretary of India, although decision makers increasingly talk about nontraditional security threats, India has yet to develop an integrated approach to deal with these problems.[66] Thus, the increasing references to these threats in Indian policy pronouncements may amount to little more than lip service. Alternatively, they may reflect a growing awareness of the emerging threats that may engender significant policy changes in the years to come.

Thus, the globalization era has increased the security challenges that South Asian states are facing. There has been an upsurge in terrorism in the region, and LICs, particularly in Kashmir, have occurred on an ongoing basis. In addition, the region faces a plethora of new challenges, including AIDS and other contagious diseases, organized crime, and the narcotics trade. Nonetheless, the doctrinal focus of the Indian and Pakistani military establishments remains on interstate warfare, with a secondary emphasis on counterterrorism. Thus, the security establishment has retained a largely traditional focus during the contemporary era, even if there are signs that its security agenda may broaden in the future.

THE STRATEGIES STATES PURSUE

If there is relatively weak support from South Asian states for the claim that globalization has altered the threats that national security establishments are countering, the region offers even less support for the claim that it has transformed the security strategies that they use. For example, the leading regional competitors both have defensive and deterrent declaratory policies on national defense (proposition PS4), but do not completely exclude offensive options. According to the nuclear doctrine approved by the Indian government in January 2003, India aims to create a credible minimum deterrent and the "posture of no-first use, i.e., nuclear weapons will only be used in retaliation against a nuclear attack on Indian territory or on Indian forces anywhere." Nevertheless, it states "in the event of a major attack against India, or Indian forces anywhere, by biological or chemical weapons, India will retain the option of retaliating with nuclear weapons," suggesting a dilution in the no-first use pledge.[67]

India's official conventional forces doctrine had been similarly defensive, retaining as objectives: national defense, confidence-building measures, arms control, and dialogue with other major powers.[68] In April 2004, however, India unveiled a new military doctrine titled "Cold Start," which would be better characterized as a deterrent/offensive posture. This doctrine envisages a "blitzkrieg" strategy vis-à-vis Pakistan in a future conflict, which would harness the full-strike potential of India's defensive and offensive forces, and mandate the permanent forward deployment of Indian divisions from their current interior locations, thereby shortening the time required for offensive operations. The Indian objectives are to reduce the length of time for mobilization and attack so as not to allow external intervention, to encourage the political leadership to take decisive action, and to achieve tactical and strategic surprise.[69] The forward deployment nearer to the border of Indian land, air, and naval forces certainly suggests the possibility of more offensive-minded military options.

Moreover, with ongoing insurgencies in Jammu and Kashmir encouraged by forces in Pakistan, and counterterrorist operations against Pakistani-based militant groups, it is possible that the professed Indian commitment to deterrence and defense could lead to a wider confrontation with its regional rival. Of course, Pakistan's possession of nuclear weapons still acts as a constraint on the offensive use of force by India.[70]

Pakistani strategy, recognizing that its conventional forces are too weak for a direct challenge to India, relies on its small nuclear arsenal to deter an Indian conventional offensive.[71] Thus, official Pakistani policy is defensive and designed to "restore the strategic balance in the interest of peace and security in South Asia."[72] In practice, though, Pakistan's commitment "to extend full political, diplomatic and moral support to the legitimate Kashmiri struggle for their right to self-determination" could amount to an attempt to change the status quo by lower level military challenges and, therefore, is potentially offensive, as well.[73] Pakistan's nuclear doctrine relies on "first use" and deterrence by punishment against a possible conventional attack by India. This is consistent with a deterrent mission. Because Pakistan views its nuclear weapons as more than just weapons of last resort and tools of deterrence, but also as "instruments that permit and facilitate low-intensity conflict against India," there is clearly an element of offensive quality to the doctrine.[74]

There is limited support from the region for proposition PS5 (*soft balancing*). The two regional states have pursued active balance-of-power politics, especially hard balancing through arms buildups and alignments since the 1950s. Pakistan has maintained an all-weather relationship with China, and occasional friendship with the United States, primarily to balance against India. In the wake of the Cold War, India has replaced its quasi-alliance relationship with the USSR with increasingly closer ties to the United States. This relationship has been driven in part by balance-of-power considerations, particularly the need to balance against the Chinese power to threaten the region. To some extent, these relationships can be understood as soft balancing, because they center around limited diplomatic and military cooperation, rather than formal alliances. It is possible, though, that the India–United States relationship could be transformed into a traditional hard balancing coalition in the event that China develops an aggressive posture toward both the United States and India. Thus, it would be incorrect to say that either state has abandoned hard balancing in the contemporary era. At the same time, India is pursuing a policy of engagement with all great powers, especially China, suggesting that the region, at best, is witnessing partial balancing efforts or prebalancing.

In South Asia, despite the predictions of proposition PS6 (*manpower*), regional manpower in the armed forces shot up from more than 2.2 million in 1988 to a high of more than 2.8 million in 1996, before stabilizing at around 2.5 million active service people, where it remained in 2007. Both leading participants increased their armed forces during this period. Although India initially reduced its manpower from 1.26 million in 1989 to less than 1.15 million in 1995, as the decade drew to a close, manpower began to increase once more. By 2003, Indian manpower had climbed to more than 1.3 million, where it has remained, with minor fluctuations, since. During the same time period, the Pakistani armed forces have grown from 580,000 active servicemen in 1989 to 619,000 in 2007.[75] Thus, there is no evidence that globalization is leading to smaller armies in the region.

Defense spending in the region (proposition PS7) also defied the globalization school's expectations, as military expenditures increased steadily during the past fifteen years. In 1992, the region spent $15.1 billion on defense; by 2006, that figure had almost doubled to less than $30 billion.[76] The principal regional rivals both increased their defense budgets, although to different degrees. During this period, India more than doubled its military spending (from $10.7 billion to more than $23.9 billion). In contrast, Pakistani military spending initially declined from less than $3.5 billion in 1992 to less than $3.3 billion in 1997 and 1998, before climbing to more than $4.6 billion in 2006. The regional trend, therefore, has been upward, rather than downward.

In terms of proposition PS8 (*shift from war fighting to policing*), the militaries in this region have engaged in both interstate and internal security functions since they came into existence in the 1940s, and continue to do so in the contemporary era. States have resorted to the military to quell the myriad of internal insurgencies they have faced. India, especially, has used its army to engage the insurgent movements in Kashmir, Punjab, and northeastern states, as well as in the occasional communal clashes that engulf other parts of the vast nation. In 1990, the Indian army set up a special force of six battalions, known as the Rashtriya Rifles, to engage in counterinsurgency warfare, along with specialized police and paramilitary units, especially in Kashmir and the northeastern states. By 2002, this force had grown to 48 battalions and was actively involved in policing operations throughout the country's trouble spots. The army's main focus, however, remains interstate conflict, and the growth of the counterinsurgency forces has only helped to increase the army's budget, without undermining the financial allocations for the regular forces.[77]

The Pakistani army had also been engaging in police functions before the onset of the globalization era. As the main custodian of the country's foreign and defense policies and the real power behind any government, the Pakistani army has engaged in both the suppression of domestic opponents and the propping up of certain Islamic groups to increase its legitimacy and control. As a result of U.S. pressure in the aftermath of the September 11 terrorist attacks, Pakistan changed its policy of support for the Taliban, who controlled Afghanistan from 1996 to 2001, and deployed its forces on the Afghan border. In this capacity, the Pakistani army has battled occasionally with remnants of Taliban and al Qaeda forces, and has selectively engaged other Islamic groups and ethnic groups waging insurgencies, such as the Baluchistan Peoples Liberation Front, which has spearheaded an independence movement in Baluchistan.[78] Nonetheless, these domestic policing operations constitute only a very small part of the military's mission. The army's main *raison d'être* still remains national defense against India, which Pakistani strategists believe still rejects the two-nation theory, the source of its sovereign legitimacy.[79]

In terms of strategies states pursue, therefore, the two leading states in South Asia have largely defied the globalization school's expectations. Although their declarative doctrines are deterrent and defensive, they both retain the possibility of offense. Neither state has completely eschewed hard balancing as an option in the region. Both states have increased their defense spending and their military manpower during the past fifteen years. And, although they both engage in policing-type operations, the primary purpose of their military apparatuses remains national defense against an interstate invasion.

THE MONOPOLY OF THE STATE AS A SECURITY PROVIDER

South Asian states do not appear to be willingly yielding any control over their national security to actors either within or without the state to help them manage contemporary threats. With regard to proposition PS9 (*nonstate actors*), for example, the pursuit of security in the region remains largely conducted through state forces. It is true that Pakistan, despite its strong military, has not been able to control its tribal areas, giving rise to parallel authorities and militia forces that have taken charge in the Northwest Frontier Province and Waziristan. For the Pakistani government, though, the Pakistani army remains the predominant security force, even if the growing power of Islamic groups suggests that they may also be playing an increasing role in the security dynamics of Pakistan.[80]

Neither in Pakistan nor in India do NGOs or private security providers perform any meaningful security functions. To be sure, a number of NGO groups, such as the Pakistan India Peoples Forum for Peace and Democracy, have emerged in the aftermath of the 1998 nuclear tests. Several women's groups and NGOs interested in finding a solution to the Kashmir problem have also sought to involve themselves in regional security affairs. It may well be possible that the peace initiatives of Prime Minister Manmohan Singh may have been influenced by some of these NGOs.[81] Nonetheless, the official Indian and Pakistani defense statements do not allocate any role for NGOs or private military organizations. Although the Indian government may rely on some of the several thousand NGO groups active in peace and development issues in India for information and analysis on India's multifarious conflicts both internal and external, national security policy remains very much a state-centric issue area. On the whole, then, neither country relies on non-state actors much in the pursuit of security.

Nor do these states utilize regional security-providing institutions (proposition PS10) to any significant degree. South Asia, as a region, lacks the kind of ambitious, overarching, regional institutions that exist in Europe, the North Atlantic, or Southeast Asia. The most relevant institution that does exist, the South Asian Association for Regional Cooperation (SAARC) forum has not traditionally dealt with security questions. Recently, however, it has started to address some of the region's security challenges, as evident in the declaration after the thirteenth summit meeting in Dhaka in November 2005. In particular, SAARC is trying to carve out a role for itself on issues such as small-state security, terrorism, environmental challenges, and natural disasters.[82] Nonetheless, the rivalry between India and Pakistan frequently gets in the way of the organization's other efforts. A good example is the refusal of Pakistan to open up trade with India under the 2006 South Asia Free Trade Agreement (SAFTA), based on the argument that it would have to settle bilateral border disputes first.[83] Furthermore, India and Pakistan frequently pursue their peace process outside this venue, which indicates that it does not yet play a major role in addressing the region's primary security challenges.

Although SAFTA might itself alter security calculations in the region, it will take time to establish. For the time being, the volume of India–Pakistan trade remains very low, despite efforts to increase it, and security largely impedes such possibilities. Changes in economic relations could come if the proposed Iran–India gas pipeline (via Pakistan) deal were to materialize.[84]

Both India and Pakistan have also been members of the ASEAN Regional Forum (ARF), which has also attempted to promote security dialogue in the region. Its scope and impact in the region, though, has been minimal. In general, there are few regional institutions, those that exist in the security theater are not very well entrenched, and the two rivals put little stock in them to advance their principal security objectives. Indeed, the doctrines of these states make scant references to institutions. Thus, India and Pakistan continue to use traditional self-help strategies, relying on their own armed forces and, at times, on interested third parties to secure themselves.

With the exception of efforts by South Asian states to combat terrorism and secessionist movements, often employing policing-type operations, the region offers almost no support for the globalization school's hypotheses on national security. The leading states of the region continue to prepare for interstate warfare as their primary security challenge and continue to structure their policy responses in traditional manners, relying on hard and soft

TABLE 5.1 Unstable Regions and Propositions Regarding Globalization

Propositions	Middle East	South Asia	Overall
PS1: shift to low-intensity conflicts	Largely inconsistent with proposition	Largely inconsistent with proposition	Largely inconsistent with proposition
PS2: shift to postindustrial warfare	Consistent with proposition	Somewhat consistent with proposition	Largely consistent with proposition
P3: face new threats	Inconsistent with proposition	Largely inconsistent with proposition	Inconsistent with proposition
P4: defensive doctrines	Consistent declaratory doctrine/ inconsistent practice and planning	Largely inconsistent with proposition	Largely inconsistent with proposition
P5: soft balancing	Inconsistent with proposition	Largely inconsistent with proposition	Largely inconsistent with proposition
P6: less manpower	Inconsistent with proposition	Inconsistent with proposition	Inconsistent with proposition
P7: lower defense budgets	Inconsistent with proposition	Inconsistent with proposition	Inconsistent with proposition
P8: shift to policing actions	Somewhat consistent with proposition	Somewhat consistent with proposition	Somewhat consistent with proposition
P9: privatize to nonstate actors	Inconsistent with proposition	Inconsistent with proposition	Inconsistent with proposition
P10: pursue security through regional institutions	Inconsistent with proposition	Largely inconsistent with proposition	Largely inconsistent with proposition

Dark shading indicates propositions that are largely consistent with evidence. Light shading indicates propositions that are somewhat consistent with evidence. Propositions that are largely inconsistent with evidence are unshaded.

balancing, high levels of defense spending and military manpower, and potentially offensive strategies. They do not appear to be willing to delegate any authority over national security either to nonstate actors or to regional security institutions.

Conclusions

As expected, regions of enduring rivalry are the least hospitable to the globalization and security propositions. The existential threats faced by states in these regions make them reluctant to alter their security frameworks radically. They are especially unwilling to relinquish any control over national security to international institutions, NGOs, or private security actors. To the extent that they identify additional security threats in the new era, they still prioritize the traditional threat of interstate warfare, and continue to address these threats with traditional methods, including hard balancing, manpower-based armies, and possible resort to offensive strategies.

As Table 5.1 indicates, the only propositions that conform to the experiences of states in unstable regions are those relating to combating terrorism and insurgencies. It would be difficult to attribute this to globalization, however, because the preoccupation with terrorism and subnational conflict in these regions long predates the advent of a global economy, as states and nonstate actors in the Middle East and South Asia have used terrorist tactics for decades to try to advance their agendas.

The fact that the experiences of unstable regions are at odds with the globalization school's predictions is not, in itself, strong evidence against the globalization and security argument. After all, these are the least likely states to make radical departures in the pursuit of security. Had we seen any degree of convergence of these states toward the new security agenda, it would have bolstered the case for a globalization-transforms-security conclusion. The complete absence of support from these regions, however, may simply be epiphenomenal of their instability and, consequently, is meaningless unless compared with other states facing different security environments. To balance out our study, then, the next chapter investigates the degree to which globalization has altered the pursuit of security by very weak and failing states.

CHAPTER 6

Weak and Failing States

IN CHAPTERS 4 AND 5 WE LOOKED at two types of regions—one stable and the other plagued by enduring rivalry—to examine how the globalization propositions apply in those very different settings. The analyses showed that the impact of globalization varies between the two types of regions, with stable regions conforming to the expectations of globalization theorists to a far greater degree. This chapter explores a final category of states: weak, failing, and failed states. Our empirical focus is specifically on the states in the sub-Saharan African region, based on a belief that the African continent contains more weak states than any other region and, therefore, offers us sufficient diversity in terms of cases. The findings in this chapter, though, may apply to other weak states in Asia and Latin America.

One caveat we propose is that state weakness varies from state to state even in Africa. For instance, states such as South Africa, Mozambique, and Botswana have higher levels of state capacity than Somalia or Sierra Leone, where parts of the territory have been controlled by warlords, and the central governments have not been able to assert authority throughout their national territories. Similarly, during the 1990s, states like Uganda and Ghana have registered high economic growth, despite recurring political conflicts. Moreover, some weak states have become stronger over time whereas some formerly strong states have joined the ranks of weak states, indicating that status is not static, but dynamic.[1] However, despite variations, almost all sub-Saharan African states exhibit characteristics of weakness, albeit in varying degrees.

In this chapter, we also depart from our practice in previous chapters of examining the behavior of the leading states in the region. Because we are investigating the implications of globalization for weak and failing states, it is precisely the smaller, less dominant states in which we are interested. So our emphasis in this chapter will be less on the Nigerias and South Africas of the region, and more on the Ivory Coasts and Ugandas.

What Is a Weak State?

According to Robert Rotberg, a weak state is characterized by the following conditions:

1. *Security deficiency:* The state is often unable to provide basic security to its citizens; to "prevent cross-border invasions and infiltrations" or "loss of territory"; to "eliminate domestic threats to or attacks upon the national order and social structure; to prevent crime and any related dangers to domestic human security; [or] to enable citizens to resolve their dispute with the state and with their fellow inhabitants without recourse to arms or other forms of physical coercion."[2] The militaries and police forces of weak states tend to be feeble, predatory, and often not interested in or capable of protecting the citizen from daily security threats. Their security forces themselves could be part of the insecurity problem that citizens encounter.

2. *Participation deficiency:* In weak states, free and open political participation is limited or absent. This means the control of political power is in the hands of an oligarchy or multiple centers, such as warlords. The expression of popular will is heavily curtailed and citizens may rarely have chances to air their grievances peacefully, resulting in day-to-day violence.

3. *Infrastructure deficiency:* The physical infrastructure of the state is poorly maintained. With resources not properly extracted or taxes collected, state coffers are very limited or heavily indebted to foreign donors. This means there is little money available for infrastructure development and maintenance, and other expenditures on public goods such as public health and education.[3]

To this list, we would add extreme external vulnerability. Weak states, in general, are more vulnerable to external shocks than their stronger counterparts.[4] For instance, the impact of the Cold War was considerable in the less developed world, where intense superpower competition inspired proxy wars and other disruptions.[5] The end of the Cold War was also especially turbulent for weak states, especially those such as Cuba, which had been propped up by one of the superpowers and then lost the support of their primary benefactor. Similarly, there is reason to believe that the onset of the new globalization era, an externally driven process, would affect Africa considerably, in both economic and security terms.[6]

However, not all weak states are failed or failing states. Although a weak state may have a mixed record when it comes to the previously mentioned characteristics, "fulfilling expectations in some areas and performing poorly in others,... the more poorly weak states perform, criterion by criterion, the weaker they become, and the more that weakness tends to edge toward failure, hence the subcategory of weakness that is termed failing."[7] The next level is "failed states," which in Rotberg's terminology are

> tense, deeply conflicted, dangerous, and contested bitterly by warring factions. In most failed states, government troops battle armed revolts led by one or more rivals. Occasionally, the official authorities in a failed state face two or more insurgencies, varieties of civil unrest, different degrees of communal discontent, and a plethora of dissent directed at the state and at groups within the state.[8]

It is clear that a failed state is the extreme case of state weakness. It has little capacity to intervene and end the internal conflicts that engulf the state. A failing state eventually approaches failure unless remedial measures are taken to stem the tide of decline and disintegration. A state may remain weak and stagnate in that position without much progress either way. However, there also exists a possibility that correct policies and favorable conditions can lift a state from the "failed" category to "failing" or even stronger.

Sub-Saharan Africa

The region of sub-Saharan Africa, stretching from the Sahel to South Africa, contains forty-two states. Most of them are weak, and a few can be classified as "failed" and "failing" states. The region consists of five loosely defined subregions: the Horn, West, North, East, and Southern Africa.[9] The failed states in the region are, in descending order of weakness, Sudan, the Democratic Republic of Congo, Cote d'Ivoire, Zimbabwe, Chad, and Somalia. The states with the highest level of stability are, in descending order, South Africa, Ghana, Senegal, Botswana, Namibia, and Benin.[10] Indeed, South Africa is often taken to be qualitatively different from other sub-Saharan

African states in possessing a relatively capable state; the analysis in this chapter, therefore, only deals with South Africa to the extent that its policies have affected other states in the region.[11]

The African states emerged in the international arena during the 1960s and '70s, at the end of the decolonization process. Many states were cobbled together into multiethnic territories, in part because they were under the control of one colonial power or the other. Sub-Saharan Africa avoided intense interstate war until the late 1970s. Some explain this outcome as the product of a norm of territoriality adopted by the Organization of African Unity (OAU) in the 1960s, whereas others attribute it to a lack of military capabilities to fight external wars.[12]

Although chapters 3 through 5 in this book are divided into states/regions (i.e., we discuss the United States, China, and Russia in separate sections, rather than look at the three of them together by proposition; we use the same strategy for the regions in chapters 4 and 5), this chapter discusses only one region—sub-Saharan Africa—and hence we divide it only by proposition group. We seek to explore how the different propositions identified in chapter 1 apply to the weak states of this region.

THE NATURE OF THREATS

With regard to proposition PS1 (*changing nature of wars*) the sub-Saharan African region has experienced a continuously low frequency of traditional interstate conflict since independence. By one reckoning, in the thirty years between 1960 and the end of the Cold War, only two traditional interstate wars (Somalia–Ethiopia and Tanzania–Uganda) occurred.[13] This trend has continued during the post-Cold War era, with only one interstate war (Ethiopia–Eritrea) in the seventeen years since 1990.[14] The war in the Great Lakes region involving Congo exhibited some characteristics of conventional war, but it was, at its core, a struggle among ethnic groups vying for domination—one in which troops from seven different African countries participated.[15] Unlike other regions, there has been no noticeable decline in traditional interstate war, simply because there was not much interstate war to begin with.

Instead, the major change in conflict patterns is the increasing number of internal wars in the region. Many of these wars have interstate dimensions, but are not properly classified as interstate wars. The involvement of a few African states in the internal conflicts of their neighbors has caused some wars to escalate (e.g., the Democratic Republic of the Congo) whereas others subside (e.g., Burundi in 2003).[16] Indeed, because many of the states lack both capacity and regime legitimacy, they have been unable to curtail civil wars (such as those in Angola and the former Zaire), ethnic conflicts (like the war between the Hutus and the Tutsis that spilled from Rwanda and Burundi into the former Zaire and Uganda), and battles by local militias (such as those in Liberia, Sierra Leone, and Somalia) for prolonged periods.[17] The other wars with some interstate characteristics were as follows: frontier clashes between Senegal and Mauritania (1989–1991), the Chad–Central African Border Conflict (2002), and the war in the Democratic Republic of the Congo (1990–present), which started as a civil war, but spread to eleven African states.[18] Other armed conflicts are listed in Table 6.1. The most recent example is the 2006–2007 Ethiopian military intervention in support of the official Somali government to expel invading Islamic forces from Mogadishu, the capital. The invaders were supported by Ethiopia's traditional rival, Eritrea.[19] These conflicts show the predominance of civil strife in Africa as opposed to regular interstate warfare, although some of these conflicts involved multiple states.

The end of the Cold War had both positive and negative impacts on the region's conflict patterns. During the Cold War, both superpowers supported regimes or opponents of regimes by giving military and economic aid, which allowed many conflicts to fester, such as the one in southern Africa involving South Africa and the frontline states. However, since the end of the Cold War, this source of external support has diminished, making some states weaker, and reducing the conflict potentials of others. The dearth of external support "tipped local balances away from the state and toward insurgent organizations," whereas the absence of superpower support "destabilized personalist states." Demands on African states by donor countries and international institutions for structural reforms such as ending subsidies have increased during the post-Cold War era, generating higher than normal instabilities.[20] In addition, the end of the Cold War has raising weapons transfers to the region, especially through illegal channels, increasing the number of armed combatants in multiple factions. Arms transfers, the resurgence of ethnic conflict, economics-driven or money-motivated insurgencies, and a decreasing interest in humanitarian intervention and peacekeeping operations by outside powers all contributed to increased substate violence in the region after the Cold War.[21]

The association between globalization and the rise of these new threats is profound. Economic factors have increasingly influenced conflict patterns. The conflict over diamonds, for instance, has played a big role in regional violence. Sierra Leone's diamonds have funded that country's conflict for both government and insurgent groups. The most prominent example is that of

TABLE 6.1 African Internal Conflicts Active in the 1990s and 2000s

Conflict	Years
Angola–UNITA	1975–2002 (R)
Angola–Cabinda	1991–2004 (R)
Burundi	1991–2005 (R)
Central African Republic	2001–2002
Chad	1965–2005 (R)
Comoros–Anjouan	1997
Congo (Republic)	1993–2002 (R)
Côte d'Ivoire	2002–2004 (R)
Democratic Republic of the Congo	1996–2001
Djibouti	1991–1999 (R)
Eritrea–Islamic Jihad	1997–2003 (R)
Ethiopia–Tigray	1976–1991
Ethiopia–Eritrea	1962–1991*
Ethiopia–Ogaden	1996–2005 (R)
Ethiopia–Afar	1989–1996 (R)
Ethiopia–al-Itahad	1996–1999 (R)
Ethiopia–Oromo	1989–2005 (R)
Guinea	2000–2001
Guinea–Bissau	1998–1999
Lesotho	1998
Liberia	1989–2003 (R)
Mali	1990–1994 (R)
Mozambique	1981–1992
Niger–Azawad	1992–1997 (R)
Niger–Eastern Niger	1996–1997
Nigeria–North	2004
Nigeria—Niger Delta	2004
Rwanda	1990–2002 (R)
Senegal	1990–2003 (R)
Sierra Leone	1991–2000
Somalia	1981– (R)
Sudan–South	1983–2004
Sudan-Darfur	2003–
Togo	1991
Uganda–LRA	1989– (R)

*Refers only to the Eritrean secessionist conflict; (R) denotes *recurrent*, a conflict with clear, discrete breaks.

Source: Peace Research Institute of Oslo, "Armed Conflicts 1946–2005," http://new.prio.no/ CSCW-Datasets/Data-on-Armed-Conflict/UppsalaPRIO-Armed-Conflicts-Dataset/ (accessed July 1, 2007). Details about conflict codings are available in Nils Petter Gleditsch, Peter Wallensteen, Mikael Eriksson, Margareta Sollenberg, and Håvard Strand, "Armed Conflict 1946–2001: A New Dataset," *Journal of Peace Research*, 39, no. 5 (September 2002): 615–637. The latest update on this project is Lotta Harbom, Stina Högbladh, and Peter Wallensteen, "Armed Conflict and Peace Agreements," *Journal of Peace Research*, 43, no. 5 (September 2006): 617–631.

the rebel group the National Union for the Total Independence of Angola (UNITA), which accounted for "75 to 90% of Angola's total diamond production and reportedly employed 100,000 miners in 1996."[22] Informal economic activity such as the illegal diamond trade and drug trafficking has increased during the globalization era. As two analysts point out: "[I]t is through informal economic activity, most obviously in the narcotics trade, that the poor world has actually become more closely integrated into globalization. The merging of development and security, together with the prevalence of informal economic activity, leads to the spectacle of wars closely connected to control of the drugs or diamond trades."[23] As James Ferguson has observed, globalization has most frequently meant the concentration of capital in enclave economies in Africa, as "capital does not flow through African countries"; it "hops" between specific sites in Africa, such as gold mines in Ghana, oil rigs off the coast of Angola, and diamond and coltan enclaves in the Democratic Republic of Congo.[24] Because concentrated sites of capital are most easily looted by rebellions,[25] the result has been a proliferation of attractive economic opportunities for insurgencies. A good example is Charles Taylor's exploitation of a Firestone rubber contract in Liberia to finance his military expenditures.[26]

Moreover, as insurgent threats have arisen, weak regimes have often responded by adopting methods similar to those of the rebellions they face, relying on illicit sources of revenue, using their soldiers to defend economic enclaves, allowing troops to loot indiscriminately to supplement their incomes, and employing private security firms (discussed later in the chapter). This has led to the phenomenon of the "shadow state": a formally legitimate state apparatus resting on clandestine commercial networks in the context of civil war. Classic examples include the Mobutu regime in Zaire and the Momoh regime of Sierra Leone.[27]

It is clear, then, that the wars African states fight today are primarily LICs, rather than interstate wars. Furthermore, it is also clear that globalization has served to increase and intensify these insurgencies. Thus, although low-level conflicts have been endemic to the region long before the advent of globalization as a result of the very weakness of the region's states, the evidence is consistent with proposition PS1.

There is also evidence that the region is confronting a growing threat from postindustrial warfare (PS2). Indeed, sub-Saharan Africa has registered an increase in terrorism since the end of the Cold War, as many of the warring groups in Africa have increasingly been practicing terrorist tactics and many international terrorist networks train or operate in the region.[28] From 1991 through 2003, the U.S. State Department's *Patterns of Global Terrorism* reported that Africa experienced 250 incidents of terrorism, 5.5% of the world's total, but amounting to 17% of the world's total terrorism-related casualties (6,106). According to the 2005 State Department report, in 2004, Africa experienced 253 incidents of terrorism (2.3% of the world's total), causing 875 deaths (6% of the world's total). In 2006, the number of terrorist attacks in eastern and sub-Saharan Africa rose 64%, from the approximately 256 attacks reported for 2005 (2.3% of the world's total attacks with 6% of the world's total deaths) to 422 reported attacks.[29] The number of attacks in Africa rose an additional 96% in 2007, totaling 835 attacks with a reported 2,187 fatalities (almost 10% of the world's 22,685 terrorism-related deaths in that year).[30] Although that percentage seems low when compared with the total number of global incidents, it is the result of a massive upsurge in terrorist incidents in Iraq and Afghanistan, rather than evidence that Africa is witnessing a major decline in absolute numbers.

Most of these incidents have been concentrated in the subregion of the Horn of Africa and surrounding states, consisting of Kenya, Ethiopia, Djibouti, Somalia, Eritrea, and Sudan. Since the September 11 attacks against the United States, international attention to the problem has increased, but terrorism has been an ongoing challenge in the region for more than a decade. The seizing of power in Sudan by the National Islamic Front in 1989 offered a fertile ground for Islamic terrorists, including the al Qaeda group of Osama Bin Laden, which had its base there for a period of time until it moved to Afghanistan. Major terrorist incidents include the killing of eighteen American soldiers in Mogadishu in 1993; the simultaneous bombing in 1998 of U.S. embassies in Nairobi and Dar-es-Salaam, which killed 200 and injured 4,000; the attack on the *USS Cole* near the Yemeni port city of Aden in October 2000, which killed seventeen American sailors; and the November 2002 hotel bombing and failed attempt to bring down an Israeli jet liner with surface-to-air missiles near Mombassa, Kenya. Most of these were high-profile precursors to the September 11 terrorist strike.[31]

In the Horn of Africa, Somalia remains particularly vulnerable to terrorism, given the occasional ascendancy of Islamists in the power struggle within the state. The local Somali partner of al Qaeda, al Itihaad (named by the United States as one of the twenty-seven entities linked to al Qaeda), was active in Somalia even before September 11.[32] However, al Qaeda and other external terrorist groups have not had tremendous success in Somalia despite the near anarchy prevailing there. The temporary victory of Islamic groups in the civil war in 2006 and their occupation of Mogadishu and surrounding regions threatened to change this trend. The Shabbab, a youth militia, whose members are trained by al Qaeda and are drawn from Somali expatriates from countries such as Canada, has emerged as a destabilizing force targeting foreign aid and humanitarian workers.[33]

The September 11 attack prompted the states in the region to confront the terrorist challenge. Twenty-seven African leaders met at Dakar, Senegal, in October 2001 to adopt a modest declaration against terrorism and to appeal to all African states to ratify the OAU and UN conventions on the prevention and combating of terrorism.[34] Some states in the region have made significant efforts to combat terrorism. The Kenyan government, for example, established an antiterrorism police unit in June 2003, and its Ministry of Finance set up a task force on money laundering to combat terrorist financing. To complement its efforts, the United States has increased financial support and training of Kenyan forces engaged in antiterrorism activities. Ethiopia has been more successful in the terrorism fight, given its tough national security-oriented regime. It has achieved this through coordinated efforts with the United States, especially in Somalia, where it has engaged in a war with the Islamic courts attempting to control the war-torn country.[35] Other states have also attempted to deal with the terrorist threat by cooperating more closely with the United States. Djibouti, for example, responded by accepting more than 800 U.S. soldiers in increasingly close relations with the United States, whereas Eritrea offered base facilities to the Americans. Even Sudan, whose Islamist regime is sympathetic to many of the terrorist groups identified by the United States, has been compelled to reign in terrorists operating on its soil in recent years. Although Sudan had offered training camps to al Qaeda, Egyptian Islamic Jihad, Hezbollah, Hamas, Palestinian Islamic Jihad, Abu Nidal, and Gama'at al Islamiyya in the past, after the first World Trade Center bombing in 1993, Khartoum buckled under to intense U.S. pressure and expelled Osama Bin Laden in 1996, after giving him safe haven for five years. In the post-September 11 environment, Sudan has increased its cooperation with U.S. counterterrorist efforts.[36]

Not all African "counterterrorist" efforts are genuine, though. By labeling their domestic political opponents as "terrorists," many African regimes have sought international sanction or even support for repressive policies that would ordinarily be condemned as human rights abuses. For instance, Eritrea's President Isaias Afewerki cracked down on opposition and media after September 11 and linked the Alliance of Eritrean National Forces with al Qaeda, Liberia's Charles Taylor called his domestic opponents terrorists, and Tanzania has been criticized for drawing up antiterrorism laws to clamp down on dissent. Ethiopia has branded its insurgents in the Oromo region as having terrorist links, whereas Zimbabwe's Robert Mugabe used antiterrorism language for internal repression, with the expectation of avoiding a negative international response.[37] Even without calling their domestic opponents terrorists, many African countries that provided the United States with access to intelligence, air fields, and military bases to assist the "War on Terror" have been able to escape western criticism of their human rights abuses and suppression of political freedom.[38] Despite this frequent abuse of counterterrorist operations, there is abundant evidence that such operations have made the challenge of postindustrial warfare an important component of the national security agendas of the weak and failing states of sub-Saharan Africa.

Regarding proposition PS3 (*changing threats*), African states certainly do face a host of nontraditional threats. To begin with, they are underdeveloped and their populations suffer from debilitating poverty. The physical infrastructures of these countries are very weak and they are often unable to cope with different kinds of threats—economic, ecological, and health related. Threats to physical security are probably more prominent than national security in most of these countries. Because nationalism is not fully developed, loyalties in most of Africa lie at the subnational level. This makes traditional notions of state-centric security problematic, and elevates human security issues to a higher level than in more developed nation-states.[39]

Disease is one threat that deserves special attention, given its dual connection to state security and human security. Diseases that have been eradicated or contained in the developed world and most parts of Asia, such as tuberculosis, malaria, polio, cholera, and a whole host of waterborne ailments, have been killing millions of Africans every year. Their prevalence has increased throughout the years as a result of migration, poor sanitary conditions, and inadequate health care facilities. Most prominent, the African states are increasingly ravaged by the scourge of HIV/AIDS. At the end of 2001, sub-Saharan Africa contained nearly 28 million HIV/AIDS patients, 70% of the world's total. The twelve Southern African Development Community (SADC) member states have the highest HIV prevalence rate in the world (20.6% of the population), and the sub-Saharan Africa region as a whole has a prevalence rate of 9% against a world rate of 1.2%.[40] It is clear that various aspects of globalization have been closely connected to the outbreak, especially an increase in long-haul transportation.[41]

HIV/AIDS affects many aspects of the new security complex. Not only does it directly threaten the lives of those infected with the virus, it also has secondary effects throughout the state. It threatens economic security in areas such as production, consumption, and investment, as the workforce is decimated by AIDS; it undermines food security, as many casualties are occurring among farmers, which is further reducing the substandard crop yields of the region; it yields governance crises, as the magnitude of the infection rates challenges states' abilities to deliver basic services to the affected population; and it threatens political instability, as AIDS-induced migration and urbanization pressures destabilize the volatile social fabric of African societies. HIV/AIDS has also increased crime rates in many countries as the number of orphans and economic refugees has increased during the past two decades.[42] In light of these profound challenges, many commentators believe that HIV/AIDS is the single greatest peril that the African continent faces.[43]

The disease creates important second-order threats to more traditional spheres of national security as well, as the HIV/AIDS crisis dramatically weakens the resources at the disposal of African states to undertake many of their principal functions.[44] According to Alex de Waal, government policy is often premised on an assumption of life expectancy—of its personnel and of its population—that is simply no longer sustainable in much of sub-Saharan Africa.[45] With crippled governments comes a host of new security threats, as other states seek to take advantage of their rivals' AIDS-induced weakness.[46] Because of the fear of HIV/AIDS, western countries have been reluctant to commit to peacekeeping operations in Africa, which has further undermined security in the region.[47] Moreover, the disease creates unique avenues for rebellion. The staggering numbers of AIDS orphans younger than the age of 15—estimated in 2003 at more than 1 million in South Africa alone, or about 48% of South Africa's orphan population, whose numbers could swell to 2.5 million by 2010[48]—presents a potential crisis of the highest order as more and more child soldiers are drawn from this population.

Of particular relevance to our inquiry is the impact of HIV/AIDS on regional armed forces. Vast numbers of armed personnel across Africa have been infected by this disease. This not only affects the number of active troops available, but also increases the incidence of personnel spreading the disease to the civilian population.[49] Thus, the disease has negatively impacted the morale of the soldiers, affected civil–military relations because societies view armed forces as bringing diseases to their midst, and the fighting ability of the forces has weakened considerably.[50] In addition, the organizational effectiveness of African militaries has declined significantly in the wake of the pandemic.[51] As a result, as Pieter Fourie and Martin Schonteich observe: "Foreign and domestic threats to a country's national security are aggravated by the security vacuum left by weakened military forces."[52]

Among other regional security threats are the prevalence of land mines in many conflict zones and the spread of small arms. The pervasiveness of small arms as a weapon of war is difficult to assess systematically, but anecdotal evidence continually points to its ubiquity. Some efforts at quantifying their prevalence have been made. The International Institute for Strategic Studies (IISS) has accumulated data about the use of small arms in warfare, concluding that "no other weapon category is as ubiquitous."[53] The IISS also surveyed eight internal conflicts from June to October 2004 to assess the prevalence of small arms as a cause of combat deaths. Three of these were in sub-Saharan Africa: Burundi, Cote d'Ivoire, and Uganda. Of 477 deaths in these African conflicts whose causes could be identified, 466 were inflicted by small arms (97.7%). This figure is substantially higher than the average of all eight conflicts: 89.8%.[54]

The region has also been heavily affected by the global market for armaments. The global legitimate transfer of small arms was estimated by the UN to be $2.1 billion in 2002; the problem of underreporting suggests that the real figure may have been closer to $4 billion.[55] It is estimated that Africa is home to more than 100 million pieces of small arms out of a total of 500 million in circulation worldwide. It is also the number one continent for the import of small arms. The AU had adopted several resolutions on controlling small arms and took an active role at the UN Conference on Small Arms and Light Weapons in July 2001. Progress in implementing the plans remains limited.[56] Thus, the global market has helped fuel many of the insurgencies raging on the African continent.[57]

Weak states are also heavily influenced by global economic pressures that have direct human and national security implications. For instance, if fully implemented, the World Trade Organization (WTO)-led agreements on intellectual property rights are expected to multiply the price of pharmaceuticals even when Africans are unable to purchase most life-saving medicines that are available under current prices.[58] High levels of debt have also affected African states' ability to provide basic services including security.

State responses to these challenges by the national security establishments have been highly variable. In some instances, for example, states have significantly reoriented their national security structures to combat HIV and AIDS. Much depends on the very definition of HIV/AIDS as a security threat; with this recognition, AIDS policy frequently moves up the bureaucratic ladder to more powerful agents—for example, from health ministries (frequently weak) to the head of state or government.[59] For example, Ugandan President Yoweri Museveni has stated that he was prompted to vigorous action on AIDS when, in 1986, he learned from Cuban President Fidel Castro of high infection rates among Ugandan soldiers sent to Cuba for training.[60] Ethiopia's AIDS policy has likewise focused on combating the threat to its armed forces.[61] At the regional level, the seriousness with which HIV/AIDS is regarded is codified in the AU's 2000 declaration treating the AIDS situation as a "State of

Emergency."[62] In its 2006 declaration, the link between disease and security was made more explicit, as the AU asserted that AIDS, along with tuberculosis and malaria, constituted "major threats to our national and continental socioeconomic development, peace and security."[63]

Despite these declarations, however, action at the state level has been lacking in most African countries; comprehensive AIDS policies like Uganda's that focuses on education, the propagation of abstinence, and the supply of condoms remain exceptional.[64] Uganda's success in rolling back AIDS depended upon centralized policy coordination as well as on the sort of engagement with civil society that weak and illegitimate states frequently lack.[65] Thus, many other states in the region have largely abdicated a comprehensive role in combating the pandemic, and their security apparatuses remain unengaged.

In general, facing a lack of capacity as well as the constant peril of rebellion and civil war, the weak states of sub-Saharan Africa frequently do not have the luxury of defining their security in terms of nontraditional security threats, and respond instead to the more immediate threat of rebellion. Although it is true that improving economic circumstances and containing the spread of pandemics could reduce the likelihood of rebellion, the leaders of failed states rarely concern themselves with the basic needs of their population, and enrich themselves instead at the population's expense.[66] New security threats, therefore, have only a limited influence on their national security efforts. Although they are becoming more aware of the security implications of nontraditional challenges,[67] the very state weakness, which underpins many of these threats, makes states in the region ill equipped to manage threats effectively. Responses, therefore, have been mixed if not wholly inadequate.

At the regional–institutional level, however, there is a new appreciation of the wide-ranging security challenges Africa faces. In the Common Defense and Security Policy adopted by the AU in February 2004, a "newer, multidimensional security" concept was adopted, which encompasses traditional state-centric security as well as issues such as human rights; the plight of refugees and other displaced persons; the use of land mines; the proliferation of small arms, pandemic diseases such as HIV/AIDS, tuberculosis, and malaria; environmental degradation; organized crime; child soldiers; terrorism; and human trafficking, drug trafficking and money laundering.[68] How effectively these general statements are translated into policy frameworks by national governments is still an open question.

In terms of new threats to security in the globalization era, then, Africa is perhaps the most visibly affected of all regions of the world. Threats are changing in the region with the intermingling of traditional security issues with nontraditional threats, such as diseases, which are spread as a result of conflict. Nonetheless, national security doctrines in the region have not yet caught up to these developments. The region is also prone to terrorism in different manifestations. Moreover, states in the region are embroiled in internal conflicts to a far greater extent than they fight interstate wars. It remains unclear, though, whether these nontraditional challenges can be fully attributed to globalization or whether they stem from persistent state weakness that is endemic to the region.

THE STRATEGIES STATES PURSUE

Turning to proposition PS4 (*defensive and deterrent doctrines*), we are unable to locate clear statements of military doctrine and national security strategy from the weak or failed states in sub-Saharan Africa. Nonetheless, given that these states cannot afford the most sophisticated modern technology and live with the constant fear of war and rebellion, there is no reason to expect that the forces of globalization have made their military establishments defensive and deterrent in nature. Indeed, in 2000, Africa contained the largest number of conflicts (mostly internal, although some with interstate dimensions) of any region of the world.[69] The sheer frequency of these conflicts suggests that at least some African states have adopted offensive military policies. Moreover, the active involvement of several states in the Great Lakes regional conflict suggests that many African states are seeking to prevent the spread of LICs to their territory through outward-looking, offensive-type strategies. That some African states are increasingly adopting offensive postures is visible in intervention patterns. Barring notable exceptions like Somalia's invasion of Ethiopia in 1977, and Tanzania's intervention to overthrow Uganda's Idi Amin in 1979, most Cold War-era interventions were in defense of beleaguered regimes. However, the interventions of the 1990s have involved the increasing use of offensive military doctrines and predatory behavior,[70] showing changes in the doctrinal approaches of the armies.[71]

Nonetheless, the majority of African forces are poorly equipped and poorly trained to fight regular wars compared with their counterparts in Asia or the Middle East. The infantries of smaller African countries tend to be "lightly equipped and [their] armor limited to light armored cars," and are, therefore,

little more than gendarmerie, and the larger armies require a number of weeks' intensive training and preparation for effective ground combat. It is because of these weaknesses that a number of African conflicts,

Sudan versus the Sudan Peoples' Liberation Army, Ethiopia versus Eritrea, UNITA versus the Angolan army, the civil warfare in Chad and Somalia, Uganda's war with the Lord's Resistance Army, all become protracted and stalemated, no side having the military capacity for all-out victory.[72]

Because most regional wars are mixtures of both internal and asymmetric conflicts, set-piece battles are the norm. "Overall conflict in Africa, whether conventional national warfare or faction street fighting, increasingly resembles precolonial warfare, bodies of men usually but by no means invariably ethnically bonded, fighting for economic assets and resources in areas not demarcated by agreed borders, the warfare of frontiersmen."[73] Furthermore, the main focus of armed forces in several countries has been internal power as opposed to external security. In West Africa, for instance, several states (including Benin, Cote d'Ivoire, Gambia, Guinea-Bissau, Mali, Niger, Nigeria, and Sierra Leone) have experienced military coups—some, multiple numbers—even after the end of the Cold War when the global democratization process had taken root throughout most of the world. Thus, the military is often more directly focused on the state and internal politics than it is on outside threats.[74] All this suggests that official military doctrines have little meaning, even if they exist in documented forms in the odd case.[75] That proposition PS4 seems to have little relevance to sub-Saharan Africa suggests that we must go beyond existing theories about globalization and national security to grasp properly the special problems that weak states face.

Regarding proposition PS5 (*soft balancing*), states in Africa have resorted to limited hard balancing against those regional states threatening to disrupt regional order and peace. However, they have also resorted to limited forms of soft balancing against each other through the AU and the UN. In terms of hard balancing, in the Great Lakes area the states aligned in two antagonistic camps in the Congo war. Intervention in the conflict was aimed at either supporting or opposing the Kabila regime. It was also meant to prevent any single state from emerging as the most powerful regional actor as a result of the war. In recent times, Ethiopia has been intervening in Somalia's civil war in an effort to contain and balance against the Islamists supported by Eritrea. However, the most powerful states in the region, South Africa and Nigeria, have not elicited any balance-of-power coalitions directed at them. Instead, these states have been major players in Africa's regional institutions aimed at generating stability in the region.

Much of the limited balancing taking place is a mixture of hard and soft balancing. The dominant patterns of balance-of-power politics are subregional in nature and they involve both states and nonguerrilla armies. For instance, in West Africa, Nigeria has engaged in a regional balance-of-power game supporting different sides in the civil wars of Liberia and Sierra Leone. In the Horn of Africa, both Ethiopia and Eritrea have engaged in a balance-of-power rivalry by supporting different factions in Somalia as well as Sudan. They have also sponsored each others' internal oppositions. Throughout the 1990s, competition between Eritrea and Ethiopia escalated, culminating in the 1998–2000 war.[76] In southern Africa, Zimbabwe and South Africa engaged in limited balance-of-power politics in the context of the SADC intervention in Congo.[77] In central Africa, Uganda and Rwanda formed a coalition against Zimbabwe, Angola, and Sudan during the civil war in the Democratic Republic of Congo (1998–2003) by supporting the rebel armies and the regime of Laurent Kabila respectively.[78]

The principal level of balancing discussed here is against regional powers and alignments, rather than against global hegemony. Indeed, Africa has long been peripheral to great power politics—occasionally involved as an arena for conflict, but not as a major player in its own right.[79] Indeed, to the extent that the region is involved in counterhegemonic balancing, it is indirectly, as a result of the rise of Chinese influence in sub-Saharan Africa. Seeking energy sources, export markets, and international prestige, China's economic, diplomatic, and military presence in sub-Saharan Africa has increased dramatically. Trade between China and the region almost tripled in five years, from $10 billion in 2000 to $28 billion in 2005, and then to $32.17 billion during the first ten months of 2006. China appears to be diplomatically aligned with states, such as Zimbabwe and Sudan, and has even spoken on their behalf in the UN. Its arms sales (to clients, including, most prominently, Sudan) and unprecedented peacekeeping presence in Liberia and the Democratic Republic of Congo, add a dimension of military force to this campaign.[80] One could argue, therefore, that the African states continue to use hard balancing against each other, while China is using Africa as a soft balancing tool against U.S. hegemony, and the continent may emerge as a key source of contention between the United States and China if the trend continues.

Regarding proposition PS6 (*manpower*) official armed forces manpower in sub-Saharan Africa increased from 958,000 in 1985 to more than 1.4 million in 1999. However, by 2006, the number declined slightly to almost 1.3 million, before falling again to just more than 1.2 million in 2007.[81] There has been no uniform trend across the region, though. From 1987 to 1997, for example, eighteen countries had witnessed a decline in the number of soldiers per thousand citizens, ten witnessed no increase at all, whereas fifteen showed major increases. The largest increases took place in Benin, Botswana, Uganda, Burundi, and Rwanda.[82] From 1999 to 2007, twenty-eight armed forces declined relative to population,[83] twelve remained unchanged or posted small increases,[84] and four posted large increases (Djibouti, Liberia, Rwanda, and Sierra Leone). Throughout the period, the armed forces of twelve countries in the region declined in absolute size,[85] fourteen remained the same,[86] fourteen had small increases in absolute size,[87] and four had large increases (Eritrea, Rwanda, Sudan, and Uganda).[88] It is clear, though, that the failed states have not uniformly reduced their militaries, as globalization theorists would have expected.[89]

With respect to propositions PS7 (*defense spending*)[90] in sub-Saharan Africa, official governmental military spending has fluctuated during the past decade. In 1990, it stood at $9.4 billion, but it dropped steadily to $5.8 billion in 1997, before rising consistently to $9 billion by 2006.[91] Of course, these figures would be higher if they included arms purchases by the nongovernmental militias, gangs, and chieftains that plague the region. Patterns are difficult to discern. For some countries, the figures are highly sensitive to the incidence of local wars. Thus, for example, defense spending in Eritrea increased from $214 million in 1996 to $400 million in 1999, before declining to $230 million by 2003, the latest figures available. In Ethiopia, it shot up sixfold from an estimated $134 million in 1996 to $822 million in 1999 and declined to $316 million in 2006. Sierra Leone reduced its spending in the 2000s as its civil war wound down—from $25.5 million in 2000 to $13.2 million in 2006. Other countries experienced apparently trendless fluctuation that is difficult to interpret, such as Angola ($1,186 million in 1997, $423 million in 1998, $1,546 million in 1999) and Rwanda (ranging from $69.6 million in 1999 to $48.3 million in 2004). Thus, the region is a mess of differing trends and, consequently, offers little support for the globalization proposition on military expenditures.

In one subregion of Africa, states have made a commitment to reduce their military power in recent years. Southern African countries engaged in a major demobilization after the end of the apartheid era. For its part, South Africa reduced its defense budget and active personnel. Between 1989–1990 and 1997–1998, South Africa's defense budget was reduced by 50% in real terms (an average of about 8% annually) and from 4% of GDP in 1989–1990 to 1.6% of GDP by 1997–1998. The end of the Cold War and demobilization in southern Africa, the end of apartheid, and an economic decline all account for this cutback.[92] As a result, during the 1990s, eleven southern African states agreed to reduce their forces or maintain them at their 1995–1996 levels: Angola (82,000 to 50,000), Lesotho (2,000 to 2,000), Malawi

(10,000 to 7,000), Mozambique (12,000 to 11,000), South Africa (136,000 to 90,000), Swaziland (3,000 to 3,000), Tanzania (49,600 to 25,000), Zambia (24,000 to 20,000), and Zimbabwe (42,000 to 25,000). Botswana and Namibia would be allowed to increase their forces from 7,500 to 10,000 in the first case and 8,100 to 10,000 in the second. The UN and western international donors played a key role in securing these force reduction agreements.[93]

In some countries, African armies have experienced reductions not only in numbers, but also in capabilities, especially war-fighting capacities. Often, rebels are able to control vast chunks of land precisely because of the weak capacity of armed forces. In many instances, equipment remains outmoded, training is very weak, and the capacity of the state is correlated with the capacity of the armed forces.[94] Paradoxically, some countries (such as Angola, Uganda, Rwanda, Zimbabwe, and Namibia) have been able to acquire capabilities for forward positions (e.g., in Congo), even while the armies of these states have been unable to suppress internal insurgents.[95]

Overall, then, although the region's states have had different experiences, the region as a whole shows no clear trend and, therefore, provides little support for the globalization school's expectations of reduced military manpower.

With regard to proposition PS8 (*shift from war fighting to policing*), in states that lack legitimacy, maintaining domestic order is often the military establishment's primary purpose. Thus, the national armed forces of Zimbabwe, Angola, Congo, and other failed African states are, in effect, brutal police forces at the service of corrupt governments.[96] It would be difficult to attribute this phenomenon to globalization, though. After all, corrupt African governments have long used their national security establishments to maintain their domestic power positions. If anything, globalization should restrain these police actions by bringing international pressure to bear against regimes that abuse human rights. Thus, the police operations of failed states should not necessarily be interpreted as consistent with the globalization school's predictions.

In general, then, it is difficult to evaluate the accuracy and the relevance of the globalization school's hypotheses regarding the strategies states use to meet their security needs in the context of sub-Saharan Africa. It would seem that African states still engage in offensive strategies, although many lack adequate military equipment and training for that purpose. They still engage in hard balancing vis-à-vis regional challengers, and have not reduced military spending or manpower in any consistent manner. And, although one of the primary missions of African military apparatuses is to engage in policing and domestic order operations, this does not appear to be a change brought upon by globalization.

THE MONOPOLY OF THE STATE AS A SECURITY PROVIDER

If the strategies that sub-Saharan African states are pursuing in the contemporary era have not altered as globalization theorists predict, there is some evidence that these weak states have reached out to other actors to assist them in the provision of security. Regarding proposition PS9 (*nonstate actors*) the weak, failing, and failed states of Africa, having little legitimacy and lacking the resources to maintain effective fighting forces, are increasingly relying on private security forces to fight rebels and defend their governments, their supporters, and their institutions. Indeed, in sub-Saharan Africa, police functions have deteriorated in most countries. Even in supposedly stronger states like South Africa, effective policing remains rather absent as evident in the soaring crime rates in that country, especially in its urban centers. Continuous LICs also have created a "weakening and fragmentation of regime power," blurring "distinctions between insurgency and counterinsurgency, and between military, police and civilians."[97] As a result, states such as South Africa, Kenya, Uganda, and Angola have been turning to private security providers, including Executive Outcomes and Sandline International, to fill in for a failing security apparatus. In a particularly notorious 1995 incident, the government of Sierra Leone contracted Executive Outcomes to suppress the resistance by rebel forces.[98]

Some argue that privatization in the security arena occurred during the 1990s, as a number of countries in sub-Saharan Africa downsized their militaries. In a way, states in the region could not maintain a monopoly over force, and the weak police forces in the region helped accelerate the process.[99] William Reno notes that the end of the apartheid regime in South Africa led that country's massive intelligence service to go into private business, a transition made easier by the longstanding use of businesses as cover for intelligence operations. He argues that this provided an immense contribution to the availability and use of private armies across sub-Saharan Africa.[100]

In addition to the use of private security companies by African states, warlords and groups that extract resources from the land have employed private militias extensively in the region. Child soldiers form a major component of these private militias. These militias often engage in the forceful acquisition of property and resources, especially mineral wealth, the defense of ethnic groups and clans, the waging of feuds between warlords, and the "simple amusement and self-assertion of the young men who compose them."[101] In addition, MNCs (including most of the foreign and local mining companies), insurgents, and criminal groups in this chaotic region also use private security forces to protect themselves and their property, because s the states' own military establishments and police forces often lack the capacity to perform these functions.

Furthermore, because they are unable to achieve their security goals independently, governments and people of the region look to several hundred humanitarian NGOs to assist them in providing food, medicine, and world attention.[102] Self-interested regimes and rebels can use such organizations as a substitute for functions that they are unable or unwilling to provide, and, in conflict zones, can even acquire a patina of legitimacy for objectionable actions. For example, several commentators have raised concerns about the manipulation of humanitarian NGOs in providing relief assistance to refugee camps that serve as hotbeds for political recruitment.[103] Thus, globalization has led weak states to embrace nongovernmental security providers to a greater extent than any other category of states.

With regard to proposition PS10 (*regional institutions*), there has been a flurry of regional efforts to form associations and institutional setups to provide both economic and security cooperation. According to Paul-Henri Bischoff, "globalization, peripheralization, and conflict as well as Africa's integration into an emergent world political structure explain this seeming growth in transnational activity."[104] Many African leaders began to realize that foreign governmental aid is unlikely to come without genuine efforts at regional cooperation and conflict resolution. The number of regional institutions mushroomed at the end of the Cold War, and existing ones were transformed. Most notably, efforts were made to revitalize the OAU (founded in 1963), which was renamed the AU in July 2002, when it was also amalgamated with the African Economic Community. The chief purposes of the OAU have been to foster cooperation, unity, and solidarity between the African states; protect their sovereignty; and resolve disputes among them.[105] It played a significant role in the decolonization of Africa, which was largely achieved by 1980. It also was credited with the creation of economic groupings in western, eastern, central, and southern Africa. However, the organization has had little success in preventing, managing, and resolving the widespread conflicts in the region.[106]

During the early 1990s, the OAU underwent a revival. In 1992 it established a mechanism for conflict resolution and a peace fund to deal with regional conflicts, and it dispatched peacekeepers to Liberia in support of ECOMOG.[107] Most notably, the AU created a protocol to establish a Peace and Security Council in July 2002 and, in February 2004, it made a declaration on a common African defense and security policy. The Peace and Security Council is a fifteen-member standing decision-making organ of the AU for the "prevention, management and resolution of conflicts." The other objectives of the council are to promote peace, security, and stability; to anticipate and prevent conflict; to implant peace-building and postconflict reconstruction activities; to combat international terrorism; and to promote democratic practices and good governance among African states. Among the principles that will guide the Council's activities is the right of the AU to intervene in the internal affairs of a country in the face of grave circumstances such as war crimes, genocide, and crimes against humanity—a new posture for Africa's primary regional institution.[108]

Most significant, the African Chiefs of Defense Staff met in Addis Ababa in May 2003 and decided to establish a regionally based standby force of 3,500 to 5,000 troops to undertake monitoring missions and to act as a rapid reaction force for intervention and peace enforcement operations sanctioned by the AU or the UN. By 2010, the AU is expected to have acquired the capacity to engage in complex peacekeeping and peace enforcement operations. A number of issues plague the plans, such as lack of adequate funding, coordination, and integration of disparate African forces; lack of training, and an insufficient political commitment of the participating countries.[109] The AU intervention in 2003 in Burundi is seen as one of the rare successes, where 3,000 troops were able to maintain stability during a cease-fire period and lay the foundation for the insertion of a subsequent UN-led peacekeeping force.[110]

The AU's peacekeeping activities in the Darfur region of Sudan deserve special mention. Since 2003, the AU has been upholding its right to intervene in member states to avert a humanitarian crisis, and to protect a cease-fire agreement it brokered between the government of Sudan and rebel groups. During the early part of its involvement, 7,000 AU troops attempted to maintain peace and stability in the region, despite their weak mandate (because they were not able to use force except when in "immediate threat").[111] As of the latter half of 2007, the AU mission in Sudan is now a joint mission authorized by Security Council Resolution 1769 (July 2007) known as the AU/UN Hybrid operation in Darfur (UNAMID). UNAMID is expected to involve as many as 19,555 military officers, including 360 military observers and liaison officers, 3,772 civilian police officers, plus nineteen formed police units of as many as 140 personnel each, and 5,105 civilians—for a total of 31,042 personnel. However, as of March 31, 2008, a total of only 9,213 uniformed personnel supported by 129 UN volunteers were on the ground in Darfur.[112] Clearly, this is an important mission for the AU, even if it needed to coordinate with the UN to be effective.

Beyond the AU, a number of regional organizations in Africa have been created or revitalized since the end of the Cold War. They include l'Union Economique et Monetaire Ouest Africaine in 1994, consisting of Benin, Burkina Faso, Cote d'Ivoire, Mali, Niger, Senegal, and Togo, which also had a nonaggression pact known as l'Accord de nonaggression et d'assistance en matèire de défense (originally signed between Mali and Burkina Faso); and the relaunching of la Communauté économique des états de l'Afrique centrale in 1998, which includes members such as Burundi, Cameroon, the Central African Republic, Chad, the Republic of Congo, the Democratic Republic of Congo, Equatorial Guinea, Gabon, Rwanda, and São Tome and Principe.

However, the most significant regional economic organization with a security mandate has been the Economic Community of West African States (ECOWAS), which has been in existence since 1975, involving fifteen states with nearly 120 million people, and its armed monitoring group, ECOMOG, which was established in 1990 to intervene in Liberia and Sierra Leone. In 1998, it established a Mechanism for Conflict Prevention, Management, Resolution and Security.[113] This may be the most active peacekeeping operation launched by African countries drawing on regional forces. Its intervention in Liberia helped to end the civil war and remove the Charles Taylor regime, but the considerable cost in both men and materiel led some to judge it a failed mission.[114] The intervention in Sierra Leone in 1997 was a more obvious failure, because it took UN forces to mount a temporary peacekeeping operation in the country.[115] Nigeria has been the lead nation in these initiatives.

The SADC was established in 1992 with the intention of establishing a free-trade area in the region. It also has attempted to promote regional stability and security by setting up an Inter-State Defense and Security Council for regional security cooperation. The SADC has made serious efforts to create a regional security community by establishing an Organ on Politics, Defense, and Security in June 1996 to harmonize national political institutions. It has also held active annual summit meetings despite differences of opinion arising from the fighting in the Democratic Republic of the Congo and South Africa's unilateral intervention in Lesotho. The members have signed twenty-two protocols on human security issues.[116] The active role that SADC's key member state, South Africa, has been playing must be noted. In May 1997, President Nelson Mandela convinced President Mobutu to leave power in Zaire and facilitated the installation of the Kabila regime. In August 1998, Zimbabwe, Angola, and Namibia intervened to save this regime, despite South African initial opposition, showing the weakness of the SADC to take common positions. South Africa and Botswana intervened in Lesotho in September 1998 to suppress an army mutiny and coup attempt.[117] These instances show that the SADC has attempted to establish regime security in the region, although it lacks sufficient unity on security issues to constitute an effective security-providing organization.

Other regional institutional efforts include the initiative by the Intergovernmental Authority on Development—comprising Sudan, Somalia, Ethiopia, Eritrea, Djibouti, Kenya, and Uganda—to end the Sudanese conflict, and the Common Market for Eastern and Southern Africa, which was established in 1994, with a common security policy. The East Africa Community, consisting of Kenya, Uganda, and Tanzania, revived in 1991, includes joint military exercises and coordination of police.[118] It should be noted that the UN also has been actively involved in regional peacekeeping and stabilization operations, most often in liaison with regional organizations such as the AU. The UN was involved in the conflicts in Rwanda, Burundi, Angola, Somalia, Liberia, and western Sahara in the mid 1990s. UN peacekeeping and peace-building operations have been fairly successful in Namibia and Mozambique, where warring factions ended their conflict and demobilized; but in Somalia, Rwanda and Angola, the UN failed in its peace mission.[119]

Because there are few widely available national security doctrines for the weak states of sub-Saharan Africa, it is difficult to evaluate the degree to which they rely on the OAU/AU and other regional organizations to achieve their security goals. Because the members of these institutions are states, and these institutions have historically supported governments against rebels, it is reasonable to assume, though, that they do value the AU and the economic institutions.[120] Nonetheless, the general picture remains that despite a mushrooming of regional institutions in Africa, and some limited successes, African states have not been able to engage in effective collective security management under the auspices of regional security institutions because of the weak state syndrome.[121] Regional peacekeeping missions have been plagued by poor funding, low levels of training and morale, and problems associated with subnationalism, ethnicity, and general apathy resulting from the weak capacity of sub-Saharan African states, and, above all, low levels of international support. Much higher levels of international involvement may be necessary for Africa to build regional institutional capacity, especially in the areas of conflict management and prevention.

Some positive developments have taken place since 2001, when the G8 leaders pledged a $64 billion investment in Africa under the AU-proposed plan called NEPAD (New Partnership for Africa's Development), which commits African leaders to pursue democratic ideals, respect of basic freedoms, sound economic management and, more important, the "establishment of peace, law and order."[122] However, a truly effective network of African security-providing institutions remains elusive.

The utility of institutions is realized by most states of Africa, then, but as a result of a lack of state capacity, it is difficult to say they are able to create or enforce institutional norms. External participation is needed for any peacekeeping operations to succeed. In the globalization era, the role of private security providers and NGOs has also increased in a major way. Thus, the globalization school's propositions about the centrality of the state as a security provider do correspond to the sub-Saharan African experience. Nevertheless, it is not entirely clear how to interpret this finding, as states in the region, because of their weakness, never enjoyed a monopoly over the provision of security. It does seem clear, though, that globalization has accelerated the participation of nonstate actors and institutions.

Conclusion

On the whole, then, the weak, failing, and failed states category presents mixed evidence for the globalization school. These states clearly have changed the type of wars they fight and have reached out to nonstate actors and institutions to help them achieve their security objectives. In addition, there indeed does seem to be an increase in nontraditional security threats in sub-Saharan Africa, although traditional interstate threats persist. The majority of the states in the region, though, have not reduced their armed forces or defense expenditures, nor have they abandoned traditional security concerns to address new threats. Furthermore, they continue to pursue strategies at odds with the prevailing view of globalization, including hard balancing against regional opponents and military offense. Although they do use their defense apparatuses for policing-type operations, this has always been the case and has more to do with the weakness of states in the region than with globalization.

Table 6.2 captures the pattern of security in the sub-Saharan African region from 1991 to 2008. The general conclusion is that the intensified era of globalization since the early 1990s has brought along major security challenges to the region, increasing the number of and type of conflicts, introducing new security challenges, bolstering the role of private security providers, and fostering attempts to rely on regional institutional mechanisms for security management. In this regard, the globalization school's propositions fit

TABLE 6.2 Weak States and Propositions Regarding Globalization

Propositions	Weak States
P1: shift to low-intensity conflicts	Consistent with proposition
P2: shift to postindustrial warfare	Consistent with proposition
P3: face new threats	Somewhat consistent with proposition
P4: defensive and deterrent doctrines	Inconsistent with proposition
P5: hard balancing to soft balancing	Largely inconsistent with proposition
P6: less manpower	Inconsistent with proposition
P7: lower defense budgets	Inconsistent with proposition
P8: shift to policing actions	Partially consistent with proposition
P9: privatize security to include nonstate actors	Consistent with proposition
P10: pursue security through regional institutions	Partially consistent with proposition

Dark shading indicates propositions that are largely consistent with evidence. Light shading indicates propositions that are somewhat consistent with evidence. Propositions that are largely inconsistent with evidence are unshaded.

the region's experience better than any other category of states, except for second-rank states in stable regions. It is the very weakness of the states of sub-Saharan Africa that have made them more susceptible to the pressures of globalization. Yet, this same weakness makes them simultaneously unable to harness other aspects of globalization in the pursuit of security. Thus, for example, these states have largely proved incapable of pursuing security through technologically sophisticated means that require less manpower.

Conclusion: State Adaptation to a New Global Environment

THE ONSET OF INTENSIFIED globalization during the past two decades has prompted scholars to question the relevance and role of the state in the contemporary era. Even in the realm of national security, which has been the quintessential domain of states, many have claimed that globalization has eroded the centrality of the state. In this book, we sought to investigate the disparate claims of globalization theorists systematically, because most writings on globalization and security operate in the realm of theory, rather than rigorous empirical analysis. Specifically, we examined whether the economic, political, and social globalization that has swept the world during the past two decades has had an impact on the way states pursue security. We investigated this question at two levels with an evaluation of security behavior from 1991 to 2008. First, we considered the global level, by assessing whether globalization has engendered markedly different international patterns, particularly with respect to the frequency of international conflicts, global military spending, military manpower, and the salience of international terrorism. Second, we examined the security behavior of major powers and several leading states in key regions of the world to assess whether globalization has altered the security threats states face, the strategies they use to combat these threats, or the monopoly of the state as a security provider. We looked at both official source materials and secondary literature and, whenever possible, supplemented them with interviews with decision makers.

Our research strategy was as follows. In chapter 1 we identified various propositions emerging from the literature on globalization and its impact on international security and state behavior in the security realm. In chapter 2 we conducted a macro-level assessment of the core global-level security propositions, specifically relating to the level of interstate warfare, global military spending, the participation of international institutions in the security area, and the relevance of transnational terrorism to the global security agenda. We then turned our attention to the experiences of different categories of states in regions facing diverse security environments to determine whether globalization has a differential effect on these states. To this end, in chapter 3 we tested these propositions against the security policies of three major power states: the United States, China, and Russia. Because these states are central actors in the international system, they pay enormous attention to national security. If globalization has affected their security policies, they indeed could offer cogent evidence on its impact on the national security state.

In chapter 4 we examined three regions of relative peace—western Europe, Latin America, and Southeast Asia—to determine whether the security strategies of states in stable regions are influenced by globalization to a greater degree than great powers with multifaceted interests and commitments. In chapter 5 we turned our attention to two key regions of enduring rivalries and protracted conflicts—the Middle East and South Asia—to assess whether intense conflict and security dilemmas lead states to pursue more traditional security policies, or whether they adjust their policies to the requirements of globalization. Then, in chapter 6, we assessed a region of weak states—sub-Saharan Africa—to determine whether these states with extremely limited capacities—both material and institutional—are affected by new global forces more or less than their stronger counterparts.

As we discuss next, our findings indicate that globalization has not yet radically transformed the international security environment to the degree forecasted by many globalization theorists. To the extent that globalization has affected the pursuit of security, it has done so unevenly across states and regions. The situations and contexts in which states find themselves have affected their responses to globalization and the challenges it has posed in the security arena.

Key Findings

GENERAL PROPOSITIONS

At the global level, our findings provide little unambiguous support for the globalization hypotheses on the national security behavior of states. To be sure, the period under investigation has witnessed a decline in the number of interstate wars and the rise of combating terrorism to the forefront of the international security agenda. With regard to the former, however, there are several compelling alternative explanations of this phenomenon, including the end of the Cold War and the rise of American hegemony in the military domain. We have no conclusive evidence that states are abstaining from wars as a result of globalization. First, in the past, there have often been periods of long peace in the international arena—especially after an era of intense conflict—which were followed by periods of rivalry and conflicts. Second, the rise of American hegemony and the near unipolarity in the international system constitutes an important pacifying condition, because minor powers do not often consider undertaking military action for fear of economic and military reprisals by the hegemon and its allies. There may well be a number of other causes, such as the presence of nuclear weapons, other lethal conventional capabilities that make quick victory difficult to obtain, the rise of nationalism, the emergence of antibelligerence and territorial integrity norms, and the maturing of states that emerged from colonial rule, which are making efforts to avoid wars over territorial disputes.[1]

Thus, the reduction in interstate wars is overdetermined and cannot easily be attributed to globalization. We do not, however, fully rule out the possibility that economic globalization may be one of the factors that constrains states from undertaking military offensives against their actual and potential enemies. The costs of war have increased during the globalization era while the benefits of military force to settle disputes have correspondingly decreased, because war creates considerable unpredictability and opportunity costs for states indulging in it. But it does not appear to be the single-most significant cause for the relative calm in the contemporary international system.

Second, we found no evidence of a sustained reduction in global military spending. Although it initially dipped in the direction that globalization theorists expected during the early post-Cold War era, military spending and war preparedness climbed back again toward the end of the twentieth century and spiked after September 11. As evidenced by the increased arms spending by the major powers, as well as the steady growth of the global arms trade since 1998, it is reasonable to conclude that global security competition in terms of military spending and arms buildups is not going away, but has begun to increase, and it is likely to accelerate during the coming decade. Dramatic increases in U.S. spending on defense and rapid innovations in military technology, especially in missile defense and competition in outer space, are likely to force other major powers to catch up as much as they can. More important, the economic prosperity brought by globalization has increased the wealth of many states (such as China and India, as well as oil-producing Gulf countries) and has sparked a buying spree on the global market for new arms. In fact, to the extent that globalization has influenced defense spending, it has been by revolutionizing defense economics, with states eschewing autarchy and purchasing weapons increasingly from the heavily globalized international market for arms. This is an area where economic globalization is having a counterintuitive outcome in the security sphere.

Third, there has been a proliferation of international institutions and IGOs operating in the security theater in recent decades, and their impact remains quite limited and dependent on the support of major powers. The role of international institutions also seems to have gone through periods of ups and downs during the period we are studying. Overall, however, these institutions seem to serve secondary roles after the key states have already made the significant decisions on security matters. Moreover, the EU, ASEAN, Mercosur, and other regional organizations and institutions have acquired only limited security functions and cannot credibly compete with the nation-state as a security provider.

Fourth, the rise of transnational terrorism to global prominence is a significant change that can be traced to the revolutions in communication and transportation associated with globalization. States are increasingly focusing on new types of security threats, particularly the threat of global terrorism. Here, too, though, the state is at the forefront of the response to the terrorist threat. Moreover, the strong counterterrorism measures enacted by states, including stricter border controls and immigration rules, have actually strengthened the state and bolstered its centrality. In this respect, the state's capacity to adapt to a new environment is a remarkable testimony to its resilience as a security-providing institution.

Fifth, the role of NGOs and other transnational actors does seem to have increased in some dimensions of security policy. Yet, this seems episodic and confined to specific issues, such as land mines and small arms. Their role in global disarmament and arms control, especially in the nuclear area, appears to have waned. Moreover, they, too, are dependent on the most powerful nation-states and have not significantly affected the pursuit of security. As Harvey Starr contends, states and transnational forces can and will coexist; the limited growth in NGO activity does not present a fundamental challenge to the nation-state.[2] And, although states are increasingly using private military contractors to assist their national security efforts, they typically do so only to a limited extent and retain control of the national security effort. The increase in the number of these contractors is visible, especially in certain traditional areas where the state had monopoly before, such as armed and unarmed operational and logistical support, as well as police functions, including crime fighting and intelligence.[3] Even here, in most instances, the functions are largely ancillary and, in most cases, under strict state controls.

SPECIFIC STATE-CENTERED AND REGIONAL PROPOSITIONS

The state-level propositions appear to be similarly overstated at this point. In fact, using our fourfold framework to assess the impact of globalization on the national security state leads us to two main observations. First, there is little evidence that globalization has yet transformed the pursuit of national security (Table C.1) by nation-states. States still endeavor to protect themselves with traditional national military apparatuses and privilege traditional defense activities over combating the "new security" threats that globalization theorists emphasize. Indeed, most states of all categories, except the weakest states of Africa, retain a doctrinal focus on traditional interstate wars, even if some of them are increasingly confronting low-intensity challenges. As far as doctrine is concerned, only among stable, cooperative regions do we find a clear trend away from offense. In other categories of states, strategic circumstances seem to be a greater determinant of strategy and doctrine than globalization. States in regions of enduring rivalry continue to use hard balancing strategies against regional and extraregional rivals. Except in stable regions (and, perhaps, in weak or failed states), there would appear to be little support for the proposition that states rely on regional security organizations to achieve their security goals, nor do states in turbulent regions eschew hard balancing strategies. Great powers do look to these institutions, but only to a limited degree when it is consistent with their strategic goals, and states in conflict-ridden regions find them to be largely irrelevant. And the globalization proposition about defense spending fails across all four categories of states, as defense budgets continue to reflect strategic conditions, rather than the pressures of globalization.

Furthermore, in some areas (such as the identification of new security threats) in which we did find limited support for the globalization school, it was clear that these concessions to the new security environment were complementary to traditional security missions, rather than a replacement for them. Of all the globalization school's propositions, then, only its predictions about an increasing focus on policing operations and postindustrial warfare are borne out across the categories of states, primarily because of international reactions to the September 11 attacks on the United States.

TABLE C.1 Four Categories of States and Globalization

Propositions	Major Powers	Stable Regions	Enduring Rivalries	Weak States
P1: shift to low-intensity conflicts	No trend	No trend	Largely inconsistent with proposition	Consistent with proposition
P2: shift to postindustrial warfare	Consistent with proposition	Largely consistent with proposition	Largely consistent with proposition	Consistent with proposition
P3: new threats	Somewhat consistent	Consistent with proposition	Inconsistent with proposition	Somewhat consistent with proposition
P4: defensive and deterrent doctrines	Largely inconsistent with proposition	Consistent with proposition	Largely inconsistent with proposition	Inconsistent with proposition
P5: soft balancing	Partially consistent with proposition	Partially consistent with proposition	Largely inconsistent with proposition	Largely inconsistent with proposition
P6: reduced manpower	Consistent with proposition	Partially consistent with proposition	Inconsistent with proposition	Inconsistent with proposition
P7: lower defense budgets	No trend	Inconsistent with proposition	Inconsistent with proposition	Inconsistent with proposition
P8: shift to policing actions	Consistent with proposition	Largely consistent with proposition	Somewhat consistent with proposition	Partially consistent with proposition
P9: nonstate actors	Largely inconsistent with proposition	Inconsistent with proposition	Inconsistent with proposition	Consistent with proposition
P10: regional institutions	Inconsistent with proposition	Partially consistent with proposition	Largely inconsistent with proposition	Partially consistent with proposition

Dark shading indicates propositions that are largely consistent with evidence. Light shading indicates propositions that are somewhat consistent with evidence. Propositions that are largely inconsistent with evidence are unshaded.

Second, to the extent that globalization has affected the pursuit of national security, it has done so unevenly. States in stable regions appear to have embraced the changes of globalization to the greatest extent. Facing no real existential threats, they have been able to broaden their conceptions of security to include a range of nontraditional threats, such as those to the environment and the economy. They have been able to adopt defensive postures, avoid hard balancing to a great extent, and rely increasingly on regional security organizations and alliances. In contrast, the national security establishments of states in regions of enduring conflict have been the least affected by the pressures of globalization. Because war remains a real and threatening possibility for them, they continue to maintain large, well-funded military apparatuses; they use traditional hard balancing strategies; and they resist the pull of regional security arrangements, private security firms, and NGOs, preferring to secure themselves. Although they are increasingly engaged in police actions and counterterrorism operations, they prioritize traditional defense-related activities over the environment, the economy, and other "new security" issues.

The major powers have responded in a mixed fashion, depending upon the threats and opportunities they face. In the contemporary environment, all of them have made fighting terrorism one of the primary purposes of their security establishments, but they have exhibited different patterns of conformity with the globalization hypotheses. The United States, for example, relies on multilateral alliances and institutions to advance its security interests to a greater extent than Russia or China, although it is willing to act independently if these institutions fail to advance Washington's goals. In addition, U.S. military doctrine emphasizes other nontraditional security threats to a far greater extent than Russia or China, although these clearly take a back seat to nuclear and conventional defense and fighting terrorism. Moreover, although it keeps these actors working in concert with its military apparatus and subordinate to it, the United States employs private security firms to a greater extent than Russia or China. For its part, China has continued to increase its military spending and, to a limited degree, its manpower, whereas its counterparts have cut manpower and, at least until 2001, reduced defense spending. In all other areas, all three major powers have retained their traditional national security priorities, concentrating on the potential for interstate warfare and great power competition. Most notable, they all continue to utilize offense or the prospect of offense and hard balancing tools to advance their interests. The United States has used its war on terrorism to craft a new offensive military doctrine. Chinese doctrine also implies the possibility of offense to resolve the dispute over Taiwanese independence. And

Russia has been behaving in a more assertive manner and utilizing offense and military threats in its Near Abroad, especially during the past two years or so. Before then, Russia's behavior was much more muted as a result of its material decline since 1991. It would seem, therefore, that the great powers have retained traditional national security states, embracing globalization in the security theater only when compelled to do so (as in the case of terrorism), in rather secure threat environments (e.g., Russian and American defense spending), and when doing so offers them potential advantages (e.g., the episodic American reliance on multilateral security institutions).

Finally, the very weak or failed states have been profoundly affected by globalization, despite the fact that they benefit least from it. Globalization has altered their national security environments by pushing them to look to private actors, such as private security firms and NGOs, and international institutions to provide their security. Nonetheless, we cannot blame globalization for the collapse of sub-Saharan Africa's national security establishments. State failure, rather than globalization, is the principal cause of the crisis of the national security state in Africa.

Thus, we conclude that globalization *has* affected the pursuit of national security, but unevenly (depending on the security environments particular states face and their degree of state coherence) and, in most cases, only to a limited degree. It has expanded the scope of threats with which national security establishments contend and the range of instruments they use to combat these threats, but—except to some extent among states in stable regions—it has not altered the primary emphasis of states on traditional security matters, nor has it dramatically altered the architecture of the national security state.

Nor do we find evidence that any particular strand of the globalization school arguments that we discuss in chapter 1 fits the evidence better than others. Although the soft globalization argument is easier to reconcile with the current security policies of our four categories of states than its hard-globalization/demise-of-the-state counterpart, they do not square with the remarkable resilience of the state and traditional security practices that we see to this point. We do not see evidence that trading states have shied away from traditional practices more than others; if anything, we see that the increasing wealth and market integration of states such as China and India have led to greater defense spending and a more formidable security presence than commercial liberalism or the rise of the trading state school would lead us to expect. If the contractions in their economies resulting from the global economic crisis since 2008 force them to reduce defense expenditures, it may also support this argument further. Furthermore, we see little evidence that the growth of global norms or culture has substantially reduced the relevance of traditional security practices or competition.

In fact, only two strands of the globalization school are not challenged by our results. Our findings have little to say about the democratic globalization hypothesis. Certainly, we see no evidence that democratic states are actively contemplating the use of force against other democracies, nor are they engaged in meaningful security competition with them. It remains possible, therefore, that the further spread of democracy around the globe will eventually transform security practices by making traditional state competition a relic of the past, although our findings neither support nor refute this conclusion. We find strong support, though, for the argument that global terrorism has transformed the nature of the global security agenda, as states of all categories have embraced counterterrorism and policing-type operations as principal missions in the post-September 11 era and are increasingly collaborating internationally to combat transnational terrorist groups.

The State: An Adapting Institution

Why has the national security state endured to this point, despite the onslaught of globalization? On one level, our findings will appear consistent with the realist approach to international relations. Realists argue that states are the central actors in the international system and seek security as their primary goal. Although they may engage in international trade and participate in international institutions to further their own interests, states are jealous of their sovereignty and thus are unwilling to cede control over their security to transnational institutions or processes.[4] Consequently, although globalization may represent an economically efficient mode of exchange, it ought not to influence the security behavior of states in any meaningful way. Moreover, given the centrality of interstate war in realist theory, which realists assert is the *ultima ratio* of international politics, states should be ill advised to abandon the traditional capacity to wage such wars.

For this reason, Dale Copeland argues that economic and political globalization may coincide with stability and cooperation in the international systems, as liberals would expect, only until the United States perceives that rising China presents a real threat to its status as the international system's leading status. At that point, concerns of relative power and interstate warfare will trump all other consideration.[5] Kenneth Waltz and John Mearsheimer similarly dismiss the economic, institutional, and democratic "constraints" of the contemporary globalized world as artifacts of the current distribution of power. Thus, they expect that globalization is unlikely to restrain states from pursuing power in traditional ways.[6] For this reason, Patrick James concludes that, although globalization adds greater complexity to international politics, it does not fundamentally undermine the utility of a realist theory of international politics.[7]

Our findings that states have been reluctant to delegate meaningful authority over national security to nonstate actors or regional institutions and continue to pursue traditional security agendas that privilege the capacity to wage interstate wars partially support the realist view of international politics. Nonetheless, we are hesitant to conclude that our research confirms the realist worldview, mainly because it may still be too early to reach definitive judgments about the impact of globalization. We accept the possibility that our findings may simply be an artifact of our vantage point in time. Our period of assessment—from the end of the Cold War in 1991 through 2008—roughly coincides with the intensified phase of globalization. Eighteen years, though, may not be sufficient to assess fully the impact of a phenomenon such as globalization, which amounts to a powerful structural/macro-level process that is still in progress. Therefore, our assessment is, of necessity, of an interim nature, and some of our conclusions might change as globalization advances and new security challenges emerge. Thus, unlike realists, who would argue that globalization is unlikely to affect the state- and war- centric nature of the international system, we acknowledge that although globalization has, to this point, only had marginal effects on the national security state, it could—if it endures—have more profound transformative effects in the decades to come. Interestingly, since 2008, the deep globalization seems to be contracting as the global meltdown caused by the financial crisis is affecting every leading industrialized state that relies upon trade. It is too early to predict how states will react or what shape the next stage in globalization will take.

To be sure, we have found some evidence of incremental changes in national responses to globalization. In our earlier work, we found that many of the leading states, such as China and the United States, did not pay much attention to new security threats in their national security doctrines.[8] Since then, however, new national security doctrines have been issued that are couched in the language of globalization to a greater extent than before, even if, in practical terms, security practice remains traditionally grounded. Thus, for example, the 2006 U.S. national security strategy includes a section on national security in the era of globalization (not included in the earlier 2002 document), which acknowledges that pandemics, environmental disasters, and the illicit trade in drug and sex are all potential security threats in the new era.[9] Similarly, the 2006 Chinese security blueprint departed from its 2002 iteration by identifying energy security, national disasters, serious communicable diseases, environmental degradation, and international crime as growing threats to Chinese security.[10]

Incrementalism by states would even be an understandable response, because to enact a significant change in approach would require governments to overcome not inconsiderable domestic forces of inertia. Mancur Olson, for example, blames failure to adapt to changing circumstances on distributional coalitions that entrench themselves over time in polities and resist policy changes affecting their interests.[11] The bureaucratic politics literature also identifies bureaucratic inertia and budgetary interests as factors leading to policy continuity.[12] There would, indeed, appear to be such entrenched interests resisting a more globalized security agenda in favor of a more traditional program. In the United States, for example, interviews we conducted at the State Department and even the Pentagon suggested that one reason why the globalized language of the new American security blueprint was not yet matched by commensurate policy changes is that significant entrenched interests in Congress and the DoD prefer to tout the China threat, rather than retool to deal with problems of disease and economic or environmental threats. The weapons in which the military is interested are largely high-tech weapons, including big-ticket items such as aircraft, aircraft carriers, battle tanks, armored vehicles, and precision-guided missiles that are useful to fight other armed forces, and not terrorist groups or insurgents in Iraq or Afghanistan.[13] Thus, it remains possible that, if the current economic slowdown were not to retard or reverse the process of globalization, in time, after domestic obstacles are overcome, globalization will have transformative effects on the way states pursue security.

We must, however, temper our expectations about future trends. Based on our assessment, the nature of security threats could change, but it is very unlikely that the primacy of the state as the key security provider will decline in the foreseeable future. This is because no comparable institution has emerged and is likely to emerge that can command individual loyalty and allegiance as states do. States still remain the focal point of individuals when it comes to security and welfare, especially during times of crisis. Individuals instinctively look up to the state in times of unforeseen crises that need collective response. And crises do tend to recur in world politics periodically.[14] The state is the only institution that maintains ultimate legitimate coercive power, even though this power is undergoing changes.[15]

The state is also perhaps the most feasible institution to deal with "inefficiencies" and distributional anomalies created by market forces, especially as a result of economic globalization. However, unlike firms that can offer several services better than or equal to states, in the security arena no such institutions exist that can effectively compensate for what the state can provide. Furthermore, there has been a deep connection between nationalism, patriotism, military, and loyalties, and these traditions are very difficult to wither away.

Moreover, the state is a very resilient institution. As we shall see, it has adapted to previous challenges that threatened to render it obsolete, such as the inventions of gunpowder, dynamite, and nuclear weapons. In each case, the state, especially the strong ones, harnessed these new technologies in a manner that kept itself at the forefront of the security game. Similar predictions about the state's demise have been made in the economic arena as well. Yet the state endured. We shall briefly look at some of these other challenges to the state and the state's response to consider the likelihood of state adaptation to globalization.[16]

Past Predictions of State's Demise

The prediction that globalization will undermine the state's role as a national security provider rings familiar, because it evokes the ghosts of past predictions of the demise of the state's security function. Prior to World War I, Norman Angell predicted that commerce would replace conquest in the industrial era, a prediction that has not yet come true.[17] After the development of nuclear weapons, John Herz concluded that the state was no longer impermeable to outside threats and, hence, was obsolete as a security-providing unit. As he put it, "the nuclear age seemed to presage the end of territoriality and of the unit whose security had been based upon it."[18] However, this prediction, too, proved to be incorrect, as states adopted nuclear deterrent postures and the national security function of the state increased under the weight of the Cold War nuclear competition.

During the 1970s, some interdependence scholars argued that economic interdependence had made the security function of the state less prominent. They believed that increased economic interdependence had a positive impact on the likelihood of peace, with economic interests overcoming the desire for military conquest. States, especially those connected by multiple social, political, and economic relations, were considered to be less focused on military security and military force in their relations with one another.[19] Richard Rosecrance even suggested that "trading states" that specialized in particular industrial activities and relied on access to the international marketplace were the wave of the future. In his view, "[t]rading states recognize that they can do better economically through internal economic development sustained by a world-wide market for their goods and services than by trying to conquer and assimilate large tracts of land."[20] Although some states focused on trading as opposed to pure security approaches, under the powerful impact of the systemic competition ushered in by the Soviet invasion of Afghanistan and the consequent Carter–Reagan arms buildup, the national security state reasserted itself. Those that sustained a trading approach (such as Japan and Germany) also had security protection offered by the U.S.-led alliance systems, obviating the need for overspending on defense. Free riding was possible under intense systemic competition, and the trading states made ample use of this opportunity.

Where did these previous predictions go wrong? First, they neglected to take into account the adaptability of the state as a sociopolitical institution. The state has been able to adjust to changes in its economic and military environment, and to maintain its supremacy as a security-providing institution largely because it has the most resources, it can command the highest levels of loyalty, and, facing competition from other similar units, it has powerful incentives to show resilience. Second, predictions based on economic changes, such as Angell's and the interdependence school's, neglect the security underpinnings of economic exchange.[21] If economic cooperation and interdependence flourished in the West during the Cold War, for example, this can be attributed to a great extent to the bipolar alliance structure, American leadership, and the security cooperation it engendered.[22] If world trade has expanded during the post-Cold War era, that can be greatly attributed to American global hegemony and the institutional order it has helped to create to conduct trade and other economic activities in an orderly manner, especially among the western states. However, others such as China have now carried this process forward to their advantage. Changing security structures are more likely to transform economic patterns, than economic relations are to transform the pursuit of security completely. Finally, forecasters of the state's demise tend to make hasty long-term assumptions based on the experience of short historical periods. During the past three centuries, pauses in interstate competition have occurred during different historical epochs, but such interregnums proved to be only temporary.

The predictions of the globalization school are somewhat different from those of other theorists heralding the demise of the national security state. It is true, for example, that the breadth and depth of global social forces are more profound than previous engines of predicted changes. In the past, predictions were made on the basis of a narrow set of variables, such as lethality of weapons, philosophical aversion to war, and economic cost-benefit calculations. During the contemporary era, the changes are perceived to have multiple sources and they seem less transient in nature. The importance of factors of production (i.e., land, labor, and capital) is changing, with information and technology being added to the mix. Competition over land may not be as intense as it is used to be, thus wars of conquest are unnecessary or even counterproductive.

Nonetheless, the globalization school may suffer from the same three shortcomings. First, those who expect the state to wither away in the face of global pressures neglect the ability of the state to adapt, which is confirmed by our study. If the state can continue to develop behavioral repertoires and appropriate security practices that keep it at the forefront of the security agenda, then the dramatic predictions by some of the state being made obsolete by globalization may be overblown.

Second, globalization theorists ignore the ability of the state to shape globalization and the challenges unleashed by new global forces. Indeed, the geopolitical underpinnings of globalization as an economic, political, and cultural force lie in American hegemony and the limits on great power security cooperation it provides. By suggesting that globalization is a force independent of both American power and this relatively stable security environment, globalization theorists may be overstating its likely impact. Under certain circumstances, the United States and its major power allies may even be able to control globalization. For example, if a new U.S. president opted for a protectionist agenda and a renegotiation of international trade agreements, as both President Barack Obama and his Secretary of State Hillary Clinton intimated regarding NAFTA during the Democratic primaries, that could lead to a contraction of the global economy. Similarly, although drastic changes to economic relations are difficult to undertake hastily, it is very probable that the United States–China relations could deteriorate if a longer downturn occurs in the U.S. economy and the relative gains that China has been making are not matched by increased openness. Moreover, sustained increases in oil prices may dampen globalization as firms suffer high transportation costs and prefer home economies or nearby countries instead of far-away locations such as China and India, even if they offer cheap production facilities. States could actively encourage such relocation. Indeed, since the global economic crisis began in 2008, it has been states, not firms, that are taking the leadership role in formulating policies to weather the crisis and bring the global economy out of a feared prolonged slump. Many of the leading American companies in the vanguard of globalization needed U.S. government money to avoid bankruptcy.

A major weakness of the globalization literature is its inattention to considerations of power competition among major powers in the international arena. Globalization is itself largely a product of American hegemony and cooperative major power relations in the wake of the Cold War, and could be further shaped by major powers for their own interests. Moreover, major powers could utilize globalization as a means of bolstering security competition. They could, for example, actively participate in economic globalization with the intent of increasing their national power, especially in the military and economic arenas. They could use the wealth they generate through increased participation in global economic order to increase their relative position vis-à-vis other major powers. Today, China and India, although participating in economic globalization, are also actively seeking military capabilities to attain global power status, and are seeking to harness globalization for this purpose.

Third, although globalization has been in the making for decades, it is a relatively new phenomenon in terms of its breadth and depth on the world stage. As a result, it is far too hasty to make predictions about its endurance—it could be challenged by political nationalism, economic collapse, or ecological disaster—or its effects, especially because current trends do not bear out their predictions. Indeed, the economic crisis of 2008 should inject a note of caution into the assumption that globalization will endure. As the asset-backed commercial paper crisis spread throughout the global economy, toppling banks and financial institutions in its wake, two features of state responses had ominous implications for globalization. First, although globalization has been characterized by a largely laissez-faire approach by governments, which have allowed global markets to regulate themselves to avoid being punished by mobile capital, states have responded to the current crisis with massive state ventures. Even in the United States, the bastion of free market enterprise, the Bush administration initiated massive bailouts of financial institutions, buying stakes in companies such as Citicorp, Bank of America, Goldman Sachs, J. P. Morgan, AIG, and others. To prevent a labor market crisis, it further entertained a government bailout of the Big Three automobile manufacturers. For its part, the Obama administration initiated a multitrillion dollar stimulus package to escape the risk of economic collapse. This form of state intervention and de facto nationalization of private industries poses a distinct challenge to the market logic of globalization, especially because national governments should face considerable domestic pressure to get an appropriate national return on the large investments made with taxpayer money. Moreover, because the Obama stimulus package was passed with explicit "Buy American" provisions, the risk that these national bailouts will undermine the free-trade engine of globalization is high.

Second, although world governments coordinated elements of their response to the crisis internationally (such as the coordinated interest rate cut on October 8, 2008), the differing national responses to the global collapse have revealed important tensions between close economic partners that may undermine closer collaboration in the future. Nowhere was this dynamic more apparent than in the EU, a group of states tightly enmeshed in a single European market. Tensions have mounted in Europe because British Prime Minister Gordon Brown has responded to the instability of financial markets with large government injections of cash and a 2.5% cut to the value-added tax. In contrast, German Chancellor Angela Merkel has resisted spending plans that she believed would take generations to pay for and has derided the British approach.[23] To the extent that differing national strategies clash with trading partners—especially if a large and powerful country such the United States were to seek to protect its labor force with trade-inhibiting measures, such as the "Buy American" provisions or the Obama Administration's quota on Chinese tire imports—this crisis could deal a considerable setback to the onslaught of globalization.

It is, therefore, too soon to write off the national security state or the foundational principle of its existence: protection of its citizens. It also seems highly speculative to write off competition over arms, spheres of influence and power, and the potential for violence in the international system. At the same time, it would be dogmatic to argue that states currently cling to the military security function exactly the same way they did for centuries and will continue to do so in the future. Every social and political organization has to adapt to changing circumstances if it wants to survive, and the state is no exception to this rule. The recent trend of the "securitization" of nontraditional areas of national security thus amounts to a largely successful attempt by some of the states to adapt to the new globalized environment, rather than the demise of the state that globalization theorists predicted.[24]

Not only may states attempt to adapt to the new global changes, they may even paradoxically strengthen their centrality as a response to globalization. We have already noted in chapter 2 that the terrorist challenge has led states to develop extensive counterterrorism capabilities that enable them to monitor communications, interdict suspects, and restrict activities to an unprecedented extent. In this regard, the paradoxical effect of globalization has frequently been akin to Karl Polayani's "double movement." As Polanyi describes, whenever adverse consequences of a liberal market economy affected the state, it activated a countervailing state response, rendering the state much stronger than it was previously.[25] Others have argued in a similar vein that government expenditures in open economies have been higher than in closed ones, that states are being "reengineered," and "recalibrated" in the face of economic changes, and that the market has acted as an enabler and an agent of "empowerment" for the state.[26] Baldev Raj Nayar sums up this paradox: What may be

> involved here is not the erosion of the state, but rather its re-configuration or readaptation in the context of globalization.... However, as between "the end-of-the-state" thesis and the notion of a possibly strengthened state because of globalization, the issue is one that needs to be resolved not a priori but through empirical examination.[27]

Theoretical Implications

Our study has several theoretical implications. First, none of the dominant international theoretical perspectives seem fully able to capture the current state of the world with respect to globalization. To begin with, liberal perspectives, particularly commercial liberalism and complex interdependence, which stress the economic foundations of state behavior, are not ideal guides to national security behavior in the contemporary environment.[28] Instead, our findings suggest that although states are increasingly focusing on trade, development, and interdependence, political economic calculations have not supplanted traditional security calculations. Although states in stable regions appear to be prioritizing economic considerations and privileging the constraints and opportunities of globalization, other categories of states have not followed suit. States in regions of enduring rivalry still prioritize traditional security concerns, and the major powers also have not subordinated traditional security concerns to the constraints of globalization. Thus, the economic logic of liberalism in the national security realm may, at best, be confined to parts of Europe, North America, and Oceania, even when increasing number of states are adopting neoliberal economic policies.

Our findings also challenge those who, drawing upon liberal institutionalism, assume that the proliferation of multilateral cooperative institutions in the contemporary international system will stabilize and dominate the pursuit of security.[29] We conclude that regional security institutions have indeed increased in number and activity, and are performing new security-related tasks, roles such as co-coordination of counterterrorist operations, peacekeeping, and humanitarian intervention. States, too, have increasingly turned to these regional institutions as both a means of increasing their wealth and the economic and political stability of their regions and as instruments of soft balancing to counter U.S. hegemony.[30] Yet, as security providers, regional institutions are still playing a secondary role, often at the mercy of politics among great powers and dominant regional states. Moreover, states of all varieties—even the weak ones—are jealously guarding their primacy in the security realm and are reluctant to delegate their security functions to these transnational entities. Thus, the degree of multilateral cooperation shows patterns of ebbs and flows, and it is largely dependent on the perceived imminence of threats, domestic politics, and other such factors.

Realist approaches are also somewhat challenged by our analysis. Although it is true that states continue to prize security and sovereignty above all else in the contemporary era, the increased reliance of states in stable regions on regional institutions and their retreat from traditional national security strategies represent something of a departure from a realist world. Moreover, all varieties of structural realism, save hegemonic stability theory, would be hard-pressed to explain why very little hard balancing is taking place against the most dominant power.[31] States in the era of intensified globalization have not engaged in military behavior akin to that expected by structural realists. Instead, most states have bandwagoned with the United States, and others have engaged only in limited soft balancing, often using institutional means. Although this is largely consistent with the expectations of hegemonic stability theory, the rapid growth of China and India, the resurgence of Russia under Putin, and the growing coherence of the EU all suggest that impending multipolarity should provide far more evidence of hard balancing than we have seen, even for proponents of hegemonic stability theory.[32]

Constructivist approaches, emphasizing the impact of common norms on international behavior also fail to capture the security practices of states in the contemporary environment.[33] The fact that most states still privilege national sovereignty and independence over multilateral cooperation, and that norms of humanitarian intervention still take a back seat to national security interests, especially in regions of enduring rivalry, suggest that global norms have not yet shaped security practices in a meaningful way.

We conclude, therefore, that we must reach beyond the dominant paradigms to understand the security behavior of states in the current international system. Specifically, we believe that more nuanced and eclectic approaches, which combine the insights of different theoretical approaches, may be most relevant.[34] Alternatively, because realist approaches provide the greatest purchase since they alone can explain the persistence of traditional approaches to security, we would expect that more nuanced forms of realism should provide the greatest explanatory payoff. In particular, neoclassical realism, which enhances realism's focus on the constraints and opportunities of the structure of the international system with an appreciation of the complexities of domestic politics and the political economic environment, may be able to capture the security responses of different states to the globalized environment most effectively.[35]

Future Trends and Prospective Research Agendas

Based on our interim assessment of globalization's impact on national security state, it would be useful to explore the relationship between systemic structures, globalization, and the security behavior of states. This entails a set of complex questions. To begin with, is globalization a phenomenon all its own, or is it merely the product of American hegemony and a conscious effort by the United States to open and integrate world markets? If globalization is merely Americanization, then what happens if the United States becomes protectionist? This is a particularly important question, as the Obama administration and the "Buy American" provisions of his stimulus plan may be evidence of a shift away from the free-trade policies championed by American presidents in recent decades. Alternatively, if near unipolarity offers the condition under which globalization could flourish and obtain relative peace, what would happen when the United States is no longer the world's leading power and countries such as China and India emerge as dominant economic and political actors? These latter states are progressively enmeshing themselves in the global economy and are beneficiaries of it. However, they are also engaging in major arms buildups using the resources they are accumulating through international trade. Barring a few historical instances, power transitions in the international system have generally been associated with war. Will increased economic globalization temper the urge to fight to obtain greater power in the international system or will it be a source of increased friction, especially if there are winners and losers in the economic arena as a result of globalization? Will these rising challengers continue to cooperate with the United States and the West as they expand in power, or will they begin to engage in hard balancing and competition, and work to shatter the consensus that has brought about globalization under U.S. leadership?

A second issue worth exploring is the relationship between globalization and nuclear weapons. Is globalization, in part, a function of nuclear deterrence? Does the existential deterrence offered by nuclear weapons provide great powers with an unprecedented level of security, freeing them from worry about survival and hence allowing them to engage in greater economic interactions?[36] If so, how long will this trend continue? Can nuclear deterrence ensure the geopolitical stability to foster globalization even after American hegemony recedes? Or will the technological and information aspects of globalization facilitate the spread of nuclear weapons into the hands of states and terrorist groups willing to accept the costs of their use, thereby thrusting us into a highly unstable, insecure world?

A third area of research interest would be to see how competition for natural resources fueled by the growing economic wealth of the rising middle classes in countries such as China, India, and Brazil can fuel security competition as well. In past epochs, the great powers divided up the continents and fought internecine warfare to obtain resources in accordance with the mercantilist policies they were pursuing. Today, competition for oil, natural gas, and precious metals have led to increased activism by countries such as China and India in Africa, Central Asia, and Latin America. This competition has been peaceful thus far, but will it continue this way as demand for strategic resources outstrips supply, or will it ultimately lead to military competition? Will globalization and nuclear weapons help the major powers to manage resource scarcity, or will they exacerbate tensions?

The story of globalization is an ongoing one. It definitely has unleashed many forces that are likely to have far-reaching consequences in the coming decades. However, our analysis indicates that it has not yet deeply reshaped the security environment or swept away the state as the principle security actor. Indeed, the state has fought with tenacity to shape globalization and has adapted to retain its primacy as a focal point in world politics, especially in the provision of security. It may well fail in the end, but during the past two decades of intensified globalization, the national security state has retained its core, even though it has tempered its behavior in the military arena.

NOTES

Introduction

1. Although these viewpoints are not embodied in a single, coherent theory, a set of common propositions tie them together, similar to a paradigm of research in international relations (e.g., realism or liberalism). Some key works include Thomas L. Friedman, *The Lexus and the Olive Tree* (New York: Farrar, Strauss and Giroux, 1998); Thomas L. Friedman, *The World Is Flat: A Brief History of the Twenty-First Century* (New York: Farrar, Strauss and Giroux, 2005); Anthony Giddens, *The Consequences of Modernity* (Cambridge: Polity Press, 1990); Ronnie D. Lipschutz, *After Authority: War, Peace and Global Politics in the 21st Century* (Albany: State University of New York Press, 2000); James H. Mittelman, *The Globalization Syndrome: Transformation and Resistance* (Princeton, N.J.: Princeton University Press, 2000); Kenichi Ohmae, *The End of the Nation Sate* (New York: Free Press, 1995): vii; and Martin van Creveld, *The Rise and Decline of the State* (Cambridge: Cambridge University Press, 1999): chap. 6. For the softer, more nuanced versions, see James N. Rosenau, "New Dimensions of Security: The Interaction of Globalizing and Localizing Dynamics," *Security Dialogue*, 25, no. 3 (1994): 255–281; Tony Spybey, *Globalization and World Society* (Cambridge, Polity Press, 1996); Hans-Henrik Holm and George Sorensen, *Whose World Order? Uneven Globalization and the End of the Cold War* (Boulder, Colo.: Westview Press, 1995); David Held, et al., *Global Transformations: Politics, Economics and Culture* (Stanford, Calif.: Stanford University Press, 1999); Anne-Marie Slaughter, "The Real New World Order," *Foreign Affairs*, 76, no. 5 (1997): 183–197; Michael Mandelbaum, *The Ideas That Conquered the World* (New York: Public Affairs, 2002); T. V. Paul, "The National Security State and Global Terrorism: Why the State Is not Prepared for the New Kind of War," in *Globalization, Security, and the Nation-State*, eds. Ersel Aydinli and James Rosenau (Albany, N.Y.: SUNY Press, 2005), ch. 3.

2. We accept the possibility that globalization is an ongoing process with no immediate end point in sight and that, therefore, its impact on the national security state may change as time passes. Nonetheless, we believe it is useful to determine whether any evidence of a systematic change in the pursuit of security has manifested itself to this point.

3. Axel Hülsemeyer, "Introduction: Globalization in the Twenty-First Century," in *Globalization in the Twenty-First Century: Convergence or Divergence?*, ed. Axel Hülsemeyer (London: Palgrave Macmillan, 2003), 3–4; Mark R. Brawley, *The Politics of Globalization: Gaining Perspectives, Assessing Consequences* (Peterborough, Ontario: Broadview Press, 2003), chap. 1.

4. Martin Shaw, *Theory of the Global State: Globality as an Unfinished Revolution* (Cambridge: Cambridge University Press, 2000), 6.

5. Jagdish Bhagwati, *In Defense of Globalization* (New York: Oxford University Press, 2004), 3.

6. See Jeffry A. Frieden and Ronald Rogowski, "The Impact of the International Economy on National Policies: An Analytic Overview," in *Internationalization and Domestic Politics*, eds. Robert O. Keohane and Helen V. Milner (New York: Cambridge, 1996), 26–27; David Goldblatt, David Held, Anthony McGrew, and Jonathan Perraton, "Economic Globalization and the Nation-State: Shifting Balances of Power," *Alternatives*, 22, no. 3 (1997): 269–285; Philip G. Cerny, "Globalization and the Changing Logic of Collective Action," *International Organization*, 49, no. 4 (Autumn 1995): 596–597; Victor Cha, "Globalization and the Study of International Security," *Journal of Peace Research*, 37, no. 3 (1999): 392; and Thomas L. Friedman, *The Lexus and the Olive Tree: Understanding Globalization* (New York: Anchor Books, 2000). To Prakash and Hart, "economic globalization is the increasing integration of input, factor, and final product markets coupled with the increasing salience of [multinational corporations] in the world economy and their creation of cross-national value-chain networks." Economic globalization is most visible in the integration of markets, finance, trade, technology, and foreign direct investment. Aseem Prakash and Jeffrey A. Hart, "Introduction," pp. 1–24 in *Globalization and Governance*, eds. Prakash and Hart (London: Routeledge, 1999), p. 2.

7. See Norrin M. Ripsman, "False Dichotomy: Why Economics Has Always Been High Politics," in *Guns and Butter: The Political Economy of the International Security*, ed. Peter Dombrowski (Boulder, Colo.: Lynne Reinner, 2005), 15–31.

8. Jean-Marc F. Blanchard and Norrin M. Ripsman, "Rethinking Sensitivity Interdependence: Assessing Trade, Financial and Monetary Linkages Between States," *International Interactions*, 27, no. 2 (June 2001): 95–127. A more potent form of economic interdependence is vulnerability, which implies that states would suffer severe and unavoidable harm in the event of a termination of their economic relationship. See Robert O. Keohane and Joseph S. Nye, Jr., *Power and Interdependence* (Boston: Little, Brown,

1977), 11–16; Jean-Marc F. Blanchard and Norrin M. Ripsman, "Measuring Vulnerability Interdependence: A Geopolitical Perspective," *Geopolitics*, 1, no. 3 (Winter 1996): 225–246.

9. Gerald Schneider, Katherine Barbieri, and Nils Petter Gleditsch, "Does Globalization Contribute to Peace?: A Critical Survey of the Literature," pp. 3–30 in *Globalization and Armed Conflict*, eds. Gerald Schneider, Katherine Barbieri, and Nils Petter Gleditsch (Lanham, Md.: Rowman & Littlefield, 2003), 1.

10. Holm and Sørensen, *Whose World Order?*, 5.

11. See Frieden and Rogowski, 26–27. For more political definitions of transnationalism, see Robert O. Keohane and Joseph S. Nye, Jr., eds., *Transnational Relations and World Politics* (Cambridge: Harvard University Press, 1973); and Thomas Risse-Kappen, ed., *Bringing Transnational Relations Back In: Non-State Actors, Domestic Structures, and International Institutions* (Cambridge: Cambridge University Press, 1995).

12. Paul Hirst and Grahame Thompson, *Globalization in Question: The International Economy and the Possibilities of Governance* (Cambridge, UK: Polity Press, 1996), 27; and Robert Gilpin, *The Challenge of Global Capitalism: The World Economy in the 21st Century*, (Princeton, N.J.: Princeton University Press, 2000), 294–296, 323–324.

13. On this debate, see Baldev Raj Nayar, *The Geopolitics of Globalization* (New Delhi: Oxford University Press, 2005), chap. 2. Scholars in between the two positions believe that "there is indeed a distinctive process under way of a sharper integration of the world economy," and that "the process is of a deeper nature than the one that existed before World War I." Furthermore, "while powerful social forces favor the advance of economic globalization, there are also strong forces—not least, states and their geopolitics—that serve to constrain it. As a consequence, while there is considerable diffusion of economic globalization across the world, there is (at the same time) a heavy concentration of its central features among a few key economies. The spread of globalization is thus uneven and asymmetrical." (Nayar, *The Geopolitics of Globalization*, 5).

14. All figures in 2005 constant U.S. dollars. This represents a threefold increase from 1985 trade levels. *The Economist*, WorldData, Economic Intelligence Unit, http://www.eiu.com/site_info.asp?info_name=corporate_landing_united_nations (accessed February 23, 2009).

15. Cited in Nayar, *The Geopolitics of Globalization*, 26. This figure continued to increase until 2001, when it hit a high of more than 79%, until it started to decline, reflecting the increasing proportion of world exports taken up by services. See United Nations, UN Comtrade Publication, http://comtrade.un.org/pb/SpecialTables.aspx?y=2006 (accessed May 31, 2008).

16. The 2004 figures represent an astonishing twelvefold increase from the 1980 figure! Foreign direct investment (outward stock) increased by a similar

proportion. UNCTAD, *Development and Globalization*, 35, http://www.unctad.
org/Templates/Download.asp?docid=4848&lang=1&intItemID=3096 (accessed
January 3, 2007).

17. UNCTAD, *World Investment Report 1992: Transnational Corporations as Engines of
Growth—Executive Summary* (New York: United Nations, 1992), 1; idem.,
UNCTAD. 2007. *World Investment Report 2007: Transnational Corporations,
Extractive Industries and Development*. Annex Table A.I.5. "Number of parent
corporations and foreign affiliates, by region and economy, latest year available
(concluded)." New York: UNCTAD. http://www.unctad.org/Templates/web-
flyer.asp?docid=9001&intItemID=4361&lang=1&mode=downloads (accessed
April 29, 2008), 218.

18. UNCTAD, *World Investment Report 2006: FDI from Developing and Transition
Economies*, 9.

19. Hülsemeyer, "Introduction," 3; and Cerny, "Globalization and the Changing
Logic of Collective Action."

20. Held, *Democracy and Global Order*; Francis Fukuyama, *The End of History and the
Last Man* (London: Penguin, 1992); Mandelbaum, *The Ideas That Conquered the
World*.

21. Shaw, *Theory of the Global State*, 10.

22. See, for example, Dani Rodrik, *Has Globalization Gone Too Far?* (Washington,
D.C.: Institute for International Economics, 1997); Richard Falk, *Predatory
Globalization: A Critique* (Cambridge: Polity Press, 1999).

23. Hülsemeyer, "Introduction," 3–4.

24. James H. Mittelman, *The Globalization Syndrome: Transformation and Resistance*
(Princeton, N.J.: Princeton University Press, 2000), 6.

25. Alex Inkeles, *One World Emerging* (Boulder, Colo.: Westview Press, 1998), xiv.

26. Holm and Sørensen, "Introduction: What Has Changed?," in *Whose World
Order?*, 4.

27. Jan Aart Scholte describes it as the transcendence of national borders. Jan Aart
Scholte, "Global Capitalism and the State," *International Affairs*, 73, no. 3 (July
1997): 430–431.

28. Our understanding of globalization, therefore, is similar to that of Christopher
Coker, who describes it as follows: "It refers in the first place to the many different complex patterns of interconnectiveness and interdependence that have
arisen in the late twentieth century. It has implications for all spheres of social
existence: the economic, political, and even the military. In all three it ties
local life to global structures, processes and events." Christopher Coker,
"Globalisation and Insecurity in the Twenty-First Century: NATO and the
Management of Risk," *Adelphi Paper*, no. 345 (June 2002), The International
Institute for Strategic Studies, 19. In this regard, we reject the contention that
globalization can be conflated with Americanization. After all, although the
United States may have been one of the driving forces behind the spread of
markets and western institutions beyond national borders, it is not in the driv-

er's seat of globalization. Indeed, as the Seattle World Trade Organization protests, pressure that compelled the United States to end its steel tariffs, and other incidents indicate, the United States, too, is subject to the pressures of globalization.

29. See Ian Clark, *Globalization and International Relations Theory* (Oxford: Oxford University Press, 1999), chaps. 2 and 3.

30. Some attribute it to the Reagan–Thatcher revolutions, and claim that the EU spread some of these free trade ideas, which were extended to the developing world by the World Bank and the IMF. For these arguments, see Eric Helleiner, *States and the Reemergence of Global Finance* (Ithaca, N.Y.: Cornell University Press, 1994).

31. Geofffrey Garrett, "The Causes of Globalization," *Comparative Political Studies*, 33, nos. 6–7 (August–September 2000): 941–991.

32. As Luisita Cordero and Richard N. Rosecrance suggest, however, authoritarian regimes have proved to be better or equally adept in embracing economic globalization compared with their democratic counterparts. "The 'Acceptance' of Globalization," in *No More States? Globalization, National Determination and Terrorism*, eds. Richard N. Rosecrance and Arthur A. Stein (Lanham, Md.: Rowman & Littlefield, 2006): 23–34. Others have argued that the mechanisms of global diffusion of liberal market-oriented economic reforms and the spread of liberal democratic ideas occurred as a result of coercion, competition, and emulation. Beth A. Simmons, Frank Dobbin, and Geoffrey Garrett, "Introduction: The International Diffusion of Liberalism," *International Organization*, 60, no. 4 (Fall 2006): 781–810.

33. Jeffry A. Frieden, *Global Capitalism: Its Fall and Rise in the Twentieth Century* (New York: W. W. Norton, 2006), xvi–xvii.

34. *Security* is a contested concept. Traditional definitions consider everything pertaining to national sovereignty and the sanctity of borders and territory (so-called "high politics") to be "national security" matters, whereas all other "low politics" concerns (including the economy, the environment, labor standards, migration, domestic order, and so forth) are not considered "security" affairs. Stephen M. Walt, "The Renaissance of Security Studies," *International Studies Quarterly*, 35, no. 2 (June 1991): 211–239. Of course, this overestimates the degree to which factors such as the economy can be separable from security. See Ripsman, "False Dichotomy." More recently, however, a wide variety of theorists have argued that the definition of security must be (or has been) expanded to include new dimensions of security, relating to economics, development, health, migration, and security of the person (human security). See Barry Buzan, Ole Wæver, and Jaap de Wilde, *Security: A New Framework for Analysis* (Boulder, Colo.: Lynne Rienner, 1998); Keith Krause and Michael C. Williams, eds., *Critical Security Studies* (Minneapolis: University of Minnesota Press, 1997). Michael T. Klare and Daniel C. Thomas, eds., *World Security: Challenges for a New Century* (New York: St. Martin's Press, 1994). We identify much of

the latter perspective with the growing globalization school, which argues that, during the era of globalization, national security is increasingly being set by nontraditional security concerns (see chapter 1, this volume). Therefore, to test these competing arguments, we begin with a rather traditional definition of the national security state and explore whether and how its institutions have opened up to the newer challenges of globalization.

35. Daniel Deudney, "Nuclear Weapons and the Waning of the Real-State," *Daedalus*, 124, no. 2 (Spring 1995): 209–231.

36. Kenneth N. Waltz, *Theory of International Politics* (Reading, Mass.: Addison-Wesley, 1979).

37. Keohane and Nye, *Power and Interdependence*, 20.

38. Regarding the centrality of the state's national security function, see Charles Tilly, "Reflections on the History of European State-Making," in *The Formation of National States in Western Europe*, ed. Charles Tilly (Princeton, N.J.: Princeton University Press, 1975), 42; Felix Gilbert, ed., *The Historical Essays of Otto Hintze* (New York: Oxford University Press, 1975), chap. 5; Michael Mann, *The Sources of Social Power* (Cambridge: Cambridge University Press, 1993), 412–413; van Creveld, *The Rise and Decline of the State*; Peter Evans, *Embedded Autonomy: States and Industrial Transformation* (Princeton, N.J.: Princeton University Press, 1995), 5.

39. Barry Buzan, *People, States and Fear*, 2nd ed. (Boulder, Colo.: Lynne Rienner, 1991), 22.

40. See Daniel Yergin, *Shattered Peace* (Boston, Mass.: Houghton Mifflin, 1977); and Marcus G. Raskin, *Essays of a Citizen: From National Security State to Democracy* (Armonk, N.Y.: Sharpe, 1991).

41. See, for example, Aaron Friedberg, "Why Didn't the United States Become a Garrison State?" *International Security*, 16, no. 4 (Spring 1992): 109–142.

42. Richard Rosecrance, *The Rise of the Trading State* (New York: Basic Books, 1986).

43. This is the approach taken in Norrin M. Ripsman, *Peacemaking by Democracies: The Effect of State Autonomy on the Post-World-War Settlements* (University Park, Pa.: Penn State University Press, 2002), chap. 2.

44. Coker, "Globalisation and Insecurity in the Twenty-First Century," 20–21. For this reason, Holm and Sørensen also differentiate the effects of economic globalization across regions. Holm and Sørensen, *Whose World Order?*

45. Edward H. Carr, *The Twenty Years' Crisis 1919–1939: An Introduction to the Study of International Relations* (New York: Harper and Row, 1946); Hans J. Morgenthau, *Politics among Nations*, 6th ed. (New York: McGraw-Hill, 1985); John J. Mearsheimer, *The Tragedy of Great Power Politics* (New York: W. W. Norton, 2001).

46. For a traditional definition, see Jack Levy, *War in the Modern Great Power System, 1495–1975* (Lexington: The University Press of Kentucky, 1983), 16.

47. Regarding structural power, see Susan Strange, "The Persistent Myth of Lost Hegemony," *International Organization*, 41, no. 4 (Autumn 1987), 565. Nayar

and Paul include ten elements in their concept of comprehensive national capability. A great power is a state that has dominance in a majority of these elements in comparison with minor powers. There are four hard power resources (military, economic, technological/knowledge, and demographic) and six soft power resources (normative power, leadership role in international institutions, culture, state capacity, strategy/diplomacy, and national leadership). See Baldev Raj Nayar and T. V. Paul, *India in the World Order: Searching for Major Power Status* (Cambridge: Cambridge University Press, 2003), 32.

48. Robert Gilpin, *War and Change in International Politics* (Princeton, N.J.: Princeton University Press, 1981); and A. F. K. Organski and Jacek Kugler, *The War Ledger* (Chicago, Ill.: University of Chicago Press, 1980).

49. See Jeffrey Taylor, "Russia Is Finished," *The Atlantic Monthly*, 287 (May 2001): 35–52; Zoltan Barany, *Democratic Decline and the Decline of the Russian Military* (Princeton, N.J.: Princeton University Press, 2007); Anatoly M. Khazanov, "A State without a Nation? Russia after Empire," in *The Nation-State in Question*, eds. T. V. Paul, G. John Ikenberry, and John A. Hall (Princeton, N.J.: Princeton University Press, 2003), 79–105.

50. For a discussion of security communities, see Karl W. Deutsch et al., *Political Community and the North Atlantic Area: International Organization in the Light of Historical Experience* (Princeton, N.J.: Princeton University Press, 1957); and Emanuel Adler and Michael Barnett, eds., *Security Communities* (Cambridge: Cambridge University Press, 1998). For a detailed discussion of contemporary western Europe as a pluralistic security community, see Ole Wæver, "Insecurity, Security, and Asecurity in the West European Non-war Community," in *Security Communities*, eds. Emanuel Adler and Michael Barnett (Cambridge: Cambridge University Press, 1998), 69–118.

51. Paul F. Diehl and Gary Goertz, *War and Peace in International Rivalry* (Ann Arbor: University of Michigan Press, 2001); Paul F. Diehl, ed., *The Dynamics of Enduring Rivalries* (Urbana: University of Illinois Press, 1998). An important source of data on enduring rivalries is the International Crisis Behavior Project database, http://www.cidcm.umd.edu/icb (accessed January 12, 2009).

52. Robert I. Rotberg, "Failed States, Collapsed Sates, Weak States: Causes and Indicators," in *State Failure and State Weakness in a Time of Terror*, ed. Robert I. Rotberg (Washington, D.C.: Brookings Institution Press, 2003), 3.

53. Joel S. Migdal, *Strong Societies and Weak States* (Princeton, N.J.: Princeton University Press, 1998), xiii.

54. Michael Mann, *The Sources of Social Power*, Vol. II (Cambridge: Cambridge University Press, 1993), 59. See also Organski and Kugler, *The War Ledger*, 4–8.

55. Ted Robert Gurr, Monty G. Marshall, and Deepa Khosla, eds., *Peace and Conflict 2001* (College Park: The Center for International Development and Conflict Management, University of Maryland, 2001), 2. See also Ted Robert Gurr and Monty G. Marshall, *Peace and Conflict 2003* (College Park: The Center for

International Development and Conflict Management, University of Maryland, 2003).

56. Rotberg, "Failed States, Collapsed Sates, Weak States: Causes and Indicators," 5.

57. See, for example, Stephen Van Evera, *A Guide to Methodology for Students of Political Science* (Ithaca, N.Y.: Cornell University Press, 1997), 56–63; Alexander L. George and Andrew Bennett, *Case Studies and Theory Development in the Social Sciences* (Cambridge, Mass.: MIT Press, 2005).

Chapter 1

1. See, for example, Robert O. Keohane, ed., *Neorealism and Its Critics* (New York: Columbia University Press, 1986); David A. Baldwin, ed., *Neorealism and Neoliberalism: The Contemporary Debate* (New York: Columbia University Press, 1993); and Andrew Moravcsik, "Taking Preferences Seriously: A Liberal Theory of International Politics," *International Organization*, 51, no. 4 (Autumn 1997): 513–553.

2. Martin Shaw, *Theory of the Global State: Globality as an Unfinished Revolution* (Cambridge: Cambridge University Press, 2000), 7.

3. Kenichi Ohmae, *The End of the Nation State* (New York: Free Press, 1995), vii. See also Thomas L. Friedman, *The World Is Flat: A Brief History of the Twenty-First Century* (New York: Farrar, Straus and Giroux, 2005).

4. Susan Strange, *The Retreat of the State: The Diffusion of Power in the World Economy* (Cambridge: Cambridge University Press, 1996), 4. See also, William Greider, *One World, Ready or Not: The Manic Logic of Global Capitalism* (New York: Simon & Schuster, 1997). For a critical perspective, see Linda Weiss, *The Myth of the Powerless State: Governing the Economy in a Global Era* (Ithaca, N.Y.: Cornell University Press, 1998).

5. See, for example, Jan Aart Scholte, *Globalization: A Critical Introduction* (London: Palgrave, 2000); Kenichi Ohmae, *The Borderless World: Power and Strategy in the Interlinked Economy* (New York: Harper Business, 1990); Richard O'Brien, *Global Financial Integration: The End of Geography* (London: Pinter, 1992). For contrary perspectives, see Miles Kahler, "Territoriality and Conflict in an Era of Globalization," in *Territoriality and Conflict in an Era of Globalization*, eds. Miles Kahler and Barbara F. Walter (Cambridge: Cambridge University Press, 2006), 1–21; David Newman, "The Resilience of Territorial Conflict in an Era of Globalization," in *Territoriality and Conflict in an Era of Globalization*, eds. Miles Kahler and Barbara F. Walter (Cambridge: Cambridge University Press, 2006), 85–110.

6. Ohmae, *The End of the Nation State*.

7. Robert Gilpin, *The Challenge of Global Capitalism: The World Economy in the 21st Century* (Princeton, N.J.: Princeton University Press, 2000), 18.

8. Ronnie D. Lipschutz, *After Authority: War, Peace and Global Politics in the 21st Century* (Albany: State University of New York Press, 2000).

9. See Joseph E. Stiglitz, *Globalization and Its Discontents* (New York: W. W. Norton, 2002); Stephen G. Brooks, *Producing Security: Multinational Corporations, Globalization, and the Changing Calculus of Conflict* (Princeton, N.J.: Princeton University Press, 2005). Conflicts affect economic prosperity in different ways: by "impeding economic relations and commercial dealings between countries," by "discouraging economic actors from pursuing business opportunities in an environment of higher risk and uncertainty," and by causing supply shortages, "hikes in transport costs, loss of access to market, and even losses of territory." See Luisita Cordero and Richard N. Rosecrance, "The 'Acceptance' of Globalization," in *No More States: Globalization, National Self-Determination, and Terrorism*, eds. Richard N. Rosecrance and Arthur A. Stein (Lanham, Md.: Rowman & Littlefield, 2006), 25.

10. Jonathan Kirshner, "Globalization and National Security," in *Globalization and National Security*, ed. Jonathan Kirshner (New York: Routledge, 2006), 24.

11. See, for example, James H. Mittelman, *The Globalization Syndrome: Transformation and Resistance* (Princeton, N.J.: Princeton University Press, 2000).

12. See, for example, Robert W. Cox, "A Perspective on Globalization," in *Globalization: Critical Reflections*, ed. James H. Mittelman (Boulder, Colo.: Lynne Rienner, 1996), 26–27; Philip G. Cerny, "What Next for the State?" in *Globalization: Theory and Practice*, eds. Eleonore Kofman and Gillian Youngs (New York: Pinter, 1996), 123–137; Philip G. Cerny, "International Finance and the Erosion of State Policy Capacity," in *Globalization and Public Policy*, ed. Philip Gummett (Cheltenham, UK: Elgar, 1996), 83–104.

13. For the softer versions, see James N. Rosenau, "New Dimensions of Security: The Interaction of Globalizing and Localizing Dynamics," *Security Dialogue*, 25, no. 3 (1994): 255–281; Tony Spybey, *Globalization and World Society* (Cambridge, Polity Press, 1996); Hans-Henrik Holm and George Sørensen, *Whose World Order? Uneven Globalization and the End of the Cold War*, (Boulder, Colo.: Westview Press, 1995); David Held et al., *Global Transformations: Politics, Economics and Culture* (Stanford, Calif.: Stanford University Press, 1999); James H. Mittelman, ed., *Globalization: Critical Reflections* (Boulder, Colo.: Lynne Rienner, 1996); Anne-Marie Slaughter, "The Real New World Order," *Foreign Affairs*, 76, no. 5 (September–October 1997): 183–197.

14. In this regard, they describe a situation akin to Keohane and Nye's "complex interdependence," in which the primacy of security for states disappears. See Robert O. Keohane and Joseph S. Nye, Jr., *Power and Interdependence* (Boston, Mass.: Little Brown, 1977), chap. 1.

15. See Richard Rosecrance, *The Rise of the Trading State* (New York: Basic Books, 1986), chap. 2; Carl Kaysen, "Is War Obsolete? A Review Essay," *International Security*, 14, no. 4 (Spring 1990): 42–64; Richard Rosecrance and Peter Thompson, "Trade, Foreign Investment and Security," *Annual Review of Political Science*, 6, no. 1 (2003): 377–398. See also Bruce Russett and John Oneal, *Triangulating Peace: Democracy, Interdependence, and International Organizations*

(New York: W. W. Norton, 2001), 145–155; Christopher R. Way, *Manchester Revisited: Economic Interdependence and Conflict* (Ithaca, N.Y.: Cornell University Press, forthcoming). An opposite view points out that territorial attachments have less to do with the notional value of land than the symbolic role it constitutes in shaping identities and a sense of belonging in an increasingly globalizing world. See Miles Kahler and Barbara F. Walter, eds., *Territoriality and Conflict in an Era of Globalization* (Cambridge: Cambridge University Press, 2006).

16. Regarding the effects of nationalism, see Ernest Gellner, *Nations and Nationalism* (Ithaca, N.Y.: Cornell University Press, 1983); Carl Kaysen, "Is War Obsolete?," 52. Regarding asymmetric warfare strategies making conquest difficult, see Ivan Arreguin-Toft, *How the Weak Win Wars: A Theory of Asymmetric Conflict* (Cambridge: Cambridge University Press, 2005); T. V. Paul, *Asymmetric Conflicts: War Initiation by Weaker Powers* (Cambridge: Cambridge University Press, 1994); Gene Sharp, *Making Europe Unconquerable: The Potential of Civilian-Based Deterrence and Defense* (Cambridge, Mass.: Ballinger, 1985); Gene Sharp, *Civilian-Based Defense* (Princeton, N.J.: Princeton University Press, 1990).

17. Michael Mann, "Has Globalization Ended the Rise and Rise of the Nation-State?" pp. 237–261 in *International Order and the Future of World Politics*, eds. T. V. Paul and John A. Hall (Cambridge: Cambridge University Press, 1999), 238.

18. See, for example, Mittelman, *The Globalization Syndrome*, 68–72.

19. Peter Stoett, *Human and Global Security: An Exploration of Terms* (Toronto: University of Toronto Press, 1999); Jessica Mathews, "Power Shift," *Foreign Affairs*, 76, no. 1 (January–February 1997): 51; Rosenau, "New Dimensions of Security," 258. For a critical perspective, see Roland Paris, "Human Security: Paradigm Shift or Hot Air?" *International Security*, 26, no. 2 (2001): 87–102. It is noteworthy, however, that even in Canada, where Foreign Affairs Minister Lloyd Axworthy championed the concept, human security has fallen out of favor in the foreign policy of the Conservative government of Stephen Harper.

20. Peter Andreas and Richard Price, "From War Fighting to Crime Fighting: Transforming the American National Security State," *International Studies Review*, 3, no. 3 (Fall 2001): 31–52.

21. Kalevi J. Holsti, *The State, War, and the State of War* (Cambridge: Cambridge University Press, 1996).

22. See, for example, Christopher Coker, "Globalisation and Insecurity in the Twenty-First Century: NATO and the Management of Risk," *Adelphi Paper*, no. 345 (June 2002), 54–56; Victor D. Cha, "Globalization and the Study of National Security," *Journal of Peace Research*, 37, no. 3 (May 2000): 391–403.

23. See Robert O. Keohane, "Economic Liberalism Reconsidered," in *The Economic Limits to Politics*, ed. John Dunn (Cambridge: Cambridge University Press, 1990), 165–194; Arthur A. Stein, "Governments, Economic Interdependence, and International Cooperation," in *Behavior, Society, and Nuclear War*, Vol. 3,

eds. Philip E. Tetlock et al. (New York: Oxford University Press, 1993), 241–324; and Michael W. Doyle, *Ways of War and Peace: Realism, Liberalism, and Socialism* (New York: W. W. Norton, 1997), 230–250. For an empirical critique, see Norrin M. Ripsman and Jean-Marc F. Blanchard, "Commercial Liberalism under Fire: Evidence from 1914 and 1936," *Security Studies*, 6, no. 2 (Winter 1996–1997): 4–50. Another, largely skeptical, work on the link between globalization (defined primarily in terms of economic interdependence) and military restraint is that by Gerald Schneider, Katherine Barbieri, and Nils Petter Gleditsch, eds., *Globalization and Armed Conflict* (Lanham, Md.: Rowman & Littlefield, 2003). Marxist scholars, such as Lenin and Hobson, expect the opposite causal effect. They argue that a global capitalist economy will lead to imperialist wars as states compete for overseas markets for raw materials and markets for surplus goods and capital. See Vladimir I. Lenin, *Imperialism: The Highest Stage of Capitalism (a Popular Outline)* (Moscow: Foreign Languages Publishing House, 1947); John A. Hobson, *Imperialism: A Study* (London: Allen & Unwin, 1948 [1902]).

24. See, for example, Norrin M. Ripsman, "False Dichotomy: Why Economics Has Always Been High Politics," pp. 15–31 in *Guns and Butter: The Political Economy of the New Security Environment*, eds. Peter Dombrowski, Susan Eckert, and William Keller (Boulder, Colo.: Lynne Rienner, 2005).

25. Peter F. Drucker, "The Global Economy and the Nation-State," *Foreign Affairs*, 76, no. 5 (September–October 1997): 170–171; Mark W. Zacher, "The Decaying Pillars of the Westphalian Temple: Implications for International Order and Governance," pp. 58–101 in *Governance without Government: Order and Change in World Politics*, eds. James N. Rosenau and Ernst-Otto Czempiel (Cambridge: Cambridge University Press, 1992), 60.

26. Stephen G. Brooks, "The Globalization of Production and the Changing Benefits of Conquest," *Journal of Conflict Resolution*, 43, no. 5 (October 1999): 646–670.

27. Rosecrance, *The Rise of the Trading State*. See also Richard N. Rosecrance, *The Rise of the Virtual State* (New York: Basic Books, 2000).

28. In Rosecrance's estimation, "[t]rading states recognize that they can do better economically through internal economic development sustained by a worldwide market for their goods and services than by trying to conquer and assimilate large tracts of land." See Rosecrance, *The Rise of the Trading State*, pp. 24–25. Stephen Van Evera similarly suggests that we have entered "the end of the age of extraction," as territorial conquest undermines, rather than facilitates, wealth creation. See Stephen Van Evera, "Primed for Peace: Europe after the Cold War," *International Security*, 15, no. 3 (Winter 1990–1991): 7–57. Stephen Brooks also argues that MNC-led production is stabilizing major powers, but need not promote peace in other parts of the world, especially among the developing states. See Brooks, *Producing Security*, 12–13. For a contrary perspective, see Peter Liberman, *Does Conquest Pay? The Exploitation*

of Occupied Industrial Societies (Princeton, N.J.: Princeton University Press, 1996).

29. Rosecrance maintains that where "capital, labor and information are mobile and have risen to predominance, no land fetish remains." Richard N. Rosecrance, "The Rise of the Virtual State," *Foreign Affairs*, 75, no. 4 (July/August 1996): 46–47.

30. Etel Solingen, *Regional Orders at Century's Dawn* (Princeton, N.J.: Princeton University Press, 1998), 46.

31. See, for example, Bruce Russett, *Grasping the Democratic Peace* (Princeton, N.J.: Princeton University Press, 1993); Steve Chan, "In Search of Democratic Peace: Problems and Promises," *Mershon International Studies Review*, 41, no. 1 (May 1997): 59–85; Michael Doyle, "Liberalism and World Politics," *American Political Science Review*, 80, no. 4 (December 1986): 1151–1169; Fred Chernoff, "The Study of Democratic Peace and Progress in International Relations," *International Studies Review*, 6, no. 1 (2004): 49–77.

32. See, for example, Margaret G. Hermann and Charles W. Kegley, Jr., "Rethinking Democracy and International Peace: Perspectives from Political Psychology," *International Studies Quarterly*, 39, no. 4 (December 1995): 514; Russett, *Grasping the Democratic Peace*, 38–40; James Lee Ray, "A Lakatosian View of the Democratic Peace Research Programme: Does It Falsify Realism (or Neorealism)?," in *Progress in International Relations Theory: Appraising the Field*, eds. Colin Elman and Miriam Fendius Elman (Cambridge, Mass.: MIT Press, 2003), 230–235.

33. William J. Dixon, "Democracy and the Peaceful Settlement of International Conflict," *American Political Science Review*, 88, no. 1 (1994): 14–32; John M. Owen, "How Liberalism Produces the Democratic Peace," *International Security*, 19, no. 2 (Fall 1994): 87–125; Bruce Russett and Zeev Maoz, "Normative and Structural Causes of Democratic Peace," *American Political Science Review*, 87, no. 3 (September 1993): 624–638.

34. This rationale has led both theorists and policy makers to conclude that the transnational spread of democracy is the surest way to global peace and stability. See, for example, Joshua Muravchik, *Exporting Democracy: Fulfilling America's Destiny* (Washington, D.C.: AEI Press, 1991); Larry Diamond, "Promoting Democracy," *Foreign Policy*, 87 (1992): 25–46; Russett, *Grasping the Democratic Peace*, 124–138. This argument, however, has been challenged by scholars such as Edward Mansfield and Jack Snyder, and Fareed Zakaria, who have noted the propensity of democratic states in their early stages to engage in conflict more often and the "illiberal" nature of many of the new democracies. See Edward D. Mansfield and Jack Snyder, *Electing to Fight: Why Emerging Democracies Go to War* (Cambridge, Mass.: MIT Press, 2005); Fareed Zakaria, *The Future of Freedom: Illiberal Democracy at Home and Abroad* (New York: W. W. Norton, 2004).

35. Mark W. Zacher, "The Territorial Integrity Norm: International Boundaries and the Use of Force," *International Organization*, 55, no. 2 (Spring 2001): 215–250.

36. For instance, see Thomas Risse et al., eds., *The Power of Human Rights: International Norms and Domestic Change* (Cambridge: Cambridge University Press, 1999).

37. Regarding the norm of nuclear nonuse, see T. V. Paul, *The Tradition of Non-Use of Nuclear Weapons* (Stanford, Calif.: Stanford University Press, 2009); Nina Tannenwald, *The Nuclear Taboo: The United States and the Non-Use of Nuclear Weapons since 1945* (Cambridge: Cambridge University Press, 2007). Regarding the nuclear nonproliferation regime, see Zachary S. Davis, "The Realist Nuclear Regime," *Security Studies*, 2, nos. 3 & 4 (September 1993): 79–99; Keith Krause and Andrew Latham, "Constructing Non-proliferation and Arms Control: The Norms of Western Practice," *Contemporary Security Policy*, 19, no. 1 (April 1998): 23–54. Regarding the land mine ban, see Richard Price, "Reversing the Gun Sights: Transnational Civil Society Targets Land Mines," *International Organization*, 52, no. 3 (Summer 1998): 613–644; Kenneth R. Rutherford, "The Evolving Arms Control Agenda: Implications of the Role of NGOs in Banning Antipersonnel Landmines," *World Politics*, 53, no. 1 (October 2000): 74–114.

38. For these positions, see Price, "Reversing the Gun Sights"; Martha Finnemore, "Constructing Norms of Humanitarian Intervention," in *The Culture of National Security: Norms and Identity in World Politics*, ed. Peter J. Katzenstein (New York: Columbia University Press, 1996), 153–185.

39. Peter L. Berger, "Four Faces of Global Culture," *The National Interest*, 49 (Fall 1997): 23–30.

40. Mittelman, *The Globalization Syndrome*, 6. See also Anthony Giddens, *The Consequences of Modernity* (Cambridge: Polity Press, 1990), 64; Mittelman, *Globalization: Critical Reflections*, chap. 6.

41. See Held et al., *Global Transformations*, chap. 7; Martin Albrow, *The Global Age: State and Society beyond Modernity* (Stanford, Calif.: Stanford University Press, 1997). For a more nuanced view of the relationship between globalization and culture, see John Tomlinson, *Globalization and Culture* (Chicago, Ill.: University of Chicago Press, 1999).

42. Stanley Hoffmann, "Clash of Globalizations," *Foreign Affairs*, 81, no. 4 (July/August 2002): 112. With regard to September 11 and its implications, see Ashton B. Carter, "The Architecture of Government in the Face of Terrorism," *International Security*, 26, no. 3 (Winter 2001–2002): 5–23; Stephen M. Walt, "Beyond bin Laden: Reshaping US Foreign Policy," *International Security*, 26, no. 3 (Winter 2001–2002): 56–78; Michael Howard "What Is in a Name? How to Fight Terrorism," *Foreign Affairs*, 81, no. 1 (January/February 2002): 8–13; Audrey Kurth Cronin, "Behind the Curve: Globalization and International Terrorism," *International Security*, 27, no. 3 (Winter 2002–2003): 30–58.

43. We recognize that these propositions are not entirely independent of each other, because one variable inherent in a proposition may affect another one

and vice versa. Nonetheless, for analytical purposes, it is useful to separate them.

44. Zaki Laidi, *A World without Meaning: The Crisis of Meaning in International Politics*, trans. June Burnham and Jenny Coulon (London: Routledge, 1998), 94; quoted in Ian Clark, *Globalization and International Relations Theory* (Oxford: Oxford University Press, 1999), 107.

45. John Mueller, *Retreat from Doomsday: The Obsolescence of Major War* (New York: Basic Books, 1989).

46. David Held and Anthony McGrew, "Globalization and the Liberal Democratic State," *Government and Opposition*, 28, no. 2 (Spring 1993): 267. See also Mary Kaldor, "Reconceptualizing Organized Violence," pp. 91–112 in *Re-imagining Political Community: Studies in Cosmopolitan Democracy*, eds. Daniele Archibugi, David Held, and Martin Köhler (Cambridge: Cambridge University Press, 1998), 103; Clark, *Globalization and International Relations Theory*, 108–109.

47. See, for example, Robert Mandel, *Deadly Transfers and the Global Playground* (New York: Praeger, 1999); Dilip K. Das and Peter C. Kratcoski, eds., *Meeting the Challenges of Global Terrorism: Prevention, Control, and Recovery* (Lanham, Md.: Lexington, 2003); Walter Enders and Todd Sandler, *The Political Economy of Terrorism* (Cambridge: Cambridge University Press, 2006), 158–159.

48. Graeme Allison, *Nuclear Terrorism: The Ultimate Preventable Catastrophe* (New York: Henry Holt, 2004).

49. Held et al., *Global Transformations*, 101. This is especially true of nuclear states, but is also true of all states with access to modern conventional arsenals. See Mueller, *Retreat from Doomsday*. For a critical perspective, see Robert Jervis, "The Political Effects of Nuclear Weapons," *International Security*, 13, no. 2 (Fall 1988): 80–90.

50. Loren B. Thompson, "Low-Intensity Conflict: An Overview," in *Low-Intensity Conflict: The Pattern of Warfare in the Modern World*, ed. Loren B. Thompson (Lexington, Mass.: Lexington Books, 1989); 1–23; Holsti, *The State, War, and the State of War*, 36–41.

51. Martin Van Creveld, *The Rise and Decline of States* (Cambridge: Cambridge University Press, 1999), 394–408. For a discussion of a different set of economic threats to the nation-state, see Ohmae, *The End of the Nation Sate*; Lipschutz, *After Authority*.

52. Lawrence Freedman, "International Security: Changing Targets," *Foreign Policy*, 110 (Spring 1998): 48–63.

53. Michael T. Klare, "Waging Postindustrial Warfare on the Global Battlefield," *Current History*, 100, no. 650 (December 2001): 433–437.

54. See, for example, Mandel, *Deadly Transfers and the Global Playground*.

55. Regarding the "securitization" of nontraditional threats, see Barry Buzan, Ole Wæver, and Jaap de Wilde, *Security: A New Framework for Analysis* (Boulder, Colo.: Lynne Rienner, 1998).

56. Giddens, *The Consequences of Modernity*, 74–75; Van Creveld, *The Rise and Decline of States*, 352–353.

57. Regarding these strategies, see T. V. Paul, James J. Wirtz, and Michel Fortmann, eds., *Balance of Power: Theory and Practice in the 21st Century* (Stanford, Calif.: Stanford University Press, 2004). Regarding soft balancing, see T. V. Paul, "Soft Balancing in the Age of U.S. Primacy," *International Security*, 30, no. 1 (Summer 2005): 46–71; Robert A. Pape, "Soft Balancing against the United States," *International Security*, 30, no. 1 (Summer 2005): 7–45; Stephen M. Walt, *Taming American Power: The Global Response to U.S. Primacy* (New York: W. W. Norton, 2005), 126–132.

58. Paul, "Soft Balancing in the Age of U.S. Primacy," 54–55.

59. Smaller armies have an additional advantage in the modern world, where democracies no longer have the stomach for war, at least if they anticipate casualties. Edward Luttwak attributes this to shrinking family size and, therefore, the decreased willingness of families to part with loved ones in war. See Edward Luttwak, "Toward Post-Heroic Warfare," *Foreign Affairs*, 74, no. 3 (May/June 1995): 109–122. See also Mann, "Has Globalization Ended the Rise and Rise of the Nation-State?"

60. Van Creveld, *The Rise and Decline of States*, 412–414. Among globalization theorists, Anthony Giddens is the exception, arguing that a shift to a higher tech military should actually increase defense spending, because even poorer states must purchase expensive, high-tech weaponry to survive. See Anthony Giddens, *The Consequences of Modernity*, 74–75.

61. Jessica T. Mathews, "Power Shift," *Foreign Affairs*, 76, no. 1 (January/February 1997): 50–51; Lipschutz, *After Authority*, 43; Andreas and Price, "From War Fighting to Crime Fighting," 31–52.

62. Robert Mandel, *The Changing Face of National Security* (Westport, Conn.: Greenwood, 1994), 1–8.

63. Cha, "Globalization and the Study of National Security."

64. Deborah D. Avant, *The Market for Force: The Consequences of Privatizing Security* (Cambridge: Cambridge University Press, 2005); Christopher Coker, "Outsourcing War," *Cambridge Review of International Affairs*, 13, no. 3 (Autumn/Winter 1999): 95–113; Van Creveld, *The Rise and Decline of States*, 404–407; Robert Mandel, "The Privatization of Security," Presented at the ISA Conference, Los Angeles, California, March 14–18, 2000.

65. See, for example, David Shearer, "Private Armies and Military Intervention," *Adelphi Paper*, 316 (February 1998), Jakkie Cillers and Peggy Mason, eds., *Peace, Profit, or Plunder? The Privatization of Security in War-Torn African Societies* (South Africa: Institute for Security Studies, 1999).

66. Deborah Avant, "The Implications of Marketized Security for IR Theory: The Democratic Peace, Late State Building, and the Nature and Frequency of Conflict," *Perspectives on Politics*, 4, no. 3 (September 2006), 507.

67. Coker, "Globalisation and Insecurity in the Twenty-First Century," 54–56; Cha, "Globalization and the Study of National Security"; Ann Marie Clark, "Non-Governmental Organizations and Their Influence on International Society," *Journal of International Affairs*, 48, no. 2 (Winter 1995): 507–525; Margaret Keck and Katherine Sikkink, *Activists beyond Borders: Advocacy Networks in International Politics* (Ithaca, N.Y.: Cornell University Press, 1998); Ann Florini, ed., *The Third Force: The Rise of Transnational Civil Society* (Washington, D.C.: Japan Center for International Exchange and Carnegie Endowment, 2000).

68. Holsti, *The State, War, and the State of War*, 129; Held et al., *Global Transformations*, 124–135; Cha, "Globalization and the Study of National Security."

69. Holm and Sørensen, *Whose World Order?*, 15.

Chapter 2

1. See, for example, Kalevi J. Holsti, *The State, War, and the State of War* (Cambridge: Cambridge University Press, 1996), 36–41.

2. Ted Robert Gurr, Monty G. Marshall, and Deepa Khosla, eds., *Peace and Conflict 2001* (College Park: Center for International Development and Conflict Management, University of Maryland, 2001): 9.

3. Stockholm International Peace Research Institute, *SIPRI Yearbook 2000* (Oxford: Oxford University Press, 2001), 324.

4. The 2001 figures are from http://editors.sipri.se/pubs/yb02/app01a.html (accessed September 21, 2009). The 2006 figures come from Stockholm International Peace Research Institute, *SIPRI Yearbook 2007* (Oxford: Oxford University Press, 2008), 79. SIPRI does not count the conflict between Israel and Hezbollah in Lebanon in 2006 as a major armed conflict because the estimated death toll was less than a thousand individuals. The number of major armed conflicts has declined steadily since 1999, and the figures for 2005 and 2006 are the lowest for the entire post-Cold War period (1990–2005). Stockholm International Peace Research Institute, *SIPRI Yearbook 2006* (Oxford: Oxford University Press, 2007), 108.

5. Raimo Väyrynen, "Globalization and Local Violence," Presented at the APSA Conference, San Francisco, California, September 2001.

6. Ted Robert Gurr and Monty Marshall, *Peace and Conflict 2003: A Global Survey of Armed Conflicts, Self-Determination Movements, and Democracy* (College Park: Center for International Development and Conflict Management, University of Maryland, 2003), 13.

7. Mohammed Ayoob, *The Third World Security Predicament: Statemaking, Regional Conflict, and the International System* (Boulder, Colo.: Lynne Rienner, 1995); Bruce D. Porter, *The USSR in Third World Conflicts* (Cambridge: Cambridge University Press, 1986); William Blum, *Killing Hope: US Military and CIA Interventions since World War II* (Eastbourne, UK: Gardner's Books, 2003).

8. According to one study, the conclusion of the Cold War rivalry helped to end about one third of all ongoing conflicts, both interstate and intrastate, by the early 1990s. See Human Security Center, *Human Security Report, 2005* (Oxford: Oxford University Press, 2005), 8.

9. The best statement of this argument is found in Robert Gilpin, *War and Change in World Politics* (Cambridge: Cambridge University, 1981). See also Stephen D. Krasner, "State Power and the Structure of International Trade," *World Politics*, 28, no. 3 (April 1976): 317–347; Charles P. Kindleberger, *The World in Depression, 1929–1939* (Berkeley: University of California Press, 1973), chap. 14; and A. F. K. Organski and Jacek Kugler, *The War Ledger* (Chicago, Ill.: University of Chicago Press, 1980).

10. William C. Wohlforth, "The Stability of a Unipolar World," *International Security*, 24, no. 1 (Summer 1999): 5–41.

11. Robert Jervis, "Cooperation under the Security Dilemma," *World Politics*, 30, no. 2 (January 1978): 167–214. Regarding the significance of the offense–defense balance in determining patterns of war and peace, see Sean M. Lynn-Jones, "Does Offense–Defense Theory Have a Future?," Working paper 12 (Montreal: University of Montreal-McGill Research Group in International Security, October 2000).

12. Jervis, "Cooperation under the Security Dilemma," p. 214.

13. Regarding the role of ideas, see John Mueller, *Retreat from Doomsday: The Obsolescence of Major War* (New York: Basic Books, 1989). For discussions of these and other factors, see chapters in Raimo Varnynen, ed., *The Waning of Major War: Theories and Debates* (New York: Routledge, 2005), especially Väyrynen, "The Waning of Major Wars: Contending Views" (pp. 1–30); John Mueller, "Does War Still Exist?" (pp. 64–79); and Kalevi J. Holsti, "The Changing International System and the Decline of Major War" (134–149).

14. Jean-Marc F. Blanchard, Edward D. Mansfield, and Norrin M. Ripsman, "The Political Economy of National Security: Economic Statecraft, Interdependence and International Conflict," *Security Studies*, 9, no. 1 (Autumn 1999): 1–15. The classic work on economic statecraft is found in David A. Baldwin, *Economic Statecraft* (Princeton, N.J.: Princeton University Press, 1985).

15. See, for example, David A. Cortright, ed., *The Price of Peace: Incentives and International Conflict Prevention* (Lanham, Md.: Rowman & Littlefield, 1997); Patricia A. Davis, *The Art of Economic Persuasion: Positive Incentives and German Economic Diplomacy* (Ann Arbor: University of Michigan Press, 1999); Daniel W. Drezner, *The Sanctions Paradox: Economic Statecraft and International Relations* (Cambridge: Cambridge University Press, 1999); Randall Newnham, *Deutsche Mark Diplomacy: Positive Economic Sanctions in German–Russian Relations* (University Park, Pa.: Pennsylvania State University Press, 2002).

16. Kimberly Ann Elliott and Barbara Oegg, "Economic Sanctions Reconsidered—Again: Trends in Sanctions Policy in the 1990s," Presented at the International Studies Association Convention, New Orleans, Louisiana, March 23–26, 2002.

Regarding the increasing use of UN sanctions, see also George A. Lopez and David Cortright with Julia Wagler. 2000. "Learning from the Sanctions Decade," http://www.fourthfreedom.org/Applications/cms.php?page_id=41 (accessed February 23, 2009).

17. See David Cortright and George A. Lopez, with Linda Gerber, *Sanctions and the Search for Security: Challenges to UN Action* (London: Lynne Rienner, 2002).

18. One notable exception to this trend was the successful use of both economic incentives and sanctions to end the Libyan weapons of mass destruction programs and bring about Libyian cooperation with the Lockerbee bombing trial. The threat of force, however, contributed to this successful use of economic statecraft. See Bruce W. Jentleson and Christopher A. Whytock, "Who 'Won' Libya? The Force–Diplomacy Debate and Its Implications for Theory and Policy," *International Security*, 30, no. 3 (Winter 2005–2006): 47–86.

19. Gary Clyde Hufbauer, Jeffrey J. Schott, Kimberly Ann Elliott, and Barbara Oegg, *Economic Sanctions Reconsidered*, 3rd ed. (Washington, D.C.: Peterson Institute for International Economics, 2007), 34–38.

20. See Robert A Pape, "Why Economic Sanctions Do Not Work," *International Security*, 22, no. 2 (Fall 1997): 90–136. For a more nuanced view, see Jean-Marc F. Blanchard and Norrin M. Ripsman, "Asking the Right Question: *When* Do Economic Sanctions Work?" *Security Studies*, 9, no. 1 (Autumn 1999): 228–264; Jean-Marc F. Blanchard and Norrin M. Ripsman, "A Political Theory of Economic Statecraft," *Foreign Policy Analysis*, 4, no. 4 (October 2008): 373–400.

21. See, for example, Johan Galtung, "On the Effects of International Economic Sanctions: With Examples from the Case of Rhodesia," *World Politics*, 19, no. 3 (April 1967): 378–416; Peter Wallensteen, "Economic Sanctions: Ten Modern Cases and Three Important Lessons," in *Dilemmas of Economic Coercion*, eds. Miroslav Nincic and Peter Wallensteen (New York: Praeger, 1983): 87–129; Richard N. Haass, "Sanctioning Madness," *Foreign Affairs*, 76, no. 6 (November/ December 1997): 74–85.

22. The definitive large-n study by Gary Clyde Hufbauer et al. (*Economic Sanctions Reconsidered*, 3rd ed.), for example, concludes that sanctions are effective only about one third of the time. Although A. Cooper Drury's critical reevaluation of their study challenges some of their proposed theoretical linkages, it does not dispute their general categorization of success. See A. Cooper Drury, *Economic Sanctions and Presidential Decisions: Models of Political Rationality* (New York: Palgrave Macmillan, 2005), 32–58.

23. Baldwin, *Economic Statecraft*, chaps. 7–8.

24. See Stephen Brooks, *Producing Security: Multinational Corporations, Globalization, and the Changing Nature of Conflict* (Princeton, N.J.: Princeton University Press, 2005). For research challenging his findings, see Norrin M. Ripsman and Christopher Way, "International Political Tensions and Foreign Investment," Presented at the 2007 annual meeting of the American Political Science Association, Chicago, Illinois, August 30–September 2, 2007.

25. Thomas L. Friedman, *The World Is Flat* (New York: Farrar, Straus and Giroux, 2005), 425–427.

26. Among globalization theorists, Anthony Giddens is the exception, arguing that a shift to a higher tech military during the contemporary era should actually increase defense spending, because even poorer states must purchase high-tech weaponry to survive. See Anthony Giddens, *The Consequences of Modernity* (Stanford, Calif.: Stanford University Press, 1990), 74–75.

27. SIPRI Military Expenditure Database, http://www.sipri.org/contents/milap/milex/mex_wnr_table.html (accessed June 9, 2008).

28. Human Security Center, *Human Security Report 2005*, 8–9. Regarding the general impact of the end of major wars, see G. John Ikenberry, *After Victory* (Princeton, N.J.: Princeton University Press, 2001).

29. Stockholm International Peace Research Institute, *SIPRI Yearbook 2007*, 278.

30. Congressional Budget Office, "An Analysis of the President's Budgetary Proposals for Fiscal Year 2009," March 2008, http://www.cbo.gov/ftpdocs/89xx/doc8990/03-19-AnalPresBudget.pdf (accessed June 7, 2008), 17–20.

31. Stockholm International Peace Research Institute, *SIPRI Yearbook 2000*, 245–247. In 2002, China increased its defense spending by nearly 18% for the second year in succession. See "China's Defense Budget," http://www.globalsecurity.org/military/world/china/budget.htm (accessed October 3, 2005).

32. Stockholm International Peace Research Institute, *SIPRI Yearbook, 2001*, 257.

33. This might explain why the rising power, China, pursues policies to boost both trade and military modernization, whereas a newly liberalizing economy such as India's is seeking more trade, and at the same time increasing its defense expenditures. In 2001, for example, China emerged as the largest arms recipient, after registering an increase of 44% from 2000, whereas imports by India increased by 50% for the same period, making it the third largest recipient for the year. See Bjorn Hagelin et al., "International Arms Transfers," chapter 8 in *SIPRI Yearbook, 2002*, http://editors.sipri.se/pubs/yb02/ch08.html (accessed October 3, 2005).

34. Congressional Research Service, Report to Congress, "Conventional Arms Transfers to Developing Nations, 1999–2006," September 26, 2007, http://www.fas.org/sgp/crs/weapons/RL34187.pdf (accessed June 7, 2008), p. 81.

35. Ibid., 78.

36. Stockholm International Peace Research Institute, *SIPRI Yearbook 2004*, 418–421.

37. Regarding the relative advantages of autarky and market-based security policy, see Alan S. Millward, *War, Economy and Society* (Berkeley: University of California Press, 1977); William Carr, *Arms, Autarky and Aggression* (New York: Norton, 1973); David A. Baldwin, *Economic Statecraft* (Princeton, N.J.: Princeton University Press, 1985), chap. 5; Edward Mead Earle, "Adam Smith, Alexander Hamilton, Friedrich List: The Economic Foundations of Military Power," in *Makers of Modern Strategy*, ed. Peter Paret (Oxford: Clarendon Press, 1986),

217–261; Norrin M. Ripsman, "False Dichotomy: Why Economics Has Always Been High Politics," pp. 15–31 in *Guns and Butter: The Political Economy of the New Security Environment*, ed. Peter Dombrowski (Boulder, Colo.: Lynne Rienner, 2005),

38. Figures are from International Institute for Strategic Studies, *The Military Balance*, annual editions from 1995/1996 through 2007 (London: International Institute for Strategic Studies).

39. For a detailed discussion of the size of national armed forces on a country-by-country and regional basis, see chapters 3 through 6 in this volume.

40. Siddharth Srivastava, "A US$10bn Scramble for India's Fighter Jets," *Asia Times*, July 12, 2007, http://www.atimes.com/atimes/South_Asia/IG12Df03. html (accessed July 25, 2007); Jonathan Watts, "Asian Arms Race Fear as Beijing Raises Spending," *The Guardian*, March 5, 2007, http://www.guard-ian.co.uk/china/story/0,,2026729,00.html (accessed July 25, 2007).

41. Thus, for example, Margaret P. Karns and Karen A. Mingst maintain that even the United States has, on occasion, been constrained by the rules and decisions of IGOs to which it belongs. See Margaret P. Karns and Karen A. Mingst, *The United States and Multilateral Institutions* (Boston, Mass.: Unwin Hyman, 1990), 1–10. See also, Todd Sandler, *Global Collective Action* (Cambridge: Cambridge University Press, 2004).

42. See Holsti, *The State, War, and the State of War*, 129; and David Held et al., *Global Transformations: Politics, Economics and Culture* (Stanford, Calif.: Stanford University Press, 1999), 124–135.

43. See, for example, Kenneth A. Oye, "Beyond Postwar Order and New World Order: American Foreign Policy in Transition," in *Eagle in a New World: American Grand Strategy in the Post-Cold War Era*, eds. Kenneth A. Oye, Robert J. Lieber, and Donald Rothchild (New York: HarperCollins, 1992), 3–34; Meena Bose and Rosanna Perotti, eds., *From Cold War to New World Order: The Foreign Policy of George H. W. Bush* (Westport, Conn.: Greenwood, 2002).

44. See the 1997–2003 editions of the *SIPRI Yearbook*. For a critical discussion of these UN missions, see David M. Malone and Karin Wermester, "Boom or Bust? The Changing Nature of UN Peacekeeping," *International Peacekeeping*, 7, no. 4 (2000): 37–54.

45. For these data, see UN Peacekeeping Department, "Facts and Figures," http://www.un.org/Depts/dpko/dpko/factsfigs.shtml (accessed May 7, 2008).

46. For a discussion of post-Cold War interventions, see Karen A. Mingst and Margaret P. Karns, *The United Nations in the Post-Cold War Era*, 2nd ed. (Boulder, Colo.: Westview Press, 2000), 111.

47. As S. Neil MacFarlane and Thomas Weiss argue: "In fact there exists an intimate relationship between politics and humanitarianism which the practitioners of humanitarian intervention often tend to ignore" (p. 112). See S. Neil MacFarlane and Thomas Weiss, "Political Interests and Humanitarian Action," *Security Studies*, 10, no. 1 (Autumn 2000): 112–142.

48. See the 1998–2003 editions of the *SIPRI Yearbook*.

49. For a discussion of these institutions, see Paul-Henri Bischoff, "Regionalism and Regional Cooperation in Africa: New Century Challenges and Prospects," pp. 121–146 in *Africa at the Crossroads: Between Regionalism and Globalization*, eds. John Mukum Mbaku and Suresh Chandra Saxena (Westport, Conn.: Praeger, 2004), 121.

50. For a description of these efforts, see Stephen F. Burgess, "African Security in the 21st Century: The Challenges of Indigenization and Multilateralism," *African Studies Review*, 41, no. 2 (September 1998): 44.

51. These strategies are discussed in Margaret E. Keck and Kathryn Sikkink, *Activists Beyond Borders: Advocacy Networks in International Politics* (Ithaca, N.Y.: Cornell University Press, 1998), 1–37; Thomas Risse-Kappen, "Bringing Transnational Relations Back In: Introduction," in *Bringing Transnational Relations Back In: Non-State Actors, Domestic Structures and International Institutions*, ed. Thomas Risse-Kappen (Cambridge: Cambridge University Press, 1995), 3–33; Steven F. Bernstein and Benjamin Cashore, "Globalization, Four Paths of Internationalization and Domestic Policy Change: The Case of EcoForestry in British Columbia, Canada," *Canadian Journal of Political Science*, 33, no. 1 (March 2000): 67–99.

52. Sidney Tarrow, *The New Transnational Activism* (Cambridge: Cambridge University Press, 2005), 44–45.

53. Mingst and Karns, *The United Nations*, 111; Price, "Reversing Gun Sights"; Kenneth R. Rutherford, "The Evolving Arms Control Agenda: Implications of the Role of NGOs in Banning Antipersonnel Landmines," *World Politics*, 53, no. 1 (October 2000): 74–114. There has been an increase in the number of individuals and organizations acting on the world stage "directly, unmediated by a state." For instance, Jody Williams was able to mobilize more than one thousand NGOs in support of the land mine ban through e-mail against the opposition from the P-5 members of the UN Security Council. See Thomas L. Friedman, "The Impact of Globalization on World Peace," Working paper 27 (Los Angeles: Burkle Center for International Relations, UCLA, January 2001): 6.

54. Rebecca Johnson, "Indefinite Extension of the Non-proliferation Treaty: Risks and Reckonings," http://www.acronym.org.uk/a07ext.htm (accessed October 3, 2005).

55. Stanley Hoffmann, "Clash of Globalizations," *Foreign Affairs*, 81, no. 4 (July/August 2002): 109.

56. In June 2001, the IMF signed an agreement with Pakistan to provide special drawing rights for $465 billion. In return, Pakistan agreed to reduce its defense spending by PKR 2 billion. See

International Monetary Fund, "Pakistan—Letter of Intent, Memorandum of Economic and Financial Policies, and Technical Memorandum of Understanding," June 27, 2001, http://www.imf.org/external/np/loi/2001/pak/02/index.htm (accessed October 3, 2005).

57. Laurie R. Blank, "The Role of International Financial Institutions in International Humanitarian Law," *Peaceworks*, 42, Washington D.C., US Institute of Peace (January 2002), 16.

58. See for example, David Rapkin and Jonathan Strand, "Reforming the IMF's Weighted Voting System," http://www.g24.0rg/Rapkin.pdf (accessed October 3, 2005).

59. See, for example, Martin van Creveld, *The Rise and Decline of the State* (Cambridge: Cambridge University Press, 1999), 394–408.

60. Ashton B. Carter, "The Architecture of Government in the Face of Terrorism," *International Security*, 26, no. 3 (Winter 2001/2002): 6.

61. See, for example, Holsti, *The State, War, and the State of War*, 36–41.

62. National Counterterrorism Center, "Annex of Statistical Information," *Country Reports on Terrorism, 2007*, http://www.state.gov/s/ct/rls/crt/2007/103716.htm (accessed May 7, 2008). This represents an increase of more than 25% on the number of incidents in 2005, with more than 50% more casualties. See National Counterterrorism Center, *Report on Incidents of Terrorism, 2005*, April 11, 2006, http://wits.nctc.gov/reports/crot2005nctcannexfinal.pdf (accessed April 17, 2008), ix.

63. John Mueller, for example, argues that terrorism has taken a comparatively insignificant toll on the Unites States. See John Mueller, *Overblown: How Politicians and the Terrorism Industry Inflate National Security Threats, and Why We Believe Them* (New York: Free Press, 2006).

64. Regarding the toughening of French immigration laws, see Virginie Guiraudon, "Immigration Politics and Policies," in *Developments in French Politics 3*, eds. Jonah Levy, Alistair Cole, and Patrick Le Galès (New York: Palgrave Macmillan, 2005), 154–169. Regarding changes to the Dutch treatment of immigrants, which includes revoking residency permits for aliens that break the law and an integration test for prospective citizens, see "Harsher Treatment for Alien Offenders," http://www.government.nl/actueel/nieuwsarchief/2005/09September/30/0–42–1_42–71997.jsp (accessed April 2, 2007); "Government Adopts New Integration System," http://www.government.nl/actueel/nieuwsarchief/2004/12December/07/0–42–1_42–51591.jsp (accessed April 2, 2007).

65. For a discussion of this topic see T. V. Paul, "The National Security State and Global Terrorism: Why the State Is Not Prepared for the New Kind of War," in *Globalization, Security and the Nation-State*, eds. Ersel Aydinli and James N. Rosenau (Albany: SUNY Press, 2005), 49–64.

66. Regarding the challenge of international piracy and its comparison with the challenge of terrorism, see Oded Löwenheim, *Predators and Parasites: Persistent Agents of Transnational Harm and Great Power Authority* (Ann Arbor: University of Michigan Press); Angus Konstam, *Piracy: The Complete History* (Oxford: Osprey Publishing, 2008).

67. Hedley Bull, "The State's Positive Role in World Affairs," *Daedalus*, 108, no. 4 (Fall 1979), 111–123.

68. See George W. Bush, *The National Security Strategy of the United States of America* (Washington, D.C.: The White House, 2002).

69. See, for example, Steven M. Fish, *Democracy Derailed in Russia: The Failure of Open Politics* (New York: Cambridge University Press, 2005).

70. For a database of all counterterrorism legislation and policy changes by UN members, see http://www.un.org/Docs/sc/committees/1373/submitted_reports. html (accessed January 9, 2007).

71. See Philip G. Cerny, "The New Security Dilemma: Divisibility, Defection and Disorder in the Global Era," *Review of International Studies*, 26, no. 4 (October 2000): 623–646.

Chapter 3

1. Department of Defense, *Quadrennial Defense Review Report* (Washington, D.C.: Department of Defense, 2006), 36.

2. George W. Bush, *The National Security Strategy of the United States of America* (Washington, D.C.: The White House, 2002).

3. See George W. Bush, *The National Security Strategy of the United States of America* (Washington, D.C.: The White House, 2006), 1.

4. U.S. State Department, "Trends in Global Terrorism," April 2006, http:// hosted.ap.org/specials/interactives/wdc/documents/terrorism/keyjudgments_ 092606.pdf (accessed June 4, 2008).

5. National Intelligence Council, "The Terrorist Threat to the US Homeland," National Intelligence Estimate, July 2007, http://www.dni.gov/press_ releases/20070717_release.pdf (accessed July 21, 2007).

6. Bush, *National Security Strategy*, 2002, 17–20, 23.

7. Bush, *National Security Strategy*, 2006, 25–35. The document argues that "[d]evelopment reinforces diplomacy and defense, reducing long-term threats to our national security by helping to build stable, prosperous and peaceful societies" (p. 33).

8. Ibid., 47–48.

9. Department of Defense, *Quadrennial Defense Review*, 41–61.

10. Interviews with Christopher "Ryan" Henry, Under Secretary of Defense (Policy), U.S. Department of Defense, August 30, 2005; Robert A. Manning, Senior Counselor, Energy Technology and Science Policy, U.S. Department of State; and Richard D. Sokolsky, Policy Planning Staff, U.S. Department of State, August 29, 2005.

11. Anthony Lake, "From Containment to Enlargement," Address to the School of Advanced International Studies, Johns Hopkins University, September 21, 1993, http://www.mtholyoke.edu/acad/intrel/lakedoc.html (accessed June 6, 2008).

12. Bush, *National Security Strategy*, 2002, 6.

13. Bush, *National Security Strategy*, 2006, 1.

14. Ibid., 5.

15. Ibid., 6.

16. Ibid., 23.

17. David C. Mulford, "U.S.–India Relationship to Reach New Heights," March 31, 2005, http://newdelhi.usembassy.gov/ambmar312005.html (accessed April 30, 2007); Condoleeza Rice, "Our Opportunity with India," *Washington Post*, March 13, 2006, A15.

18. Data on national manpower for this chapter come from International Institute for Strategic Studies, *The Military Balance*, 1989–2007 issues (London: International Institute for Strategic Studies).

19. The 1990–2006 defense spending figures for all countries and regions (in 2005 constant U.S. dollars) are from Stockholm International Peace Research Institute, *SIPRI Yearbook 2007*, http://www.sipri.org/contents/milap/milex/mex_wnr_table.html (accessed June 26, 2007).

20. See Department of Defense, *Quadrennial Defense Review*, 43–45.

21. See, for example, William C. Wohlforth, "The Stability of a Unipolar World," *International Security*, 24, no. 1 (Summer 1999): 5–41.

22. Department of Defense, *Quadrennial Defense Review*, 41–61.

23. Anthony Giddens, *The Consequences of Modernity* (Cambridge: Polity Press, 1990), 74–75.

24. See Bush, *National Security Strategy*, 2002, 29–31; Bush, *National Security Strategy*, 2006, 43–44.

25. Bush, *National Security Strategy*, 2002, 10.

26. Bush, *National Security Strategy*, 2006. These groups were conspicuously absent in the 2002 iteration, as well.

27. Sue E. Eckert, "Protecting Critical Infrastructure: The Role of the Private Sector," in *Guns & Butter: The Political Economy of National Security*, ed. Peter Dombrowski (Boulder, Colo.: Lynne Rienner, 2005), 179–201.

28. See Deborah Clay-Mendez, *Public and Private Roles in Maintaining Military Equipment at Depot Level* (Washington, D.C.: Congressional Budget Office, 1995).

29. Department of Defense, *Quadrennial Defense Review*, 75. This document does not focus much on the role of these contractors, and its discussion efforts to streamline management and supply chain issues revolve exclusively around internal reorganization, rather than external contractors and NGOs (pp. 63–73).

30. For the argument that "Mercenary Incorporated" is playing an increasing role in support of U.S. operations abroad, see Ken Silverstein, *Private Warriors* (New York: Verso, 2000), chap. 4.

31. Deborah D. Avant, *The Market for Force: The Consequences of Privatizing Security* (Cambridge: Cambridge University Press, 2005), 147–148.

32. See Renae Merle, "Census Counts 100,000 Contractors in Iraq," *Washington Post* (December 5, 2006), D1.

33. Scott Shane and Ron Nixon, "U.S. Contractors becoming a Fourth Branch of Government," *International Herald Tribune*, February 4, 2007, http://www.iht.com/bin/print.php?id=4460796 (accessed June 7, 2007).

34. Bush, *National Security Strategy*, 2006, 18, 22, 35.

35. Ibid., 37–42.

36. Ibid., 35.

37. Ibid., 37.

38. Robert Gilpin, *War and Change in International Politics* (Princeton, N.J.: Princeton University Press, 1981); and A. F. K. Organski and Jacek Kugler, *The War Ledger* (Chicago, Ill.: University of Chicago Press, 1980).

39. China, *China's National Defense in 2006*, sect. II, http://english.peopledaily.com.cn/whitepaper/defense2006/defense2006(2).html (accessed January 9, 2007).

40. Michael D. Swaine and Ashley J. Tellis, *Interpreting China's Grand Strategy: Past, Present and Future* (Santa Monica, Calif.: RAND, 2000), 121.

41. China, *China's National Defense in 2006*, sect. I, http://english.peopledaily.com.cn/whitepaper/defense2006/defense2006(1).html (accessed January 9, 2007).

42. For a relevant discussion, see James Millward, "Violent Separatism in Xinjiang: A Critical Assessment," *Policy Studies*, 6 (2004).

43. See Willy Wo-Lap Lam, "Terrorism Fight Used to Target China Secessionists," October 23, 2001, http://www.cnn.com/2001/WORLD/asiapcf/east/10/23/willy.china.split (accessed October 16, 2005); Seth Faison, "In Beijing: A Roar of Silent Protesters," *New York Times*, April 27, 1999, http://partners.nytimes.com/library/world/asia/042799china-protest.html (accessed January 8, 2007).

44. Regarding the Chinese approach to Tibetan separatists, see Carole McGranahan, "Kashmir and Tibet: Comparing Conflicts, States, and Solutions," *India Review*, 2, no. 3 (July 2003), 145–180; Chien-peng Chung, "Confronting Terrorism and Other Evils in China: All Quiet on the Western Front?" *China and Eurasia Forum Quarterly*, 4, no. 2 (2006), 75–87. Regarding the recent pre-Olympic crackdown, see "China Steps up Tibetan Crackdown," BBC News, March 20, 2008, http://news.bbc.co.uk/2/hi/asia-pacific/7306096.stm (accessed June 6, 2008).

45. See, for example, China, *China's National Defense in 2006*, sects. I and II.

46. See Norrin M. Ripsman and T. V. Paul, "Globalization and the National Security State: A Framework for Analysis," *International Studies Review*, 7, no. 2 (June 2005): 207.

47. China, *China's National Defense in 2006*, sect. I.

48. The White Paper states: "China's national defense, in keeping with and contributing to the country's development and security strategies, aims at maintaining national security and unity, and ensuring the realization of the goal of building a moderately prosperous society in an all-round way." China, *China's National Defense in 2006*, preface, http://english.peopledaily.

com.cn/whitepaper/defense2006/defense2006forward.html (accessed June 6, 2008).

49. China, *China's National Defense in 2006*, sect. II.

50. See, for example, Erik Eckholm, "Spread of SARS Acts as a Rude Awakening for China," *New York Times*, May 13, 2003, http://query.nytimes.com/gst/health/article-page.html?res=9806E0D9103FF930A25756C0A9659C8B63 (accessed November 6, 2005).

51. China, *China's National Defense in 2006*, preface.

52. See National Intelligence Council, "China," http://www.cia.gov/nic/graphics/battilega/china.pdf (accessed May 25, 2003); China, *China's National Defense in 2006*, sect. II.

53. The 2006 White Paper asserts: "China remains firmly committed to the policy of no first use of nuclear weapons at any time and under any circumstances. It unconditionally undertakes not to use or threaten to use nuclear weapons against non-nuclear-weapon states or nuclear-weapon-free zones, and stands for the comprehensive prohibition and complete elimination of nuclear weapons. China upholds the principles of counterattack in self-defense and limited development of nuclear weapons, and aims at building a lean and effective nuclear force capable of meeting national security needs." China, *China's National Defense in 2006*, sect. II.

54. See, for example, China, *China's National Defense in 2006*, sect. I.

55. Swaine and Tellis, *Interpreting China's Grand Strategy*, chap. 4.

56. Michael Pillsbury, *China Debates the Future Security Environment* (Honolulu, Hawaii: University Press of the Pacific, 2005), xxxix.

57. See Richard Weitz, "Why Russia and China Have Not Formed an Anti-American Alliance," *Naval War College Review*, 56, no. 4 (Autumn 2003): 39–57.

58. For a discussion of these efforts, see T. V. Paul, "Soft Balancing in the Age of U.S. Primacy," *International Security*, 30, no. 1 (Summer 2005): 46–71.

59. For a discussion, see Marc Lanteigne, *China and International Institutions: Alternate Path to Global Power* (London: Routledge, 2005).

60. China, *China's National Defense in 2006*, sect. IV, http://english.peopledaily.com.cn/whitepaper/defense2006/defense2006(4).html (accessed January 9, 2007). Earlier in the white paper, a discussion of the context of Chinese security observes the following: "A revolution in military affairs is developing in depth worldwide. Military competition based on informationization is intensifying. There has not been major change in the imbalances in relative military strength. Some developed countries have increased their input into the military and speeded up R & D of high-tech weaponry to gain military superiority. Many developing countries are also upgrading their armaments and modernizing their military forces." China, *China's National Defense in 2006*, sect. I. As with all manpower figures in this book, data on Chinese manpower comes from

International Institute for Strategic Studies, *The Military Balance*, 1989–2007 issues.

61. Moreover, these official figures may underestimate Chinese defense expenditures, which are said to be higher, because the "published defense budget does not include large categories of expenditure, including expenses for strategic forces, foreign acquisitions, military-related research and development, and China's paramilitary forces." "China's Defense Budget," http://www.globalsecurity.org/military/world/china/budget.htm (accessed June 23, 2008).

62. China, *China's National Defense in 2006*, sect. IX, http://english.peopledaily. com.cn/whitepaper/defense2006/defense2006(9).html (accessed June 6, 2008).

63. Indeed, the Chinese defense policy statement explicitly links the dramatic increase to Chinese economic development. Ibid.

64. These figures may be slightly exaggerated, given that we evaluated Chinese GDP based on IMF statistics in current U.S. dollars, which does not factor in inflation. Nonetheless, this is still a remarkable rate of growth, even discounting for inflation. By comparison, the U.S. rate of growth for the same period was only 215%. International Monetary Fund, "World Economic Outlook Database," April 2007, http://www.imf.org/external/pubs/ft/weo/2007/01/ data/index.aspx (accessed April 18, 2007).

65. Office of the Secretary of Defense, *Annual Report to Congress: The Military Power of the People's Republic of China 2005* (Washington D.C.: Office of the Secretary of Defense, 2005), http://www.dod.mil/news/Jul2005/d20050719china.pdf (accessed June 17, 2006); Giusepe Anzera, "The Modernization of the Chinese Navy," *Power and Interest News Report*, September 12, 2005, http://www.pinr. com/report.php?ac=view_printable&report_id=364&language_id=1 (accessed June 17, 2006).

66. China, *China's National Defense in 2006*, sect. II.

67. China, *China's National Defense in 2006*, sect. V, http://english.peopledaily. com.cn/whitepaper/defense2006/defense2006(5).html (accessed January 9, 2007).

68. We thank Pradeep Taneja for bringing this to our attention.

69. China, *China's National Defense in 2006*, sects. I and X.

70. See, for example, Dmitri Trenin, "Russia Leaves the West," *Foreign Affairs*, 85, no. 4 (July/August 2006): 87–96, which argues that Moscow has revived the concept of "Near Abroad" in recent years to indicate its heightened interest in former Soviet republics, such as Georgia and the Ukraine.

71. See Dov Lynch, *Russian Peacekeeping Strategies in the CIS: The Cases of Moldova, Georgia and Tajikistan* (New York: St. Martin's Press, 2000); Rajan Menon, "In the Shadow of the Bear: Security in Post-Soviet Central Asia." *International Security*, 20, no. 1 (Summer 1995): 149–181. Putin's government used his involvement in Georgia as part of its pressure tactics to prevent Georgia from

joining NATO. See "Georgia–Russia Tensions Ramped Up," BBC News, April 30, 2008, http://news.bbc.co.uk/2/hi/europe/7374546.stm (accessed April 30, 2008). Although Russia officially endorsed the UN action against Iraq in 1991, it did not send troops to participate in the Gulf War coalition.

72. "Russia's Military Doctrine 2000," sect. I, para. 7, http://www.armscontrol.org/act/2000_05/dc3ma00.asp (accessed May 26, 2003).

73. Regarding the Georgian War, see Roy Allison, "Russia Resurgent? Moscow's Campaign to 'Coerce Georgia to Peace,'" *International Affairs*, 84, no. 6 (November 2008): 1145–1171. For the latest iteration of the dispute between Russia and the Ukraine, which led to the disruption of natural gas supplies to all of western Europe, see David Jolly, "Russia–Ukraine Gas Dispute Enters 10th Day," *New York Times*, January 15, 2009, http://www.nytimes.com/2009/01/16/world/europe/16gazprom.html?partner=rss&emc=rss (accessed January 16, 2009). Regarding the threat to Poland by a leading Russian general, see Chris Baldwin, "Russia Could Strike Poland over Shield: Report," *Reuters*, August 16, 2008, http://www.reuters.com/article/newsOne/idUSLF16791020080816 (accessed January 16, 2009).

74. Regarding the conflict in Chechnya, see Gail W. Lapidus, "Contested Sovereignty: The Tragedy of Chechnya," *International Security*, 23, no. 1 (Summer 1998): 5–49; Tracey D. German, *Russia's Chechen War* (New York: Routledge Curzon, 2003); Mark Kramer, "The Perils of Counterinsurgency: Russia's War with Chechnya," *International Security*, 29, no. 3 (Winter 2004/2005): 5–62.

75. "Russia's Military Doctrine 2000," sect. I, para. 16b.

76. Ibid., sects. V, VI.

77. Ibid., sect. I, para. 8.

78. See Andrew E. Kramer, "Peace Plan Offers Russia an Opportunity to Advance," *New York Times*, August 13, 2008, http://www.nytimes.com/2008/08/14/world/europe/14document.html (accessed January 21, 2009).

79. Paul T. Mitchell, "The First Information War? Russia's Cyberwar against Estonia," *RSIS Commentaries*, vol. 43, May 12, 2007, pp. 1–3; "Russia Could Strike Poland over Shield: Report."

80. For a discussion of these efforts, see Paul, "Soft Balancing in the Age of U.S. Primacy"; William C. Wohlforth, "Russia's Soft Balancing Act," in *Strategic Asia, 2003–4: Fragility and Crisis*, eds. Richard Ellings and Aaron Fridberg, with Michael Wills (Seattle, Wash.: National Bureau of Asia Research, 2003), 165–179; Andrei P. Tsygankov, "Vladimir Putin's Vision of Russia as a Normal Great Power," *Post-Soviet Affairs*, 21, no. 2 (April–June 2005): 132–158.

81. See http://encarta.msn.com/encyclopedia_761553017/union_of_soviet_socialist_republics.html (accessed June 6, 2008).

82. "Russia's Military Doctrine 2000," sect. I, para. 6.

83. Peter W. Singer, *Corporate Warriors: The Rise of the Privatized Military Industry* (Ithaca, N.Y.: Cornell University Press, 2003), 11, 258, note 44. In Russia

today, more than 9,000 companies employ more than 120,000 employees, most of whom are former members of the Russian armed forces. Kevin A. O'Brien, "PMCs, Myths and Mercenaries: The Debate on Private Military Companies," *Royal United Service Institute Journal*, February (2000), http://www.globalpolicy.org/nations/sovereign/military/02debate.htm (accessed January 16, 2007).

84. "Russia's Military Doctrine 2000," sect. III, para. 8.

85. Ibid., para. 6.

86. Specifically, NATO consults with Russia in the NATO–Russia Council, whereas the EU has held EU–Russia summits since 2000. Regarding the NATO–Russia Council, see "Russia Views N.A.T.O. Expansion as a Strategic Threat," *Power and Interest News Report*, May 5, 2004, http://www.pinr.com/report.php?ac=view_report&report_id=166&language_id=1 (accessed April 20, 2007). Regarding the EU–Russia summits, see "EU–Russia Relations," http://ec.europa.eu/comm/external_relations/russia/intro/index.htm (accessed April 20, 2007).

87. See, for example, Yuliya Tymoshenko, "Containing Russia," *Foreign Affairs*, 8, no. 3 (May/June, 2007): 69–82.

88. Regarding the military–industrial complex, see C. Wright Mills, *The Power Elite* (New York: Oxford University Press, 2000). The argument here is similar to Mancur Olson's, who claims that distributional coalitions that grow in strength as a result of past successes often serve as a brake on the state's future progress and, therefore, frequently require a crisis to shatter their destructive influence on the state. Mancur Olson, *The Rise and Decline of Nations: Economic Growth, Stagflation, and Social Rigidities* (New Haven, Conn.: Yale University Press, 1982).

89. See note 10 in this chapter.

Chapter 4

1. Regarding the dynamics of western Europe's transition, see Norrin M. Ripsman, "Two Stages of Transition from a Region of War to a Region of Peace: Realist Transition and Liberal Endurance," *International Studies Quarterly*, 49, no. 4 (December 2005): 669–693; Ole Wæver, "Insecurity, Security, and Asecurity in the West European Non-war Community," in *Security Communities*, eds. Emanuel Adler and Michael Barnett (Cambridge: Cambridge University Press, 1998), 69–118. For a discussion of pluralistic security communities, see Emanuel Adler and Michael Barnett, "Security Communities in Theoretical Perspective," in *Security Communities*, eds. Emanuel Adler and Michael Barnett (Cambridge: Cambridge University Press, 1998), 3–28; Karl W. Deutsch et al., *Political Community and the North Atlantic Area: International Organization in the Light of Historical Experience* (Princeton, N.J.: Princeton University Press, 1957).

2. Wæver, "Insecurity, Security, and Asecurity in the West European Non-war Community." Benjamin Miller contends that war between them is "unlikely, if

not unthinkable." Benjamin Miller, "Explaining Variations in Regional Peace: Three Strategies for Peace-making," *Cooperation and Conflict*, 35, no. 2 (June 2000): 155–191.

3. United Kingdom, Ministry of Defence, *Defence White Paper 2003 (CM 6697): Delivering Security in a Changing World*, December 2003, http://www.official-documents.gov.uk/document/cm66/6697/6697.pdf (accessed February 26, 2009), sect. 3, para. 1; sect. 1, para. 2.

4. République Française, Présidence de la République, Speech by Jacques Chirac, President of the French Republic, during his visit to The Strategic Air and Maritime Forces at Landivisiau, L'Île Longue, January 19, 2006, http://www.cedoc.defense.gouv.fr/IMG/pdf/Discours_President_2006_en.pdf (accessed June 24, 2006).

5. Regarding the continuity of thinking in Sarkozy's strategic vision, see Justin Vaisse, "A Gaullist by Any Other Name," *Survival*, 50, no. 3 (June 2008): 5–10.

6. David C. Rapoport, "The Fourth Wave: September 11 in the History of Terrorism," *Current History*, December (2001): 420–422.

7. Etienne de Durand, "French Defense Policy under the New Government," in *US–France Analysis Series* (Washington, D.C.: Brookings Institution, 2002), http://www.brookings.edu/~/media/Files/rc/articles/2002/11france_durand/dedurand.pdf. (accessed September 22, 2009), 2.

8. République Française, Ministère de la Défense, "Projet de loi de programmation militaire 2003–2008," http://www.defense.gouv.fr/actualites/dossier/d140/index.htm (accessed June 18, 2003), chaps. 1 and 3. A shorter version of this report, which is no longer available on the French government's website, is available at http://www.defense-aerospace.com/article-view/reports_ar/16405/projet-de-loi-programmation-militaire-2003_2008.html (accessed September 22, 2009).

9. United Kingdom, Ministry of Defence, *Defence White Paper 2003*, sect. 2, paras. 2–4.

10. In a report on the bombings by the Intelligence and Security Committee, for example, the chief of the British Secret Intelligence Service concluded: "We need to do more of what we were planning to do anyway [to fight terrorism] and we need to do it faster." Intelligence and Security Committee, "Report on the London Terrorist Attacks on 7 July 2005," http://news.bbc.co.uk/2/shared/bsp/hi/pdfs/11_05_06_isc_london_attacks_report.pdf (accessed September 18, 2006), 34.

11. United Kingdom, Ministry of Defence, *Defence White Paper 2003*, sect. 3, para. 1.

12. Ibid, sect. 2, para. 9.

13. Ibid., sect. 2, para. 8.

14. UK Ministry of Defense, Development, Concepts and Doctrines Centre, "Strategic Trends, 2007–2036," December 2006, http://www.dcdc-strategic-trends.org.uk/viewdoc.aspx?doc (accessed July 21, 2007).

15. République Française, Ministère de la Défense, "Projet de loi de programmation militaire 2003–2008," chap. 3. It is interesting, though, that these non-traditional security threats did not receive much emphasis in Chirac's major 2006 speech on defense policy. République Française, Présidence de la République, "Speech by Jacques Chirac."

16. United Kingdom, Ministry of Defence, "The Future Strategic Context for Defence: The Political Context," http://www.mod.uk/issues/strategic_context/political.htm (accessed June 8, 2003.); United Kingdom, Ministry of Defence, "The Future Strategic Context for Defence: The Military Context," http://www.mod.uk/issues/strategic_context/military.htm (accessed June 8, 2003).

17. United Kingdom, Ministry of Defence, *Defence White Paper 2003*, sect. 3, para. 2.

18. République Française, Présidence de la République, "Speech by Jacques Chirac," 2–3.

19. Sten Rynning, *Changing Military Doctrine: Presidents and Military Power in Fifth Republic France* (Westport, Conn.: Praeger, 2002), chap. 5.

20. Regarding British support for American policy, which earned former British Prime Minister the derisive nickname "Bush's poodle," see Inderjeet Parmar, " 'I'm Proud of the British Empire': Why Tony Blair Backs George W. Bush," *The Political Quarterly*, 76, no. 2 (April 2005), 218–231; Lawrence D. Freedman, "The Special Relationship, Then and Now," *Foreign Affairs*, 85, no. 3 (May/June 2006), 61–73.

21. See, for example, Patrick Basham, "French President Sarkozy, the American?" April 26, 2007, http://www.cato.org/pub_display.php?pub_id=8213 (accessed June 19, 2008).

22. See T. V. Paul, "Soft Balancing in the Age of U.S. Primacy," *International Security*, 30, no. 1 (Summer 2005): 46–71.

23. Data on national manpower for all countries and regions come from International Institute for Strategic Studies, *The Military Balance*, 1989–2007 issues(London: International Institute for Strategic Studies). This publication reports on manpower for "NATO Europe," rather than western Europe per se.

24. The 1990–2006 defense spending figures for all countries and regions (in 2005 constant U.S. dollars) are from Stockholm International Peace Research Institute, "SIPRI Yearbook 2007," http://www.sipri.org/contents/milap/milex/mex_wnr_table.html (accessed June 26, 2007).

25. It is interesting that British planners, themselves, expect globalization to increase both regional and global defense spending in the future, because rapidly changing technologies and cross-border collaborations require large outlays of cash to keep up. More important, they expect proliferation of WMD to continue unabated as a result of globalization, which may imply a global arms race. U.K. Ministry of Defense, Development, Concepts and Doctrines Centre, *Strategic Trends, 2007–2036*, esp. pp. 17, 72–75.

26. United Kingdom, Ministry of Defence, *Defence White Paper 2003*, sect. 1, para. 5.

27. Ibid., sect. 3, para. 8.

28. République Française, Ministère de la Défense, "Projet de loi de programmation militaire 2003–2008," chap. 3. It is interesting, though, that political pressure prevented the French government from using French military personnel to cope with widespread rioting in Parisian suburbs and the capital itself in late 2005 and 2006.

29. République Française, Ministère de la Défense, "Projet de loi de programmation militaire 2003–2008," chap. 3.

30. United Kingdom, Ministry of Defence, *Defence Industrial Strategy: Defence White Paper, 2005*, sect. C, para. 1.4.

31. Ibid., sect. C, para. 1.16.

32. République Française, Ministère de la Défense, "The Defense Procurement Policy (2004): For a Competitive Autonomy in Europe," http://www.cedoc. defense.gouv.fr/IMG/pdf/ENG-achat-2.pdf (accessed June 24, 2006).

33. United Kingdom, Ministry of Defence, "The Future Strategic Context for Defence: The Military Context," 28.

34. République Française, Ministère de la Défense, "Projet de loi de programmation militaire 2003–2008," chap. 1.

35. United Kingdom, Ministry of Defence, *Defence White Paper 2003*, sect. 2, para. 18.

36. Ibid., sect. 2, para. 19.

37. "President Sarkozy Marches France Back to NATO with Military Shake-up," *Timesonline*, June 18, 2008, http://www.timesonline.co.uk/tol/news/world/europe/article4160462.ece (accessed June 19, 2008).

38. United Kingdom, Ministry of Defence, "The Future Strategic Context for Defence: The Political Context," 22–23.

39. United Kingdom, Ministry of Defence, *Defence White Paper 2003*, sect. 2, para. 16.

40. République Française, Ministère de la Défense, "Projet de loi de programmation militaire 2003–2008," chap. 3.

41. See Arie M. Kacowicz, *Zones of Peace in the Third World: South America and West Africa in Comparative Perspective* (Albany: SUNY Press, 1998); Jorge I. Dominquez, ed., *International Security and Democracy: Latin America and the Caribbean in the Post-Cold War Era* (Pittsburgh, Pa.: University of Pittsburgh Press, 1998); Douglas Lemke, *Regions of War and Peace* (Cambridge: Cambridge University Press, 2002).

42. Andrew Hurrell argues that, although the region does not yet constitute a security community, it may be in the process of developing into one. Andrew Hurrell, "An Emerging Security Community in South America?" in *Security Communities*, eds. Emanuel Adler and Michael Barnett (Cambridge: Cambridge University Press, 1998), 228–264.

43. See the discussion in T. V. Paul, *Power Versus Prudence: Why Nations Forgo Nuclear Weapons* (Montreal: McGill-Queen's University Press, 2000), 99–112.

44. David R. Mares, *Violent Peace: Militarized Interstate Bargaining in Latin America* (New York: Columbia University Press, 2001). During the 1990s, a number of boundary disputes were settled, including those between Argentina and Chile, Chile and Peru, and Brazil and its neighboring countries. Disputes linger on, however, between Guyana, Venezuela, and Columbia in Central America; Nicaragua with four of its neighbors; between Venezuela and Honduras; El Salvador and Guatemala; and Guyana and its neighbors. See Jorge I. Dominguez et al., "Boundary Disputes in Latin America," *Peaceworks*, 50 (September 2003).

45. Federative Republic of Brazil, "National Defense Policy, 2002," sect. I, para. 2.11, http://www.oas.org/csh/english/docwhitepapers%20Brasil.asp (accessed June 18, 2003).

46. Republica Federativa do Brasil, Ministerio da Defesa, "Politica de defesa nacional 2005," sect. I, para. 1.3, http://www.defesanet.com.br/docs/LDN-2005.pdf (accessed July 4, 2006).

47. Federative Republic of Brazil, "National Defense Policy, 2002," sect. 4.

48. The document begins by noting that "[i]n Asia, China receives much of the strategic focus because this country is increasingly transforming itself into an important political, economic and military actor. China is growing in power and influence; it maintains a nuclear capability that allows it to reach North America; it will not stop its military modernization program and has decided to accelerate its nuclear development program. China has further declared that it will not allow any nation to 'threaten its strategic interests or to alter the international balance.' Also, North Korea, India, Pakistan, Iran, and Iraq have shown the capacity to build nuclear armaments and delivery vectors. For these reasons, the strategic concerns of the Western world are located in the Middle-East and Central-Asia." Republica Argentina, Ministerio de Defensa, "Revision de la Defensa 2001: Consideraciones acerca del Marco Estratégico, Escenario Mundial," http://www.pdgs.org.ar/Archivo/revi-part1.htm#a (accessed September 22, 2009).

49. Ibid.

50. Argentina, "White Paper on National Defense, January 2000," part II, chap. V, sect. 3, http://www.defensenet.ser2000.org.ar/Archivo/libro-argentina-eng/ (accessed June 8, 2003).

51. Republica Federativa do Brasil, Ministerio da Defesa, "Politica de defesa nacional 2005," sect. 2, para. 2.6.

52. See, for example, ibid., sect. 3, paras. 3.4–3.5.

53. See Argentina, "White Paper on National Defense, January 2000," part II, chap. V, sect. 3; part I, chap. III, sect. 2. The 2001 revision acknowledges that "international terrorism continues to be a constant source of risks and, indirectly, a threat to world peace." Republica Argentina, Ministerio de Defensa, "Revision de la Defensa 2001: Consideraciones acerca del Marco Estratégico, Escenario Mundial." Argentina's worst terrorist attack was a car bombing at the Buenos

Aires AMIA Jewish Community center in July 1994, which killed more than 80 people and injured 200. Iran was blamed for planning the attack. See "Iran Blamed for Argentine Bomb," *BBC News Online*, November 6, 2003, http://news.bbc.co.uk/2/hi/middle_east/3245641.stm (accessed June 19, 2008).

54. Mark P. Sullivan, "Latin America: Terrorism Issues, Congressional Research Service Report to Congress," http://fpc.state.gov/documents/organization/ 5192. pdf (accessed April 28, 2006).

55. Argentina, "White Paper on National Defense," part II, chap. V, sect. 3.

56. Ibid., part III, chap. IX, sect. 3.

57. Republica Argentina, Ministerio de Defensa, "Revision de la Defensa 2001, Consideraciones acerca del Marco Estratégico, Escenario Mundial."

58. K. Larry Storrs and Connie Veillette, "Andean Regional Initiative (ARI): FY2003 Supplemental and FY2004 Assistance for Colombia and Neighbors," July 25, 2003, http://bogota.usembassy.gov/wwwfari1.pdf (accessed October 17, 2006).

59. Federative Republic of Brazil, "National Defense Policy."

60. Republica Federativa do Brasil, Ministerio da Defesa, "Politica de defesa nacional 2005," sect. II, paras. 2.2 and 2.4.

61. Argentina, "White Paper on National Defense, January 2000," part II, sect. 2. The 2001 revision elaborates on Argentine security goals: "As an independent nation, the Republic of Argentina has to be self-sufficient for the accomplishment of its military missions. It must be able to deter attacks against its territory, protect its natural resources and practice surveillance over its sea and air lines of communication, with the help of armed forces which must possess an adequate operational capability, high mobility and sufficient levels of instruction." Republica Argentina, Ministerio de Defensa, "Revision de la Defensa 2001: Prioridades Estratégicas para el siglo que se inicia," http://www.pdgs.org.ar/Archivo/revi-part2.htm (accessed February 26, 2009).

62. Argentina, "White Paper on National Defense, January 2000," part III, sect. 5.

63. Republica Federativa do Brasil, Ministerio da Defesa, "Politica de defesa nacional 2005," sect. 6, para. 6.2.

64. Ibid., sect. 6, para. 6.3.

65. J. Samuel Fitch, *The Armed Forces and Democracy in Latin America* (Baltimore, Md.: The Johns Hopkins University Press, 1998).

66. Mark Eric Williams, "Soft Balancing: Much Ado about Nothing?," Middlebury College, Vt., October 2006, unpublished.

67. The IISS reports on "Caribbean, Central, and Latin America," rather than South America.

68. In contrast, Argentine spending dropped by about 15% during the same period, but this seems to be at odds with the broader regional trend.

69. Federative Republic of Brazil, "National Defense Policy."

70. Republica Federativa do Brasil, Ministerio da Defesa, "Politica de defesa nacional 2005," sect. 6, para. 6.22.

71. Ibid., sect. IV, para. 4.4.

72. Republica Argentina, Ministerio de Defensa, "Revision de la Defensa 2001: Consideraciones acerca del Marco Estratégico, Amenazas no tradicionales," http://www.resdal.org/Archivo/revi-part1.htm (accessed February 26, 2009).

73. Republica Argentina, Ministerio de Defensa, "Revision de la Defensa 2001: Misiones y Funciones de la Defensa," http://www.mindef.gov.ar/secciones/revision/misiones.htm (accessed July 4, 2006).

74. The only mention of private actors in the 2005 Brazilian white paper is a cursory reference to securing "the permanent engagement of governmental, industrial and academic sectors" in support of national security operations. Republica Federativa do Brasil, Ministerio da Defesa, "Politica de defesa nacional 2005," sect. 6, para. 6.9. This routine consultation, however, hardly amounts to the outsourcing envisioned by the globalization school.

75. See Alvaro S. Pinheiro, "Narcoterrorism in Latin America: A Brazilian Perspective," http://www.defesanet.com.br/docs/MG_Alvaro_JSOU_Paper374.pdf (accessed October 17, 2006); Peter W. Singer, *Corporate Warriors: The Rise of the Privatized Military Industry* (Ithaca, N.Y.: Cornell University Press, 2003), 14.

76. Argentina, "White Paper on National Defense, January 2000," part III, chap. VII, sect. 5.

77. Ibid., part I, chap. II, sects. 1 and 2.

78. Organization for American States, "The OAS and the Inter-American System," http://www.oas.org/documents/eng/oasinbrief.asp (accessed March 14, 2009).

79. Argentina, "White Paper on National Defense, January 2000," part I, chap. II, sects. 1 and 2. In May 2007, Argentina and Brazil, along with other member states Paraguay, Uruguay, and Venezuela, attempted to deepen regional integration with the inauguration of the Mercosur Parliament. "Parliament Inaugurated," BBC News, May 7, 2007, http://news.bbc.co.uk/go/pr/fr/-/2/hi/americas/6633457.stm (accessed May 11, 2007).

80. The document asserts: "During the last years, the ancient tensions prevailing in the South Cone of the American continent between Argentina, Chile and Brazil, have been eliminated by the strong and significant regional integration process arrived at through MERCOSUR (between Argentina, Brazil, Uruguay and Paraguay) and connected agreements with Bolivia and Chile. Cooperation has replaced rivalry." Republica Argentina, Ministerio de Defensa, "Revision de la Defensa 2001: El marco hemisférico y regional," http://www.mindef.gov.ar/secciones/revision/consideraciones2.htm (accessed July 4, 2006).

81. Republica Federativa do Brasil, Ministerio da Defesa, "Politica de defesa nacional 2005," sect. 3, para. 3.3.

82. Ibid., sect. 3, para. 3.6.

83. Part of the motivation for this institution came from civilian rulers who wanted to retain their control over security matters and relegate the role of the military

establishments in security policy making. See Paul, *Power Versus Prudence*, 99–112; Arturo C. Sotomayor Velazquez, "Civil–Military Affairs and Security Institutions in the Southern Cone: The Sources of Argentina–Brazilian Nuclear Cooperation," *Latin American Politics and Society*, 46, no. 4 (Winter 2004): 29–60.

84. Erik Martinez Kuhonta, "Walking a Tightrope: Democracy Versus Sovereignty in ASEAN's Illiberal Peace," *The Pacific Review*, 19, no. 3 (September 2006): 338.

85. See Anja Jetschke, "Democratization: A Threat to Peace and Stability in Southeast Asia," in *Asia–Pacific Economic and Security Cooperation*, ed. Christopher M. Dent (Houndmills, UK: Palgrave-Macmillan, 2003), 176–177.

86. See Jean-Marc F. Blanchard, "Maritime Issues in Asia: The Problem of Adolescence," in *Asian Security Order: Instrumental and Normative Features*, ed. Muthiah Alagappa (Stanford, Calif.: Stanford University Press, 2003), 438–441.

87. R. James Ferguson, "New Norms of Southeast Asian Regional Governance: From 'Codes of Conduct' to 'Greater East Asia,'" in *Non-Traditional Security Issues in Southeast Asia*, eds. Andrew T. H. Han and J. D. Kenneth Boutin (Singapore: Select Publishing, 2001), 127.

88. Lawrence W. Prabhakar, Joshua H. Ho, and Sam Bateman, eds., *The Evolving Maritime Balance of Power in the Asia–Pacific* (Singapore: World Scientific Publishing Company, 2006).

89. See P. Chalk, "Separatism and Southeast Asia: The Islamic Factor in Southern Thailand, Mindanao, and Aceh," *Studies in Conflict and Terrorism*, 24, no. 1 (July 2001), 241–269.

90. See Marc Askew, *Conspiracy, Politics, and a Disorderly Border: The Struggle to Comprehend Insurgency in Thailand's Deep South*, vol. 29 of *Policy Studies* (Washington, DC: East-West Center, 2007). The military junta that came to power in September 2006 adopted a repressive policy but with little success in quelling the insurgency. Seth Mydans, "Muslim Insurgency Stokes Fear in Southern Thailand," *International Herald Tribune*, February 25, 2007, http://nytimes.com/2007/02/25/world/asia/25iht-thailand.4712619.html (accessed September 22, 2009).

91. Regarding terrorist presence in Indonesia, see Council on Foreign Relations, "Backgrounder, Terrorist Havens: Indonesia," http://www.cfr.org/publication/9361/ (accessed July 5, 2007).

92. Rohan Gunaratna, "Southeast Asia: The Terrorist Threat," in *Asia–Pacific Security Outlook 2004*, ed. Charles Morrison (Tokyo: Japan Center for International Exchange, 2004), 36. See also, Barry Deskar and Kumar Ramakrishna, "Forging a Indirect Strategy in Southeast Asia," *The Washington Quarterly*, 25, no. 2 (Spring 2002): 161–176.

93. *The Fight against Terror: Singapore's National Security Strategy* (Singapore: National Security Coordination Centre, 2004), 12.

94. Regarding the status of cooperation with the United States by different countries in Southeast Asia, see Office of the Coordinator for Counterterrorism, *Country Reports on Terrorism* (Washington, D.C.: U.S. State Department, Office of the Coordinator for Counterterrorism, April 30, 2007), chap. 2, http://www.state.gov/s/ct/rls/crt/2006/82731.htm (accessed July 5, 2007).

95. Gunaratna, "Southeast Asia: The Terrorist Threat," 34.

96. Seth Mydans, "Indonesia Redefines Itself by 'Rolling up' Terrorist Leaders," *International Herald Tribune*, June 17, 2007, http://www.iht.com/articles/2007/06/17/news/terror.php (accessed June 17, 2007).

97. Kusuma Snitwongse and Suchit Bunbongkarn, "New Security Issues and Their Impact on ASEAN," in *Reinventing ASEAN*, eds. Simon S. C. Tay, Jesus P. Estanislao, and Hadi Soesastra (Singapore: Institute of Southeast Asian Studies, 2001), 148–162.

98. See David Glover and Timothy Jessup, *Indonesia's Fires and Haze: The Cost of Catastrophe* (Singapore: Institute of Southeast Asian Studies, 1999).

99. Carolina G. Hernandez, "Challenges for Security and Politics," in *Reinventing ASEAN*, eds. Simon S. C. Tay, Jesus P. Estanislao, and Hadi Soesastra (Singapore: Institute of Southeast Asian Studies, 2001), 108. Among the political refugees are nearly 300,000 Burmese in Thailand, nearly 90,000 Muslim Filipinos in eastern Malaysia, and 10,000 Irianese from Indonesia in Papua New Guinea. See Graeme Hugo, "Asia and the Pacific on the Move: Workers and Refugees, A Challenge to Nation States," *Asia Pacific Viewpoint*, 38, no. 3 (December 1997): 267–286.

100. See Joseph Y. S. Cheng, "Broadening the Concept of Security in East and Southeast Asia: The Impact of Asian Financial Crisis and the September 11 Incident," *Journal of Contemporary China*, 15, no. 46 (February 2006): 89–111.

101. Ralf Emmers, *Non-Traditional Security in the Asia–Pacific* (Singapore: Eastern Universities Press, 2004): 35–60.

102. Snitwongse and Bunbongkarn, "New Security Issues and Their Impact on ASEAN," 160. ASEAN Vision 2020 states: "We envision the evolution in Southeast Asia of agreed rules of behaviour and cooperative measures to deal with problems that can be met only on a regional scale, including environmental pollution and degradation, drug trafficking, trafficking in women and children, and other transnational crimes." "ASEAN Vision 2020," December 15, 1997, http://www.aseansec.org/1814.htm (accessed April 30, 2008); "Hanoi Plan of Action," n.d., http://www.aseansec.org/8754.htm (accessed April 29, 2008).

103. David B. Dewitt and Carolina G. Hernandez, "Defining the Problem and Managing the Uncertainty," in *Development and Security in Southeast Asia*, vol. I, eds. David B. Dewitt and Carolina G. Hernandez (Hants, UK: Ashgate, 2003), 5.

104. Kusnanto Anggoro, "Globalization and the Military in Indonesia," in *Development and Security in Southeast Asia*, vol. 3, eds. David B. Dewitt and Carolina G. Hernandez (Hants, UK: Ashgate, 2003), 263–264.

105. Indonesia, "Indonesia: Defense White Paper 2003: Defending the Country Entering the 21st Century," http://merln.ndu/Whitepapers/Indonesiawhitepaper.pdf (accessed June 25, 2007) 11.

106. Ibid., 19–23.

107. Marvin C. Ott, "Southeast Asian Security Challenges: America's Response?" *Strategic Forum*, 222 (October 2006): 4.

108. Government of Cambodia, "Defending the Kingdom of Cambodia: Security and Development 2000," http://merln.ndu.edu/Whitepapers/Cambodia-2000.pdf (accessed June 25, 2007), 27–30.

109. Teerawat Putamanonda, "The Strategy of Conflict: A Royal Thai Army Perspective," http://www.ndu.edu/inss/books/Books%20_%201997/Strength%20Through%20Cooperation%201997/stcch11.html (accessed June 27, 2007).

110. Putamanonda, "The Strategy of Conflict."

111. Emmers, *Non-Traditional Security in the Asia–Pacific*, 9–34.

112. Vietnam Ministry of Foreign Affairs, "Vietnam's Present Foreign Policy," http://www.mofa.gov.vn/en/cs_doingoai/cs/ns041025165700 (accessed July 13, 2007). Our interviews with Vietnamese officials in Hanoi and Ho Chi Minh City suggested that Vietnam has changed its policies during the past fifteen years to accommodate new security threats. Interview with Ta Minh Tuan, Foreign Ministry Official, Hanoi, January 26, 2005.

113. William T. Tow, "Alternative Security Models: Implications for ASEAN," in *Non-Traditional Security Issues in Southeast Asia*, eds. Andrew T. H. Tan and J. D. Kenneth Boutin (Singapore: Institute of Defense and Strategic Studies/Select Publishing, 2001), 268.

114. Singapore, Ministry of Defense, "Total Defence 2006," http://home.totaldef-ence.org/abt/abt.html (accessed December 12, 2006).

115. Putamanonda, "The Strategy of Conflict."

116. "ABRI—Armed Forces of the Republic of Indonesia," http://www.globalsecu-rity.org/military/world/indonesia/abri.htm (accessed July 5, 2007).

117. Malaysia, Ministry of Defence, "National Defence Policy," Portal Kementerian Pertahanan Malaysia, http://www.mod.gov.my/index.php?Itemid=173&id=89&option=com_content&task=blogcategory&lang=en (accessed June 20, 2007).

118. Interview with Ta Minh Tuan.

119. Allan S. Whiting, "ASEAN Eyes China: The Security Dimension," *Asian Survey*, 37, no. 4 (April 1997): 299–322.

120. The Philippines, for instance, has revitalized its defense ties with Washington, which include joint military exercises and training, a resumption of U.S. military assistance to improve Manila's counterterrorism capability, and the stationing of American troops and special forces in the country. See Renato Cruz De Castro, "Philippine Defense Policy in the 21st Century: Autonomous

Defense or Back to the Alliance?," *Pacific Affairs*, 78, no. 3 (Fall 2005): 403–422. Thailand also believes that the "U.S. presence in the Asia–Pacific region is critical to peace and stability," because the "region as a whole [has] no collective security arrangement like NATO or WEU [the Western European Union] in Europe. ARF or other multilateral security dialogues in the Asia–Pacific region require a strong countervailing power against any unilateralism or nationalism; the United States is suitable for this role." Putmanonda, "The Strategy of Conflict."

121. Other scholars who study the region also concur with this argument. Acharya and Seng state that, in Southeast Asia, "balance of power" and "regional community dynamics" seem to be coexisting, and this trend is likely to continue in the foreseeable future. Amitav Acharya and See Seng Tan, "Betwixt Balance and Community: America, ASEAN, and the Security of Southeast Asia," *International Relations of the Asia Pacific*, 6, no. 1 (2006): 40. See, also, Prabhakar, Ho, and Bateman, *The Evolving Maritime Balance of Power in Asia–Pacific*, chap. 13.

122. These figures are not entirely accurate, as SIPRI was unable to report figures for Laos and Myanmar in 1988 and Vietnam in 2006. Nonetheless, as Vietnam spends considerably more than Laos and Myanmar combined, the net increase should actually be even larger.

123. For an early assessment, see Amitav Acharya, "Governance and Security in Southeast Asia: Assessing the Impact of Defense Spending," in *Eastern Asia Policy Papers* 9 (Toronto: University of Toronto–York University Joint Center for Asia–Pacific Studies, 1995). Regarding maritime disputes in Asia that affect regional security calculations, see Blanchard, "Maritime Issues in Asia."

124. Christopher M. Dent, "New Economic and Security Cooperation in the Asia–Pacific: An Introduction," in *Asia–Pacific Economic and Security Cooperation*, ed. Christopher M. Dent (Houndmills, UK: Palgrave-Macmillan, 2003), 8.

125. Han and Boutin, *Non-Traditional Security Issues in Southeast Asia*, 3.

126. CSCAP is credited with the ARF adopting certain principles on confidence building and preventive diplomacy at the July 2001 ARF summit. Alan Collins, *Security and Southeast Asia* (Boulder, Colo.: Lynne Rienner, 2003), 174.

127. For the activities and impact of these groups, see Mely Caballero-Anthony, "Revisioning Human Security in Southeast Asia," *Asian Perspectives*, 28, no. 3 (2004): 155–189.

128. Brian L. Job, "Track 2 Diplomacy: Ideational Contribution to the Evolving Asian Security Order," in *Asian Security Order: Instrumental and Normative Features*, ed. Muthiah Alagappa (Stanford, Calif.: Stanford University Press, 2003), 241–279.

129. See Carolin Liss, "Private Security Companies in the Fight against Piracy in Asia," working paper no. 120 (Singapore: Asia Research Center, Murdoch University, June 2005).

130. Lianita Prawindarti, "The First ASEAN Defence Ministers Meeting: An Early Test for the ASEAN Security Community?" *IDSS Commentaries*, 34 (May 16, 2006), 1–3.

131. Hanoi Plan of Action, http://www.aseansec.org/10382.htm (accessed July 5, 2007).

132. Ibid.

133. http://www.aseansec.org/92.htm (accessed July 5, 2007).

134. For instance, see the statement at the end of the twelfth ARF meeting in July 2005 in Laos, "Annex 4," http://www.aseansec.org/ARF/12ARF/12th-ARF/Annex-4.pdf (accessed July 5, 2007).

135. Jurgen Ruland, "Asian Regionalism Five Years after the 1997/98 Financial Crisis: A Case of 'Cooperative Realism?'," in *Asia-Pacific Economic and Security Cooperation, Asia–Pacific Economic and Security Cooperation*, ed. Christopher M. Dent (Houndmills, UK: Palgrave-Macmillan, 2003), 65–66.

136. Marvin C. Ott, "Southeast Asian Security Challenges: America's Response?," *Strategic Forum*, 222 (October 2006), 1–8.

137. Malaysian Ministry of Foreign Affairs, "An Overview of Malaysia's Foreign Policy," http://www.kln.gov.my/?m_id=2 (accessed June 26, 2007).

138. Republic of the Philippines, Department of Foreign Affairs, "DFA Accomplishment Report for 2003," January 2004, http://www.dfa.gov.ph/archive/accreport2003.htm (accessed December 12, 2006).

139. Statement by H. E. Thongloun Sisoulith, Minister of Foreign Affairs, at the general debate of the sixty-first session of the UN General Assembly, New York, September 25, 2006, http://www.mofa.gov.la/ (accessed July 13, 2007).

140. Malaysian Ministry of Defence, "National Defence Policy," n.d., Portal Kementerian Pertahanan Malaysia, http:www.mod.giv.my/ (accessed June 20, 2007).

141. Amitav Acharaya, *Constructing a Security Community in Southeast Asia: ASEAN and the Problem of Regional Order* (London: Routledge, 2001); Amitav Acharaya, *The Quest for Identity: International Relations of Southeast Asia* (Singapore: Oxford University Press, 2000).

142. Alastair Iain Johnston, "Socialization in International Institutions: The ASEAN Way and International Relations Theory," in *International Relations Theory and the Asia–Pacific*, eds. G. John Ikenberry and Michael Mastanduno (New York: Columbia University Press, 2003): 108.

143. See Kuhonta, "Walking a Tightrope," 337–358.

144. Acharya, *Constructing a Security Community in Southeast Asia*, 26. ASEAN officials reject criticism of ASEAN's "passive" peace, as opposed to an "active peace" agenda. To one official, ASEAN's February 1976 Treaty of Amity and Cooperation requires states to renounce use of force, and members both old and new have been abiding by this principle. Interview with M. C. Abad, Head Regional Forum Unit, ASEAN Secretariat, Jakarta, February 11, 2005.

According to Abad, ASEAN is "norms rich" even though it is "resource poor."

145. Herman Kraft, "The Principle of Non-Intervention: Evolution and Challenges for the Asia–Pacific Region," pp. 23–41 in *Non-Intervention and State Sovereignty in the Asia–Pacific*, eds. David Dickens and Guy Wilson-Roberts (Wellington, NZ: Center for Strategic Studies, 2000).

146. Acharya and Tan, "Betwixt Balance and Community," 40.

Chapter 5

1. Paul F. Diehl, "Introduction: An Overview and Some Theoretical Guidelines," in *The Dynamics of Enduring Rivalries*, ed. Paul F. Diehl (Urbana: University of Illinois Press, 1998), 1–25; Charles S. Gochman and Zeev Maoz, "Militarized Interstate Disputes, 1916–1976," *Journal of Conflict Resolution*, 28, no. 4 (December 1984): 585–616; Paul Diehl and Gary Goertz, *War and Peace in International Rivalry* (Ann Arbor: University of Michigan Press, 2001); John A. Vasquez, "Distinguishing Rivals That Go to War from Those That Do Not," *International Studies Quarterly*, 40, no. 4 (December 1996): 531–558. An important source of data on enduring rivalries is the International Crisis Behavior Project database, http://www.cidcm.umd.edu/icb (accessed January 12, 2009). See, also, Michael Brecher and Jonathan Wilkenfeld, *A Study of Crisis* (Ann Arbor: University of Michigan Press, 1997).

2. Regarding the 1956 campaign, see Jack S. Levy and Joseph R. Gochal, "Democracy and Preventive War: Israel and the 1956 Sinai Campaign," *Security Studies*, 11, no. 2 (Winter 2001/2002): 1–49. Regarding the preemptive war of 1967, see Michael B. Oren, *Six Days of War: June 1967 and the Making of the Modern Middle East* (Oxford: Oxford University Press, 2002); Anthony Clark Arend, "International Law and the Preemptive Use of Military Force," *The Washington Quarterly*, 26, no. 2 (Spring 2003): 89–103.

3. The roots of the conflict are discussed in Ian J. Bickerton and Carla Klausner, *A Concise History of the Arab–Israeli Conflict*, 4th ed. (New York: Prentice Hall, 2002); Walter Laqueur and Barry Rubin, eds., *The Israeli–Arab Reader: A Documentary History of the Middle East Conflict* (New York: Penguin Books, 1995); William B. Quandt, *Peace Process: American Diplomacy and the Arab–Israeli Conflict since 1967* (Washington, D.C.: Brookings/University of California, 2001). Benjamin Miller characterizes the peace settlements as "cold peace," where war remains possible, if not likely. Benjamin Miller, *States, Nations and Great Powers: The Sources of Regional War and Peace* (Cambridge: Cambridge University Press, 2007).

4. Regarding tensions within the Arab world, see Bruce Maddy-Weitzman, "The Inter-Arab System and the Arab–Israeli Conflict: Ripening for Resolution," *Perceptions*, 5, no. 1 (March–May 2000): 44–54.

5. The Middle East and South Asia accounted for 90% of the nearly 300 high-casualty attacks in 2006 that killed ten or more people. Of the 14,000 reported terrorist attacks for 2006, 45% (about 6,600) of them occurred in Iraq. For more details see, National Counterterrorism Center, "Report on Terrorist Incidents, 2006," April 30, 2007, http://wits.nctc.gov/reports/crot2005nct-cannexfinal.pdf (accessed April 22, 2008), 2.

6. David Rodman, "Israel's National Security Doctrine: An Introductory Overview," *Middle East Review of International Affairs*, 5, no. 3 (September 2001), http://meria.idc.ac.il/journal/2001/issue3/jv5n3a6.html (accessed June 19, 2003); Aharon Ze'evi, "Israel's Strategic Environment," *Strategic Assessment*, 5, no. 2 (August 2002), http://www.tau.ac.il/jcss/sa/v5n2p7Zee.html (accessed July 10, 2006).

7. Hillel Frisch, "Guns and Butter in the Egyptian Army," in *Armed Forces in the Middle East: Politics and Strategy*, eds. Barry Rubin and Thomas A. Keaney (London: Frank Cass, 2002), 102.

8. Daniel L. Byman, "The Implications of Leadership Change in the Arab World," in *The Future Security Environment in the Middle East: Conflict, Stability, and Political Change*, eds. Nora Bensahel and Daniel L. Byman (Santa Monica, Calif.: RAND, 2004), 187–190; Barry Rubin, *Islamic Fundamentalism in Egyptian Politics* (New York: Palgrave-Macmillan, 2002).

9. "Iranian Defense Minister on Iran's Defense Doctrine," *The Middle East Media Research Institute, Special Dispatch Series*, no. 502, May 9, 2003, http://www.memri.org/bin/articles.cgi?Page=countries&Area=iran&ID=SP50203 (accessed April 22, 2008).

10. Daniel Byman et al., *Iran's Security Policy in the Post-Revolutionary Era* (Santa Monica, Calif.: The Rand Corporation, 2001), 12.

11. In October 2005, Iranian President Mahmoud Ahmadinejad declared that Israel "must be wiped off the map," a position he has not retreated from since. Nazila Fathi, "Iran's New President Says Israel 'Must Be Wiped Off the Map,'" *New York Times*, October 27, 2005, http://trave12.nytimes.com/2005/10/27/international/middleeast/27iran.html?ex=1162443600&en=cfc17eacb4f7be4c&ei=5070 (accessed April 22, 2008).

12. Anoushiravan Ehteshami, "Iran–Iraq Relations after Saddam" *The Washington Quarterly*, 26, no. 4 (Autumn 2003): 115–129; Sanam Vakil, "Iran: Balancing East against West," *The Washington Quarterly*, 29, no. 4 (Autumn 2006): 51–65.

13. Israel Ministry of Foreign Affairs, "Victims of Palestinian Violence and Terrorism since 2000," http://www.mfa.gov.il/MFA/Terrorism-%200bsta-cle%20to%20Peace/Palestinian%20terror%20since%202000/Victims%20Of%20Palestinian%20Violence%20and%20Terrorism%20sinc (accessed April 22, 2008).

14. See, for example, Thomas L. Friedman, "War on Daddy's Dime," *New York Times*, August 18, 2006, A17.

15. Nachman Tal, "Islamic Terrorism in Egypt: The Challenge and the Response," *Strategic Assessment*, 1, no. 1 (March 1998), http://www.tau.ac.il/jcss/sa/v1n1p4_n.html (accessed April 22, 2008).

16. "Iranian Defense Minister on Iran's Defense Doctrine."

17. Israel Defense Forces, n.d., "IDF Doctrine," http://dover.idf.il/IDF/English/about/doctrine/ (accessed June 9, 2003).

18. Rodman, "Israel's National Security Doctrine."

19. Efraim Halevy, "Israel's National Security Agenda in the Coming Year," *Strategic Assessment*, 6, no. 2 (September 2003), http://www.tau.ac.il/jcss/sa/v6n2p6Hal.html (accessed April 22, 2008).

20. Aharon Ze'evi, "Israel and the Middle-East, 2005: A Strategic Overview," *Strategic Assessment*, 8, no. 3 (November 2005), http://www.tau.ac.il/jcss/sa/v8n3p1Far.html (accessed April 22, 2008).

21. AMI International Naval Analysts and Advisors, "Egypt," May 2001, http://www.amiinter.com/samples/egypt/general.html (accessed April 22, 2003).

22. Frisch, "Guns and Butter in the Egyptian Army," 106.

23. "Iranian Defense Minister on Iran's Defense Doctrine."

24. "IDF Doctrine."

25. See, for example, David E. Sanger, "Cheney Says Israel Might 'Act First' on Iran," *New York Times*, January 21, 2005, A6; "Military Rumblings on Iran," *New York Times*, January 27, 2005, A24; Whitney Raas and Austin Long, "Osirak Redux? Assessing Israeli Capabilities to Destroy Iranian Nuclear Facilities," *International Security*, 31, no. 4 (Spring 2007): 7–33.

26. AMI International Naval Analysts and Advisors, "Egypt."

27. Frisch, "Guns and Butter in the Egyptian Army," 97.

28. "Iranian Defense Minister on Iran's Defense Doctrine."

29. International Institute for Strategic Studies, *The Military Balance, 2006* (London: International Institute for Strategic Studies, 2006), 174.

30. Anthony H. Cordesman, "Iran's Developing Military Capabilities," December 9, 2004, Center for Strategic & International Studies, http://www.csis.org/component/option,com_csis_press/task,view/id,422/ (accessed June 8, 2008).

31. Regarding the Israeli–American relationship, see Yaacov Bar-Siman-Tov, "The United States and Israel since 1948: A 'Special Relationship?'" *Diplomatic History*, 22, no. 2 (Spring 1998): 231–262.

32. See Said Aly, Abdel Moneim, and Robert H. Pelletreau, "U.S.–Egyptian Relations," *Middle East Policy*, 8, no. 2 (June 2001): 45–58.

33. Regarding the American claims that Iran was supplying Shia insurgents in Iraq, see comments by General Casey, Commander of the Multinational Force in Iraq, June 16, 2006, http://www.defenselink.mil/Transcripts/Transcript.aspx?TranscriptID=3752 (accessed April 22, 2008); and Sudarsan Raghavan, "Iran Said to Support Shiite Militias in Iraq: Proxy Groups Involved, U.S.

Asserts," *Washington Post Foreign Service*, August 15, 2006, A09, http://www. washingtonpost.com/wp-dyn/content/article/2006/08/14/AR2006081400477. html (accessed April 22, 2008). The English language texts of Ahmadinejad's speeches, which are frequently anti-American and balancing in tone, can be found at http://www.president.ir/eng/ahmadinejad/speeches (accessed April 22, 2008). Regarding Iranian support for groups that the United States considers terrorist organizations, see Council on Foreign Relations, "Backgrounder, State Sponsors: Iran," August 2007, http://www.cfr.org/publication/9362 (accessed April 22, 2008).

34. See Dingli Shen, "Iran's Nuclear Ambitions Test China's Wisdom," *The Washington Quarterly*, 29, no. 2 (Spring 2006): 57–58. Shen lists two other motives for Iranian nuclear weapons: deterrence against the reputed Israeli nuclear arsenal and deterrence against Iraq, which it believed was acquiring nuclear capability prior to the downfall of Saddam Hussein. Of course, the latter motive is now belied, as the collapse of the Iraqi regime and evidence of the absence of an Iraqi nuclear program has not altered Teheran's desire to proliferate.

35. Keir A. Lieber and Gerard Alexander refer to the Iranian nuclear program as classic "asymmetric balancing." See Keir A. Lieber and Gerard Alexander, "Waiting for Balancing: Why the World Is Not Pushing Back," *International Security*, 30, no. 1 (Summer 2005): 109–139.

36. Data on national manpower for all countries and regions come from International Institute for Strategic Studies, *The Military Balance*, 1989–2007 issues (London: International Institute for Strategic Studies). This publication reports on manpower for "The Middle East and North Africa."

37. The 1991–2006 defense spending figures for all countries and regions (in 2006 constant dollars) are from Stockholm International Peace Research Institute, "SIPRI Yearbook 2007," http://www.sipri.org/contents/milap/milex/mex_ wnr_table.html (accessed April 22, 2008).

38. See, for example, Barry Rubin, "The Military in Contemporary Middle East Politics," *Middle East Review of International Affairs*, 5, no. 1 (March 2001), http:// meria.idc.ac.il/journal/2001/issue1/jv5n1a4.html (accessed June 8, 2008).

39. Byman, "The Implications of Leadership Change in the Arab World," 188–190; Nora Bensahel, "Political Reform in the Middle East," in *The Future Security Environment in the Middle East: Conflict, Stability, and Political Change*, eds. Nora Bensahel and Daniel L. Byman (Santa Monica, Calif.: RAND, 2004), 38–39.

40. Ayelet Savyon, "Iran's Student Riots—June 2003," *Middle East Media Research Institute (MEMRI) Inquiry and Analysis Series*, 142 (July 16, 2003), http://www. memri.org/bin/articles.cgi?Page=countries&Area=iran&ID=IA14203 (accessed April 22, 2008); Anthony H. Cordesman, *The Military Balance in the Middle East* (Westport, Conn.: CSIS–Praeger, 2004), 266.

41. Council on Foreign Relations, "Backgrounder."

42. See article 2 of the Arab League's charter at http://www.yale.edu/lawweb/ avalon/mideast/arableag.htm (accessed April 22, 2008).

43. See, for example, Avraham Sela, *The Decline of the Arab–Israeli Conflict: Middle East Politics and the Quest for Regional Order* (Albany: SUNY Press, 1997).

44. Regarding the different dimensions of the India–Pakistan rivalry, see T. V. Paul, ed., *The India–Pakistan Conflict: An Enduring Rivalry* (Cambridge: Cambridge University Press, 2005).

45. The region also contains several small, weak states that are beset with internal conflicts. Since 1976, the island state of Sri Lanka waged a brutal war with Tamil separatists that ended in 2009, although the peace is yet to be won. Nepal, another small Himalayan kingdom, has witnessed intense violence involving Maoists and state forces, which came to a halt in November 2006 after a power-sharing accord was signed. Although Bangladesh has not faced the same degree of internal conflict, it, too, is beset by several ethnic and political struggles (e.g., tribal conflicts in the Chittagong Hill Tracts and Chakma). Moreover, Bangladesh's unsettled and porous border with India also engenders occasional violent interactions with Indian border security forces. It is also home to several Islamic terrorist groups who are linked to al Qaeda.

46. Regarding this conventional definition of war, see Melvin Small and J. David Singer, *Resort to Arms: International and Civil Wars 1816–1980* (Thousand Oaks, Calif.: Sage, 1982).

47. See Mehtab Ali Shah, "Sectarianism: A Threat to Human Security: A Case Study of Pakistan," *The Round Table*, 94, no. 382 (October 2005): 613–628.

48. See Rizwan Hussain, *Pakistan and the Emergence of Islamic Militancy in Afghanistan* (Aldershot, Hampshire, UK: Ashgate Publishing, 2005).

49. Rahul Roy-Chaudhury, "The United States' Role and Influence on the India–Pakistan Conflict," *Disarmament Forum*, 2 (June 2004): 31–39. Some Pakistanis have argued for improved trade as a confidence-building measure. See, for instance, S. Akbar Zaidi, "India–Pakistan Trade," *South Asian Journal*, 4 (April–June 2004), http://www.southasianmedia.net/Magazine/Journal/indiapakistan_ trade. htm (accessed April 22, 2008).

50. See Sarah Bokhari, "Indo-Pak 'New Peace,'" *Journal on Science and World Affairs*, 1, no. 2 (2005): 149. States one report: "Fearful of India's emergence as a major destination for international investment and its growing geo-political partnership with Washington, many in Pakistan's business and political elite argue it is better to seek a deal with New Delhi now, when Pakistan remains a valued ally of the Bush administration in its 'war on terrorism,' than to risk having to deal with a stronger India in the future." Keith Jones, "India and Pakistan to Pursue 'Composite Dialogue,'" *Countercurrents.Org*, January 30, 2004, http://www.countercurrents.org/ipk-jone300104.htm (accessed April 22, 2008).

According to Hassan-Azkari Rizvi, the Pakistani Army has come to the conclusion that normalization of India–Pakistani relations will improve

Pakistan's economy, which will increase the power base of the Army. See Hassan-Azkari Rizvi, *India Abroad*, 35 (May 27, 2005): 14.

51. Saeed Ismat, "Strategy for Total Defence: A Conceptual Nuclear Doctrine," *Defence Journal* March (2000), http://www.defencejournal.com/2000/mar/doctrine.htm (accessed April 22, 2008). In the post-September 11 war on terrorism, Pakistan has also focused on Afghanistan to some extent. Its efforts, however, have been quite limited, and its Northwest Frontier Provinces remain safe heavens for Taliban and al Qaeda forces.

52. See Gurmeet Kanwal, "India's National Security Strategy in a Nuclear Environment," *Strategic Analysis*, http/www.ciaonet.org/olj/sa/sa_dec00kag01.html (accessed September 23, 2009).

53. Indian Army, "Indian Army, Doctrine for Subconventional Operations," October 2004, http://www.indianarmy.gov.in/indar_doctrine.htm (accessed February 26, 2009, 2008). See also, Gautam Navlakha, "Doctrine for Sub-Conventional Operations: A Critique," *Economic and Political Weekly*, April 7, 2007, 1242–1246.

54. Indian Army, "Indian Army Doctrine,", October 2004, from http://www.ids.nic.in/doctrine.htm, 7 (accessed September 22, 2009).

55. Other stated objectives include protecting the country against war, terrorism, nuclear threats, and militant activities, as well as "protecting the country from instability and religious and other forms of radicalism and extremism emanating from neighboring states." Ministry of Defense, Government of India, "Security Environment: An Overview," http://mod.nic.in/aforces/body.htm (accessed April 22, 2008).

56. Interview with Sathish Kumar, Defense Analyst, New Delhi, August 20, 2005.

57. See Aamer Ahmed Khan, "Can Musharraf Contain the Militant Threat?," *BBC News*, July 13, 2007, http://news.bbc.co.uk/2/hi/south_asia/6897683.stm (accessed April 22, 2008).

58. See Zahid Hussain, *Frontline Pakistan: The Struggle with Militant Islam* (New York: Columbia University Press, 2007), 51–52.

59. Indian government officials disputed a UN report in 2005, which estimated 5.7 million cases of HIV/AIDS in India and which meant the South Asian country overtook South Africa and Nigeria in the number of cases. Estimates by the government put the number at 2 to 3.1 million. *Earth Times*, "India's Estimated HIV/AIDS Caseload Drops by More Than Half," July 6, 2007, http://www.earthtimes.org/articles/show/79959.html (accessed April 22, 2008). Regarding Pakistan, see Omar A. Khan and Adnan A. Hyder, "Responses to an Emerging Threat: HIV/AIDS Policy in Pakistan," *Health Policy and Planning*, 16, no. 2 (2001): 214–218.

60. See, for example, Kanwal, "India's National Security Strategy in a Nuclear Environment."

61. Bokhari, "Indo-Pak 'New Peace,'" 150.

62. For instance, in an important speech in February 2004, General Musharraf identified external threats and safeguarding Pakistani sovereignty as principal security issues, followed by internal threats, which were confined to a brief discussion of economic security. See, "Address by General Pervez Musharraf," *Inaugural Session of Third National Security Workshop*, National Defense College, Islamabad, February 12, 2004, http://www.millat.com/president/defense/1018200430248PMnational%20defense%20college.pdf (accessed February 26, 2009).

63. Khan and Hyder, "Responses to an Emerging Threat," 214–217.

64. Indian Army, "The Indian Army Doctrine," October 6, 2004, http://www.indianarmy.gov.in/indar_doctrine.htm (accessed April 22, 2008). It adds: "With market forces playing an important role, economic strength is likely to become the currency of power. National economies are undergoing liberalisation to cater to globalisation. The dominance of the developed world over the global economy is, nonetheless, likely to continue. Even so, China and India have been acknowledged as emerging economic powers. Economic linkages and interdependence amongst countries are likely to result in mutual security becoming an important issue. Water, energy sources (mainly oil) and even environmental issues may emerge as causes of future conflict between states." Ibid.

65. Ministry of Defense, Government of India, "Security Environment: An Overview," http://mod.nic.in/aforces/welcome.html (accessed April 22, 2008).

66. Kanwal, "India's National Security Strategy in a Nuclear Environment," interview with Salman Haider, New Delhi, July 21, 2005.

67. Press Information Bureau, Government of India, "Cabinet Committee on Security Reviews Progress in Operationalizing India's Nuclear Doctrine," January 4, 2003, http://pib.nic.in/archieve/Ireleng/lyr2003/rjan2003/04012003/r040120033.html (accessed June 9, 2003).

68. Ibid. According to the Defense Ministry, India's "defence policy and force postures remain defensive in orientation." Ministry of Defense, Government of India, "Security Environment: An Overview," 3.

69. Subhash Kapila, "India's New 'Cold Start' War Doctrine Strategically Reviewed," paper no. 991, South Asia Analysis Group, May 4, 2004, http://www.southasiaanalysis.org/%5Cpapers10%5Cpaper991.html (accessed September 22, 2009).

70. It is possible, therefore, that Indian leaders expect that permanent deployment of forces nearer the border and quick response would compel a relatively weaker Pakistan to spread its forces thinly and, consequently, compel Pakistani leaders to refrain from limited probes into Kashmir similar to those that provoked the Kargil episode. On this, see T.V. Paul, "Why Has the India–Pakistan Rivalry Been So Enduring? Power Asymmetry and an Intractable Conflict," *Security Studies*, 15, no. 4 (October–December, 2006): 600–630.

71. Ismat, "Strategy for Total Defence."

72. Pakistan, Ministry of Foreign Affairs, "Pakistan's Foreign Policy," http://www.forisb.org/ForeignPolicy.html (accessed June 19, 2003).

73. Pakistan, Ministry of Foreign Affairs, "Kashmir Dispute: Background," http://www.mofa.gov.pk/Pages/Brief.htm (accessed June 19, 2003).

74. Peter R. Lavoy, "Pakistan's Nuclear Doctrine," in *Prospects for Peace in South Asia*, eds. Rafiq Dossani and Henry S. Rowen (Stanford, Calif.: Stanford University Press, 2005): chap. 11. See also Zafar Iqbal Cheema, "Pakistan's Nuclear Use Doctrine and Command and Control," in *Planning the Unthinkable*, eds. Peter R. Lavoy, Scott C. Sagan, and James J. Wirtz (Ithaca, N.Y.: Cornell University Press, 2001), 158–181; Timothy D. Hoyt, "Pakistani Nuclear Doctrine and the Dangers of Strategic Myopia," *Asian Survey*, 41, no. 6 (2001): 956–977.

75. The 1990–2006 defense spending figures for all countries and regions (in 2005 constant U.S. dollars) are from Stockholm International Peace Research Institute, "SIPRI Yearbook 2007," http://www.sipri.org/contents/milap/milex/mex_wnr_table.html (accessed June 26, 2007).

76. Because SIPRI and the IISS define their regions in different ways, the military spending figures are for South Asia, whereas the manpower figures are for central and southern Asia.

77. See Rajesh Rajagopalan, "Innovations in Counterinsurgency: The Indian Army's Rashtriya Rifles," *Contemporary South Asia*, 13, no. 1 (March 2004): 25–37.

78. See Stephen Philip Cohen, "The Jihadist Threat to Pakistan," *The Washington Quarterly*, 26, no. 3 (Summer 2003): 7–25. Baluchis are irked by the Pakistani central government's lack of focus on the region's economic development and extraction of its mineral wealth. Mohamad N. Osman, "Baluchistan: A Miscalculated Killing," *IDSS Commentaries*, 93 (September 1, 2006) 1–3.

79. Regarding the Pakistani army's conception, see Stephen Philip Cohen, *The Idea of Pakistan* (Washington D.C.: Brookings Institution Press, 2004), 62.

80. The support base of some of these groups seems to be growing since the Afghan war started. In the October 2002 elections, Muttahida Majlis-e-Amal, a coalition of six Islamic parties, garnered fifty-three seats in the Pakistani National Assembly (17% of the total membership) and thereby achieved chief opposition party status. It also formed the government in the Northwest Frontier Province. Other groups that have played a significant role in Pakistan include Jama'at-i-Islmai, Tablighi jama'at, Islmai Jaiat-i-Tulabah, and Jamiat-e-Ulema-e-islam. Terrorist groups such as Harkat ul-Mujahideen, Jaish-e-Mohammed, and Laskar-e-Taiba have stepped up their activities, especially in the Indian side of Kashmir, and have been banned, only to resurface under other names. Some of these groups have also been associated with warring sectarian groups involving Shias, Sunnis, and Deobandis, and have been the instigators of much of violence that recurs in Pakistani society. See Cohen, "The Jihadist Threat to Pakistan,"

8–11. States Cohen: "Paradoxically, it has almost always been the state, especially the Pakistani Army, that has allowed most radical Islamic groups to function on a wider stage—equipping and training them when necessary and providing overall strategic guidance for their activities." Ibid., 14.

81. See NGO Committee on Disarmament, Peace and Security, "India/Pakistan: NGOs and Activism," (New York: United Nations), http://disarm.igc.org/indiapakistan-ngos.php (accessed April 22, 2008). The peace process has increased the people-to-people contact across the border.

82. Dhaka Declaration, 13th SAARC Summit, November 13, 2005, http://www.mofa.gov.np/uploads/news/20060309153959.pdf (accessed February 26, 2009).

83. India granted Pakistan Most Favored Nation (MFN) status in 1995, which has not yet been reciprocated. Bilateral trade figures in 2005–2006 were around $800 million, whereas informal trade was estimated at $2 billion, a paltry sum compared with what they could achieve if trade liberalization were to occur. Nirupama Subramanian, "India–Pakistan Trade Stuck on SAFTA," *The Hindu*, July 31, 2006, http://www.thehindu.com/2006/07/31/stories/2006073101901100.htm (accessed September 22, 2009). Regarding the January 2006 SAFTA agreement, see "South Asian Free Trade Area (SAFTA)," n.d., http://www.saarc-sec.org/main.php?t=2.1.6 (accessed April 22, 2008).

84. Some argue the proposed pipeline has the potential to transform the "social and political discourse between the countries, perhaps even leading to mediation and resolution of regional conflicts." See Shamila N. Chaudhary, "Iran to India Natural Gas Pipeline: Implications for Conflict Resolution & Regionalism in India, Iran, and Pakistan," *TED Case Studies*, 11, no. 1 (January 2001), 1, http://www.american.edu/TED/iranpipeline.htm (accessed April 22, 2008).

Chapter 6

1. For examples, see Herbert M. Howe, *Ambiguous Order: Military Forces in African States* (Boulder, Colo.: Lynne Rienner, 2001), 3.

2. Robert I. Rotberg, "Failed States, Collapsed Sates, Weak States: Causes and Indicators," in *State Failure and State Weakness in a Time of Terror*, ed. Robert I. Rotberg (Washington D.C.: Brookings Institution Press, 2003), 3.

3. For these characteristics, see Rotberg, "Failed States, Collapsed Sates, Weak States," 3.

4. A staggering 77% of all international crises in the post-Cold War era have involved at least one unstable or failing state. See Joseph Hewitt, Jonathan Wilkenfeld, and Ted Robert Gurr, *Peace and Conflict 2008*, "Executive Summary," http://www.cidcm.umd.edu/pc/executive_summary/pc_es_200706 13.pdf (accessed April 27, 2008), 1.

5. See, for example, S. Neil MacFarlane, "The Superpowers and Third World Security," in *The Insecurity Dilemma: National Security of Third World States*, ed. Brian L. Job (Boulder, Colo.: Lynne Rienner, 1992), 209–230.

6. See, for example, Severine M. Rugumamu, *Globalization Demystified: Africa's Possible Development Futures* (Dar es Salaam: Dar es Salaam University Press, 2005).

7. Rotberg, "Failed States, Collapsed Sates," 4.

8. Ibid., 5.

9. Paul-Henri Bischoff, "Regionalism and Regional Cooperation in Africa: New Century Challenges and Prospects," pp. 121–146 in *Africa at the Crossroads: Between Regionalism and Globalization*, eds. John Mukum Mbaku and Suresh Chandra Saxena (Westport, Conn.: Praeger, 2004), 121.

10. The Fund for Peace, "Failed States Index 2006," http://www.fundforpeace.org/programs/fsi/fsindex2006.php (accessed October 10, 2006).

11. For an argument against this view of South African exceptionalism in government, see Mahmood Mamdani, *Citizen and Subject: Contemporary Africa and the Legacy of Late Colonialism* (Princeton, N.J.: Princeton University Press, 1996).

12. Robert H. Jackson and Carl G. Rosberg "Why Africa's Weak States Persist: The Empirical and the Juridical in Statehood," *World Politics*, 35, no. 1 (1982): 1–24; Jeffrey Herbst, *States and Power in Africa* (Princeton, N.J.: Princeton University Press, 2000).

13. "The Correlates of War Project," http://www.correlatesofwar.org/cow2%20data/WarData/InterState/Inter-State%20Wars%20 (V%203–0).htm (accessed October 10, 2006).

14. Kristian Gleditsch, "A Revised List of Wars between and within Independent States, 1816–2002," *International Interactions*, 30 (2004): 231–262.

15. Guy Martin, *Africa in World Politics: A Pan African Perspective* (Trenton, N.J.: Africa World Press, 2002): 199–204. Many suggest that most internal war/civil wars in the region are extensively supported by external actors, blurring the inter-/intra-state distinction. See, for example, Monty G. Marshall, "Conflict Trends in Africa, 1946–2004: A Macro-Comparative Perspective," Report prepared for the Africa Conflict Prevention Pool, Government of the United Kingdom, October 14, 2005, http://www.systemicpeace.org/africa/AfricaConflictTrendsMGM2005us.pdf (accessed September 22, 2009).

16. Esther Pan, "African Peacekeeping Operations," December 2, 2005, *Council on Foreign Relations*, http://www.cfr.org/publication/9333/african_peacekeeping_operations.html (accessed October 10, 2006).

17. As Herbst observes, the prevalence of civil and ethnic wars has eroded the possibility of African states emerging as strong entities, unlike the European state formation experience. As a result, only a few African states have been successful in mobilizing their populations for external war. Jeffrey Herbst, "States and War in Africa," in *The Nation-State in Question*, eds. T.V. Paul, G. John Ikenberry, and John A. Hall (Princeton, N.J.: Princeton University Press, 2003), 166.

18. This war deserves special mention because it is often called Africa's *Great War*, in terms of the number of casualties (estimates vary from 350,000–1,000,000).

It began in the early 1990s, but became intense in 1994, when more than a million Hutus fled from the Rwandan genocide. In 1996, rebel leader Laurent Kabila, with the support of Rwanda, overthrew the Mobutu Sese Seko regime. Rwandan support for the Kabila regime was withdrawn as a result of operations of Hutus from the eastern Congo against Tutsis in Rwanda, and Rwanda and Uganda supported the rebel group Congolese Rally for Democracy, which tried to depose Kabila. Other African states, such as Zimbabwe, Angola, and Namibia, provided military support to the Kabila regime. A ceasefire was signed in July 1999, but violations continue. This war has both civil war and interstate characteristics. See Carolyn Pumphrey and Rye Schwartz-Barcott, eds., *Armed Conflict in Africa, A Chronology of Armed Conflict: Prehistory to Present* (Lanham, Md: Scarecrow Press, 2003), 275.

19. Mohamed Olad Hassan, "Ethiopians Said to Patrol Somali Road," *Washington Post*, November 23, 2006, A26.

20. Howe, *Ambiguous Order*, 77–78.

21. Ibid., 77–112.

22. Ibid., 89.

23. Stephen Ellis and David Killingray, "Africa after 11 September 2001," *African Affairs*, 101, no. 402 (January 2002): 8.

24. James Ferguson, *Global Shadows: Africa in the Neoliberal World Order* (Durham, N. Caro.: Duke University Press, 2006), 38.

25. For a general argument, see Paul Collier, "Rebellion as a Quasi-Criminal Activity," *Journal of Conflict Resolution*, 44, no. 6 (December 2000): 839–853.

26. William Reno, *Warlord Politics and African States* (Boulder, Colo.: Lynne Rienner, 1998), 100.

27. William Reno, "Clandestine Economies, Violence and States in Africa," *Journal of International Affairs*, 53, no. 2 (2000): 433–459.

28. These include many insurgent groups fighting governments, such as "UNITA and RENAMO in Angola and Mozambique, the Mai Mai, Lord's Resistance ARMY [in Uganda], the LURD, MODEL, [Liberia]" in addition to governments that follow terrorist means such as "Liberia under Charles Taylor, Zimbabwe," under Mugabe, Angola, and, most conspicuous, the Sudanese government in the southern Darfur region. See Jakkie Ciliers, "Terrorism and Africa," *African Security Review*, 12, no. 4 (2003): 93.

29. National Counterterrorism Center, "Reports on Terrorist Incidents," 2006, http://www.terrorisminfo.mipt.org/pdf/Country-Reports-Terrorism-2006-NCTC-Annex.pdf (accessed May 2, 2008).

30. National Counterterrorism Center, "2007 Report on Terrorism," http://www.terrorisminfo.mipt.org/pdf/NCTC-2007-Report-on-Terrorism.pdf (accessed May 2, 2008).

31. United States Institute of Peace, "Terrorism in the Horn of Africa," Washington D.C., United States Institute of Peace, *Special Report*, 113 (January 2004): 2.

32. Harvey Glickman, "Africa in the War on Terrorism," *Journal of Asian and African Studies*, 38, nos. 2–3 (August 2003): 167.

33. "Somali Jihadis May be Coming from Canada," *The Gazette*, October 14, 2006, A27.

34. Mark Malan, "The Post-9/11 Security Agenda and Peacekeeping in Africa," *African Security Review*, 11, no. 3 (2002): 3.

35. John W. Harbeson, "Ethiopia and the Global Antiterrorism Campaign," *CSIS AFRICA Policy Forum*, February 27, 2007, http://forums.csis.org/africa/?p=26 (accessed May 1, 2008).

36. For a discussion of the state of terrorism in these countries, see "Terrorism in the Horn of Africa," 4–15. Beyond the Horn, both Nigeria (with its twelve Muslim majority states) and South Africa have Islamic terrorist cells on their soil. See Glickman, "Africa in the War on Terrorism," 168.

37. J. Stephen Morrison, "Somalia's and Sudan's Race to the Fore in Africa," *The Washington Quarterly*, 25, no. 2 (Spring 2002): 203; Adikeye Adebajo, "Africa and America in an Age of Terror," *Journal of Asian and African Studies*, 38, nos. 2–3 (August 2003): 181.

38. Malan, "The Post-9/11 Security Agenda and Peacekeeping in Africa," 3.

39. Robert L. Ostergard, "Politics in the Hot Zone: AIDS and National Security in Africa," *Third World Quarterly*, 23, no. 2 (2002): 333–350.

40. Robyn Pharaoh and Martin Schonteich, *AIDS, Security and Governance in Southern Africa*, Occasional paper no. 65 (Pretoria: Institute for Security Studies, January 2003).

41. For example, long-haul truckers appear to have spread HIV in Uganda in its early years. See James Putzel, "The Politics of Action on AIDS: A Case Study of Uganda," *Public Administration and Development*, 24, no. 1 (February 2004): 21; and, more generally, Lee-Nah Hsu, "Building Dynamic Democratic Governance and HIV-Resilient Societies," *International Social Science Journal*, 57, no. 186 (December 2005): 709–710.

42. For these consequences of the disease, see Pieter Fourie and Martin Schonteich, "Africa's New Security Threat: HIV/AIDS and Human Security in Southern Africa," *African Security Review*, 10, no. 4 (2001): 29–44.

43. Stephen Lewis, *Race against Time: Searching for Hope in AIDS-Ravaged Africa*, 2nd ed. (Toronto: Anansi Press, 2006); Alex de Waal, "How Will HIV/AIDS Transform African Governance?" *African Affairs*, 102, no. 406 (January 2003): 1.

44. For a good overview of the main arguments on this point, see Harley Feldbaum, Kelley Lee, and Preeti Patel, "The National Security Implications of HIV/AIDS," *PLoS Medicine*, 3, no. 6 (June 2006): 771–778.

45. See de Waal, "How Will HIV/AIDS Transform African Governance?" 11–17.

46. See Rotberg, "Failed States, Collapsed States, Weak States" 13.

47. Gregory R. Copley, "AIDS and African Armies: A Crisis Worse Than War," *Defense & Foreign Affairs Strategic Review*, 27, no. 11 (November 1999): 4–6.

48. UNAIDS/ UNICEF/ USAID, *Children on the Brink 2004: A Joint Report of New Orphan Estimates and a Framework for Action* (New York: United Nations Children's Fund, 2004), 26; http://www.unicef.org/publications/files/cob_layout6–013.pdf (accessed May 2, 2008); Lindy Heinecken, "Living in Terror: The Looming Security Threat to Southern Africa," *African Security Review*, 10, no. 4 (2001): 2.

49. Indeed, soldiers have become an important AIDS vector. It has been argued that conflict in Angola in the 1970s and '80s helped in the dissemination of HIV/AIDS in different parts of the region. To a large extent, HIV/AIDS has been spread through widespread rape in civilian areas, and through unprotected sex by regular armies, especially in large refugee camps. Consequently, rape—long used as a weapon of war, or at least an attendant evil associated with war—causes even greater damage in an age of AIDS than it ever did, and now AIDS has come to be regarded as itself a weapon of war. See Stefan Elbe, "HIV/AIDS and the Changing Landscape of War in Africa," *International Security*, 27, no. 2 (Fall 2002): 167–171; Dennis Altman, "AIDS and Security," *International Relations*, 17, no. 4 (2003): 421.

50. Gregory R. Copley, "AIDS and African Armies: A Crisis Worse Than War," *Defense & Foreign Affairs Strategic Review*, 27, no. 11 (November 1999): 4–6.

51. John Kemoli Sagala, "HIV/AIDS and the Military in Sub-Saharan Africa: Impact on Military Organizational Effectiveness," *Africa Today*, 53, no. 1 (2006): 53–77.

52. Fourie and Schonteich, "Africa's New Security Threat."

53. International Institute for Strategic Studies, *Small Arms Survey 2005: Weapons at War* (Geneva: Graduate School of International Studies, 2005): 248.

54. Ibid., 249. These data come with several caveats, including small sample size and the time period surveyed. Moreover, conflict deaths are inherently hard to measure because of the chaotic circumstances in which they occur.

55. Ibid., 98.

56. Regarding the efforts of the AU, see African Union, "Small Arms and Light Weapons," http://www.africa-union.org/root/au/AUC/Departments/PSC/Small_Arms.htm (accessed July 19, 2007).

57. Different insurgencies have different sourcing patterns of weapons. For example, the 1990–1996 Tuareg insurgency in Mali relied on looting existing army stockpiles, whereas Liberian rebels procured weapons through international channels to a greater degree, with sources as close as Cote d'Ivoire and as far away as China. To a large extent, Liberian rebels' greater access to international sources stemmed from their access to capital from natural resource predation. Jakkie Cillers, *Human Security in Africa: A Conceptual Framework for Review* (Nairobi, Kenya: African Human Security Initiative, 2004), 165–169. This further suggests the interrelationships among components of state weakness. However, the looting of stockpiles is also connected to global trade flows.

58. Ostergard, "Politics in the Hot Zone," 345.

59. Altman, "AIDS and Security," 422.

60. Putzel, "The Politics of Action on AIDS," 23.

61. De Waal, "How Will HIV/AIDS Transform African Governance?," 21.

62. African Union, "Abuja Declaration on HIV/AIDS, Tuberculosis and Other Related Infectious Diseases," 2000, http://www.uneca.org/ADF2000/Abuja% 20Declaration.htm (accessed September 13, 2009), para. 22.

63. African Union, "Abuja Call for Accelerated Action towards Universal Access to HIV and AIDS, Tuberculosis and Malaria Services in Africa," 2006, http:// www.africa-union.org/root/au/conferences/past/2006/may/summit/doc/en/ ABUJA_CALL.pdf (accessed September 13, 2009), para. 8.

64. De Waal, "How Will HIV/AIDS Transform African Governance?," 21–22.

65. Putzel, "The Politics of Action on AIDS," 19–30; Justin O. Parkhurst, "The Response to HIV/AIDS and the Construction of National Legitimacy: Lessons from Uganda," *Development and Change*, 36, no. 3 (2005): 571–590.

66. See Robert I. Rotberg, "Failed States in a World of Terror," *Foreign Affairs*, 81, no. 4 (July/August 2004): 127–140.

67. According to an Ethiopian general we interviewed, the end of the Cold War brought soft security issues to the forefront in Africa, and regimes have become increasingly aware of the need for acknowledging them to receive international legitimacy. Interview with Lt. Gen. (Retd.) Tensae Tsadkhan, Former Chief of Staff of Ethiopian Armed Forces, Addis Ababa, January 6, 2006.

68. African Union, Assembly of the Union, 2nd Extraordinary Session, February 27–28, 2004, Sirte, Libya, http://www.africa-union.org/root/au/Documents/ Decisions/hog/DECISIONS_Sirte_2004.pdf (accessed September 13, 2009).

69. Department for International Development, *The Causes of Conflict in Sub-Saharan Africa* (London: Department for International Development, 2001), 8; http://www. dfid.gov.uk/Pubs/files/conflict_subsaharanafrica.pdf (accessed June 19, 2003).

70. See Boaz Atzili, "When Good Fences Make Bad Neighbours: Fixed Borders, State Weakness, and International Conflict," *International Security*, 31, no. 3 (Winter 2006–2007): 139–173.

71. Howe, *Ambiguous Order*, 113.

72. Tony Clayton, "African Military Capabilities in Insurrection, Intervention and Peace Support Operations," in *African Interventionist States*, eds. Oliver Furley and Roy May (London: Ashgate, 2001): 53.

73. Ibid., 55–56.

74. Jimmy D. Kandeh, "Civil–Military Relations," in *West Africa's Security Challenges*, eds. Adekeye Adebajo and Ismail Rashid (Boulder, Colo.: Lynne Rienner, 2004), 148–149.

75. South Africa is one state in which defense doctrines present a tractable point of analysis. See Rocklyn Williams, "A Postmodern Military: Mission Redefinition and Defensive Restructuring," pp. 71–86 in *Defensive Restructuring of Armed Forces in Southern Africa*, eds. Gavin Cawthra and Bjorn Moller (London:

Ashgate, 1997); and Martin Rupiya, "Post War Restructuring: The Region's Defence Structures," in *Defensive Restructuring of Armed Forces in Southern Africa*, eds. Gavin Cawthra and Bjorn Moller (London: Ashgate, 1997), 44–54. However, the importance of defense doctrines in South Africa exists precisely because it is not as weak a state as most other states in the region.

76. John Abbink, "Ethiopia–Eritrea: Proxy Wars and Prospects of Peace in the Horn of Africa," *Journal of Contemporary African Studies*, 21, no. 3 (September 2003): 407–426; Lionel Cliffe, "Regional Dimensions of Conflict in the Horn of Africa," *Third World Quarterly*, 20, no. 1 (1999): 89–111.

77. Mark Malan, "Regional Power Politics under Cover of SADC," Institute for Security Studies occasional paper no. 35, October 1998, http://www.iss.co.za/Pubs/PAPERS/35/Paper35.html (accessed May 1, 2008).

78. John F. Clark, "Explaining Ugandan Intervention in Congo: Evidence and Interpretations," *Journal of Modern African Studies*, 39, no. 2 (2001): 261–287.

79. An exception, as noted, is Nigeria's ambitions for regional hegemony, displacing France.

80. Chris Alden, "China in Africa," *Survival*, 47, no. 3 (2005): 147–164; Denis M. Tull, "China's Engagement in Africa: Scope, Significance and Consequences," *Journal of Modern African Studies*, 44, no. 3 (2006): 459–479.

81. Data on national manpower come from International Institute for Strategic Studies, *The Military Balance*, 1989–2007 issues.

82. See Jeffrey Herbst, "African Militaries and Rebellion: The Political Economy of Threat and Combat Effectiveness," *Journal of Peace Research*, 41, no. 3 (2004): 357–369. Herbst's figures are calculated from U.S. Arms Control and Disarmament Agency, *World Military Expenditures and Arms Transfers, 1999* (Washington, D.C.: United States State Department, 2001)

83. These states were Angola, Benin, Burkina Faso, Cameroon, Central African Republic, Chad, Congo-Brazzaville, Democratic Republic of the Congo, Equatorial Guinea, Eritrea, Ethiopia, Gambia, Ghana, Guinea, Guinea-Bissaw, Kenya, Madagascar, Malawi, Mali, Namibia, Niger, Nigeria, Seychelles, South Africa, Sudan, Tanzania, Zambia, and Zimbabwe.

84. "Small increases" are defined as less than one soldier per 1,000 people. These states were Botswana, Burundi, Cape Verde, Cote d'Ivoire, Gabon, Lesotho, Mauritius, Mozambique, Senegal, Somalia, Togo, and Uganda.

85. These states were Angola, Benin, Central African Republic, Ethiopia, Kenya, Madagascar, Nigeria, Seychelles, South Africa, Tanzania, Zambia, and Zimbabwe.

86. These states were Botswana, Chad, Congo-Brazzaville, Equatorial Guinea, Gabon, Gambia, Ghana, Guinea, Guinea-Bissau, Lesotho, Mali, Mauritius, Niger, and Somalia.

87. Defined as increasing by fewer than 10,000 personnel. These states were Burkina Faso, Burundi, Cameroon, Cape Verde, Cote d'Ivoire, Democratic Republic of the Congo, Djibouti, Liberia, Malawi, Mozambique, Namibia, Senegal, Sierra Leone, and Togo.

88. These figures are compiled from Christopher Langton, ed., *The Military Balance 2006* (London: International Institute for Strategic Studies, 2006), 353–394; and from Terence Taylor, ed., *The Military Balance 1999–2000* (London: International Institute for Strategic Studies, 1999), 252–279.

89. It should, however, be noted that the size of military forces in this region has been very small. Only four had 80,000 or more troops, twenty-one averaged fewer than 10,000, seventeen states with coastal access had fewer than 500 troops in the navy, and twenty-five states had fewer than 500 in the air force.

90. We do not report the same countries for the defense expenditure and manpower portions of this section, because data on many of the failed African states is scarce and, at times, contradictory. Thus, we provide what we can to give a picture of developments in the region.

91. The 1990–2006 defense spending figures for the region, in 2005 constant U.S. dollars, are from Stockholm International Peace Research Institute, "SIPRI Yearbook 2007," http://www.sipri.org/contents/milap/milex/mex_wnr_table.html (accessed June 26, 2007). The 1991–2005 defense spending figures for all countries (in 2005 constant U.S. dollars) are from The SIPRI Military Expenditure Database, http://www.sipri.org/contents/milap/milex/mex_database1.html (accessed June 26, 2007).

92. Peter Batchelor, Paul Dunne, and Guy Lamb, "The Demand for Military Spending in South Africa," *Journal of Peace Research*, 39, no. 3 (2002): 339–354.

93. Rupiya, "Post War Restructuring," 46.

94. Some attribute this decline in part to combinations of shrinking budgets, international pressures to downsize and demobilize, and absence of international assistance such as that seen during the Cold War. William G. Thom, "Judging Africa's Military Capabilities," *Journal of Third World Studies*, 5, no. 2 (1988): 52–65; Jeffrey Herbst, "African Militaries and Rebellion: The Political Economy of Threat and Combat Effectiveness," *Journal of Peace Research*, 41, no. 3 (2004): 357–369.

95. Herbst, "African Militaries and Rebellion," 360.

96. It is frequently difficult to distinguish between African armies and police forces, because police forces in the region are typically quasi military and both groups have low status and are prone to violence and abuse of power. Peter Lock, "Africa: Military Downsizing and the Growth in the Security Industry," in *Peace, Profit or Plunder: The Privatization of Security in War-Torn Africa*, eds. Jackie Cillers and Peggy Mason (Pretoria: Institute for Security Studies, 1999), 11–36.

97. Alice Hills, "Policing Low Intensity Conflicts," in *Policing Africa: Internal Security and the Limits of Liberalization*, ed. Alice Hills (Boulder, Colo.: Lynne Rienner, 2000), 947.

98. Jakkie Cilliers and Peggy Mason, eds., *Peace, Profit or Plunder: The Privatization of Security in War-Torn Africa* (Pretoria: Institute for Security Studies, 1999), 1–9.

99. Lock, "Africa," 16.

100. Reno, *Warlord Politics and African States*, 57–61.

101. Charles H. Fairbanks, Jr., "Weak States and Private Armies," in *Beyond State Crisis? Postcolonial Africa and Post-Soviet Eurasia in Comparative Perspective*, eds. Mark R. Beissinger and Crawford Young (Washington, D.C.: Woodrow Wilson Center Press, 2002), 145. Private Military Companies (PMCs) themselves have been criticized as partners of arms brokers and local warlords who engage in illegitimate resource appropriation and thereby cause and contribute to many ongoing civil wars and the proliferation of weapons that accompany them. See Abdel-Fatau Musah, "Privatization of Security, Arms Proliferation and the Process of State Collapse in Africa," *Development and Change*, 33, no. 5 (2002): 911–933.

102. For a list of these NGOs, see United Nations, "Networking: Directory of African NGOs," http://www.un.org/africa/osaa/ngodirectory/ (accessed June 27 1, 2008).

103. Alex de Waal, *Famine Crimes: Politics and the Disaster Relief Industry in Africa* (Bloomington: Indiana University Press, 1997); Wafula Okumu, "Humanitarian International NGOs and African Conflicts," *International Peacekeeping*, 10, no. 1 (2003): 120–137. For a related argument about the use of NGOs to advance political objectives, see Gerald Steinberg, "NGOs Make War on Israel," *Middle East Quarterly*, 11, no. 3 (Summer 2004), http://www.meforum.org/article/633 (accessed June 27, 2008).

104. Bischoff, "Regionalism and Regional Cooperation in Africa," 124. He argues that "[t]he withdrawal of superpowers, the demise of apartheid in South Africa, changes at the United Nations, the promise of aid and trade concessions, conditionalities laid down by the structural adjustment programs of the World Bank and the IMF and a new uniformity in politics away from one-party states to multiparty democracy and a similar, 'liberal' outlook toward cooperation have all been factors in the reconstitution of regional organizations." Ibid., 125–126.

105. Regarding OAU efforts at regional conflict management, see Margaret A. Vogt, "The OAU and Conflict Management," Presented at the International Resource Group Conference, Mombasa, Kenya, November 6–9, 1996.

106. Solomon Gomes, "The OAU, State Sovereignty, and Regional Security," in *Africa in the New International Order*, eds. Edmund J. Keller and Donald S. Rothchild (Boulder, Colo.: Lynne Rienner, 1996), 38.

107. Stephen F. Burgess, "African Security in the 21st Century: The Challenges of Indigenization and Multilateralism," *African Studies Review*, 41, no. 2 (September 1998): 40.

108. "Protocol Relating to the Establishment of the Peace and Security Council of the African Union," July 9, 2002, http://www.africa-union.org/root/au/organs/psc/Protocol_peace%20and%20security.pdf (accessed June 27, 2008).

109. Vanessa Kent and Mark Malan, "The African Standby Force: Progress and Prospects," *African Security Review*, 12, no. 3 (2003): 71–81.

110. Pan, "African Peacekeeping Operations."

111. Stephanie Hanson, "The Nascent African Union," *Council on Foreign Relations*, http://www.cfr.org/publication/11616/ (accessed October 10, 2006).

112. UNAMID, "Darfur—UNAMID—Facts and Figures," http://www.un.org/Depts/dpko/missions/unamid/facts.html (accessed May 7, 2008).

113. See Bischoff, "Regionalism and Regional Cooperation in Africa," 136.

114. Howe, *Ambiguous Order*, 163. Regarding the mission in Liberia, see Robert A. Mortimer, "ECOMOG, Liberia, and Regional Security in West Africa," in *Africa in the New International Order*, eds. Edmund J. Keller and Donald S. Rothchild (Boulder, Colo.: Lynne Rienner, 1996), 149–164.

115. Howe, *Ambiguous Order*, 165.

116. See Naison Ngoma, "SADC: Towards a Security Community?," *African Security Review*, 12, no. 3 (2003): 17–28. Critics contend that states in southern Africa are unwilling to forgo national conceptions of sovereignty and are unable to see security as a broader problem, and these issues have undermined the efforts to create a security community. Sandra J. Maclean, "Peacebuilding and the New Regionalism in South Africa," *Third World Quarterly*, 20, no. 5 (1999): 943–956.

117. See Burgess, "African Security in the 21st Century," 44.

118. See Bischoff, "Regionalism and Regional Cooperation in Africa," 29.

119. Burgess, "African Security in the 21st Century," 39.

120. See Connie Peck, *Sustainable Peace: The Role of the UN and Regional Organizations in Preventing Conflict* (Lanham, Md.: Rowman and Littlefield, 1998): 155–172. One AU official considers the inclusion of internal conflicts under AU's jurisdiction as a major achievement. Interview with Ambassador Said Djinnit of Algeria, AU Headquarters, Addis Abbaba, January 3, 2005.

121. I. William Zartman, "Regional Conflict Management in Africa," in *Regional Conflict Managements*, eds. Paul F. Diehl and Joseph Lepgold (Lanham, Md.: Rowman and Littlefield, 2003): 81–103. States in more advanced regions of southern Africa are also unwilling to forgo national conceptions of sovereignty, and their inability to see security as a broader problem has undermined the efforts to create a security community. See Maclean, "Peacebuilding and the New Regionalism in South Africa," 943–956.

122. George B. N. Ayittey, "NEPAD and Africa's Leaky Begging Bowl," *Global Dialogue*, 6, nos. 3–4 (Summer/Autumn 2004): 28.

Conclusion

1. For some of these causes see Raimo Väyrynen, ed., *The Waning of Major Wars: Theories and Debates* (New York: Routledge, 2006); John Mueller, *Retreat from Doomsday: The Obsolescence of Major Wars* (New York: Basic Books, 1989); Mark W. Zacher, "The Territorial Integrity Norms: International Boundaries and the Use of Force," *International Organization*, 55, no. 2 (Spring 2001): 215–250.

2. Harvey Starr, *Anarchy, Order, and Integration* (Ann Arbor: The University of Michigan Press, 1997), 73.

3. See Deborah D. Avant, *The Market of Force: The Consequences of Privatizing Security* (Cambridge: Cambridge University Press, 2005): 16–22.

4. See, for example, John J. Mearsheimer, "The False Promise of International Institutions," *International Security*, 19, no. 3 (Winter 1994/1995): 5–49; Kenneth Waltz, *Theory of International Politics* (Reading, Mass.: Addison-Wesley, 1979).

5. Dale C. Copeland, *The Origins of Major War* (Ithaca, N.Y.: Cornell University Press, 2000), 240–245.

6. Kenneth N. Waltz, "Structural Realism After the Cold War," *International Security*, 25, no. 1 (Summer 2000): 5–41; John J. Mearsheimer, *The Tragedy of Great Power Politics* (New York: Norton, 2001): 370–372.

7. Patrick James, *International Relations and Scientific Progress: Structural Realism Reconsidered* (Columbus: The Ohio State University Press, 2002).

8. Norrin M. Ripsman and T. V. Paul, "Assessing the Uneven Impact of Global Social Forces on the National Security State: A Framework for Analysis," *International Studies Review*, 7, no. 2 (June 2005): 199–227; T. V. Paul and Norrin M. Ripsman, "Under Pressure: Globalization and the National Security State," *Millennium: Journal of International Studies*, 33, no. 2 (March 2004): 355–380.

9. George W. Bush, *The National Security Strategy of the United States of America* (Washington, D.C.: The White House, 2006), 47–48.

10. China, *China's National Defense in 2006*, sect. I, http://english.peopledaily.com.cn/whitepaper/defense2006/defense2006(1).html (accessed January 9, 2007).

11. Mancur Olson, *The Rise and Decline of Nations: Economic Growth, Stagflation, and Social Rigidities* (New Haven, Conn.: Yale University Press, 1982).

12. The classic budget maximizing model is offered by William A. Niskanen, *Bureaucracy and Representative Government* (Edison, N.J.: Transaction Publishers, 2007). See also Theodore Lowi, *The End of Liberalism*, 2nd ed. (New York: W. W. Norton, 1979).

13. Interview with Christopher "Ryan" Henry, Under Secretary of Defense (Policy), U.S. Department of Defense, August 30, 2005; Robert A. Manning, Senior Counselor, Energy Technology and Science Policy, U.S. Department of State; and Richard D. Sokolsky, Policy Planning Staff, U.S. Department of State, August 29, 2005.

14. Two key examples were the way in which individuals reacted to the September 11 attacks on the World Trade Center and the devastation caused by hurricane Katrina on New Orleans in August 2005. The focal point of attention was the state, even when the state failed in providing imminent assistance, especially in the latter case.

15. A monopoly over coercive power and the authority to make binding rules for all inhabitants, including social organizations within its territory, have been

the key attributes of nation-states. See Max Weber, *The Theory of Social and Economic Organization*, trans. A. M. Henderson and Talcott Parsons (New York: Free Press, 1968), 156. Regarding the multidimensional capacity of states to cope with changes, see T. V. Paul, G. John Ikenberry, and John A Hall, eds., *The Nation-State in Question* (Princeton, N.J.: Princeton University Press, 2003). See, also, John A. Hall and G. John Ikenberry, *The State* (Minneapolis: University of Minnesota Press, 1989).

16. Our purpose in this volume has been to provide a systematic test of the globalization school's propositions on national security in a globalized world. It would be beyond the scope of this book to develop a comprehensive theoretical alternative to the globalization paradigm. Nonetheless, it may be possible for other researchers to investigate the key attributes that allow the state as an institution to survive and adapt in the face of several challenges that it faces, especially in the modern age, but in particular in the intensified globalization era. Complex adaptive systems theory, derived from a nonlinear systems approach, has been increasingly applied in natural, behavioral, and social sciences, and may be one such approach. See Roy J. Eidelson, "Complex Adaptive Systems in the Behavioral and Social Sciences," *Review of General Psychology*, 1, no. 1 (1997): 42–71; J. Stephen Lansing, "Complex Adaptive Systems," *Annual Review of Anthropology*, 32 (2003): 183–204; J. H. Holland, *Hidden Order: How Adaptation Builds Complexity* (New York: Helix Books, 1995). For an application in international relations, see Robert Jervis, *System Effects: Complexity in Political and Social Life* (Princeton, N.J.: Princeton University Press, 1997).

17. Norman Angell, *The Great Illusion* (New York: G. P. Putnam's Sons, 1909).

18. John H. Herz, The Territorial State Revisited: Reflections on the Future of the Nation-State, *Polity*, Vol. 1, No. 1 (Autumn, 1968), pp. 11–34, at p. 13. See also John H. Herz, "Rise and Demise of the Territorial State," *World Politics*, 9 (1957): 473–493; Klaus Knorr, *On the Uses of Military Power in the Nuclear Age* (Princeton, N.J.: Princeton University Press, 1966). For a contemporary argument that the state system must eventually evolve to meet the challenge of nuclear weapons, see Daniel Deudney, *Bounding Power: Republican Security Theory from the Polis to the Global Village* (Princeton, N.J.: Princeton University Press, 2008).

19. Albert O. Hirschman, *The Passions and the Interests: Political Arguments for Capitalism before its Triumph* (Princeton, N.J.: Princeton University Press, 1977); Robert O. Keohane and Joseph S. Nye, Jr., "Power and Interdependence Revisited," *International Organization*, 41, no. 4 (Autumn 1987): 727; Robert O. Keohane and Joseph S. Nye, *Power and Interdependence*, 2nd ed. (New York: Harper Collins, 1989), 25, 27.

20. Richard Rosecrance, *The Rise of the Trading State: Commerce and Conquest in the Modern World* (New York: Basic Books, 1986), 24–25.

21. Barry Buzan, "Economic Structure and International Security: The Limits of the Liberal Case," *International Organization*, 38, no. 4 (Autumn 1984): 597–624; Benjamin Cohen, "The Revolution in Atlantic Economic Relations: A Bargain

Comes Unstuck," in *Crossing Frontiers: Explorations in International Political Economy*, ed. Benjamin Cohen (Boulder, Colo.: Westview Press, 1991), 102; Joanne Gowa, *Allies, Adversaries, and International Trade* (Princeton, N.J.: Princeton University Press, 1994).

22. See Robert Gilpin, *The Political Economy of International Relations* (Princeton, N.J.: Princeton University Press, 1987); G. John Ikenberry, *After Victory* (Princeton, N.J.: Princeton University Press, 2000); Robert Keohane, *After Hegemony* (Princeton, N.J.: Princeton University Press, 1984).

23. See, for example, Carter Dougherty, "Memo from Berlin: Allies See Germany Trying Bailout with a Thimble," *The New York Times*, December 16, 2008, http://www.nytimes.com/2008/12/17/world/europe/17germany.html?n=Top/ Reference/Times%20Topics/People/M/Merkel,%20Angela (accessed January 26, 2009).

24. For a discussion of securitization, see Barry Buzan, Ole Wæver, and Jaap de Wilde, *Security: A New Framework for Analysis* (Boulder, Colo.: Lynne Rienner, 1998). In this regard, we would conclude that, rather than being overtaken by globalization, the state's national security role has been altered.

25. Karl Polanyi, *The Great Transformation*, 2nd ed. (Boston, Mass.: Beacon Press, 2001), 130. Others have challenged the notion of "the modern state is passé." See Robert Boyer and Daniel Drache, eds. *States Against Markets: The Limits of Globalization* (London: Routledge, 1996).

26. Dani Rodrik, "Why Do More Open Economies Have Bigger Governments?," *Journal of Political Economy*, 106, no. 5 (1998): 997–1032; Linda Weiss, ed., *States in the Global Economy: Brining Domestic Institutions Back In* (New York: Cambridge University Press, 2003), chap. 1; Stephan Haggard and Robert R. Kaufman, "The State in the Initiation and Consolidation of Market-Oriented Reform," in *State and Market in Development: Synergy or Rivalry?*, eds. Louis Putterman and Dietrich Rueschemeyer (Boulder, Colo.: Lynne Rienner, 1992), chap. 11.

27. Baldev Raj Nayar, *The Myth of the Shrinking State: Globalization and the State in India* (New Delhi: Oxford University Press, 2009), 15. In his study on the Indian state, Nayar concludes: "[T]he relationship between market and the state is not a zero-sum game, and it can be empowering for both. Contrary to the fears or expectations of the critics, liberalization has not made for the erosion of the state. There has been no hollowing out of the state, and there has been no retrenchment of the state from either its economic role or its welfare role. Indeed, liberalization has been 'empowering' for the state; it has strengthened state capacity as a result of the increased resources that the state has been able to gain access to because of the growth acceleration that has accompanied liberalization." Ibid., 225.

28. For a discussion of commercial liberalism, see Robert O. Keohane, "International Liberalism Revisited," in *The Economic Limits to Modern Politics*, ed. John Dunn (Cambridge: Cambridge University Press, 1990), 186–187; and Michael W. Doyle, *Ways of War and Peace: Realism, Liberalism, and Socialism* (New York:

Norton, 1997), 230–250; Rosecrance, *The Rise of the Trading State*. For a discussion of complex interdependence, see Keohane and Nye, Jr., *Power and Interdependence*, 20–31.

29. See, for example, David R. Davis, John R. Oneal, and Bruce Russett, "The Third Leg of the Kantian Tripod for Peace: International Organizations and Militarized Disputes, 1950–85," *International Organization*, 52, no. 3 (Summer 1998): 441–467.

30. See, T. V. Paul, "Soft Balancing in the Age of U.S. Primacy," *International Security*, 30, no. 1 (Summer 2005): 46–71; Stephen Walt, *Taming American Power: The Global Response to U.S. Primacy* (New York: W. W. Norton, 2005).

31. For a structural realist account that anticipates the return to hard balancing, see Kenneth N. Waltz, "Structural Realism after the Cold War," *International Security*, 25, no. 1 (Summer 2000): 5–41.

32. Regarding hegemonic stability theory as an explanation for the broad-level cooperation with the United States after the Cold War, see William Wohlforth, "The Stability of a Unipolar World," *International Security*, 24, no. 1 (Summer 1999): 5–41.

33. For such norm-based approaches to security, see Martha Finnemore, *The Purpose of Intervention: Changing Beliefs about the Use of Force* (Ithaca, N.Y.: Cornell University Press, 2003); Alexander Wendt, *Social Theory of International Politics* (Cambridge: Cambridge University Press, 1999).

34. For examples of theories that combine the insights of different paradigms, see Peter J. Katzenstein, *A World of Regions: Asia and Europe in the American Imperium* (Ithaca, N.Y.: Cornell University Press, 2005); Benjamin Miller, *States, Nations, and the Great Powers: The Sources of Regional War and Peace* (Cambridge: Cambridge University Press, 2007); Norrin M. Ripsman, "Two Stages of Transition from a Region of War to a Region of Peace: Realist Transition and Liberal Endurance," *International Studies Quarterly*, 49, no. 4 (December 2005): 669–693; T. V. Paul, *The Tradition of Non-use of Nuclear Weapons* (Stanford, Calif.: Stanford University Press, 2009).

35. See Steven E. Lobell, Norrin M. Ripsman, and Jeffrey W. Taliaferro, eds., *Neoclassical Realism, the State, and Foreign Policy* (Cambridge: Cambridge University Press, 2009); Gideon Rose, "Neoclassical Realism and Theories of Foreign Policy," *World Politics*, 51, no. 1 (October 1998): 144–172; Randall L. Schweller, "The Progressiveness of Neoclassical Realism," in *Progress in International Relations Theory: Appraising the Field*, eds. Colin Elman and Miriam Fendius Elman (Cambridge, Mass.: MIT Press, 2003): 311–347; Randall L. Schweller, *Unanswered Threats: Political Constraints on the Balance of Power* (Princeton, N.J.: University Press, 2006.

36. See Patrick M. Morgan and T. V. Paul, "Deterrence among Great Powers in an Era of Globalization," in *Complex Deterrence: Strategy in the Global Era*, eds. T. V. Paul, Patrick M. Morgan, and James J. Wirtz (Chicago, Ill.: University of Chicago Press, 2009), 259–276.

SELECT BIBLIOGRAPHY

Abbink, John. "Ethiopia-Eritrea: Proxy Wars and Prospects of Peace in the Horn of Africa." *Journal of Contemporary African Studies* 21 (3) (September 2003): 407–426.

Acharya, Amitav. *Governance and Security in Southeast Asia: Assessing the Impact Of Defense Spending*. Eastern Asia policy papers 9. University of Toronto: York University Joint Center for Asia-Pacific Studies, 1995.

———. *The Quest for Identity: International Relations of Southeast Asia*. Singapore: Oxford University Press, 2000.

———. *Constructing a Security Community in Southeast Asia: ASEAN and the Problem of Regional Order*. London: Routledge, 2001.

Acharya, Amitav, and See Seng Tan. "Betwixt Balance and Community: America, ASEAN, and the Security of Southeast Asia." *International Relations of the Asia Pacific* 6 (2006): 37–59.

Adebajo, Adikeye. "Africa and America in an Age of Terror." *JAAS* 38 (2–3) (August 2003): 175–191.

Adler, Emanuel, and Michael Barnett, eds. *Security Communities*. Cambridge: Cambridge University Press, 1998.

———. "Security Communities in Theoretical Perspective." In *Security Communities*, edited by Emanuel Adler and Michael Barnett, 3–28. Cambridge, UK: Cambridge University Press, 1998.

Albrow, Martin. *The Global Age: State and Society beyond Modernity*. Stanford, Calif.: Stanford University Press, 1997.

Alden, Chris. "China in Africa." *Survival* 47 (3) (2005): 147–164.

Allison, Graeme. *Nuclear Terrorism: The Ultimate Preventable Catastrophe*. New York: Henry Holt, 2004.

Allison, Roy. "Russia Resurgent? Moscow's Campaign to Coerce Georgia to Peace." *International Affairs* 84 (6) (November 2008): 1145–1171.

Altman, Dennis. "AIDS and Security." *International Relations* 17 (4) (2003): 417–427.

Aly, Said, Abdel Moneim, and Robert H. Pelletreau. "U.S.–Egyptian Relations." *Middle East Policy* 8 (2) (June 2001): 45–58.

Andreas, Peter, and Richard Price. "From War Fighting to Crime Fighting: Transforming the American National Security State." *International Studies Review* 3 (3) (Fall 2001): 31–52.

Angell, Norman. *The Great Illusion*. New York: G. P. Putnam's Sons, 1909.

Anggoro, Kusnanto. "Globalization and the Military in Indonesia." In *Development and Security in Southeast Asia*, vol. 3, edited by David B. Dewitt and Carolina G. Hernandez, 259–276. Aldershot, UK: Ashgate, 2003.

Arend, Anthony Clark. "International Law and the Preemptive Use of Military Force. *The Washington Quarterly* 26 (2) (Spring 2003): 89–103.

Arreguin-Toft, Ivan. *How the Weak Win Wars: A Theory of Asymmetric Conflict*. Cambridge, UK: Cambridge University Press, 2005.

Askew, Marc. *Conspiracy, Politics, and a Disorderly Border: The Struggle to Comprehend Insurgency in Thailand's Deep South*. Washington, D.C.: East-West Center, 2007.

Atzili, Boaz. "When Good Fences Make Bad Neighbours: Fixed Borders, State Weakness, and International Conflict." *International Security* 31 (3) (Winter 2006–2007): 139–173.

Avant, Deborah D. *The Market for Force: The Consequences of Privatizing Security*. Cambridge: Cambridge University Press, 2005.

———. "The Implications of Marketized Security for IR Theory: The Democratic Peace, Late State Building, and the Nature and Frequency of Conflict." *Perspectives on Politics* 4 (3) (September 2006): 507–528.

Ayittey, George B. N. "NEPAD and Africa's Leaky Begging Bowl." *Global Dialogue* 6 (3–4) (Summer/Autumn 2004): 26–36.

Ayoob, Mohammed. *The Third World Security Predicament: Statemaking, Regional Conflict and the International System*. Boulder, Colo.: Lynne Rienner, 1995.

Baldwin, David A. *Economic Statecraft*. Princeton, N.J.: Princeton University Press, 1985.

———, ed. *Neorealism and Neoliberalism: The Contemporary Debate*. New York: Columbia University Press, 1993.

Barany, Zoltan. *Democratic Decline and the Decline of the Russian Military*. Princeton, N.J.: Princeton University Press, 2007.

Bar-Siman-Tov, Yaacov. "The United States and Israel since 1948: A 'Special Relationship?'" *Diplomatic History* 22 (2) (Spring 1998): 231–262.

Batchelor, Peter, Paul Dunne, and Guy Lamb. "The Demand for Military Spending in South Africa." *Journal of Peace Research* 39 (3) (2002): 339–354.

Bensahel, Nora. "Political Reform in the Middle East." In *The Future Security Environment in the Middle East: Conflict, Stability, and Political Change*, edited by Nora Bensahel and Daniel L. Byman. Santa Monica, Calif.: The RAND Corporation, 2004.

Berger, Peter L. "Four Faces of Global Culture." *The National Interest* 49 (Fall 1997): 23–30.

Bernstein, Steven F., and Benjamin Cashore. "Globalization, Four Paths of Internationalization and Domestic Policy Change: The Case of Eco-Forestry in British Columbia, Canada." *Canadian Journal of Political Science* 33 (1) (March 2000): 67–99.

Bhagwati, Jagdish. *In Defense of Globalization*. New York: Oxford University Press, 2004.

Bickerton, Ian J., and Carla Klausner. *A Concise History of the Arab-Israeli Conflict*. 4th edition. New York: Prentice Hall, 2002.

Bischoff, Paul-Henri. "Regionalism and Regional Cooperation in Africa: New Century Challenges and Prospects." In *Africa at the Crossroads: Between Regionalism and Globalization*, edited by John Mukum Mbaku and Suresh Chandra Saxena, 121–146. Westport, Conn.: Praeger, 2004.

Blanchard, Jean-Marc F. "Maritime Issues in Asia: The Problem of Adolescence." In *Asian Security Order: Instrumental and Normative Features*, edited by Muthiah Alagappa, 424–457. Stanford, Calif.: Stanford University Press, 2003.

Blanchard, Jean-Marc F., Edward D. Mansfield, and Norrin M. Ripsman. "The Political Economy of National Security: Economic Statecraft, Interdependence and International Conflict." *Security Studies* 9 (1) (Autumn 1999): 1–15.

Blanchard, Jean-Marc F., and Norrin M. Ripsman. "Measuring Vulnerability Interdependence: A Geopolitical Perspective." *Geopolitics* 1 (3) (Winter 1996): 225–246.

———. "Asking the Right Question: *When* Do Economic Sanctions Work?" *Security Studies* 9 (1) (Autumn 1999): 228–264.

———. "Rethinking Sensitivity Interdependence: Assessing Trade, Financial and Monetary Linkages Between States." *International Interactions* 27 (2) (June 2001): 95–127.

———. "A Political Theory of Economic Statecraft." *Foreign Policy Analysis* 4 (4) (October 2008): 373–400.

Blank, Laurie R. *The Role of International Financial Institutions in International Humanitarian Law*. Peaceworks 42. Washington, D.C.: U.S. Institute of Peace, 2002.

Blum, William. *Killing Hope: US Military and CIA Interventions Since World War II*. Eastbourne, UK: Gardner's Books, 2003.

Bokhari, Sarah. "Indo-Pak 'New Peace.'" *Journal on Science and World Affairs* 1 (2) (2005): 145–151.

Bose, Meena, and Rosanna Perroti, eds. *From Cold War to New World Order: The Foreign Policy of George H.W. Bush*. Westport, Conn.: Greenwood, 2002.

Boyer, Robert, and Daniel Drache, eds. *States Against Markets: The Limits of Globalization*. London: Routledge, 1996.

Brecher, Michael, and Jonathan Wilkenfeld. *A Study of Crisis*. Ann Arbor: University of Michigan Press, 1997.

Brooks, Stephen G. "The Globalization of Production and the Changing Benefits of Conquest." *Journal of Conflict Resolution* 43 (5) (October 1999): 646–670.

———. *Producing Security: Multinational Corporations, Globalization, and the Changing Calculus of Conflict.* Princeton, N.J.: Princeton University Press, 2005.

Bull, Hedley. "The State's Positive Role in World Affairs." *Daedalus* 108 (4) (Fall 1979): 111–123.

Burgess, Stephen F. "African Security in the 21st Century: The Challenges of Indigenization and Multilateralism." *African Studies Review* 41 (2) (September 1998): 37–61.

Bush, George W. *The National Security Strategy of the United States of America.* Washington, D.C.: The White House, 2002.

———. *The National Security Strategy of the United States of America.* Washington, D.C.: The White House, 2006.

Buzan, Barry. "Economic Structure and International Security: The Limits of the Liberal Case." *International Organization* 38 (4) (Autumn 1984): 597–624.

———. *People, States and Fear.* Boulder, Colo.: Lynne Rienner, 1991.

Buzan, Barry, Ole Wæver, and Jaap de Wilde. *Security: A New Framework for Analysis.* Boulder, Colo.: Lynne Rienner, 1998.

Byman, Daniel L. "The Implications of Leadership Change in the Arab World." In *The Future Security Environment in the Middle East: Conflict, Stability, and Political Change*, edited by Daniel L. Byman and Nora Bensahel, 163–196. Santa Monica, Calif.: The RAND Corporation, 2004.

Byman, Daniel L., and Nora Bensahel, eds. *The Future Security Environment in the Middle East: Conflict, Stability, and Political Change.* Santa Monica, Calif.: The RAND Corporation, 2004.

Byman, Daniel L., Shahram Chubin, Anoushiravan Ehteshami, and Jerrold D. Green. *Iran's Security Policy in the Post-Revolutionary Era.* Santa Monica, Calif.: The Rand Corporation, 2001.

Caballero-Anthony, Mely. "Revisioning Human Security in Southeast Asia." *Asian Perspectives* 28 (3) (2004): 155–189.

Carr, Edward H. *The Twenty Years' Crisis 1919–1939: An Introduction to the Study of International Relations.* New York: Harper and Row, 1946.

Carr, William. *Arms, Autarky and Aggression.* New York: Norton, 1973.

Carter, Ashton B. "The Architecture of Government in the Face of Terrorism." *International Security* 26 (3) (Winter 2001–2002): 5–23.

Cerny, Philip G. "Globalization and the Changing Logic of Collective Action." *International Organization* 49 (4) (Autumn 1995): 595–625.

———. "International Finance and the Erosion of State Policy Capacity." In *Globalization and Public Policy*, edited by Philip Gummett, 83–104. Cheltenham, UK: Elgar, 1996.

———. "What Next for the State?" In *Globalization: Theory and Practice*, edited by Eleonore Kofman and Gillian Youngs, 123–137. New York: Pinter, 1996.

————. "The New Security Dilemma: Divisibility, Defection and Disorder in the Global Era." *Review of International Studies* 26 (4) (October 2000): 623–646.

Cha, Victor. "Globalization and the Study of National Security." *Journal of Peace Research* 37 (3) (May 2000): 391–403.

Chalk, P. "Separatism and Southeast Asia: The Islamic Factor in Southern Thailand, Mindanao, and Aceh." *Studies in Conflict and Terrorism* 24 (1) (July 2001): 241–269.

Chan, Steve. "In Search of Democratic Peace: Problems and Promises." *Mershon International Studies Review* 41 (1) (May 1997): 59–85.

Cheema, Zafar Iqbal. "Pakistan's Nuclear Use Doctrine and Command and Control." In *Planning the Unthinkable: How New Powers Will Use Nuclear, Biological, and Chemical Weapons*, edited by Scott D. Sagan, Peter R. Lavoy, and James J. Wirtz, 158–181. Ithaca, N.Y.: Cornell University Press, 2001.

Cheng, Joseph Y. S. "Broadening the Concept of Security in East and Southeast Asia: The Impact of Asian Financial Crisis and the September 11 Incident." *Journal of Contemporary China* 15 (46) (February 2006): 89–111.

Chernoff, Fred. "The Study of Democratic Peace and Progress in International Relations." *International Studies Review* 6 (1) (2004): 49–77.

Chung, Chien-Peng. "Confronting Terrorism and Other Evils in China: All Quiet on the Western Front?" *China and Eurasia Forum Quarterly* 4 (2) (2006): 75–87.

Ciliers, Jakkie. "Terrorism and Africa." *African Security Review* 12 (4) (2003): 91–103.

Cillers, Jackie, and Peggy Mason, eds. *Peace, Profit, or Plunder? The Privatization of Security in War-Torn African Societies*. Pretoria, South Africa: Institute for Security Studies, 1999.

Clark, Ann Marie. "Non-Governmental Organizations and Their Influence on International Society." *Journal of International Affairs* 48 (2) (Winter 1995): 507–525.

Clark, Ian. *Globalization and International Relations Theory*. Oxford: Oxford University Press, 1999.

Clark, John F. "Explaining Ugandan Intervention in Congo: Evidence and Interpretations." *Journal of Modern African Studies* 39 (2) (2001): 261–287.

Clay-Mendez, Deborah. *Public and Private Roles in Maintaining Military Equipment at Depot Level*. Washington, D.C.: Congressional Budget Office, 1995.

Clayton, Tony. "African Military Capabilities in Insurrection, Intervention and Peace Support Operations." In *African Interventionist States*, edited by Oliver Furley and Roy May, 51–68. London, UK: Ashgate, 2001.

Cliffe, Lionel. "Regional Dimensions of Conflict in the Horn of Africa." *Third World Quarterly* 20 (1) (1999): 89–111.

Cohen, Benjamin. "The Revolution in Atlantic Economic Relations: A Bargain Comes Unstuck." In *The United States and Western Europe: Political, Economic and Strategic Perspectives*, edited by W. F. Hanrieder. Cambridge, Mass.: Winthrop Publishers, 1974.

————. *Crossing Frontiers: Explorations in International Political Economy*. Boulder, Colo.: Westview Press, 1991.

Cohen, Stephen Philip. "The Jihadist Threat to Pakistan." *The Washington Quarterly* 26 (3) (Summer 2003): 7–25.

————. *The Idea of Pakistan*. Washington D.C.: Brookings Institution Press, 2004.

Coker, Christopher. "Outsourcing War." *Cambridge Review of International Affairs* 13 (3) (Autumn–Winter 1999): 95–113.

————. *Globalisation and Insecurity in the Twenty-First Century: NATO and the Management of Risk*. London: International Institute for Strategic Studies, 2002.

Collier, Paul. "Rebellion as a Quasi-Criminal Activity." *Journal of Conflict Resolution* 44 (6) (December 2000): 839–853.

Collins, Alan. *Security and Southeast Asia*. Boulder, Colo.: Lynne Rienner, 2003.

Copeland, Dale C., *The Origins of Major War*. Ithaca, N.Y.: Cornell University Press, 2000.

Copley, Gregory R. "AIDS and African Armies: A Crisis Worse Than War." *Defense & Foreign Affairs Strategic Review* 27 (11) (November 1999): 4–6.

Cordero, Luisita, and Richard N. Rosecrance. "The 'Acceptance' of Globalization." In *No More States? Globalization, National Determination and Terrorism*, edited by Richard N. Rosecrance and Arthur A. Stein, 23–34. Lanham, Md.: Rowman & Littlefield, 2006.

Cordesman, Anthony H. *The Military Balance in the Middle East*. Westport, Conn.: CSIS–Praeger, 2004.

Cortright, David A., ed. *The Price of Peace: Incentives and International Conflict Prevention*. Lanham, Md.: Rowman & Littlefield, 1997.

Cortright, David, and George A. Lopez (with Linda Gerber). *Sanctions and the Search for Security: Challenges to UN Action*. London, UK: Lynne Rienner, 2002.

Cox, Robert W. "A Perspective on Globalization." In *Globalization: Critical Reflections*, edited by James H. Mittelman, 21–30. Boulder, Colo.: Lynne Rienner, 1996.

Cronin, Audrey Kurth. "Behind the Curve: Globalization and International Terrorism." *Internation Security* 27 (3) (Winter 2002/2003): 30–58.

Das, Dilip K., and Peter C. Kratcoski, eds. *Meeting the Challenges of Global Terrorism: Prevention, Control, and Recovery*. Lanham, Md.: Lexington, 2003.

Davis, David R., John R. Oneal, and Bruce Russett. "The Third Leg of the Kantian Tripod for Peace: International Organizations and Militarized Disputes, 1950–85." *International Organization* 52 (3) (Summer 1998): 441–467.

Davis, Patricia A. *The Art of Economic Persuasion: Positive Incentives and German Economic Diplomacy*. Ann Arbor: University of Michigan Press, 1999.

Davis, Zachary S. "The Realist Nuclear Regime." *Security Studies* 2 (3 & 4) (September 1993): 79–99.

De Castro, Renato Cruz. "Philippine Defense Policy in the 21st Century: Autonomous Defense or Back to the Alliance?" *Pacific Affairs* 78 (3) (Fall 2005): 403–422.

de Durand, Etienne. "French Defense Policy Under the New Government." In *US–France Analysis Series*. Washington, D.C.: Brookings Institution, 2002.

Dent, Christopher M. "New Economic and Security Cooperation in the Asia-Pacific: An Introduction." In *Asia–Pacific Economic and Security Co-operation*, edited by Christopher M. Dent. Basingstoke, UK: Palgrave Macmillan, 2003.

Deskar, Barry, and Kumar Ramakrishna. "Forging a Indirect Strategy in Southeast Asia." *The Washington Quarterly* 25 (2) (Spring 2002): 161–176.

Deudney, Daniel. "Nuclear Weapons and the Waning of the Real-State." *Daedalus* 124 (2) (Spring 1995): 209–231.

——. *Bounding Power: Republican Security Theory from the Polis to the Global Village.* Princeton, N.J.: Princeton University Press, 2008.

Deutsch, Karl W., Sidney A. Burrell, and Robert A. Kann. *Political Community and the North Atlantic Area: International Organization in the Light of Historical Experience.* Princeton, N.J.: Princeton University Press, 1957.

de Waal, Alex. *Famine Crimes: Politics and the Disaster Relief Industry in Africa.* Bloomington: Indiana University Press, 1997.

——. "How Will HIV/AIDS Transform African Governance?" *African Affairs* 102 (406) (January 2003): 1–23.

Dewitt, David B., and Carolina G. Hernandez. "Defining the Problem and Managing the Uncertainty." In *Development and Security in Southeast Asia*, vol. 1, edited by David B. Dewitt and Caroline G. Hernandez, 3–18. Hants, UK: Ashgate, 2003.

Diamond, Larry. "Promoting Democracy." *Foreign Policy* 87 (1992): 25–46.

Diehl, Paul F., ed. *The Dynamics of Enduring Rivalries*. Urbana: University of Illinois Press, 1998.

——. "Introduction: An Overview and Some Theoretical Guidelines." In *The Dynamics of Enduring Rivalries*, edited by Paul F. Diehl, 1–28. Urbana: University of Illinois Press, 1998.

Diehl, Paul F., and Gary Goertz. *War and Peace in International Rivalry*. Ann Arbor: University of Michigan Press, 2001.

Dixon, William J. "Democracy and the Peaceful Settlement of International Conflict." *American Political Science Review* 88 (1) (1994): 14–32.

Dominguez, Jorge I., ed. *International Security and Democracy: Latin America and the Caribbean in the Post-Cold War Era*. Pittsburgh, Pa.: University of Pittsburgh Press, 1998.

Dominguez, Jorge I., David Mares, Manuel Orozco, David Scott Palmer, Francisco Rojas Aravena, and Andrés Serbin. *Boundary Disputes in Latin America.* Peaceworks 50. Washington, D.C.: U.S. Institute of Peace, 2003.

Doyle, Michael W. "Liberalism and World Politics." *American Political Science Review* 80 (4) (December 1986): 1151–1169.

——. *Ways of War and Peace: Realism, Liberalism, and Socialism.* New York: W. W. Norton, 1997.

Drezner, Daniel W. *The Sanctions Paradox: Economic Statecraft and International Relations.* Cambridge, UK: Cambridge University Press, 1999.

Drucker, Peter F. "The Global Economy and the Nation-State." *Foreign Affairs* 76 (5) (September–October 1997): 159–171.

Drury, Cooper A. *Economic Sanctions and Presidential Decisions: Models of Political Rationality*. New York: Palgrave Macmillan, 2005.

Earle, Edward Mead. "Adam Smith, Alexander Hamilton, Friedrich List: The Economic Foundations of Military Power." In *Makers of Modern Strategy*, edited by Peter Paret, 217–261. Oxford: Clarendon Press, 1986.

Eckert, Sue E. "Protecting Critical Infrastructure: The Role of the Private Sector." In *Guns & Butter: The Political Economy of International Security*, edited by Peter Dombrowski, 179–201. Boulder, Colo.: Lynne Rienner, 2005.

Ehteshami, Anoushiravan. "Iran–Iraq Relations after Saddam." *The Washington Quarterly* Autumn (2003): 115–129.

Elbe, Stefan. "HIV/AIDS and the Changing Landscape of War in Africa." *International Security* 27 (2) (Fall 2002): 159–177.

Elliott, Kimberly Ann, and Barbara Oegg. "Economic Sanctions Reconsidered—Again: Trends in Sanctions Policy in the 1990s." Presented at the International Studies Association Convention. New Orleans, Louisiana. March 23–26, 2002.

Ellis, Stephen, and David Killingray. "Africa after 11 September 2001." *African Affairs* 101 (2002): 5–8.

Emmers, Ralf. *Non-Traditional Security in the Asia-Pacific*. Singapore: Eastern Universities Press, 2004.

Enders, Walter, and Todd Sandler. *The Political Economy of Terrorism*. Cambridge: Cambridge University Press, 2006.

Evans, Peter. *Embedded Autonomy: States and Industrial Transformation*. Princeton, N.J.: Princeton University Press, 1995.

Fairbanks, Charles H., Jr. "Weak States and Private Armies." In *Beyond State Crisis? Postcolonial Africa and Post-Soviet Eurasia in Comparative Perspective*, edited by Mark R. Beissinger and Crawford Young, 126–160. Washington D.C.: Woodrow Wilson Center Press, 2002.

Falk, Richard. *Predatory Globalization: A Critique*. Cambridge: Polity Press, 1999.

Feldbaum, Harley, Kelley Lee, and Preeti Patel. "The National Security Implications of HIV/AIDS." *PLoS Medicine* 3 (6) (June 2006): 771–778.

Ferguson, James R. "New Norms of Southeast Asian Regional Governance: From 'Codes of Conduct' to 'Greater East Asia.'" In *Non-Traditional Security Issues in Southeast Asia*, edited by Andrew T. H. Tan and J. D. Kenneth Boutin, 122–165. Singapore: Select Books, 2001.

———. *Global Shadows: Africa in the Neoliberal World Order*. Durham, N. Caro.: Duke University Press, 2006.

Finnemore, Martha. "Constructing Norms of Humanitarian Intervention." In *The Culture of National Security: Norms and Identity in World Politics*, edited by Peter J. Katzenstein, 153–185. New York: Columbia University Press, 1996.

———. *The Purpose of Intervention: Changing Beliefs About the Use of Force*. Ithaca, N.Y.: Cornell University Press, 2003.

Fish, Steven M. *Democracy Derailed in Russia: The Failure of Open Politics*. New York: Cambridge University Press, 2005.

Fitch, J. Samuel. *The Armed Forces and Democracy in Latin America*. Baltimore, Md.: The Johns Hopkins University Press, 1998.

Florini, Ann, ed. *The Third Force: The Rise of Transnational Civil Society*. Washington, D.C.: Japan Center for International Exchange and Carnegie Endowment, 2000.

Fourie, Pieter, and Martin Schonteich. "Africa's New Security Threat: HIV/AIDS and Human Security in Southern Africa." *African Security Review* 10 (4) (2001): 29–44.

Freedman, Lawrence. "International Security: Changing Targets." *Foreign Policy* 110 (Spring 1998): 48–63.

———. "The Special Relationship, Then and Now." *Foreign Affairs* 85 (3) (May/June 2006): 61–73.

Friedberg, Aaron. "Why Didn't the United States Become a Garrison State?" *International Security* 16 (4) (Spring 1992): 109–142.

Frieden, Jeffry A. *Global Capitalism: Its Fall and Rise in the Twentieth Century*. New York: W. W. Norton, 2006.

Frieden, Jeffry A., and Ronald Rogowski. "The Impact of the International Economy on National Policies: An Analytic Overview." In *Internationalization and Domestic Politics*, edited by Robert O. Keohane and Helen V. Milner, 25–47. New York: Cambridge, 1996.

Friedman. Thomas L. *The Lexus and the Olive Tree*. New York: Farrar, Strauss and Giroux, 1998.

———. *The Impact of Globalization on World Peace*. Working paper no. 27. Burkle Center for International Relations, UCLA, January 2001. http://www.international.ucla.edu/cms/files/friedman.pdf

———. *The World Is Flat: A Brief History of the Twenty-First Century*. New York: Farrar, Strauss and Giroux, 2005.

———. "War On Daddy's Dime," *New York Times*, August 18, 2006, A17.

Frisch, Hillel. "Guns and Butter in the Egyptian Army." In *Armed Forces in the Middle East: Politics and Strategy*, edited by Barry Rubin and Thomas A. Keaney, 93–112. London: Frank Cass, 2002.

Fukuyama, Francis. *The End of History and the Last Man*. London: Penguin, 1992.

Galtung, Johan. "On the Effects of International Economic Sanctions: With Examples from the Case of Rhodesia." *World Politics* 19 (3) (April 1967): 378–416.

Garrett, Geoffrey. "The Causes of Globalization." *Comparative Political Studies* 33 (August–September 2000): 941–991.

———. "Introduction: The International Diffusion of Liberalism." *International Organization* 60 (4) (Fall 2006): 781–810.

Gellner, Ernest. *Nations and Nationalism*. Ithaca, N.Y.: Cornell University Press, 1983.

George, Alexander L., and Andrew Bennett. *Case Studies and Theory Development in the Social Sciences*. Cambridge, Mass.: MIT Press, 2005.

German, Tracey D. *Russia's Chechen War*. New York: Routledge Curzon, 2003.

Giddens, Anthony. *The Consequences of Modernity*. Cambridge: Polity Press, 1990.

Gilbert, Felix, ed. *The Historical Essays of Otto Hintze*. New York: Oxford University Press, 1975.

Gilpin, Robert. *War and Change in International Politics*. Princeton, N.J.: Princeton University Press, 1981.

———. *The Political Economy of international Relations*. Princeton, N.J.: Princeton University Press, 1987.

———. *The Challenge of Global Capitalism: The World Economy in the 21st Century*. Princeton, N.J.: Princeton University Press, 2000.

Gleditsch, Kristian. "A Revised List of Wars Between and Within Independent States, 1816–2002." *International Interactions* 30 (2004): 231–262.

Glickman, Harvey. "Africa in the War on Terrorism." *JAAS* 38 (2–3) (August 2003): 162–174.

Glover, David, and Timothy Jessup. *Indonesia's Fires and Haze: The Cost of Catastrophe*. Singapore: Institute of Southeast Asian Studies, 1999.

Gochman, Charles S., and Zeev Maoz. "Militarized Interstate Disputes, 1916–1976." *Journal of Conflict Resolution* 28 (4) (December 1984): 585–616.

Goldblatt, David, David Held, Anthony McGrew, and Jonathan Perraton. "Economic Globalization and the Nation-State: Shifting Balances of Power." *Alternatives* 22 (3) (1997): 269–285.

Gomes, Solomon. "The OAU, State Sovereignty, and Regional Security." In *Africa in the New International Order: Rethinking State Sovereignty and Regional Security*, edited by Edmund Joseph Keller and Donald S. Rothchild, 37–51. Boulder, Colo.: Lynne Rienner, 1996.

Gowa, Joanne. *Allies, Adversaries, and International Trade*. Princeton, N.J.: Princeton University Press, 1994.

Greider, William. *One World, Ready or Not: The Manic Logic of Global Capitalism*. New York: Simon & Schuster, 1997.

Guiraudon, Virginie. "Immigration Politics and Policies." In *Developments in French Politics*, edited by Jonah Levy, Alistair Cole, and Patrick Le Galès. New York: Palgrave Macmillan, 2005.

Gummett, Philip ed., *Globalization and Public Policy*. Cheltenham, UK: Elgar, 1996.

Gunaratna, Rohan. "Southeast Asia: The Terrorist Threat." In *Asia–Pacific Security Outlook 2004*, edited by Charles Morrison. Tokyo: Japan Center for International Exchange, 2004.

Gurr, Ted Robert, and Monty G. Marshall. *Peace and Conflict 2003*. College Park: The Center for International Development and Conflict Management, University of Maryland, 2003.

Gurr, Ted Robert, Monty G. Marshall, and Deepa Khosla. *Peace and Conflict 2001*. College Park: The Center for International Development and Conflict Management, University of Maryland, 2001.

Haass, Richard N. "Sanctioning Madness." *Foreign Affairs* 76 (6) (November–December 1997): 74–85.

Haggard, Stephan, and Robert R. Kaufman. "The State in the Initiation and Consolidation of Market-Oriented Reform." In *State and Market in Development: Synergy or Rivalry?*, edited by Louis Putterman and Dietrich Rueschemeyer, 221–242. Boulder, Colo.: Lynne Rienner, 1992.

Halevy, Efraim. "Israel's National Security Agenda in the Coming Year." *Strategic Assessment* 6 (2) (September 2003). http://www.inss.org.il/publications.php?cat=21&incat=&read=674.

Hall, John A., and G. John Ikenberry. *The State*. Minneapolis: University of Minnesota Press, 1989.

Han, Andrew T. H., and J. D. Kenneth Boutin, eds. *Non-Traditional Security Issues in Southeast Asia*. Singapore: Select Publishing, 2001.

Hassan, Mohamed Olad. "Ethiopians Said to Patrol Somali Road." *Washington Post*, November 23, 2006, A26.

Held, David, and Anthony McGrew. "Globalization and the Liberal Democratic State." *Government and Opposition* 28 (2) (Spring 1993): 261–288.

Held, David, Anthony McGrew, David Goldblatt, and Jonathan Perraton. *Global Transformations: Politics, Economics and Culture*. Stanford, Calif.: Stanford University Press, 1999.

Helleiner, Eric. *States and the Reemergence of Global Finance*. Ithaca, N.Y.: Cornell University Press, 1994.

Herbst, Jeffrey. *States and Power in Africa*. Princeton, N.J.: Princeton University Press, 2000.

———. "States and War in Africa." In *The Nation-State in Question*, edited by T.V. Paul, G. John Ikenberry, and John A. Hall, 166–182. Princeton, N.J.: Princeton University Press, 2003.

———. "African Militaries and Rebellion: The Political Economy of Threat and Combat Effectiveness." *Journal of Peace Research* 41 (3) (2004): 357–369.

Hermann, Margaret G., and Charles W. Kegley, Jr. "Rethinking Democracy and International Peace: Perspectives from Political Psychology." *International Studies Quarterly* 39(4) (December 1995): 511–533.

Hernandez, Carolina G. "Challenges for Security and Politics." In *Reinventing ASEAN*, edited by Simon S. C. Tay, Jesus P. Estanislao, and Hadi Soesastra, 103–120. Singapore: Institute of Southeast Asian Studies, 2001.

Herz, John H. "The Territorial State Revisited: Reflections on the Future of the Nation State." In *International Politics and Foreign Policy: A Reader in Research and Theory*, edited by James N. Rosenau, 76–89. New York: The Free Press, 1969.

———. "Rise and Demise of the Territorial State." *World Politics* 9 (1957): 473–493.

Hills, Alice. *Policing Africa: Internal Security and the Limits of Liberalization*. Boulder, Colo.: Lynne Rienner, 2000.

Hirschman, Albert O. *The Passions and the Interests: Political Arguments for Capitalism before Its Triumph*. Princeton, N.J.: Princeton University Press, 1977.

Hirst, Paul, and Grahame Thompson. *Globalization in Question: The International Economy and the Possibilities of Governance*. Cambridge, UK: Polity Press, 1996.

Hobson, J. A. *Imperialism: A Study*. London: Allen & Unwin, 1948.

Hoffmann, Stanley. "Clash of Globalizations." *Foreign Affairs* 81 (4) (July–August 2002): 104–115.

Holm, Hans-Henrik, and George Sorensen. *Whose World Order? Uneven Globalization and the End of the Cold War*. Boulder, Colo.: Westview Press, 1995.

Holsti, Kalevi J. *The State, War, and the State of War*. Cambridge: Cambridge University Press, 1996.

————. "The Changing International System and the Decline of Major War." In *The Waning of Major War: Theories and Debates*, edited by Raimo Väyrynen, 135–159. New York: Routledge, 2005.

Howard, Michael. "What Is in a Name? How to Fight Terrorism." *Foreign Affairs* 81 (1) (January–February 2002), 8–13.

Howe, Herbert M. *Ambiguous Order: Military Forces in African States*. Boulder, Colo.: Lynne Rienner, 2001.

Hoyt, Timothy D. "Pakistani Nuclear Doctrine and the Dangers of Strategic Myopia." *Asian Survey* 41 (6) (2001): 956–977.

Hsu, Lee-Nah. "Building Dynamic Democratic Governance and HIV-Resilient Societies." *International Social Science Journal* 57 (186) (December 2005): 699–713.

Hufbauer, Gary Clyde, Jeffrey J. Schott, Kimberly Ann Elliott, and Barbara Oegg. *Economic Sanctions Reconsidered*. 3rd edition. Washington, D.C.: Peterson Institute for International Economics, 2007.

Hugo, Graeme. "Asia and the Pacific on the Move: Workers and Refugees, A Challenge to Nation States." *Asia Pacific Viewpoint* 38 (3) (December 1997): 267–286.

Hülsemeyer, Axel. "Introduction: Globalization in the Twenty-First Century." In *Globalization in the Twenty-First Century: Convergence or Divergence?*, edited by Axel Hülsemeyer, 1–11. London: Palgrave Macmillan, 2003.

Hurrell, Andrew. "An Emerging Security Community in South America?" In *Security Communities*, edited by Emanuel Adler and Michael Barnett, 228–264. Cambridge: Cambridge University Press, 1998.

Hussain, Rizwan. *Pakistan and the Emergence of Islamic Militancy in Afghanistan*. Aldershot, Hampshire: Ashgate Publishing, 2005.

Hussain, Zahid. *Frontline Pakistan: The Struggle with Militant Islam*. New York: Columbia University Press, 2007.

Ikenberry, G. John. *After Victory*. Princeton, N.J.: Princeton University Press, 2001.

Inkeles, Alex. *One World Emerging*. Boulder, Colo.: Westview Press, 1998.

International Institute for Strategic Studies. *The Military Balance, 1989–2006*. London: International Institute for Strategic Studies, 1996–2006.

Jackson, Robert H., and Carl G. Rosberg. "Why Africa's Weak States Persist: The Empirical and the Juridical in Statehood." *World Politics* 35 (1) (1982): 1–24.

James, Patrick. *International Relations and Scientific Progress: Structural Realism Reconsidered.* Columbus: The Ohio State University Press, 2002.

Jentleson, Bruce W., and Christopher A. Whytock. "Who 'Won' Libya? The Force–Diplomacy Debate and Its Implications for Theory and Policy." *International Security* 30 (3) (Winter 2005–2006): 47–86.

Jervis, Robert. "Cooperation under the Security Dilemma." *World Politics* 30 (2) (January 1978): 167–214.

———. "The Political Effects of Nuclear Weapons." *International Security* 13 (2) (Fall 1988), 80–90.

Jetschke, Anja. "Democratization: A Threat to Peace and Stability in Southeast Asia." In *Asia–Pacific Economic and Security Cooperation*, edited by Christopher M. Dent, 167–184. Houndmills, UK: Palgrave-Macmillan, 2003.

Job, Brian L. "Track 2 Diplomacy: Ideational Contribution to the Evolving Asian Security Order." In *Asian Security Order: Instrumental and Normative Features*, edited by Muthiah Alagappa, 241–279. Stanford, Calif.: Stanford University Press, 2003.

Johnston, Alastair Iain. "Socialization in International Institutions: The ASEAN Way and International Relations Theory." In *International Relations Theory and the Asia–Pacific*, edited by G. John Ikenberry and Michael Mastanduno, 107–162. New York: Columbia University Press, 2003.

Kacowicz, Arie M. *Zones of Peace in the Third World: South America and West Africa in Comparative Perspective.* Albany, N.Y.: SUNY Press, 1998.

Kahler, Miles. "Territoriality and Conflict in an Era of Globalization." In *Territoriality and Conflict in an Era of Globalization*, edited by Miles Kahler and Barbara F. Walter, 1–24. Cambridge: Cambridge University Press, 2006.

Kahler, Miles, and Barbara Walter, eds. *Territoriality and Conflict in an Era of Globalization.* Cambridge: Cambridge University Press, 2006.

Kaldor, Mary. "Reconceptualizing Organized Violence." In *Re-Imagining Political Community: Studies in Cosmopolitan Democracy*, edited by Daniele Archibugi, David Held, and Martin Köhler, 91–112. Cambridge: Cambridge University Press, 1998.

Kandeh, Jimmy D. "Civil–Military Relations." In *West Africa's Security Challenges*, edited by Adekeye Adebajo and Ismail Rashid, 145–168. Boulder, Colo.: Lynne Rienner, 2004.

Kanwal, Gurmeet. "India's National Security Strategy in a Nuclear Environment," *Strategic Analysis* 24 (9) (December 2000) http://www.ciaonet.org/olj/sa/sa_dec00kag01.html.

Kapila, Subhash. *India's New 'Cold Start' War Doctrine Strategically Reviewed.* South Asia Analysis Group. Paper no. 991. May 4, 2004.

Karns, Margaret P., and Karen A. Mingst. *The United States and Multilateral Institutions.* Boston, Mass.: Unwin Hyman, 1990.

Katzenstein, Peter J. *A World of Regions: Asia and Europe in the American Imperium*. Ithaca, N.Y.: Cornell University Press, 2005.

Kaysen, Carl. "Is War Obsolete? A Review Essay." *International Security* 14 (4) (Spring 1990): 42–64.

Keck, Margaret E., and Kathryn Sikkink. *Activists Beyond Borders: Advocacy Networks in International Politics*. Ithaca, N.Y.: Cornell University Press, 1998.

Kent, Vanessa, and Mark Malan. "The African Standby Force: Progress and Prospects." *African Security Review* 12 (3) (2003): 71–81.

Keohane, Robert. *After Hegemony*. Princeton, N.J.: Princeton University Press, 1984.

————, ed. *Neorealism and Its Critics*. New York: Columbia University Press, 1986.

————. "International Liberalism Revisited." In *The Economic Limits to Modern Politics*, edited by John Dunn, 165–194. Cambridge: Cambridge University Press, 1990.

Keohane, Robert O., and Joseph S. Nye, Jr., eds. *Transnational Relations and World Politics*. Cambridge, Mass.: Harvard University Press, 1973.

————. *Power and Interdependence*. Boston, Mass.: Little, Brown, 1977.

————. "Power and Interdependence Revisited." *International Organization* 41 (4) (Autumn 1987): 725–753.

Khan, Omar A., and Hyder, Adnan A. "Responses to an Emerging Threat: HIV/AIDS Policy in Pakistan." *Health Policy and Planning* 16 (2) (2001): 214–218.

Khazanov, Anatoly M. "A State without a Nation? Russia after Empire." in *The Nation-State in Question*, edited by T. V. Paul, G. John Ikenberry, and John A. Hall, 79–105. Princeton, N.J.: Princeton University Press, 2003.

Kindleberger, Charles P. *The World in Depression, 1929–1939*. Berkeley, Calif.; University of California Press, 1973.

Kirshner, Jonathan. "Globalization and National Security." In *Globalization and National Security*, edited by Jonathan Kirshner, 1–33. New York: Routledge, 2006.

Klare, Michael T. "Waging Postindustrial Warfare on the Global Battlefield." *Current History* 100 (650) (December 2001): 433–437.

Klare, Michael T., and Daniel C. Thomas, eds. *World Security: Challenges for a New Century*. New York: St. Martin's Press, 1994.

Knorr, Klaus. *On the Uses of Military Power in the Nuclear Age*. Princeton, N.J.: Princeton University Press, 1996.

Konstam, Angus. *Piracy: The Complete History*. Oxford: Osprey Publishing, 2008.

Kraft, Herman. "The Principle of Non-Intervention: Evolution and Challenges for the Asia–Pacific Region." In *Non-Intervention and State Sovereignty in the Asia–Pacific*, edited by David Dickens and Guy Wilson-Roberts, 23–41. Wellington, NZ: Center for Strategic Studies, 2000.

Kramer, Mark. "The Perils of Counterinsurgency: Russia's War with Chechnya." *International Security* 29 (3) (Winter 2004/2005): 5–62.

Krasner, Stephen D. "State Power and the Structure of International Trade." *World Politics* 28 (April 1976): 317–347.

Krause, Keith, and Andrew Latham. "Constructing Non-proliferation and Arms Control: The Norms of Western Practice." *Contemporary Security Policy* 19 (1) (April 1998): 23–54.

Krause, Keith, and Michael C. Williams, eds. *Critical Security Studies*. Minneapolis: University of Minnesota Press, 1997.

Kuhonta, Erik Martinez. "Walking a Tightrope: Democracy versus Sovereignty in ASEAN's Illiberal Peace." *The Pacific Review* 19 (3) (September 2006): 337–358.

Laidi, Zaki. *A World Without Meaning: The Crisis of Meaning in International Politics*. London: Routledge, 1998.

Langton, Christopher, ed. *The Military Balance 2006*. London: International Institute for Strategic Studies, 2006.

Lanteigne, Marc. *China and International Institutions: Alternate Path to Global Power*. London: Routledge, 2005.

Lapidus, Gail W. "Contested Sovereignty: The Tragedy of Chechnya." *International Security* 23 (1) (Summer 1998): 5–49.

Laqueur, Walter, and Barry Rubin, eds. *The Israeli–Arab Reader: A Documentary History of the Middle East Conflict*. New York: Penguin Books, 1995.

Lavoy, Peter R. "Pakistan's Nuclear Doctrine." In *Prospects for Peace in South Asia*, edited by Rafiq Dossani and Henry S. Rowen, 280–300. Stanford, Calif.: Stanford University Press, 2005.

Lemke, Douglas. *Regions of War and Peace*. Cambridge: Cambridge University Press, 2002.

Lenin V. I. *Imperialism: The Highest Stage of Capitalism (a Popular Outline)*. Moscow: Foreign Languages Publishing House, 1947.

Levy, Jack. *War in the Modern Great Power System, 1495–1975*. Lexington: The University Press of Kentucky, 1983.

Levy, Jack S., and Joseph R. Gochal. "Democracy and Preventive War: Israel and the 1956 Sinai Campaign." *Security Studies* 11 (2) (Winter 2001–2002): 1–49.

Lewis, Stephen. *Race Against Time: Searching for Hope in AIDS-Ravaged Africa*. Toronto: Anansi Press, 2006.

Liberman, Peter. *Does Conquest Pay? The Exploitation of Occupied Industrial Societies*. Princeton, N.J.: Princeton University Press, 1996.

Lieber, Keir A., and Gerard Alexander. "Waiting for Balancing: Why the World Is Not Pushing Back." *International Security* 30 (1) (Summer 2005): 109–139.

Lipschutz, Ronnie D. *After Authority: War, Peace and Global Politics in the 21st Century*. Albany: State University of New York Press, 2000.

Liss, Carolin. *Private Security Companies in the Fight against Piracy in Asia*. Working paper no. 120. Asia Research Center, Murdoch University, June 2005. http://wwwarc.murdoch.edu.au/wp/wp120.pdf.

Lobell, Steven E., Norrin M. Ripsman, and Jeffrey W. Taliaferro, eds. *Neoclassical Realism, the State, and Foreign Policy*. Cambridge: Cambridge University Press, 2009.

Lock, Peter. "Africa: Military Downsizing and the Growth in the Security Industry." In *Peace, Profit or Plunder: The Privatization of Security in War-Torn Africa*, edited by

Jackie Cillers and Peggy Mason, 11–36. Pretoria, South Africa: Institute for Security Studies, 1999.

Löwenheim, Oded. *Predators and Parasites: Persistent Agents of Transnational Harm and Great Power Authority*. Ann Arbor: University of Michigan Press, 2006.

Lowi, Theodore. *The End of Liberalism*, 2nd edition. New York: W. W. Norton, 1979.

Luttwak, Edward. "Toward Post-Heroic Warfare." *Foreign Affairs* 74 (3) (May–June 1995): 109–122.

Lynch, Dov. *Russian Peacekeeping Strategies in the CIS: The Cases of Moldova, Georgia and Tajikistan*. New York: St. Martin's Press, 2000.

Lynn-Jones, Sean M. *Does Offense–Defense Theory Have a Future?* Working paper no. 12. University of Montreal-McGill Research Group in International Security, October 2000. https://depot.erudit.org/retrieve/851/000260pp.pdf.

MacFarlane, S. Neil. "The Superpowers and Third World Security." In *The Insecurity Dilemma: National Security of Third World States*, edited by Brian L. Job, 209–230. Boulder, Colo.: Lynne Rienner, 1992.

MacFarlane, S. Neil, and Thomas Weiss. "Political Interests and Humanitarian Action." *Security Studies* 10 (1) (Autumn 2000): 112–142.

Maclean, Sandra J. "Peacebuilding and the New Regionalism in South Africa." *Third World Quarterly* 20 (5) (1999): 943–956.

Maddy-Weitzman, Bruce. "The Inter-Arab System and the Arab–Israeli Conflict: Ripening for Resolution." *Perceptions* 5 (1) (March–May 2000), 44–54.

Malan, Mark. *Regional Power Politics Under Cover of SADC*. Occasional paper no. 35. Institute for Security Studies, October 1998. http://www.iss.co.za/Pubs/PAPERS/35/Paper35.html.

———. "The Post-9/11 Security Agenda and Peacekeeping in Africa." *African Security Review* 11 (3) (2002): 53–66.

Malone, David M., and Karin Wermester. "Boom or Bust? The Changing Nature of UN Peacekeeping." *International Peacekeeping* (7) (4) (2000): 37–54.

Mamdani, Mahmood. *Citizen and Subject: Contemporary Africa and the Legacy of Late Colonialism*. Princeton, N.J.: Princeton University Press, 1996.

Mandel, Robert. *The Changing Face of National Security*. Westport, Conn.: Greenwood, 1994.

———. *Deadly Transfers and the Global Playground*. New York: Praeger, 1999.

———. "The Privatization of Security." Presented at the ISA Conference. Los Angeles, California. March 14–18, 2000.

Mandelbaum, Michael. *The Ideas That Conquered the World*. New York: Public Affairs, 2002.

Mann, Michael. *The Sources of Social Power*. Cambridge: Cambridge University Press, 1993.

———. "Has Globalization Ended the Rise and Rise of the Nation-State?" In *International Order and the Future of World Politics*, edited by T. V. Paul and John A. Hall, 237–261. Cambridge: Cambridge University Press, 1999.

Mansfield, Edward D., and Jack Snyder. *Electing to Fight: Why Emerging Democracies Go to War*. Cambridge, Mass.: MIT Press, 2005.

Mares, David R. *Violent Peace: Militarized Interstate Bargaining in Latin America*. New York: Columbia University Press, 2001.

Marshall, Monty G. *Conflict Trends in Africa, 1946–2004: A Macro-Comparative Perspective*. Report prepared for the Africa Conflict Prevention Pool, Government of the United Kingdom, October 14, 2005. http://www.dfid.gov.uk/pubs/files/africa-conflictpp-stats-report.pdf.

Martin, Guy. *Africa in World Politics: A Pan African Perspective*. Trenton, N.J.: Africa World Press, 2002.

Mathews, Jessica. "Power Shift." *Foreign Affairs* 76 (1) (January–February 1997): 50–66.

McGranahan, Carole. "Kashmir and Tibet: Comparing Conflicts, States, and Solutions." *India Review* 2 (3) (July 2003): 145–180.

Mearsheimer, John J. "The False Promise of International Institutions." *International Security* 19 (3) (Winter 1994/1995): 5–49.

Mearsheimer, John J. *The Tragedy of Great Power Politics*. New York: W. W. Norton Press, 2001.

Menon, Rajan. "In the Shadow of the Bear: Security in Post-Soviet Central Asia." *International Security* 20 (1) (Summer 1995): 149–181.

Merle, Renae. "Census Counts 100,000 Contractors in Iraq," *Washington Post*, December 5, 2006, D01.

Migdal, Joel S. *Strong Societies and Weak States*. Princeton, N.J.: Princeton University Press, 1998.

Miller, Benjamin. "Explaining Variations in Regional Peace: Three Strategies for Peace-making." *Cooperation and Conflict* 35 (2) (June 2000): 155–191.

———. *States, Nations and Great Powers: The Sources of Regional War and Peace*. Cambridge: Cambridge University Press, 2007.

Mills, C. Wright. *The Power Elite*. New York, Oxford University Press, 2000.

Millward, Alan S. *War, Economy and Society*. Berkeley, Calif.: University of California Press, 1977.

Millward, James. *Violent Separatism in Xinjiang: A Critical Assessment*. Policy Studies 6. Washington, D.C.: East–West Center, 2004.

Mingst, Karen A., and Margaret P Karns. *The United Nations in the Post-Cold War Era*. Boulder, Colo.: Westview Press, 2000.

Mittelman, James H. *Globalization: Critical Reflections*. Boulder, Colo.: Lynne Rienner, 1996.

———. *The Globalization Syndrome: Transformation and Resistance*. Princeton, N.J.: Princeton University Press, 2000.

Moravcsik, Andrew. "Taking Preferences Seriously: A Liberal Theory of International Politics." *International Organization* 51 (4) (Autumn 1997): 513–553.

Morgan, Patrick M., and T. V. Paul, "Deterrence among Great Powers in an Era of Globalization." In *Complex Deterrence: Strategy in the Global Era*, edited by T. V.

Paul, Patrick M. Morgan, and James J. Wirtz, 259–276. Chicago, Ill.: University of Chicago Press, 2009.

Morgenthau, Hans J. *Politics Among Nations*. New York: McGraw-Hill, 1985.

Morrison, J. Stephen. "Somalia's and Sudan's Race to the Fore in Africa." *The Washington Quarterly* 25 (2) (Spring 2002), 191–205.

Mortimer, Robert A. "ECOMOG, Liberia, and Regional Security in West Africa." In *Africa in the New International Order: Rethinking State Sovereignty and Regional Security*, edited by Edmund Joseph Keller and Donald S. Rothchild, 149–164. Boulder, Colo.: Lynne Rienner, 1996.

Mueller, John. *Retreat from Doomsday: The Obsolescence of Major War*. New York: Basic Books, 1989.

———. *Overblown: How Politicians and the Terrorism Industry Inflate National Security Threats, and Why We Believe Them*. New York: Free Press, 2006.

Muravchik, Joshua. *Exporting Democracy: Fulfilling America's Destiny*. Washington, D.C.: AEI Press, 1991.

Musah, Abdel-Fatau. "Privatization of Security, Arms Proliferation and the Process of State Collapse in Africa." *Development and Change* 33 (5) (2002): 911–933.

Mydans, Seth. "Muslim Insurgency Stokes Fear in Southern Thailand." *International Herald Tribune*, February 25, 2007.

Nachman, Tal. "Islamic Terrorism in Egypt: The Challenge and the Response." *Strategic Assessment* 1 (1) (March 1998). http://www.inss.org.il/publications.php?cat=21&incat=&read=592.

Navlakha, Gautam. "Doctrine for Sub-Conventional Operations: A Critique." *Economic and Political Weekly*. April 7, 2007, 1242–1246.

Nayar, Baldev Raj. *The Geopolitics of Globalization*. New Delhi: Oxford University Press, 2005.

———. *The Myth of the Shrinking State: Globalization and the State in India*. New Delhi: Oxford University Press, 2009.

Nayar, Baldev Raj, and T. V Paul. *India in the World Order: Searching for Major Power Status*. Cambridge: Cambridge University Press, 2003.

Newman, David. "The Resilience of Territorial Conflict in an Era of Globalization." In *Territoriality and Conflict in an Era of Globalization*, edited by Miles Kahler and Barbara F. Walter, 85–110. Cambridge: Cambridge University Press, 2006.

Newnham, Randall. *Deutsche Mark Diplomacy: Positive Economic Sanctions in German–Russian Relations*. University Park: Pennsylvania State University Press, 2002.

Ngoma, Naison. "SADC: Towards a Security Community?" *African Security Review* 12 (3) (2003): 17–28.

Niskanen, William A. *Bureaucracy and Representative Government*. Edison, N.J.: Transaction Publishers, 2007.

O'Brien, Kevin A. "PMCs, Myths and Mercenaries: The Debate on Private Military Companies." *Royal United Service Institute Journal* 145 (1) (February 2000): 59–64.

O'Brien, Richard. *Global Financial Integration: The End of Geography*. London: Pinter, 1992.

Ohmae, Kenichi. *The Borderless World: Power and Strategy in the Interlinked Economy*. New York: Harper Business, 1990.

———. *The End of the Nation Sate*. New York: Free Press, 1995.

Olson, Mancur. *The Rise and Decline of Nations: Economic Growth, Stagflation, and Social Rigidities*. New Haven, Conn.: Yale University Press, 1982.

Oren, Michael B. *Six Days of War: June 1967 and the Making of the Modern Middle East*. Oxford: Oxford University Press, 2002.

Organski, Kenneth, A. F., and Jacek Kugler. *The War Ledger*. Chicago, Ill.: University of Chicago Press, 1980.

Ostergard, Robert L. "Politics in the Hot Zone: AIDS and National Security in Africa." *Third World Quarterly* 23 (2) (2002): 333–350.

Ott, Marvin C. "Southeast Asian Security Challenges: America's Response?" *Strategic Forum* 222 (October 2006): 1–8.

Owen, John M. "How Liberalism Produces the Democratic Peace." *International Security* 19 (2) (Fall 1994): 87–125.

Oye, Kenneth A. "Beyond Postwar Order and New World Order: American Foreign Policy in Transition." In *Eagle in a New World: American Grand Strategy in the Post-Cold War Era*, edited by Kenneth A. Oye, Robert J. Lieber, and Donald Rothchild. New York: Harper-Collins, 1992.

Pape, Robert A. "Why Economic Sanctions Do Not Work." *International Security* 22 (2) (Fall 1997): 90–136.

———. "Soft Balancing against the United States." *International Security* 30 (1) (Summer 2005): 7–45.

Paris, Roland. "Human Security: Paradigm Shift or Hot Air?" *International Security* 26 (2) (2001): 87–102.

Parmar, Inderjeet. "'I'm Proud of the British Empire': Why Tony Blair Backs George W. Bush." *The Political Quarterly* 76 (2) (April 2005): 218–231.

Paul, T. V. *Asymmetric Conflicts: War Initiation by Weaker Powers*. Cambridge: Cambridge University Press, 1994.

———. *Power Versus Prudence: Why Nations Forgo Nuclear Weapons*. Montreal: McGill-Queen's University Press, 2000.

———. "Soft Balancing in the Age of U.S. Primacy." *International Security* 30 (1) (Summer 2005): 46–71.

———. "The National Security State and Global Terrorism: Why the State Is Not Prepared for the New Kind of War." In *Globalization, Security, and the Nation-State*, edited by Ersel Aydinli and James Rosenau, 49–66. Albany, N.Y.: SUNY Press, 2005.

———, ed. *The India–Pakistan Conflict: An Enduring Rivalry*. Cambridge: Cambridge University Press, 2005.

———. "Why Has the India–Pakistan Rivalry Been So Enduring? Power Asymmetry and an Intractable Conflict." *Security Studies* 15 (4) (October–December, 2006): 600–630.

———. *The Tradition of Non-use of Nuclear Weapons*. Stanford, Calif.: Stanford University Press, 2009.

Paul, T. V., G. John Ikenberry, and John A. Hall, eds. *The Nation-State in Question*. Princeton, N.J.: Princeton University Press, 2003.

Paul, T. V., and Norrin M. Ripsman. "Under Pressure: Globalization and the National Security State." *Millennium: Journal of International Studies* 33 (2) (March 2004): 355–380.

Paul, T. V., James J. Wirtz, and Michel Fortmann, eds. *Balance of Power: Theory and Practice in the 21st Century*. Stanford, Calif.: Stanford University Press, 2004.

Peck, Connie. *Sustainable Peace: The Role of the UN and Regional Organizations in Preventing Conflict*. Lanham, Md.: Rowman & Littlefield, 1998.

Pharaoh, Robyn, and Martin Schonteich. *AIDS, Security and Governance in Southern Africa*. Occasional paper 65. Pretoria, South Africa: Institute for Security Studies, January 2003. http://www.iss.co.za/Pubs/Papers/65/Paper65.pdf.

Pillsbury, Michael. *China Debates the Future Security Environment*. Honolulu: University Press of the Pacific, 2005.

Polanyi, Karl. *The Great Transformation*. 2nd edition. Boston, Mass.: Beacon Press, 2001.

Porter, Bruce D. *The USSR in Third World Conflicts*. Cambridge: Cambridge University Press, 1986.

Porter, William. *Killing Hope: US Military and CIA Interventions Since World War II*. Eastbourne, UK: Gardner's Books, 2003.

Prabhakar, Lawrence W., Joshua H. Ho, and Sam Bateman, eds. *The Evolving Maritime Balance of Power in the Asia–Pacific*. Singapore: World Scientific Publishing Company, 2006.

Prawindarti, Lianita. "The First ASEAN Defence Ministers Meeting: An Early Test for the ASEAN Security Community?" *IDSS Commentaries* 34 (May 16, 2006).

Price, Richard. "Reversing the Gun Sights: Transnational Civil Society Targets Land Mines." *International Organization* 52 (3) (Summer 1998): 613–644.

Pumphrey, Carolyn, and Rye Schwartz-Barcott, eds. *Armed Conflict in Africa, A Chronology of Armed Conflict: Prehistory to Present*. Lanham, Md.: Scarecrow Press, 2003.

Putzel, James. "The Politics of Action on AIDS: A Case Study of Uganda." *Public Administration and Development* 24 (2004): 19–30.

Quandt, William B. *Peace Process: American Diplomacy and the Arab–Israeli Conflict Since 1967*. Washington, D.C.: Brookings/University of California, 2001.

Raas, Whitney, and Austin Long. "Osirak Redux? Assessing Israeli Capabilities to Destroy Iranian Nuclear Facilities." *International Security* 31 (4) (Spring 2007): 7–33.

Rajagopalan, Rajesh. "Innovations in Counterinsurgency: The Indian Army's Rashrtriya Rifles." *Contemporary South Asia* 13 (1) (March 2004): 25–37.

Rapoport, David C. "The Fourth Wave: September 11 in the History of Terrorism." *Current History* (December 2001): 419–424.

Raskin, Marcus G. *Essays of a Citizen: From National Security State to Democracy.* Armonk, N.Y.: Sharpe, 1991.

Ray, James Lee. "A Lakatosian View of the Democratic Peace Research Programme: Does It Falsify Realism (or Neorealism)?" In *Progress in International Relations Theory: Appraising the Field*, edited by Colin Elman and Miriam Fendius Elman, 205–244. Cambridge, Mass.: MIT Press, 2003.

Reno, William. *Warlord Politics and African States.* Boulder, Colo.: Lynne Rienner, 1999.

———. "Clandestine Economies, Violence and States in Africa." *Journal of International Affairs* 53 (2) (2000): 433–459.

Rice, Condoleeza. "Our Opportunity with India." *Washington Post*, March 13, 2006, A15.

Ripsman, Norrin M. *Peacemaking by Democracies: The Effect of State Autonomy on the Post-World-War Settlements.* University Park: Penn State University Press, 2002.

———. "False Dichotomy: Why Economics Has Always Been High Politics." In *Guns and Butter: The Political Economy of the International Security*, edited by Peter Dombrowski, 15–31. Boulder, Colo.: Lynne Rienner, 2005.

———. "Two Stages of Transition From a Region of War to a Region of Peace: Realist Transition and Liberal Endurance." *International Studies Quarterly* 49 (4) (December 2005): 669–693.

Ripsman, Norrin M., and Jean-Marc F. Blanchard. "Commercial Liberalism Under Fire: Evidence from 1914 and 1936." *Security Studies* 6 (2) (Winter 1996–1997): 4–50.

Ripsman, Norrin M., and T. V. Paul. "Assessing the Uneven Impact of Global Social Forces on the National Security State: A Framework for Analysis." *International Studies Review* 7 (2) (June 2005): 199–227.

Ripsman, Norrin M., and Christopher Way. "International Political Tensions and Foreign Investment." Presented at the 2007 annual meeting of the American Political Science Association. Chicago, Illinois. August 30–September 2, 2007.

Risse-Kappen, Thomas, ed. *Bringing Transnational Relations Back In: Non-State Actors, Domestic Structures, and International Institutions.* Cambridge: Cambridge University Press, 1995.

———. "Bringing Transnational Relations Back In: Introduction." In *Bringing Transnational Relations Back In: Non-State Actors, Domestic Structures and International Institutions*, edited by Thomas Risse-Kappen, 3–36. Cambridge: Cambridge University Press, 1995.

Risse-Kappen, Thomas, Stephen C. Ropp, and Kathryn Sikkink, eds. *The Power of Human Rights: International Norms and Domestic Change.* Cambridge: Cambridge University Press, 1999.

Rodman, David. "Israel's National Security Doctrine: An Introductory Overview," *Middle East Review of International Affairs* 5 (3) (September 2001): 71–86.

Rodrik, Dani. *Has Globalization Gone Too Far?* Washington, D.C.: Institute for International Economics, 1997.

———. "Why Do More Open Economies Have Bigger Governments?" *Journal of Political Economy* 106 (5) (1998): 997–1032.

Rose, Gideon. "Neoclassical Realism and Theories of Foreign Policy." *World Politics* 51 (1) (October 1998): 144–172.

Rosecrance, Richard N. *The Rise of the Trading State: Commerce and Conquest in the Modern World*. New York: Basic Books, 1986.

———. "The Rise of the Virtual State." *Foreign Affairs* 75 (4) (July–August 1996): 45–61.

Rosecrance, Richard, and Peter Thompson. "Trade, Foreign Investment and Security." *Annual Review of Political Science* 6 (1) (2003): 377–398.

Rosenau, James N. "New Dimensions of Security: The Interaction of Globalizing and Localizing Dynamics." *Security Dialogue* 25 (3) (1994): 255–281.

Rotberg, Robert I. "Failed States, Collapsed Sates, Weak States: Causes and Indicators." In *State Failure and State Weakness in a Time of Terror*, edited by Robert I. Rotberg, 1–28. Washington D.C.: Brookings Institution Press, 2003.

———. "Failed States in a World of Terror." *Foreign Affairs* 81 (4) (July–August 2004): 127–140.

Rubin, Barry. "The Military in Contemporary Middle East Politics." *Middle East Review of International Affairs* 5 (1) (March 2001). http://meria.idc.ac.il/journal/2001/issue1/jv5n1a4.html.

———. *Islamic Fundamentalism in Egyptian Politics*. New York: Palgrave Macmillan, 2002.

Rugumamu, Severine M. *Globalization Demystified: Africa's Possible Development Futures*. Dar es Salaam, Tanzania: Dar es Salaam University Press, 2005.

Ruland, Jurgen. "Asian Regionalism Five Years after the 1997/98 Financial Crisis: A Case of 'Cooperative Realism?'" In *Asia–Pacific Economic and Security Co-operation*, edited by Christopher M. Dent, 53–71. Basingstoke, UK: Palgrave Macmillan, 2003.

Rupiya, Martin. "Post War Restructuring: The Region's Defence Structures." In *Defensive Restructuring of Armed Forces in Southern Africa*, edited by Gavin Gawthra and Bjorn Moller. London: Ashgate, 1997.

Russett, Bruce. *Grasping the Democratic Peace*. Princeton, N.J.: Princeton University Press, 1993.

Russett, Bruce, and Zeev Maoz. "Normative and Structural Causes of Democratic Peace." *American Political Science Review* 87 (3) (September 1993): 624–638.

Russett, Bruce, and John Oneal. *Triangulating Peace: Democracy, Interdependence, and International Organizations*. New York: W. W. Norton, 2001.

Rutherford, Kenneth R. "The Evolving Arms Control Agenda: Implications of the Role of NGOs in Banning Antipersonnel Landmines." *World Politics* 53 (1) (October 2000): 74–114.

Rynning, Sten. *Changing Military Doctrine: Presidents and Military Power in Fifth Republic France*. Westport, Conn.: Praeger, 2002.

Sagala, John Kemoli. "HIV/AIDS and the Military in Sub-Saharan Africa: Impact on Military Organizational Effectiveness." *Africa Today* 53 (1) (2006): 53–77.

Sandler, Todd. *Global Collective Action*. Cambridge: Cambridge University Press, 2004.

Sanger, David E. "Cheney Says Israel Might 'Act First' on Iran," *New York Times*, January 21, 2005, A6.

———. "Military Rumblings on Iran," *New York Times*, January 27, 2005, A24.

Scholte, Jan Aart. "Global Capitalism and the State." *International Affairs* 73 (3) (July 1997): 427–452.

———. *Globalization: A Critical Introduction*. London: Palgrave, 2000.

Schneider, Gerald, Katherine Barbieri, and Nils Petter Gleditsch, eds. *Globalization and Armed Conflict*. Lanham, Md.: Rowman & Littlefield, 2003.

———. "Does Globalization Contribute to Peace: A Critical Survey of the Literature." In *Globalization and Armed Conflict*, edited by Gerald Schneider, Katherine Barbieri, and Nils Petter Gleditsch, 3–30. Lanham, Md.: Rowman & Littlefield, 2003.

Schweller, Randall L. "The Progressiveness of Neoclassical Realism." In *Progress in International Relations Theory: Appraising the Field*, edited by Colin Elman and Miriam Fendius Elman, 311–347. Cambridge, Mass.: MIT Press, 2003.

———. *Unanswered Threats: Political Constraints on the Balance of Power*. Princeton, N.J.: University Press, 2006.

Sela, Avraham. *The Decline of the Arab–Israeli Conflict: Middle East Politics and the Quest for Regional Order*. Albany, N.Y.: SUNY Press, 1997.

Shah, Mehtab Ali. "Sectarianism: A Threat to Human Security: A Case Study of Pakistan." *The Round Table* 94 (382) (October 2005), 613–628.

Sharp, Gene. *Making Europe Unconquerable: The Potential of Civilian-Based Deterrence and Defense*. Cambridge, Mass.: Ballinger, 1985.

———. *Civilian-Based Defense*. Princeton, N.J.: Princeton University Press, 1990.

Shaw, Martin. *Theory of the Global State: Globality as an Unfinished Revolution*. Cambridge: Cambridge University Press, 2000.

Shearer, David. *Private Armies and Military Intervention*. Adelphi paper 316. London: Routledge, 1998.

Shen, Dingli. "Iran's Nuclear Ambitions Test China's Wisdom." *The Washington Quarterly* 29 (2) (Spring 2006): 55–66.

Silverstein, Ken. *Private Warriors*. New York: Verso, 2000.

Singer, Peter W. *Corporate Warriors: The Rise of the Privatized Military Industry*. Ithaca, N.Y.: Cornell University Press, 2003.

SIPRI Yearbook 1999–2008. Oxford: Oxford University Press, 1999–2008.

Slaughter, Anne-Marie. "The Real New World Order." *Foreign Affairs* 76 (5) (1997): 183–197.

Small, Melvin, and Singer, J. David. *Resort to Arms: International and Civil Wars 1816–1980*. Thousand Oaks, Calif.: Sage, 1982.

Small Arms Survey 2005: Weapons at War. Geneva, Switzerland: Graduate School of International Studies, 2005.

Snitwongse, Kusuma, and Suchit Bunbongkarn. "New Security Issues and their Impact on ASEAN." In *Reinventing ASEAN*, edited by Simon S. C. Tay, Jesus P. Estanislao, and Hadi Soesastra, 148–162. Singapore: Institute of Southeast Asian Studies, 2001.

Solingen, Etel. *Regional Orders at Century's Dawn*. Princeton, N.J.: Princeton University Press, 1998.

Spybey, Tony. *Globalization and World Society*. Cambridge, Polity Press, 1996.

Starr, Harvey. *Anarchy, Order, and Integration*. Ann Arbor: The University of Michigan Press, 1997.

Stein, Arthur A. "Governments, Economic Interdependence, and International Cooperation." In *Behavior, Society, and Nuclear War*, vol. III, edited by Philip E. Tetlock, Charles Tilly, Robert Jervis, and Jo L. Husbands, 241–324. New York: Oxford University Press, 1993.

Steinberg, Gerald. "NGOs Make War on Israel." *Middle East Quarterly* 11 (3) (Summer 2004), http://www.meforum.org/article/633.

Stiglitz, Joseph E. *Globalization and Its Discontents*. New York: W. W. Norton, 2002.

Stoett, Peter. *Human and Global Security: An Exploration of Terms*. Toronto: University of Toronto Press, 1999.

Strange, Susan. "The Persistent Myth of Lost Hegemony." *International Organization* 41 (4) (Autumn 1987): 551–574.

———. *The Retreat of the State: The Diffusion of Power in the World Economy*. Cambridge: Cambridge University Press, 1996.

Swaine, Michael D., and Ashley J. Tellis. *Interpreting China's Grand Strategy: Past, Present and Future*. Santa Monica, Calif.: The RAND Corporation, 2000.

Tannenwald, Nina. *The Nuclear Taboo: The United States and the Non-Use of Nuclear Weapons Since 1945*. Cambridge: Cambridge University Press, 2007.

Tarrow, Sidney. *The New Transnational Activism*. Cambridge: Cambridge University Press, 2005.

Taylor, Jeffrey. "Russia Is Finished." *The Atlantic Monthly* 287 (May 2001): 35–52.

Taylor, Terence, ed. *The Military Balance 1999–2000*. London: International Institute for Strategic Studies, 1999.

Thom, William G. "Judging Africa's Military Capabilities." *Journal of Third World Studies* 5 (2) (1988): 52–65.

Thompson, Loren B. "Low-Intensity Conflict: An Overview." In *Low-Intensity Conflict: The Pattern of Warfare in the Modern World*, edited by Loren B. Thompson. Lexington, Mass.: Lexington Books, 1989.

Tilly, Charles. "Reflections on the History of European State-Making." In *The Formation of National States in Western Europe*, edited by Charles Tilly, 3–83. Princeton, N.J.: Princeton University Press, 1975.

Tomlinson, John. *Globalization and Culture*. Chicago, Ill.: University of Chicago Press, 1999.

Tow, William T. "Alternative Security Models: Implications for ASEAN." In *Non-Traditional Security Issues in Southeast Asia*, edited by Andrew T. H. Han and J. D. Kenneth Boutin, 257–287. Singapore: Select Publishing, 2001.

Trenin, Dmitri. "Russia Leaves the West." *Foreign Affairs* 85 (4) (July/August 2006): 87–96.

Tsygankov, Andrei P. "Vladimir Putin's Vision of Russia as a Normal Great Power." *Post-Soviet Affairs* 21 (2) (April–June 2005): 132–158.

Tull, Denis M. "China's Engagement in Africa: Scope, Significance and Consequences." *Journal of Modern African Studies* 44 (3) (2006): 459–479.

Tymoshenko, Yuliya. "Containing Russia." *Foreign Affairs* 8 (3) (May/June, 2007): 69–82.

Vaisse, Justin. "A Gaullist by Any Other Name." *Survival* 50 (3) (June 2008): 5–10.

Vakil, Sanam. "Iran: Balancing East against West." *The Washington Quarterly* 29 (4) (Autumn 2006): 51–65.

van Creveld, Martin. *The Rise and Decline of the State*. Cambridge: Cambridge University Press, 1999.

Van Evera, Stephen. "Primed for Peace: Europe After the Cold War." *International Security* 15 (3) (Winter 1990–1991): 7–57.

———. *A Guide to Methodology for Students of Political Science*. Ithaca. N.Y.: Cornell University Press, 1997.

Vasquez, John A. "Distinguishing Rivals That Go to War from Those That Do Not." *International Studies Quarterly* 40 (4) (December 1996): 531–558.

Väyrynen, Raimo, ed. *The Waning of Major War: Theories and Debates*. New York: Routledge, 2005.

———. "The Waning of Major Wars: Contending Views." In *The Waning of Major War: Theories and Debates*, edited by Raimo Väyrynen, 1–30. New York: Routledge, 2005.

Väyrynen, Raimo. "Globalization and Local Violence," Presented at the APSA Conference, San Francisco, California, September 2001.

Velazquez, Arturo C. Sotomayor. "Civil–Military Affairs and Security Institutions in the Southern Cone: The Sources of Argentina–Brazilian Nuclear Cooperation." *Latin American Politics and Society* 46 (4) (Winter 2004): 29–60.

Vogt, Margaret A. "The OAU and Conflict Management." Presented at the International Resource Group Conference, Mombasa, Kenya, November 6–9, 1996.

Waever, Ole. "Insecurity, Security, and Asecurity in the West European Non-war Community." In *Security Communities*, edited by Emanuel Adler and Michael Barnett, 69–118. Cambridge: Cambridge University Press, 1998.

Wafula Okumu. "Humanitarian International NGOs and African Conflicts." *International Peacekeeping* 10 (1) (2003): 120–137.

Wallensteen, Peter. "Economic Sanctions: Ten Modern Cases and Three Important Lessons." In *Dilemmas of Economic Coercion*, edited by Miroslav Nincic and Peter Wallensteen, 87–130. New York: Praeger, 1983.

Walt, Stephen M. "The Renaissance of Security Studies." *International Studies Quarterly* 35 (2) (June 1991): 211–239.

———. "Beyond bin Laden: Reshaping US Foreign Policy." *International Security* 26 (3) (Winter 2001–2002): 56–78.

———. *Taming American Power: The Global Response to U.S. Primacy*. New York: W. W. Norton, 2005.

Waltz, Kenneth N. *Theory of International Politics*. Reading, Mass.: Addison-Wesley, 1979.

———. "Structural Realism After the Cold War," *International Security* 25 (1) (Summer 2000): 5–41.

Way, Christopher R. *Manchester Revisited: Economic Interdependence and Conflict*. Ithaca, N.Y.: Cornell University Press, forthcoming.

Weber, Max. *The Theory of Social and Economic Organization*, edited by Talcott Parsons. New York: Free Press, 1964.

Weiss, Linda. *The Myth of the Powerless State: Governing the Economy in a Global Era*. Ithaca, N.Y.: Cornell University Press, 1998.

———, ed. *States in the Global Economy: Brining Domestic Institutions Back In*. New York: Cambridge University Press, 2003.

Weitz, Richard. "Why Russia and China Have Not Formed an Anti-American Alliance." *Naval War College Review* 56 (4) (Autumn 2003): 39–57.

Wendt, Alexander. *Social Theory of International Politics*. Cambridge: Cambridge University Press, 1999.

Williams, Mark Eric. "Soft Balancing: Much Ado About Nothing?" Middlebury College, Vt., unpublished, October 2006.

Williams, Rocklyn. "A Postmodern Military: Mission Redefinition and Defensive Restructuring." In *Defensive Restructuring of Armed Forces in Southern Africa*, edited by Gavin Cawthra and Bjorn Moller. London: Ashgate, 1997.

Wohlforth, William C. "The Stability of a Unipolar World." *International Security* 24 (1) (Summer 1999): 5–41.

———. "Russia's Soft Balancing Act." In *Strategic Asia, 2003–4: Fragility and Crisis*, edited by Richard Ellings and Aaron Fridberg with Michael Wills, 165–179. Seattle, Wash.: National Bureau of Asia Research, 2003.

Yergin, Daniel. *Shattered Peace*. Boston, Mass.: Houghton Mifflin, 1977.

Zacher, Mark W. "The Decaying Pillars of the Westphalian Temple: Implications for International Order and Governance." In *Governance without Government: Order and Change in World Politics*, edited by James N. Rosenau and Ernst-Otto Czempiel, 58–101. Cambridge: Cambridge University Press, 1992.

———. "The Territorial Integrity Norm: International Boundaries and the Use of Force." *International Organization* 55 (2) (Spring 2001): 215–250.

Zaidi, Akbar, S. "India–Pakistan Trade," *South Asian Journal* 4 (April–June 2004), http://www.southasianmedia.net/Magazine/Journal/indiapakistan_trade.htm.

Zakaria, Fareed. *The Future of Freedom: Illiberal Democracy at Home and Abroad.* New York: W. W Norton, 2004.

Zartman, I. William. "Regional Conflict Management in Africa." In *Regional Conflict Management*, edited by Paul F. Diehl and Joseph Lepgold, 81–103. Lanham, Md.: Rowman & Littlefield, 2003.

Ze'evi, Aharon. "Israel's Strategic Environment." *Strategic Assessment* 5 (2) (August 2002) http://www.inss.org.il/publications.php?cat=21&incat=&read=630.

———. "Israel and the Middle-East, 2005: A Strategic Overview." *Strategic Assessment* 8 (3) (November 2005), http://www.inss.org.il/publications.php?cat=21&incat= &read=155.

Government Documents

13th SAARC Summit. "Dhaka Declaration," http://www.mofa.gov.np/uploads/news/ 20060309153959.pdf (accessed March 15, 2009).

African Union. "Abuja Call for Accelerated Action towards Universal Access to HIV and AIDS, Tuberculosis and Malaria Services in Africa," 2006, http://www.africa-union.org/root/au/conferences/past/2006/may/summit/doc/en/ABUJA_CALL.pdf (accessed March 15, 2009).

African Union. "Abuja Declaration on HIV/AIDS, Tuberculosis and Other Related Infectious Diseases," 2000, http://www.uneca.org/ADF2000/Abuja%20 Declaration.htm (accessed March 15, 2009).

African Union. "Assembly of the Union 2nd Extraordinary Session," February 27–28, 2004, http://www.africa-union.org/root/au/Documents/Decisions/hog/ DECISIONS_Sirte_2004.pdf (accessed March 15, 2009).

African Union. "Protocol Relating to the Establishment of the Peace and Security Council of the African Union," http://www.africa-union.org/root/AU/organs/psc/ Protocol_peace%20and%20security.pdf (accessed March 15, 2009).

Argentina Ministry of Defense. "White Paper on National Defense, January 2000," http://www.defensenet.ser2000.0rg.ar/Archivo/libro-argentina-eng/ (accessed March 15, 2009).

Cambodia. "Defending the Kingdom of Cambodia: Security and Development 2000," http://merln.ndu.edu/whitepapers/Cambodia-2000.pdf (accessed March 15, 2009).

China Government White Paper. "China's National Defense in 2006," http://chinesejil.oxfordjournals.org/cgi/reprint/6/1/195.pdf (accessed March 15, 2009).

Congressional Budget Office. "An Analysis of the President's Budgetary Proposals for Fiscal Year 2005," http://www.cbo.gov/showdoc.cfm?index=5151&sequence=1 (accessed March 15, 2009).

Department for International Development. *The Causes of Conflict in Sub-Saharan Africa.* London: Department for International Development, 2001, http://www. dfid.gov.uk/pubs/files/conflictsubsaharanafrica.pdf (accessed March 15, 2009).

Federative Republic of Brazil. "National Defense Policy, 2002," http://www.oas.org/csh/english/docwhitepapers%20Brasil.asp (accessed June 18, 2003).

Human Security Center, University of British Columbia. *Human Security Report 2005*. Oxford: Oxford University Press, 2005, http://www.humansecurityreport.info/index.php?option=content&task=view&id=28&Itemid=63 (accessed March 15, 2009).

India. "Draft Report of National Security Advisory Board on Indian Nuclear Doctrine," http://www.indianembassy.org/policy/CTBT/nuclear_doctrine_aug_17_1999.html (accessed March 15, 2009).

India, Indian Army. "The Indian Army Doctrine," http://www.indianarmy.gov.in/indar_doctrine.htm (accessed March 15, 2009).

India, Indian Army. "Indian Army, Doctrine for Subconventional Operations," http://www.indianarmy.gov.in/indar_doctrine.htm (accessed March 15, 2009).

India, Ministry of Defense. "Security Environment: An Overview," http://mod.nic.in/aforces/body.htm (accessed March 15, 2009).

Indonesia. "Defense White Paper 2003: Defending the Country Entering the 21st Century." http://merln.ndu.edu/whitepapers/IndonesiaWhitePaper.pdf (accessed March 15, 2009).

Israel, Israeli Defense Forces. "IDF Doctrine," http://dover.idf.il/IDF/English/about/doctrine/ (accessed March 15, 2009).

Malaysia, Ministry of Defense. "National Defence Policy," http://www.mod.gov.my/index.php?Itemid=173&id=89&option=com_content&task=blogcategory&lang=en (accessed March 15, 2009).

Malaysia, Ministry of Foreign Affairs. "An Overview of Malaysia's Foreign Policy," http://www.kln.gov.my/?m_id=2 (accessed March 15, 2009).

Organization for American States. "The OAS and the Inter-American System," http://www.oas.org/documents/eng/oasinbrief.asp (accessed, March 14, 2009).

Pakistan, "Address by General Pervez Musharraf." Inaugural Session of Third National Security Workshop, National Defense College, Islamabad, February 12, 2004, http://www.millat.com/president/defense/1018200430248PMnational%20defense%20college.pdf (accessed March 15, 2009).

Pakistan, Ministry of Foreign Affairs. "Jammu & Kashmir Dispute," http://www.mofa.gov.pk/Pages/Brief.htm (accessed March 15, 2009).

Republic of the Philippines, Department of Foreign Affairs. "DFA Accomplishment Report for 2003," http://www.dfa.gov.ph/archive/accreport2003.htm (accessed March 15, 2009).

Republica Argentina, Ministerio de Defensa. "Revision de la Defensa 2001: Consideraciones acerca del Marco Estratégico, Amenazas no tradicionales," http://www.resdal.org/Archivo/revi-part1.htm (accessed March 15, 2009).

Republica Argentina, Ministerio de Defensa. "Revision de la Defensa 2001: Consideraciones acerca del Marco Estratégico, Escenario Mundial," http://www.pdgs.org.ar/Archivo/revi-part1.htm#a (accessed March 15, 2009).

Republica Argentina, Ministerio de Defensa. "Revision de la Defensa 2001: Prioridades Estratégicas para el siglo que se inicia," http://www.pdgs.org.ar/Archivo/revi-part2.htm (accessed March 15, 2009).

Republica Federativa do Brasil Ministerio da Defesa. "Politica de defesa nacional 2005," http://www.resdal.org/Archivo/brasil-politica-defensa.htm (accessed March 15, 2009).

République Française Ministère de la Défense." Projet de loi de programmation militaire 2003–2008," http://www.defense-aerospace.com/article-view/reports_ar/16405/projet-de-loi-de-programmation-militaire-2003_2008.html (accessed March 15, 2009).

République Française Ministère de la Défense. "The Defense Procurement Policy (2004): For a Competitive Autonomy in Europe," http://www.cedoc.defense.gouv.fr/IMG/pdf/ENG-achat-2.pdf (accessed March 15, 2009).

République Française, Présidence de la République. "Speech by Jacques Chirac, President of the French Republic, during his visit to The Strategic Air and Maritime Forces at Landivisiau, L'Île Longue," http://www.cedoc.defense.gouv.fr/IMG/pdf/Discours_President_2006_en.pdf (accessed March 15, 2009).

The Fight Against Terror: Singapore's National Security Strategy. Singapore: National Security Coordination Centre, 2004, www.mindef.gov.sg/imindef/resources/e-books/ebklist.-imindefPars-0004-DownloadFile.tmp/FightAgainstTerror.pdf (accessed March 15, 2009).

United Kingdom Ministry of Defence. "Defence Industrial Strategy: Defence White Paper 2005," http://www.defenceandsecurity.ca/public/docs/2006/march/UK%20defence%20industrial%20strategy%20-%20dec%2005.pdf (accessed March 15, 2009).

United Kingdom Ministry of Defence. "Defence White Paper 2003," http://www.mod.uk/NR/rdonlyres/051AF365-0A97-4550-99C0-4D87D7C95DED/0/cm6041I_whitepaper2003.pdf (accessed March 15, 2009).

United Kingdom, Ministry of Defence. "Defence White Paper 2003 (CM 6697): Delivering Security in a Changing World," http://www.official-documents.gov.uk/document/cm66/6697/6697.pdf (accessed March 15, 2009).

United Kingdom Ministry of Defence. "The Future Strategic Context for Defence: The Military Context," http://www.mod.uk/issues/strategic_context/military.htm.

United Kingdom Ministry of Defence. "The Future Strategic Context for Defence: The Political Context," http://www.mod.uk/issues/strategic_context/political.htm (accessed March 15, 2009).

United Nations Conference on Trade and Development. "Development and Globalization," 35, http://www.unctad.org/Templates/Download.asp?docid=4848&lang=1&intItemID=3096 (accessed March 15, 2009).

United Nations Conference on Trade and Development. *Development and Globalization: Facts and Figures.* New York: United Nations, 2004 (accessed March 15, 2009).

United Nations Conference on Trade and Development. *World Investment Report 1992: Transnational Corporations as Engines of Growth—Executive Summary*. New York: United Nations, 1992, http://www.unctad.org/en/docs/wir920ve.en.pdf (accessed March 15, 2009).

United Nations Conference on Trade and Development. *World Investment Report 2006: FDI from Developing and Transition Economies*. New York: United Nations, 2005, http://www.unctad.org/en/docs/wir2006ref_en.pdf (accessed March 15, 2009).

United Nations Conference on Trade and Development. *World Investment Report 2007: Transnational Corporations, Extractive Industries and Development*. New York: UNCTAD, 2008, http://www.unctad.org/en/docs/wir2008_en.pdf (accessed March 15, 2009).

United States Congressional Budget Office, "An Analysis of the President's Budgetary Proposals for Fiscal Year 2009," http://www.cbo.gov/ftpdocs/89xx/doc8990/03-19-AnalPresBudget.pdf (accessed March 15, 2009).

United States Congressional Research Service. "Conventional Arms Transfers to Developing Nations, 1999–2006," Report to Congress, September 26, 2007, http://www.fas.org/sgp/crs/weapons/RL34187.pdf (accessed March 15, 2009).

United States Council on Foreign Relations. "Backgrounder, State Sponsors: Iran," http://www.cfr.org/publication/9362 (accessed March 15, 2009).

United States Department of Defense. *Annual Report to Congress: The Military Power of the People's Republic of China 2005*. Washington D.C.: Office of the Secretary of Defense, 2005, http://www.defenselink.mil/news/Jul2005/d20050719china.pdf (accessed March 15, 2009).

United States Department of Defense. *Quadrennial Defense Review Report*. Washington, D.C.: Department of Defense, 2006, http://www.globalsecurity.org/military/library/policy/dod/qdr-2006-report.pdf (accessed March 15, 2009).

United States National Intelligence Council. "The Terrorist Threat to the US Homeland," *National Intelligence Estimate, July 2007*, http://www.dni.gov/press_releases/20070717_release.pdf (accessed March 15, 2009).

United States National Counterterrorism Center. "Annex of Statistical Information," *Country Reports on Terrorism, 2007*, http://www.state.gov/s/ct/rls/crt/2007/103716.htm (accessed March 15, 2009).

United States National Counterterrorism Center. "Report on Incidents of Terrorism, 2005," April 11, 2006, http://wits.nctc.gov/reports/crot2005nctcannexfinal.pdf (accessed March 15, 2009).

Page numbers set in italics refer to terms in tables.

incentives, economic, 39, 198n18
India
    HIV/AIDS and, 226n55
    introduction to, 124
    military spending of, 44–45, 199n33
    Pakistan and, 41, 225n50, 229n83
    security objectives of, 226n55
    as security provider, 132–35
    security strategies of, 128–32, 227n70
    threats against, 124–28
Indonesia
    ASEAN and, 100
    defense doctrine of, 104, 106
    military manpower and spending of, 107
    non-government organizations and, 108
    terrorism and, 50, 102–3
infrastructural power, 16
infrastructure deficiency, 15, 137
Inkeles, Alex, 8
Interdependence. *See* economic
        interdependence
Intergovernmental Authority on
        Development, 158
intergovernmental organizations
        (IGOs), 45–49, 164, 200nn41,47
International Campaign to Ban
        Landmines, 48
International Criminal Court, 27
international financial institutions
        (IFIs), 49 (*see also* International
        Monetary Fund (IMF); World Bank)
International Institute for Strategic Studies
        (IISS), 17, 147
international institutions, 45–50
International Monetary Fund (IMF), 9, 23,
        48, 49, 185n30, 201n56
interstate wars
    China and, 64–65
    Cold War and, 197n8
    decline in, 29, 196n4
    key findings on, 162–63
    proposition on, 36–41
    Russia and, 71–72
    South Asia and, 124–26, 225nn45,50
    Southeast Asia and, 101, 111
    sub-Saharan Africa and, 139–40, *141*,
        231n18
    United States and, 55
intrastate wars, 36–41, 196n4, 197n8,
        230nn15,17

Iran
    introduction to, 116–17
    nuclear weapons and, 224n34
    as security provider, 123–24
    security strategies of, 119–23
    threats against, 117–19
Iran-India gas pipeline, 133, 229n83
Iraq
    al Qaeda and, 50
    China and, 68
    defense spending of, 122
    France and, 88, 91
    Great Britain and, 84
    low-intensity conflicts in, 117–18
    NATO and, 47
    non-government organizations and, 62
    Russia and, 74
    sanctions against, 40
    United Nations and, 46
    United States and, 55, 58
Islmai Jaiat-i-Tulabah, 228n80
Israel
    Ahmadinejad on, 222n11
    introduction to, 115–17
    as security provider, 123–24
    security strategies of, 119–23
    threats against, 117–19

Jaish-e-Mohammed, 228n80
Jakarta, 102–3
Jama'at-i-Islmai, 228n80
James, Patrick, 170
Jamiat-e-Ulema-e-islam, 228n80
Japan, 39, 43, 59, 70, 104, 110
Jervis, Robert, 38
Job, Brian, 109

Kabila, Laurent, 151, 157, 231n18
Karns, Margaret P., 200n41
Katrina (hurricane), 240n14
Kenya, 50, 56, 143, 144, 158
Kirshner, Jonathan, 24
Klare, Michael, 32

Laidi, Zaki, 29
land, control and conquest of, 24–25,
        190n15
land mines, 27–28, 48, 146–47, 201n53
Laos, 100, 101, 111
Laskar-e-Taiba, 229n80

Mittelman, James H., 8
Mobutu Sésé Seko, 142, 157, 231n18
MODEL, 231n28
Momoh, Joseph Saidu, 142
Mubarak, Hosni, 121
Mueller, John, 202n63
Mugabe, Robert, 144, 231n28
Museveni, Yoweri, 147
Musharraf, Pervez, 51, 127, 227n62

Namibia, 138, 153, 157, 158, 231n18
national capability, 187n47
National Islamic Front, 143
National Security Act (1947), 11
national security state
    definition of term, 10–12
    theories on globalization and, 1–3, 20–29
National Union for the Total Independence
    of Angola (UNITA), *141*, 142, 150,
    231n28
Nayar, Baldev Raj, 177, 187n47, 241n27
Nepal, 124, 225n45
Netanyahu, Binyamin, 120
New Partnership for Africa's Development
    (NEPAD), 158–59
non-government organizations (NGOs)
    Brazil and, 215n74
    China and, 70
    coercive power and, 240n15
    influence of, 201n53, 201n56
    key findings on, 164–65, *166*
    major powers and, 78
    Middle East and, 123
    Pakistan and, 228n80
    Private Military Companies, 154–55,
        237n101
    proposition on, 35, 45–49
    Russia and, 76, 209n83
    South America and, 98
    South Asia and, 132–33, *134*
    Southeast Asia and, 108–09
    stable regions and, *113*
    sub-Saharan Africa and, 154–55, *160*
    United States and, 61–63
    western Europe and, 89–91
nonstate actors. *See* non-government
    organizations
norms
    global, 21, 27–28
    human rights, 27–28

North American Treaty Organization
    (NATO)
    Great Britain and, 87
    as regional security institution, 35
    Russia and, 72, 73, 74, 75, 76, 209n86
    United States and, 46, 47, 63
    western Europe and, 83, 84, 88, 91
Nuclear Non-Proliferation Treaty (NPT), 48
nuclear weapons
    China's policies on, 206n53
    France and, 87
    globalization and, 179–80
    influence of, 38
    Iran and, 224n34
Nuttahida Majlis-e Amal, 228n80

Obama, Barack, 174, 175, 176
Oegg, Barbara L., 39
Ohmae, Kenichi, 22
Olmert, Ehud, 120
Olson, Mancur, 171, 209n88
Organization of American States (OAS), 35,
        46, 94, 99 (*see also* African Union)
Organization of African Unity (OAU), 139,
        144, 155–56, 158 (*see also* African
        Union)
Organ on Politics, Defense, and Security, 157

Pakistan
    Afghanistan and, 226n51
    ASEAN and, 110
    Baluchistan and, 228n78
    defense spending of, 201n56
    India and, 15, 41, 225n50, 227n70,
        229n83
    introduction to, 124
    Iran and, 117
    non-government organizations
        and, 228n80
    as security provider, 132–35
    security strategies of, 128–32
    threats against, 124–28, 227n62
Palestine, 50, 116
Pape, Robert, 40
participation deficiency, 15, 137
Paul, T. V., 187n47
Peace, Disarmament, and Symbiosis in the
        Asia Pacific, 108
Peace and Security Council, 155–56
People's Armed Police Force (PAPF), 69

Sarkozy, Nicolas, 73, 85, 88
Schneider, Gerald, 6
Scholte, Jan Aart, 184n27
Schonteich, Martin, 146
second-tier powers
    Middle East, 116–24
    regions of enduring rivalry, 115–16, 135
    South America, 92–100
    South Asia, 124–35
    Southeast Asia, 100–12
    stable regions, 81–82, 112–13
    western Europe, 83–92
security
    deficiency, 15, 137
    definition of, 185n33
    internationalization of, 30, 45–49
    privatization of national, 34–35
    regionalization of, 35
    terrorism as challenge to, 50–52
Senegal
    armed forces of, 235n84, 236n87
    internal conflicts in, 141
    interstate wars and, 140
    regional security organizations and, 157
    as weak state, 16, 138
Shabbab, 143–44
"shadow state," 142
Shanghai Cooperation Organization
        (SCO), 47, 70
Sharon, Ariel, 120
Shaw, Martin, 8, 21–22
Sierra Leone
    balance-of-power politics and, 151
    defense spending of, 152
    defensive and deterrent doctrines
        and, 150
    internal conflicts in, 141
    interstate wars and, 140
    non-government organizations and, 154
    regional security organizations and,
        47, 157
    as "shadow state," 142
    as weak state, 16, 136
Sinai War, 116
Singapore
    ASEAN and, 100
    balance-of-power politics and, 106
    defense spending of, 107
    defensive and deterrent doctrines
        and, 105

Malaysia and, 101
    piracy and, 104
    terrorism and, 102
    as trading state, 43
Singh, Manmohan, 132
small arms, 128, 146–47, 164
Snyder, Jack, 192n34
social definitions of globalization, 8
soft balancing
    China and, 67–68
    major powers and, 78
    Middle East and, 120–21
    proposition on, 33
    Russia and, 74
    South America and, 98
    South Asia and, 130, 134
    Southeast Asia and, 106–7
    stable regions and, 113
    sub-Saharan Africa and, 150–51, 160
    United States and, 59
    western Europe and, 88
soft globalization theorists, 24–25
Solingen, Etel, 26
Somalia
    balance-of-power politics and, 151
    ethnic conflicts in, 140
    as failed state, 16, 136, 138
    internal conflicts in, 141
    interstate wars and, 139, 150
    regional security organizations and, 46,
        158
    terrorism and, 143–44
Sørensen, Georg, 6, 8
South African Development Community
        (SADC), 47, 145, 151, 157–58,
        238n116
South America
    boundary disputes in, 213n44
    China and, 213n48
    conclusions on, 100
    introduction to, 92–93
    Mercosur and, 215n80
    as security community, 212n42
    as security provider, 98–100
    security strategies of, 95–98
    threats against, 93–95
South Asia
    arms spending and, 43
    as competitive regional
        subsystem, 14–15

Middle East and, 117–18
South America and, 93–94
South Asia and, 124–26
Southeast Asia and, 101, 105–6
sub-Saharan Africa and, 139–40
United States and, 55–58
western Europe and, 84
warlords, 154–55, 237n101
Warsaw Pact, 42, 74
weak states
  characteristics of, 137–38
  commercial liberalism and, 241n27
  conclusions on, 159–60
  introduction to, 136–37
  key findings on, 165, *166*, 168
  overview of, 15–16
  as security providers, 154–59
  security strategies of, 149–54
  threats against, 139–49
  weapons and, 233n57
weapons. *See also* arms market; nuclear
      weapons; small arms
  destructive capability of, 194n49
  military doctrine and, 33
  norms regarding, 27–28

sub-Saharan Africa and, 146–47, 233n57
Weiss, Thomas, 200n47
western Europe. *See also* France; Great Britain
  introduction to, 82–83, 83–84
  as security provider, 89–92
  security strategies of, 87–89
  threats against, 84–87
Whiting, Allan, 106
Williams, Jody, 201n53
Wohlforth, William, 38
World Bank, 9, 23, 49, 185n30, 237n104

Yergin, Daniel, 11

Zacher, Mark, 27
Zaire, 140, 142, 157
Zakaria, Fareed, 192n34
Zia ul-Haq, Muhammad, 125
Zimbabwe
  Africa's Great War and, 231n18
  armed forces of, 153
  balance-of-power politics and, 151
  SADC and, 157
  terrorism and, 144
  as weak state, 138